Semantics and Poetics of the Righteous and the Wicked in the Psalms

Semantics and Poetics of the Righteous and the Wicked in the Psalms

Kevin Foth

LEXINGTON BOOKS

Lanham • Boulder • New York • London

Published by Lexington Books
An imprint of The Rowman & Littlefield Publishing Group, Inc.
4501 Forbes Boulevard, Suite 200, Lanham, Maryland 20706
www.rowman.com

86-90 Paul Street, London EC2A 4NE, United Kingdom

British Library Cataloguing in Publication Information Available

Library of Congress Cataloging-in-Publication Data

Names: Foth, Kevin, 1992- author.
Title: Semantics and poetics of the righteous and the wicked in the Psalms / Kevin Foth.
Description: Lanham : Lexington Books, [2025] | Includes bibliographical references and index. | Summary: "This book examines the common contrast between the "righteous" and the "wicked" in the Book of Psalms. Combining semantic analysis with poetics, the research contends that these contrasting figures are integral to the conventions of Hebrew psalmody, serving diverse functions within individual psalms"—Provided by publisher.
Identifiers: LCCN 2024037343 (print) | LCCN 2024037344 (ebook) | ISBN 9781666974003 (cloth) | ISBN 9781666974010 (epub)
Subjects: LCSH: Bible. Psalms—Criticism, interpretation, etc. | Righteousness—Biblical teaching. | Good and evil—Biblical teaching.
Classification: LCC BS1430.6.R54 F67 2025 (print) | LCC BS1430.6.R54 (ebook) | DDC 223/.2066—dc23/eng/20241112
LC record available at https://lccn.loc.gov/2024037343
LC ebook record available at https://lccn.loc.gov/2024037344

For my dad

Contents

Acknowledgments

This project began as my Ph.D. dissertation from McMaster Divinity College. I am grateful to my *Doktorvater*, Mark Boda, who saw this project through from the earliest stages to completion. His support, both academically and personally, enabled this project to be academically rigorous and enjoyable to complete. Paul S. Evans likewise offered quality feedback and encouragement to continue to improve. I am also grateful to William P. Brown, who served as an external examiner, for his valuable feedback and encouragement to publish this study. My thanks are owed to those professors in both my undergraduate and graduate degrees who fostered a love for biblical studies and encouraged me to pursue further education, including Ron Herms, Bob Stallman, Brad Embry, Blaine Charette, Knut Heim, Danny Carroll, Hélène Dallaire, and Rick Hess.

There are too many peers from the Ph.D. program at McMaster Divinity College who made a difference in this project to mention. Many helped with revisions, conversed about ideas, supported me in moving toward goals, or simply offered friendship, including Megan Roberts, Darlene Seal, Ambrose Thomson, Jake Burnette, Alex Stewart, Daniel Kim, Mark Hanson, Moises Zumaeta, Byungwook Choi, Julie Dykes, Matt Bovard, Ji Hyung Kim, Jake Tomc, and Paulo Caproni.

Other friends supported the work in many ways. Pride of place here goes to Andrew LiVecchi, who provided significant editing and meaningful friendship throughout the writing of this book. Gary Dumbrill and Richard Randall asked many stimulating questions about my research. Special thanks are due to Joel, Sara, Amos, and Andrew, whose friendship enriched my life during this project in immeasurable ways.

I am grateful to Megan White and Tara Donovan from Lexington/Fortress Academic for their assistance in ensuring the seamless publication of this book through clear and prompt communication.

Finally, I wish to thank my family. My wife Esther never failed to believe in me and my work. Your love means more than you know. My children, both of whom were born during the writing or production of this book, provided enormous joy. Thank you to my brothers, Brian and Paul, for ongoing friendship, even from a distance. Lastly, I wish to thank my parents for encouraging me to ask questions about the Bible even from an early age. This work is dedicated to my dad, who always showed an interest in what I was doing and never failed to let me know he is proud of me.

List of Abbreviations

AB	Anchor Bible
AcBib	Academia Biblica
AIL	Ancient Israel and Its Literature
BBB	Bonner biblische Beiträge
BBR	*Bulletin of Biblical Research*
BCOTWP	Baker Commentary on the Old Testament Wisdom and Psalms
BETL	Bibliotheca Ephemeridum theologicarum Lovaniensium
Bib	*Biblica*
BibInt	*Biblical Interpretation*
BibInt	Biblical Interpretation Series
BZAW	Beihefte zur Zeitschrift für die alttestamentliche Wissenschaft
CBQ	*Catholic Biblical Quarterly*
CC	Continental Commentaries
DCH	Clines, David J. A., ed. *The Dictionary of Classical Hebrew.* 9 vols. Sheffield, England: Sheffield Academic Press, 1993–2014.
EJL	Early Judaism and Its Literature
FAT	Forschungen zum Alten Testament
FB	Forschung zur Bibel
HS	*Hebrew Studies*
JBL	*Journal of Biblical Literature*
JBTh	*Jahrbuch für Biblische Theologie*
JETS	*Journal of the Evangelical Theological Society*
JHS	*Journal of Hebrew Scriptures*
JSOT	*Journal for the Study of the Old Testament*
JSOTSup	*Journal for the Study of the Old Testament Supplement Series*
JTS	*Journal of Theological Studies*

SK	*Skrif en Kerk*
LHBOTS	Library of Hebrew Bible/Old Testament Studies
LNTS	Library of New Testament Studies
NCBC	New Cambridge Bible Commentary
NIBC	New International Biblical Commentary
NICOT	New International Commentary of the Old Testament
OBO	Orbis Biblicus et Orientalis
OTE	*Old Testament Essays*
OTS	Old Testament Studies
PRSt	*Perspectives in Religious Studies*
RB	*Revue Biblique*
RBS	Resources for Biblical Study
SBLDS	Society of Biblical Literature Dissertation Series
SEÅ	*Svensk Exegetisk Årsbok*
SJOT	*Scandinavian Journal of the Old Testament*
SSN	Studia Semitica Neerlandica
TynBul	*Tyndale Bulletin*
TOTC	Tyndale Old Testament Commentaries
VT	*Vetus Testamentum*
VTSup	Supplements to Vetus Testamentum
WBC	Word Biblical Commentary
ZAW	*Zeitschrift für die alttestamentliche Wissenschaft*

Introduction

Psalm 1 famously includes a contrast between the two figures of the righteous and the wicked. The psalm concludes:

> For Yhwh knows the path of righteous people
> But the path of wicked people will die.[1]

Beginning with Ps 1, these two figures of the righteous and the wicked—and their counterparts[2]—claim an important role in the Psalter. These designations, צַדִּיק, "righteous," and רָשָׁע, "wicked," are present most significantly in Books 1 and 5 of the Psalter, though they appear in psalms throughout the collection.[3]

Because of the prevalence of these figures, Joseph Blenkinsopp notes: "One of the most striking features of the canonical psalms is the binary contrast between the righteous and those the righteous considered impious and wicked."[4] Similarly, Patrick D. Miller suggests that due to the presence at the outset of the Psalter and throughout the Book of Psalms, "how these two groups act, the way they go . . . is very much the subject matter of the psalms."[5] It is surprising, given this theme's prevalence and apparent importance, that there are few works on the topic as a whole in scholarship. What lacks significant engagement in particular is the variation in the usage of both terms throughout the Psalms.[6] At the same time, discussion about these figures appears as part of other arguments within psalm scholarship.

Psalm 1 is often thought of as a key text for understanding these figures, especially with its focus on the idea that the pathway to life is through obedience to Torah. Psalm 1 does offer a synopsis of how a person may become identified with the characteristics of those whose path Yhwh knows, as will be shown further below. The righteous are understood based on Ps 1 as those who are prototypically good, those who are "moral" in a fuller sense, and perhaps, as those who are faithful to the covenant. As such, in Psalm 1, "all that they do is made successful" (Ps 1:4). In light of this, John Kartje suggests that Ps 1 supports the "primary proposition" that "the righteous prosper and the wicked fail."[7] The statement accurately summarizes Ps 1, and yet, in other psalms, the righteous are the poor or are attacked (e.g., Ps 34:20, 37:16). The eventual outcome for the righteous, even in these instances, is receiving good things from God, but a disagreement exists between Ps 1 and others as to when the righteous receive blessings.[8]

A strikingly different tone for the righteous figure appears in Ps 58:11:

> The righteous person will rejoice for they will have seen vengeance;
> They will wash their feet in the blood of the wicked person.

Here, the vision for the righteous contains neither the concept of nearness to God nor clear moral categories as in Ps 1. Instead, they rejoice, rather gruesomely, in the downfall of the wicked. A contrast still exists here, yet if these figures function predominantly to create a vision for ethics or a model for prosperity,[9] what does the violent expression of rejoicing in the death of the wicked say for what the righteous ought to do? It is worth exploring whether and how presentations of these figures relate—and in what ways they do not.

The most common way scholars understand these terms is that their uses derive from a wisdom context, and the presence of the terms is seen as evidence of a category of "wisdom psalms."[10] However, several scholars have seriously questioned the categories of wisdom psalms and of wisdom literature more generally.[11] Will Kynes has problematized the genre category of wisdom outside of psalms, arguing through an extensive survey of previous research that the category of "wisdom literature" is itself a modern construct.[12] Jaqueline Vayntrub, collating a variety of introductions to Wisdom Literature, has shown the ubiquity and circularity of using Proverbs as a standard by which biblical wisdom—as a literary type—is defined.[13] Mark Sneed has also shown that scholarship has often viewed genre as a signifier of worldview, which poses the risk of imposing the meaning of words in one context to another, such as assuming what may be true for the righteous and the wicked in Proverbs is also true in Psalms.[14] Further, the language of the righteous and the wicked appears throughout the Hebrew Bible, not only in Psalms and Proverbs where the terms are most prevalent.[15] Careful attention to the uses of these terms in psalms is needed to support the ways in which they are employed.

William Brown has helpfully shown that while Proverbs and Psalms often share similar themes, language, and metaphors, these features are not always employed toward the same ends.[16] Some of the differences in the presentation of the righteous and the wicked that appear are the connection of the righteous with the poor and needy, the lack of interest in the behavior of the wicked apart from the threat to the righteous, and the "proportionally greater emphasis on the destiny and condition of the wicked and the righteous than on their general conduct."[17] Here, where the conventional language is shared between Psalms and Proverbs, is an area ripe for understanding ways that individual poems or sayings utilize this convention, namely, the figures of the righteous and the wicked, with an end that differs from other presentations—within the same corpus or outside of it.

Apart from wisdom, Psalm scholars have connected significance about the editing of the Psalter with the righteous and the wicked because of the connection with Psalm 1. Some believe that the righteous person should be identified with the king or anointed figure in psalms.[18] Others see the language of the righteous and the wicked as evidence for a late editorial layer of the Psalter.[19] However, these discussions do not include a discussion of either the semantics of the terms or a careful attention to the function of the contrast in individual psalms, pointing rather to their presence as meaningful in some way related to the editorial process by which the Psalter was compiled.

A thorough canonical engagement with the theme of the righteous and the wicked throughout the Psalms comes from Jerome Creach.[20] Creach employs a canonical approach to show a close connection between the language of Torah and the language of refuge at significant locations within the Psalter, including Pss 1–2.[21] Creach writes that the "destiny of the righteous is the primary subject of the Psalms" when it is recognized that "the prayers in the Psalter that call out to God for help are the prayers of those the Psalms call righteous."[22] While there are poetic differences between the voice of the psalmist and the righteous,[23] Creach's use of the *destiny* of the righteous as an interpretive paradigm is highly suggestive, and largely points to the need for understanding the meaning and function of these terms in individual psalms.

Other studies have focused on the functions of the righteous and the wicked within the poetry of the psalms. Claudia Sticher focuses largely on the phenomenon found in many psalms that the righteous are blessed by God but the wicked are destroyed by their own devices.[24] Sticher's goal is to understand the historical development of this theme, and she focuses specifically on this single phenomenon.[25] However, this is by no means a universal aspect of the theme of the righteous and the wicked in the Psalter (see, e.g., Pss 9:16; 28:5; 94:23; 146:9). Sticher has demonstrated helpful connections of a theological theme and argued for their emergence at a particular time, but she has not attempted to understand the underlying literary presentation of these characters across the corpus.

In some cases, the antagonism between good and bad characters has been noted to play a significant role within the structure of individual psalms. For example, P. J. Botha has argued that the function of polarity between the faithful and the enemies is a literary motif in Ps 119, where the presence of literal enemies would not be expected.[26] Additionally, Gert Prinsloo has identified the relationships between the righteous, the wicked, and Yhwh to be the "primary textual strategy" of Ps 5 as a means to reveal the connection between the faithful and Yhwh.[27] In both cases, the literary function is unique to its poetic context, but also integral to the message of the psalm.

The presence and importance of these figures in the Book of Psalms is well noted; several areas of research have proved fruitful. However, in many cases, descriptions of their functions frequently lack clarity and specificity. There are several psalms where the figures appear in the explicit context of enmity. The same figures appear in Proverbs with great frequency, and yet the presentation of these figures shows immediately noticeable differences. In line with the tension between the presentation of these figures in Ps 1 and others, William P. Brown notes that "in Psalms, the wicked represent a clear and present danger to the righteous . . . in Proverbs, the wicked are more an object of contempt than a dire source of danger."[28] Said differently, one finds in reading the psalms that the righteous and the wicked are not only placed in contrast with one another, they are in conflict with one another. In contrast with the vision in Ps 1, Jože Krašovec writes, "The opposition between the righteous and the wicked is shown most clearly in Psalms by the distress of the just psalmist who begs for divine righteousness and deliverance."[29] While there may be consistency with the function of these figures in Ps 1 and other psalms, the situations and presentations of the righteous and the wicked differ from other portions of Old Testament literature, and even, as I argue, from other psalms.

This present work argues that the figures designated by the terms רָשָׁע and צַדִּיק should be understood as part of the poetic conventions of Hebrew psalmody.[30] As conventional resources, these figures have stable semantic properties, yet are employed to serve various communicative ends on the level of discourse. Their stable properties include common activities that these figures participate in and common themes such as the eventual destruction of the wicked and the rescue of the righteous by Yhwh. For the righteous, this also includes the avoidance of direct identification of the speaker as צַדִּיק. These stable properties do not include identities that are common for each usage of the term (e.g., a historical or cultural figure) nor do they require specific contexts (e.g., covenantal or judicial). Due to the conventional properties, these figures are employed in highly creative and even diverse ways within an individual psalm. This study elucidates the meaning of these terms and the associated literary functions and highlights the uses of terms within psalms where both terms צַדִּיק and רָשָׁע appear. This study provides a synthetic overview and an analysis of the discrete uses of these literary figures.

POETICS

This work builds on the research that has sought to define the function of the righteous and the wicked by looking at the ways that these figures are used in individual psalms. The aim is to understand these figures as they belong to the conventions of psalmody and from the semantics of the terms that are used. Drawing on a focus on the function of the contrast in individual psalms, this study will reveal that, though there are several stable semantic properties, the contrast between the figures is used in various ways at the level of discourse.

The use of the righteous and the wicked is both conventional and innovative in individual psalms, and, as such, the analysis in this work addresses both semantics and poetics.[31] Regarding semantics, I argue that the use of the righteous and the wicked in the psalms conforms to similar meanings of these words in other contexts. However, they draw on certain conventions that differ from other types or modes of literature in the Old Testament, most importantly the Book of Proverbs, where these figures appear with similar (even slightly higher) frequency. In order to do this, I summarize the themes and particular topics of the totality of the presentation of the righteous and the wicked in psalms first. I draw on literary research about the concept of characterization to understand the role of the righteous and the wicked in *psalms* as a category of literature. Regarding poetics, I focus on the function of these characters within individual presentations (i.e., representative psalms) to show how the conventions of these figures are adopted and adapted within the literature in ways that highlight their importance for psalmic rhetoric.[32] These figures belong firmly in the conventions of Hebrew psalmody across various genres, modes, and possible time periods, and while the presentation of these figures is not entirely unique, it is distinctive enough to warrant a clearer understanding of their use and function across psalms as part of Hebrew psalmody. The presentations of the righteous and the wicked are not somehow divorced from any historical referent, social function, or redaction. Rather, these ideas are rooted in practices evidenced in the texts of psalms themselves. Studies on thematic conventions do not often fall under the category of Hebrew poetics, unless it uses a specific kind of imagery.[33] This does not mean that these kinds of studies have not taken place in scholarship. It is well recognized that the righteous and the wicked, along with other figures, play an important role in the poetry of psalms. Scholarship has focused largely on formal categories of poetics, especially that of parallelism, and figures of speech. A consistent trope, as with the righteous and the wicked, is also part of the verbal resources of the poetics of psalmody. These kinds of topics have been studied more extensively in narrative than in poetic texts, largely due to the greater part that character plays in narrative art.

The identification of the righteous and the wicked will thus proceed from the careful analysis of their function within the individual psalm prior to understanding to whom these figures refer. How these figures function within Hebrew psalmody should not be left to assumptions about what these words mean nor who these characters are. They should be understood from within psalmody rather than drawn from assumptions of cultic activity in ancient Israel, from some sort of hypothetical historical situation, or from assumptions of borrowing from other modes of literature of ancient Israel (e.g., "wisdom literature").

PSALMODY

Throughout this work, I refer to the concept of Psalmody. Psalmody is commonly used in scholarship as a basic term to refer to the kind of literature that encompasses psalms.[34] In this study, the primary starting point is those compositions found in the Book of Psalms. The previous section in this study indicated the importance of using poetics to understand psalms. The conventions of psalmody include not only formal and stylistic features but also thematic and theological features that can be understood as part of the conventions of this literary group. The Psalter is itself a collection of a certain type of literature,[35] of which the distinctive features have often been appreciated for their differences from others within the collection rather than for what is unique to those works in the collection in comparison to other types of literature in the Hebrew Bible.[36] In this study, I suggest that psalms exhibit features that are unique to—or, at least, distinctive of—psalmody. The Psalter is made up of a compilation of what we call psalms today, which are representative of the literary mode referred to as psalmody.

Critical scholarship on the psalms has focused on questions of which context is primary in interpreting the psalms. Many form-critical and cult-functional scholars would credit at least the origins of psalmody to the liturgy in ancient Israel and Judah.[37] This is certainly possible. However, I utilize the context of the psalms as a group as the entry point rather than the context of the Psalter. Further, while examples of psalmody exist outside the Psalter, this study focuses on the canonical psalms in the Psalter. It thus focuses on poetic convention within a defined set of compositions found in the Psalter. At the same time, this work addresses examples where both צַדִּיק and רָשָׁע appear together in compositions outside the Psalter in chapter 3. This study differs from studies that are canonical in orientation, in that the focus is on discrete psalms within the Psalter rather than on the editorial connections between psalms or redactional perspective. The purpose is not to argue that other contexts are irrelevant or unimportant. Rather, beginning with the psalms themselves (rather than the historical situation or the Psalter as a whole) has a bearing on our understanding of features present in the psalms and the differences and similarities within the collection. In other words, this work is primarily an attempt at understanding psalmic poetics, instead of psalm or Psalter exegesis.

This work proceeds from the view that psalms exhibit similar literary features that differ from other poetic texts in the Old Testament[38] and are included in the Psalter because this work is a collection of this type of literature.[39] They are not defined exclusively by their inclusion in the Psalter, though they are included in this study because of that feature. Even if there are specific types of psalms that have unique elements, as form criticism has classically proposed, there is a broader category of a type or mode of literature we know as psalms.[40]

Psalmody represents what can be understood as a mode of literary production. Sneed argues for using the concept of literary mode to approach wisdom, which is a more abstract and higher-level classification than a genre,[41] and I suggest that the same be done for psalms. Psalms are a particular kind of poem, and while there may be identifiable subgenres, approaching psalmody from the perspective of a literary mode helps to clarify that certain features may belong to this category of texts because of their relationship to each other. Viewing language within the concept of a mode of writing allows for a way to view these poems within a broad conventional category without stating that they are necessarily the same or belong to the same liturgical or historical situation.

Significant for understanding a certain literary mode or type is understanding its conventions. These conventional elements are necessarily contextually bound, yet they can influence the reading of a text outside of the immediate cultural context in which that written product was produced. Tracing conventional elements in science fiction, for example, can point to clear tropes drawn from key early examples that can be seen as establishing these stock images or types.[42] In the case of the Psalms, it is much less clear what elements are earlier than others, or even what psalms might be older than others.

The righteous and the wicked serve a specific function within the literary conventions of psalms. These could be understood as analogous to stock characters that appear in stock situations. M. H. Abrams and Geoffrey Harpham define stock characters as "types of persons that occur repeatedly in a particular literary genre, and so are recognizable as part of the conventions of the form."[43] Stock characters are immediately recognized by their appearance in the type of literature and in their presentation.[44] I will argue that the righteous and the wicked can be viewed in this way by establishing that the basic presentation of the antagonism between these characters is unique to the literature of psalms. Thus, in chapters 2 and 3, I establish both the meaning of these terms and their possible uses in psalms as distinct from other books in the Old Testament. The individual analyses of psalms will highlight the specific ways that psalms employ this aspect of the literary conventions of psalmody.

This study approaches the psalms for understanding the contrast between the righteous and the wicked as part of the "literary toolkit" of psalmody. This "literary toolkit" involves other poetic conventions, the conventions of language, social factors, and idioms belonging to common speech and to genre conventions, as well as modes of expression or themes that belong readily to a certain mode of literary production. In light of this, the contrast between the righteous and the wicked serves as part of a broader set of literary conventions.

PLAN AND ARGUMENT OF THE WORK

Thus far in scholarship, most attempts to understand the language of the righteous and the wicked have been done often in reference to something else, whether a theological theme, historical development, a hypothetical cultic situation, or usefulness for ethics. However, the language of the righteous and the wicked is not bound (exclusively) to any specific historical, form-critical, or canonical context. Other than a few articles, the focus has rarely been on the literary function of these figures in individual psalms. In fact, other than the works by Creach, there are no monograph-length attempts to understand the phenomenon throughout the Psalter, and none have focused on the definitions and functions of these terms. This work will specifically address the function of this literary comparison between characters in psalms by analyzing the function of their contrast in each psalm where both figures appear.

In this work, I approach psalms from the perspective of poetics to argue that the righteous and the wicked should be understood as stock imagery in the conventions of Hebrew psalmody; as such, the contrast between these two characters, which is central to their presentation, serves various functions in individual psalms. Approaching the contrast between these characters in the psalms from a literary perspective illuminates their function within the poem as well as the creativity with which they are employed. Each presentation of these characters has continuity and discontinuity with other presentations of these characters in other psalms. As part of the literary conventions of psalmody, the general pattern of antagonism and contrast between these two figures is utilized alongside other poetic resources to create meaning in the poem. In light of this, this work explores both the general characteristics and the uniqueness of the individual presentations of these figures in psalms.

This study differs from previous attempts to understand these figures in several ways. First, it begins to grapple with the lexical semantics of the terms צַדִּיק and רָשָׁע and the possible uses of these terms in psalms. Second, it takes an intentionally poetic approach to understanding these features both generally (as in conventions) and specifically in the individual psalm. With these two foundational contributions, the third unique contribution emerges: the צַדִּיק and רָשָׁע in psalms are not only, or even usually, employed to describe the "prototypically good" or "prototypically bad" person. Rather, the רָשָׁע is usually understood as a designation for an antagonist, and the צַדִּיק often is understood as one who is innocently wronged. Fourth, with its focus on the setting of a single psalm as primary in interpretation, this study emphasizes the differences between presentations of these figures, as well as the similarities.

By focusing on the semantics and poetics of the figures of the righteous and the wicked, this study uniquely offers clarity regarding how the contrast of these figures can function in psalms. In the following chapter, I discuss an appropriate way to view character in psalms as part of the poetics of Hebrew psalmody. In chapter 2, I detail the range of meanings for both of the terms צַדִּיק and רָשָׁע in the Hebrew Bible. This sets up the foundation for looking in chapter 3 at the unique ways these figures are used in other books that use the contrast as a literary pattern. Chapter 3 also briefly summarizes themes that emerge from the use of צַדִּיק and רָשָׁע in psalms before analyzing individual psalms.

In chapter 4, I analyze the function of the figures צַדִּיק and רָשָׁע in the eighteen psalms that include a mention of both as substantive adjectives that refer to human persons. The psalms in this study are: Pss 1; 7; 11; 31; 32; 34; 37; 55; 58; 68; 75; 92; 94; 97; 112; 140; 141; and 146. While the focus in each psalm will be on the particular use of the contrast between the righteous and the wicked, the entire psalm will be interpreted to situate the function of the characters within the overall context of the psalm. This is a study of the literary features of the righteous and the wicked and thus takes account of the instances of these figures across the psalms of the Psalter.

NOTES

1. All translations are the author's own.
2. See Hans-Joachim Kraus, *Theology of the Psalms*, trans. Keith R. Crim (Minneapolis, MN: Augsburg, 1986), 157; Patrick D. Miller, "The Beginning of the Psalter," in *The Shape and Shaping of the Psalter*, ed. J. Clinton McCann, JSOTSup 159 (Sheffield: JSOT, 1993), 88. For those connected with the wicked, see Patrick D. Miller, "Who Are the Bad Guys in the Psalms?" in *Let Us Go up to Zion: Essays in Honour of H. G. M. Williamson on the Occasion of His Sixty-Fifth Birthday*, ed. Iain W. Provan and Mark J. Boda, VTSup 153 (Leiden: Brill, 2012), 423–424;

P. J. Botha, "The Function of the Polarity Between the Pious and the Enemies in Psalm 119," *OTE* 5 (1992): 256–257.

3. Jerome F. D. Creach, *Yahweh as Refuge and the Editing of the Hebrew Psalter*, JSOTSup 217 (Sheffield: Sheffield Academic, 1996), 79–80; Christoph Levin, "Das Gebetbuch der Gerechten: Literargeschichtliche Beobachtungen am Psalter," *Zeitschrift für Theologie und Kirche* 90 (1993): 371. The singular and plural forms of the term רָשָׁע refer to the wicked eighty-one times in the Psalter, representing 30 percent of the total instances of this term in the Old Testament. The term צַדִּיק in its singular and plural forms refers to the individual forty-four times.

4. Joseph Blenkinsopp, *The Beauty of Holiness: Rereading Isaiah in Light of the Psalms* (London: T&T Clark, 2019), 109–110.

5. Miller, "Beginning," 85.

6. As is common in research, throughout this work, "psalms" written with a lowercase "p" refers to individual compositions, whereas "Psalms" refers to the Book of Psalms.

7. John Kartje, *Wisdom Epistemology in the Psalms: A Study of Psalms 1, 73, 90, and 107*, BZAW 472 (Berlin: De Gruyter, 2014), 83.

8. Brown ("Reading the Psalms Sapientially in the Writings," in *The Oxford Handbook of the Writings of the Hebrew Bible*, ed. by Donn F. Morgan [Oxford: Oxford University Press, 2018], 156) notes this difference between Ps 37 and Proverbs as well.

9. Gordon J. Wenham, "The Ethics of the Psalms," in *Interpreting the Psalms: Issues and Approaches*, ed. David Firth and Philip S. Johnston (Downers Grove, IL: InterVarsity, 2005), 187; Friederike Neumann, *Schriftgelehrte Hymnen: Gestalt, Theologie und Intention der Psalmen 145 und 146–150*, BZAW 491 (Berlin: De Gruyter, 2016), 100. Daniel C. Owens (*Portraits of the Righteous in the Psalms: An Exploration of the Ethics of Book I* [Eugene, OR: Pickwick, 2013]) also approaches ethics in the Psalms, but uses "righteous" as a general category for the faithful. Stuart Weeks ("Wisdom Psalms," in *Temple and Worship in Biblical Israel*, ed. John Day, LHBOTS 422 [London: T&T Clark, 2005], 299–300), noting significant challenges for viewing wisdom as a genre category, suggests that the focus on ethical behavior connects psalms with the concept of wisdom.

10. The terms צַדִּיק and רָשָׁע are occasionally used as criteria for determining the category of "wisdom psalms" in Hermann Gunkel and Joachim Begrich, *Introduction to Psalms: The Genre of the Religious Lyric of Israel*, trans. James D. Nogalski (Macon, GA: Mercer University Press, 1998), 296; Murphy, "Consideration," 163; R. B. Y. Scott, *The Way of Wisdom in the Old Testament* (New York: Macmillan, 1971), 198; J. Kenneth Kuntz, "The Retribution Motif in Psalmic Wisdom," *ZAW* 89 (1977): 223; Neumann, *Schriftegelehrte Hymnen*, 111; Walter Brueggemann, "Some Aspects of Theodicy in Old Testament Faith," *PRSt* 26 (1999): 255; Marko Marttila, *Collective Reinterpretation in the Psalms: A Study of the Redaction History of the Psalter*, FAT 2.13 (Tübingen: Mohr Siebeck, 2006), 206; Norman Whybray, *Reading the Psalms as a Book*, JSOTSup 222 (Sheffield: Sheffield Academic, 1996), 63; R. B. Y. Scott, "Wise and Foolish, Righteous and Wicked," in *Studies in the Religion of Ancient Israel*, ed. G. W. Anderson et al., VTSup 23 (Leiden: Brill, 1972), 160–161;

J. Kenneth Kuntz, "The Canonical Wisdom Psalms of Ancient Israel: Their Rhetori-
cal, Thematic, and Formal Dimensions," in *Rhetorical Criticism, Essays in Honor of
James Muilenburg*, ed. Jared J. Jackson and Martin Kessler, Pittsburgh Theological
Monograph Series 1 (Pittsburgh, PA: Pickwick, 1974), 211; Roland E. Murphy, "A
Consideration of the Classification, 'Wisdom Psalm,'" in *Congress Volume Bonn
1962*, ed. G. W. Anderson et al., VTSup 9 (Leiden: Brill, 1963), 159–160; J. A.
Burger, "Psalm 1 and Wisdom," *OTE* 8 (1995): 334–336; Gerstenberger, *Psalms,
Part 1*, 157. Similarly, James Luther Mays ("The Place of the Torah-Psalms in
the Psalter," *JBL* 106 [1987]: 4) suggests that Ps 1 drew its themes from Proverbs.
Other scholars see "retribution" or "retribution theology" as an indicator of wisdom
thinking in psalms, e.g., Kuntz, "Retribution Motif," 225; Sigmund Mowinckel, *The
Psalms in Israel's Worship*, trans. D. R. Ap-Thomas (Oxford: Blackwell, 1962),
2:112. These are, of course, distinguished from other formal categories for wisdom,
and most scholars would assume that both form and content be present (e.g., Murphy
"Consideration," 160). Scott (*Way of Wisdom*, 121–122) includes the two terms צַדִּיק
and רָשָׁע in his list of seventy-seven "characteristic vocabulary" of wisdom texts,
which is used as a launching point for Kuntz. Avi Hurvitz ("Wisdom Vocabulary in
the Hebrew Psalter: A Contribution to the Study of 'Wisdom Psalms," *VT* 38 [1988]:
43–44) intentionally focuses on language that is exclusive or distinctive in usage in
wisdom texts, implying that the language of righteous and wicked can only further
corroborate a wisdom categorization. Gerard von Rad (*Wisdom in Israel*, trans. James
D. Martin [London: SCM, 1972], 12), however, casts doubt on the usefulness of terminology as a way to understand wisdom texts. See also Simon P. Stocks, "'Children,
Listen to Me': The Voicing of Wisdom in the Psalms," in *Interpreting Old Testament
Wisdom Literature*, ed. David G. Firth and Lindsay Wilson (Downers Grove, IL: IVP
Academic, 2017), 196–199.

 One common way that the discussion of the righteous and the wicked appears
in scholarship is in relation to a so-called two-way theology, often considered a wisdom theme (Bernd U. Schipper, *Proverbs 1–15*, ed. Thomas Krüger, trans. Stephen
Germany, Hermeneia [Minneapolis, MN: Fortress, 2019], 176; Mark J. Boda, *A
Severe Mercy: Sin and Its Remedy in the Old Testament*, Siphrut 1 [Winona Lake,
IN: Eisenbrauns, 2009], 364, 371–373, 396; Bruce K. Waltke, *The Book of Proverbs: 1–15*, NICOT [Grand Rapids, MI: Eerdmans, 2004], 285–286). The apparent
categorization comes through the metaphorical contrast of differing pathways of the
righteous and the wicked, as one sees in Ps 1:5–6, Prov 2:20–22, 4:10–19. Certainly,
the pathway metaphor is important in Prov 1–9 (Norman C. Habel, "The Symbolism of Wisdom in Proverbs 1–9," *Interpretation* 26 [1972]: 133, 137; Raymond C.
Van Leeuwen, "Liminality and Worldview in Proverbs 1–9," *Semeia* 50 [1990]:
112–113; Raymond C. Van Leeuwen, "Theology: Creation, Wisdom, and Covenant," in *The Oxford Handbook of Wisdom in the Bible*, ed. Will Kynes [Oxford:
Oxford University Press, 2021], 75). Though this pathway imagery appears without
mention of righteous and wicked, for example, Deut 30:15–20 (Joseph Blenkinsopp, *Wisdom and Law in the Old Testament: The Ordering of Life in Israel and
Early Judaism*, Oxford Bible Series [Oxford: Oxford University Press, 1995], 87).
Markus Philipp Zehnder (*Wegmetaphorik im Alten Testament: Eine semantische*

Untersuchung der alttestamentlichen und altorientalischen Weg-Lexeme mit beson-
derer Berücksichtigung ihrer metaphorischen Verwendung, BZAW 268 [Berlin: De
Gruyter, 1999], 593–594) has shown that contrasting opposing ways is common in
the OT; it does not as consistent as other expressions of two ways in later literary
corpora, such as *Did.* 1:1.

11. For wisdom psalms, see especially James L. Crenshaw, *The Psalms: An Intro-*
duction (Grand Rapids, MI: Eerdmans, 2001), 94; James L. Crenshaw, "Wisdom
Psalms?" *Currents in Research: Biblical Studies* 8 (2000): 9–17; James L. Crenshaw,
"Gold Dust or Nuggets? A Brief Response to J. Kenneth Kuntz," *Currents in Biblical*
Research 1/2 (2003): 156; Tova Forti, "Gattung and Sitz im Leben: Methodological
Vagueness in Defining Wisdom Psalms," in *Was There a Wisdom Tradition? New*
Prospects in Israelite Wisdom Studies, ed. Mark R. Sneed, AIL 23 (Atlanta, GA:
SBL, 2015), 205–220.

12. Kynes, *Obituary*, 82–104.

13. Jacqueline Vayntrub, *Beyond Orality: Biblical Poetry on Its Own Terms*, The
Ancient Word (London: Routledge, 2019), 72–73.

14. Mark R. Sneed, "Is the 'Wisdom Tradition' a Tradition?" *CBQ* 73 (2011):
55; Mark R. Sneed, "'Grasping After the Wind': The Elusive Attempt to Define and
Delimit Wisdom," in *Was There a Wisdom Tradition? New Prospects in Israelite*
Wisdom Studies, ed. Mark R. Sneed, AIL 23 (Atlanta, GA: SBL, 2015), 40.

15. Susan E. Gillingham ("The Wisdom Tradition and the Psalms," in *Perspec-*
tives on Israelite Wisdom: Proceedings of the Oxford Old Testament Seminar, ed.
John Jarrick, LHBOTS 618 [New York: T&T Clark, 2016], 293) and Weeks ("Wisdom Psalms," 305) both note the presence of the language in other traditions.

16. William P. Brown, "Come, O Children . . . I Will Teach You the Fear of the
Lord" (Psalm 34:12): Comparing Psalms and Proverbs," in *Seeking Out the Wisdom*
of the Ancients: Essays Offered to Honor Michael V. Fox on the Occasion of His
Sixty-Fifth Birthday, ed. Ronald L. Troxel, Kelvin G. Friebel, and Dennis R. Magary
(Winona Lake, IN: Eisenbrauns, 2005), 85–103.

17. Brown, "Come, O Children," 87–88.

18. Jamie A. Grant, *The King as Exemplar: The Function of Deuteronomy's*
Kingship Law in the Shaping of the Book of Psalms, AcBib 17 (Atlanta, GA: SBL,
2004); Rolf Rendtorff, "The Psalms of David: David in the Psalms," in *The Book of*
Psalms: Composition and Reception, ed. Peter W. Flint and Patrick D. Miller, VTSup
99 (Leiden: Brill, 2005), 60–61, 63; Mays, "Torah Psalms," 11; David M. Howard,
Jr., "The Proto-MT Psalter, the King, and Psalms 1 and 2: A Response to Klaus Seybold," in *Jewish and Christian Approaches to the Psalms: Conflict and Convergence*,
ed. Susan Gillingham, 182–189 (Oxford: Oxford University Press, 2013), 186–187;
David M. Howard, Jr., *The Structure of Psalms 93–100*, Biblical and Judaic Studies
from the University of California San Diego 5 (Winona Lake, IN: Eisenbrauns, 1997),
202–207; Jerome F. D. Creach, *The Destiny of the Righteous in the Psalms* (St. Louis,
MO: Chalice, 2008), 55. However, Creach (*Destiny*, 86–98) sees the king as also distinct from the identity of the righteous as the one who protects the righteous community. Brown (*Psalms*, Interpreting Biblical Texts [Nashville, TN: Abingdon, 2010],
117) identifies the speaker of Ps 3 as the righteous king based on the context of Pss

1–2. Gerald E. Wilson ("Shaping the Psalter: A Consideration of Editorial Linkage in the Book of Psalms," in *The Shape and Shaping of the Psalter*, ed. J. Clinton McCann, JSOTSup 159 [Sheffield: JSOT, 1993], 80–81), while not directly citing the language of righteous and wicked as evidence for categorization of wisdom, sees a "wisdom frame" encompassing Pss 1–145 with those wisdom psalms (1, 73, 90, 107, and 145) in the immediate vicinity of royal psalms (2, 72, 89, and 144). Others see the צַדִּיק in individual psalms as referring to the king, apart from canonical placement. For further examples from Ps 3 see Ee Kon Kim, "Holy War Ideology and the Rapid Shift of Mood in Psalm 3," in *On the Way to Nineveh: Studies in Honor of George M. Landes*, ed. Stephen L. Cook and S. C. Winter, ASOR Books 4 (Atlanta, GA: Scholars, 1999), 86–90; Craigie, *Psalms 1–50*, 72. On Ps 11, see Stephen T. Sumner, "A Reanalysis of Psalm 11," *ZAW* 131 (2019): 86. For other instances, see Mowinckel, *Psalms*, 1:76–78. On Ps 5 see John Eaton, *The Psalms: A Historical and Spiritual Commentary with an Introduction and New Translation* (London: Continuum, 2005), 74.

19. See Levin, "Gebetbuch," which is followed by Urmas Nõmmik, "Die Gerechtigkeitsbearbeitungen in den Psalmen: Eine Hypothese von Christoph Levin formgeschichtlich und kolometrish überprüft," *Ugarit Forschungen* 31 (1999): 443 and *passim*; Oswald Loretz, *Psalmstudien: Kolometrie, Strophik, und Theologie ausgewählter Psalmen*, BZAW 309 (Berlin: De Gruyter, 2002), 13, 24–25; and in part by Urmas Nõmmik and Anu Põldsam, "Psalm 86, Its Place in the Psalter, and Group Identity in the Second Temple Period," *ZAW* 130 (2018): 411. Else K. Holt ("'Let the Righteous Strike Me; Let the Faithful Correct Me': Psalm 141 and the Enclave of the Ṣaddiqîm," *SJOT* 33 [2019]: 186, https://doi.org/10.1080/09018328.2019.1686282) also finds the presence of "psalms of the righteous" to prove the presence of a group of Persian period Judeans that see themselves as the righteous community, citing Pss 1, 36, 37, 73, 92, 141, and 146. Reinhard Gregor Kratz ("Gerechte und Frevler: die Auslegung von Psalm 37 in Qumran und bei Martin Luther," *Zeitschrift für Theologie und Kirche* 114 [2017]: 367–397, 371) sees historical referents to these terms but suggest that their identities are lost to history. Cf. Nõmmik and Põldsam ("Psalm 86," 398) who agree that it is a difficult endeavor yet seek to identify layers in the psalms that belong to different groups. See also Klaus Seybold (*Introducing the Psalms*, trans. R. Graeme Dunphy [London: T&T Clark, 1990], 175), who notes conversely that the various uses of the "negative" characters suggest these terms cannot refer to a single group. Several scholars have suggested that a community who called themselves the *Hasidim* can be seen in the Psalter, e.g., Nõmmik and Põldsam, "Psalm 86," 410; Harm Van Grol, "David and His Chasidim: Place and Function of Psalms 138–145," in *The Composition of the Book of Psalms*, ed. Erich Zenger, BETL 238 (Leuven: Peeters, 2010), 309–337. Against Levin, Blenkinsopp (*Beauty*, 109) notes that there is no external evidence for a group labeled צדיקים, unlike the חֲסִידִים.

20. Creach, *Yahweh as Refuge*; Creach, *Destiny*; Jerome F. D. Creach, "The Destiny of the Righteous and the Theology of the Psalms," in *Soundings in the Theology of the Psalms: Perspectives and Methods in Contemporary Scholarship*, ed. Rolf A. Jacobson (Minneapolis, MN: Fortress, 2011), 49–61; Jerome F. D. Creach, "The Righteous and the Wicked," in *The Oxford Handbook of the Psalms*, ed. William P. Brown (Oxford: Oxford University Press, 2014), 529–541.

21. Creach, *Yahweh as Refuge*, 74–105. Brown (*Seeing the Psalms: A Theology of Metaphor* [Louisville, KY: Westminster John Knox, 2002], 18–79) largely follows Creach's argument, yet focuses on the pathway metaphor itself.

22. Creach, *Destiny*, 1. J. Clinton McCann (*A Theological Introduction to the Psalter: The Psalms as Torah* [Nashville, TN: Abingdon, 1993], 35, 88) also sees the voice of the psalmist as one of the righteous on theological grounds. Others connect the voice with the community on historical grounds, e.g., Holt, "Psalm 141," 192: "his fellow *ṣaddiqîm*"; Blenkinsopp, *Beauty*, 109–110.

23. See Martin Ravndal Hauge, *Between Sheol and Temple: Motif Structure and Function in the I-Psalms*, JSOTSup 178 (Sheffield: Sheffield Academic, 1995), 29–30, 36–37, for helpful comments on the distinction between the designation of "I" and the righteous.

24. Claudia Sticher, *Die Rettung der Guten durch Gott und die Selbstzerstörung der Bösen: ein theologisches Denkmuster im Psalter*, BBB 137 (Berlin: Philo, 2002).

25. Sticher, *Die Rettung*, 16.

26. Botha, "Function," 262.

27. Gert T. M. Prinsloo, "Psalm 5: A Theology of Tension and Reconciliation," *SK* 19 (1998): 636–638.

28. Brown, "Reading the Psalms Sapientially," 158.

29. Jože Krašovec, *God's Righteousness and Justice in the Old Testament* (Grand Rapids, MI: Eerdmans, 2022), 62. Krašovec unhelpfully assumes a connection between the speaker and the righteous, which will be addressed in chapter 2.

30. Throughout this work, I use both the Hebrew צַדִּיק and רָשָׁע and the common English glosses "righteous" and "wicked" to refer to these terms, rather than to refer to a wider range of figures that could be classified under these English designations.

31. As Susan E. Gillingham (*The Poems and Psalms of the Hebrew Bible*, Oxford Bible Series [Oxford: Oxford University Press, 1994], 190) notes, the tension between innovation and convention is present throughout the poetry of psalms.

32. Berlin ("On Reading Biblical Poetry: The Role of Metaphor," in *Congress Volume: Cambridge, 1995*, ed. J. A. Emerton [Leiden: Brill, 1997], 31) writes that "even stock images like water can be used creatively." While the image differs, the same is true for the language of the righteous and the wicked.

33. Examples that would be considered under the broad category of poetics would be Tova Forti, *"Like a Lone Bird on a Roof": Animal Imagery and the Structure of Psalms*, Critical Studies in the Hebrew Bible 10 (University Park, PA: Eisenbrauns, 2018). However, Shubert Spero ("Variations on a Theme in Biblical Psalmody," *JBQ* 45 [2017]: 115–118) briefly notes "variations on a theme" as a poetic technique in psalms.

34. See, for examples of psalmody as opposed to prophecy, in William H. Bellinger, *Psalmody and Prophecy*, JSOTSup 27 (Sheffield: JSOT, 1984), 9 (and title), and Susan E. Gillingham, "New Wine and Old Wineskins: Three Approaches to Prophecy and Psalmody," in *Prophecy and Prophets and Ancient Israel: Proceedings of the Oxford Old Testament Seminar*, ed. John Day, LHBOTS 531 (London: T&T Clark, 2010), 370. For more general uses see also, for example, David Willgren, *The Formation of the "Book" of Psalms: Reconsidering the Transmission and*

Canonization of Psalmody in Light of Material Culture and the Poetics of Anthologies, FAT 2.88 (Tübingen: Mohr Siebeck, 2016).

35. Here, I refer to the conventions of anthologies as opposed to poems.

36. This is true when genre is discussed, stemming from form criticism. Rather than definitions of "psalms," the discussion nearly always focuses on differences. See e.g., Nancy L. DeClaissé-Walford, Rolf Jacobson, and Beth LaNeel Tanner, *The Book of Psalms*, NICOT (Grand Rapids, MI: Eerdmans, 2014), 13–21; Gillingham, *Poems and Psalms*, 206–230, etc. Form criticism has helped to identify differences between forms and smaller genres (see earlier sections on form criticism), but its continued influence has highlighted that there are different types of psalms rather than that psalmody is something distinct from other types of literature. William H. Bellinger ("Psalms and the Question of Genre," in *The Oxford Handbook of the Psalms*, ed. William P. Brown [Oxford: Oxford University Press, 2014], 322–323) concludes his summary of form-critical genres and responses by highlighting that the categories themselves are less rigid, though still affirms Westermann's division between two types of praise and lament. See Claus Westermann, *Praise and Lament in the Psalms*, trans. Keith R. Crim and Richard N. Soulen (Atlanta, GA: John Knox, 1981).

37. See esp. Mowinckel, *Psalms*, and Gerstenberger, *Psalms, Part 2*. Tremper Longman III ("The Psalms and Ancient Near Eastern Prayer Genres," in *Interpreting the Psalms: Issues and Approaches*, ed. Philip S. Johnston and David G. Firth [Downers Grove, IL: InterVarsity, 2005], 59) cautions against coming to specific conclusions about the use of prayers in certain historical settings, though focuses on prayer as an address to a deity to define genre and psalms (41). However, Boda ("'Varied and Resplendid Riches': Exploring the Breadth and Depth of Worship in the Psalter," in *Rediscovering Worship: Past, Present, and Future*, ed. Wendy J. Porter, McMaster New Testament Studies [Eugene, OR: Pickwick, 2015], 63–64) has shown through careful attention to shifts in voicing and collation of the data that in psalms "over half of the words spoken by psalmists are addressed on the horizontal plane" rather than to God. This is significant in terms of defining psalms as prayers, as Longman has done.

38. This is not to say that psalms do not appear outside the Psalter in the Old Testament, as seen in examples in James W. Watts, *Psalm and Story: Inset Hymns in Hebrew Narrative*, JSOTSup 139 (Sheffield: JSOT, 1992). Rather, there are features unique to psalms. However, works on poetry primarily address poetry as a general category rather than psalmic poetry in particular, such as Alonso-Schökel, *A Manual of Hebrew Poetics*, trans. Adrian Graffy, Subsidia Biblica 11 (Rome: Editrice Pontificio Istituto Biblico, 1988); Robert Alter, *The Art of Biblical Poetry*, rev. ed. (New York: Basic Books, 2011); Gillingham, *Poems and Psalms*; James L. Kugel, *The Idea of Hebrew Poetry: Parallelism and Its History* (New Haven, CT: Yale University Press, 1981); F. W. Dobbs-Allsopp, *On Biblical Poetry* (Oxford: Oxford University Press, 2015); J. P. Fokkelman, *Reading Biblical Poetry: An Introductory Guide* (Louisville, KY: Westminster John Knox, 2001); Wilfred G. E. Watson, *Classical Hebrew Poetry: A Guide to Its Techniques*, 2nd ed., JSOTSup 26 (Sheffield: Sheffield Academic, 1986).

39. For a similar position, see James L. Mays, *Psalms*, Interpretation (Louisville, KY: John Knox, 1994), 20–21.

40. As Harry P. Nasuti (*Defining the Sacred Songs: Genre, Tradition and the Post-Critical Interpretation of the Psalms*, JSOTSup 218 [Sheffield: Sheffield Academic, 1999], 58–59) points out, breaking down the rigid barriers between genres of psalms is key to the work of both Westermann (*Praise and Lament*) and Walter Brueggemann (e.g., "Psalms and Life of Faith: A Suggested Typology of Function," *JSOT* 17 [1980]: 3–32).

41. Sneed, "Wisdom Tradition," 57.

42. As an example, see the history and development of tropes of robotic characters in Sherryl Vint, *Science Fiction*, MIT Essential Knowledge Series (Cambridge, MA: MIT Press, 2021), 75–95, or of Alien tropes in David Seed, *Science Fiction: A Very Short Introduction* (New York: Oxford University Press, 2011), 27–46.

43. M. H. Abrams and Geoffrey Galt Harpham, *A Glossary of Literary Terms*, 10th ed. (Boston, MA: Wadsworth Cengage Learning, 2012), 378.

44. Chris Baldick, *The Oxford Dictionary of Literary Terms*, 4th ed. (Oxford: Oxford University Press, 2015), 342.

Chapter 1

An Approach to Character in Hebrew Psalms

Research on character and characterization often comes from the interpretation of fictional literary figures, yet there are elements related to the figures in the psalms that further elucidate the function of these figures in the poetics of psalms.[1] Though the righteous and the wicked are not equivalent to characters in works of fictional narrative, they are similar enough to merit the use of the analogy. While the precise wording of definitions for "character" varies, there are at least four common elements: (1) singularly identified (an individual or collective); (2) participant (meaning that they take part in some kind of action); with (3) human or human-like characteristics; (4) in a discourse, usually noted as a work of fiction or a "storyworld."[2]

In order for a character to be represented in a text, Margolin writes, "an individual entity, designated by a singular term in the narrative text, can be said to be minimally represented by this text if and only if the twin conditions of existence and predication are fulfilled with respect to it."[3] While I am not addressing "storyworlds" per se, the discourse of a psalm functions within a kind of literary world that can appropriately be compared to "storyworlds" at the most basic level. The righteous and the wicked meet these minimum requirements for consideration as characters in many psalms.[4]

THEORIES OF CHARACTERS

Theories of character are often discussed within narratology. There are several topics that could be addressed relating to character, but three are salient for this discussion: (1) character as a function of plot; (2) character as a representation of people; and (3) character as a signifier of ideas. While each of these models and definitions can help to clarify the roles and functions of

17

characters, it is the synthetic approach highlighted by Margolin and Phelan that forms the basis of the understanding utilized here.[5] These theories provide insights into relating the figures of psalms and their ontology, which must be mediated by the cultural and social understanding of these figures. The insights of characterization brought into this work derive specifically from this understanding of character and the development of the righteous and the wicked as figures in the psalms, and will thus be treated secondarily in its own section.

Characters as Function of Plot

As with most literary features, the starting point in understanding the theory of character is Aristotle. Aristotle, while also including discussion of characters as representations, sees events as the most important aspect of a story (in his case, tragedy), writing: "tragedy is a *mimesis* not of men . . . but of actions . . . events—the plot—is the *end* of tragedy, and the end is what matters most of all."[6] This same idea about character as a function of plot has been popular in modern narratological research. Both Formalist and many Structuralist attempts to understand characters reflect the idea of character as a function of narrative. Vladimir Propp saw characters as one of the commonalities of Russian folktales and argued that these figures serve a limited set of functions in the structure of the folktale.[7] This research is limited by its application to a single literary type, but Greimas took Propp's functions as a starting point to develop his Actant model of character.[8] According to Greimas, characters fit with certain functions as senders, receivers, helpers, and opponents in relation to the plot.[9] This positivistic view, that the actant model reflects a sort of deep structure "able to account for the organization of the human imaginary,"[10] breaks down with modern fiction. It accounts for the story in the story/discourse distinction, but does not fill out the possibilities of character when it comes to discourse. Further, the subordination of character to plot is itself an unnecessary and unhelpful distinction.[11]

At the same time, the two concepts of character and action are intrinsically related. Aspects related to character, in particular a character's motivation, become central to the way that a narrative plays out.[12] Sometimes these characters play a specific role within the narrative, as with Propp's research on the Russian folktale. When looking at psalms, there is a close relationship between the figures of the righteous and the wicked and the role they play in the overall story, and yet, the aspects of the story are far less clear. There are, of course, specific roles that the righteous and the wicked play, even if there is some variation in the way that these roles are expressed. The titles themselves of righteous, wicked, and God appear to fulfill particular functions in relation to each other. These specific functions, while part of the narrative structure, also have religious and rhetorical purposes. In fact, it is the rhetorical effect that appears more likely to account for the function of these figures, so while a sort of structural relational triangulation can help show what the righteous and the wicked are doing in the story,[13] it does not account for what is considered the thematic contribution of these figures.

Character as Representation of People

One of the other emphases of character highlighted originally by Aristotle is mimesis or representation. The mimetic, or representational, features of characters are in part necessary in order for a figure or element to be considered a character, a figure requiring human-like features.[14] That is, they are by definition figures representational of people, whether based on an individual figure or not. There are various degrees of mimesis at play in literature.[15] A character may be one that reflects reality closely, and yet, within a discourse, they may not be represented to such a large degree.[16] It is in light of the sentiment that all character is in some way mimetic that Schwarz describes all characterization as a kind of "trope," drawing on something real to become something meaningful in a text.[17]

There is a sense in which the righteous and the wicked are *not* the same as fictional characters, which is why I refer to them as *analogous* to characters. Characters themselves are figures in fictional worlds, and, for example, figures in a biography would not fit neatly into that categorization.[18] The lines here are rather thin, and whether a figure is considered a character depends largely on how a discourse is presented. While the "world" of the discourse of psalms may have elements that are not tied directly to an experience in reality, they do appear to attempt to say something true about the world. In some cases, the psalmists may have had a particular individual in mind when referring to a righteous or wicked figure in the psalms. But at the same time, they are not described in any identifiable manner (at least to those of us reading today).

The righteous and the wicked are only weakly mimetic figures. They are not generally intended to reflect real figures in either history or practice. They are characters that are intended to function more as symbols than as people, and their struggles are emblematic rather than factual. This does not suggest that there is nothing in history that underlies the presentation of these figures in psalms. Reflections of real people and historical events may sometimes be identified in psalms. However, this is far from the specificity found in Hebrew literature that emphasizes history. The presentation is entirely different, and the resulting function is the re-applicability of songs for a variety of events. Even if an autobiographical account of disaster or threat appears in a psalm, it is done only in vague terms, as a sort of vignette. One could not identify an author from any psalm based on its contents. A time period is also difficult to identify because of these conventions. And yet, they are clearly reflections of real people. While the mimetic function of psalms is not the same as that of literary figures, or even Hebrew characters, they do often reflect human nature in terms of their activities and emotions. Thus, they are mimetic in other ways.

Character as Signifier of Ideas

Characters are more than functions of plot and representations of people. As part of a discourse that serves to signify a theme or idea, characters are determined by this theme and act as signifiers of it.[19] That is, characters are able to express ideas about the world outside of the text, such as values or morality. Characters are used toward particular ends, often beyond that of entertainment. Rather than express themes explicitly, characters allow for these values or ideas to be expressed in modes that make concepts tangible.[20] The righteous and the wicked are weakly mimetic but are thematically significant.

Character types, including but not limited to stock characters, develop through the use of figures with consistent characteristics over time and in light of the literature and culture in which a text is produced. The types of characters that a text employs are one indication of a text's genre, as certain types typify one or another.[21] Because the figures of the righteous and the wicked are conventional, they bring with them certain characteristics that are not explicitly present in the text. In part, this is due to the cultural lenses that are brought to bear on the figures within a particular genre. Margolin writes, "By writing their narratives, authors determine rather than describe the properties of their characters."[22] While there is a degree to which this is true for the psalmists writing about the righteous and the wicked, there are also historical and theological factors at play. The authors of psalms do define, in part, what the righteous and the wicked are like, but they are also bound by literary convention. Each expression of the righteous and the wicked includes elements that are drawn from cultural expectations, but it also has a particular purpose in a given psalm. As religious literature from a particular people across centuries of time, the psalms themselves had particular functions for the community, and the figures presented within the psalms are part of that overall purpose.

Summary of Theory of Character

James Phelan argues that characters can function simultaneously as possible persons (mimetic), as signifiers of ideas (thematic), and as a construction of discourse (synthetic), and do not necessarily adhere to an either/or distinction.[23] Here, he draws a helpful distinction between the dimensions (or attributes) of characters and their functions, as these elements need not become functions.[24] This study takes Phelan's work as a starting point regarding character, noting the attributes in the following chapters, then relates their functions in chapters 4–5. James Phelan's theory allows for a connection between these functions.[25] These three aspects relate to the various functions of these figures in psalms. While seeing the righteous and the wicked as mimetic figures has its challenges, in that they by definition function as representative entities—the precise point where mimetic and thematic functions diverge in Phelan's articulation—they are nonetheless figures that contain each of these concepts.[26] The nature of these figures as signifiers of meaning is, at the same time, a heightened feature, given that they are designated by intentional thematic titles.

CHARACTERS IN PSALMIC POETRY

This work seeks to understand the ways Hebrew psalmists employ character and characterization, utilizing the figures of the righteous and the wicked. Characters are both built on experiences with real people and constructions of a literary world, drawn within literary conventions.[27] The features are culturally mediated and genre specific—the specific types of character or models that are part of the conventions of the literature and the elements that influence the specific knowledge necessary to understand characters.[28] Conventions of character in literary fiction differ from those of Western lyric poetry just as Hebrew narrative conventions differ from Hebrew psalms. Thus, any discussion of character in psalms must accurately describe characters in light of a psalm's own literary style.

Most theoretical contributions to the study of character come from narratology and focus on character within narrative, specifically narrative fiction. Characterization, however, is a poetic device in its own right.[29] Winko, writing on character in poetry, concludes that "the constitution of characters in poems does not show any essential differences from the constitution of characters in narrative texts."[30] At the same time, Winko suggests, they are presented in distinctly poetic ways.[31] When adequately qualified, the theories of character from the field of narratology have much to offer for poetic texts, including psalms.

For characters to be constructed in a literary text, they must fit within the logic of the world of the text. Looking to narratology to understand character does not require a strict adherence to finding a narrative within a poem, however. Character and narrative (or sequentiality) are intrinsically related, but they are distinct. Seymour Chatman writes, "Both character and event are logically necessary to narrative; where chief interest falls is a matter of the changing taste of authors and their publics."[32] To develop an appropriate understanding of character within poetry requires more than a borrowing of theories of character from narratology, as the ways that characters function in narrative and in lyric differ. Hillebrandt, writing on the nature of character in poetry, suggests that characters in lyric poetry tend to be clear character "types," and more flat than round, largely due to the nature of the lyric mode.[33] An approach to character in lyric—and Hebrew psalms in particular—cannot simply borrow ideas about character and characterization from narratological theory without modifying them for use in understanding poetry.

To analyze character in psalms, as Eder has cautioned,[34] one must take into account the imagery, as well as other poetic devices, used to characterize them. To reiterate the point, the presentation of character in the lyric (or the psalm) is not the same as character is presented in narrative, though insights from narratology can help elucidate character function.

CHARACTERIZATION

In a broad sense, characterization is the phenomenon of ascribing a certain stable property to a figure.[35] In many older studies, characterization has meant a focus on the psychological features of a character in a text.[36] However, characterization is far more than psychological features; as Jannidis notes, it includes both "physiological and locative" descriptions.[37] The ascription of stable properties in fictional narratives takes place in concrete descriptions, as well as the habitual actions that a figure participates in within a discourse.[38]

Two general categories of characterization are (1) the direct or explicitly stated attribution of elements to figures within the text (e.g., "she was shy") and (2) the indirect attribution of elements which can only be inferred or extrapolated from other descriptions of a figure (e.g., "she attempted to avoid conversation at all costs").[39] For this work, these two features will be referred to as "portraiture" and "emplotment."[40] Though there are variations between how direct and indirect characterization occur, generally, indirect characterization requires inference, whereas direct characterization is plainly stated.[41] The focus of characterization tends to be on *traits*, though characterization also can come to mean all pieces of information in the text that are related to a single character.[42]

TACTICS OF CHARACTERIZATION IN PSALMS

In this work, I am drawing on research regarding character from narratology to analyze the figures of the righteous and the wicked as characters in psalms. Though characters in psalms differ in many ways from those in narrative texts, characters are constituted, predicated, and described in psalms. Though few speak of "characters" in psalms, Strawn notes their possibility but suggests that "even when characters are present, the portrait thereof is synchronic, not diachronic."[43] To elaborate, Strawn rightly points out that character development as one would see in narrative texts is almost entirely absent. This should be expected, as the righteous and the wicked appear in poetic, not narrative or dramatic texts. As such, they are poetic characters rather than narrative or dramatic characters. Any attempt to understand them must approach them as they appear within the poetics of Hebrew psalmody.

The resources of meaning-making in Hebrew psalmody are different from those of Hebrew narrative, and thus, the resources for characterization are different. The tools used for meaning in psalms generally are also present in the construal and development of characters. I argue here that the existence and use of stock figures, namely the righteous and the wicked, are themselves part of the toolkit of psalmody. The summary below provides a brief identification of features that relate to characterization in Hebrew psalmody and provides the basis for features that are relevant in the analyses of chapter 5. Rather than outlining all of the ways that these poetic features interact with the righteous and the wicked, I list and describe these here to provide a clear marker of methodological influences on the analysis of the psalms in general when discussing the ways that the figures function in the discourse.

Imagery

One of the primary literary resources in psalms is imagery. Adele Berlin writes, "metaphor is as important a constituent of poetry as parallelism."[44] A number of recent works have utilized metaphor theory to explore meaning in the Bible and, in particular, the psalms.[45] For Brown, metaphor is a centralizing component of the theology of the psalms.[46] Both metonymy and metaphor are prevalent in the psalms,[47] and are often used to depict or to characterize figures. This is true of human figures (righteous, wicked, etc.) as well as the divine. One feature that will become clear is the use of animal imagery, both positive and negative, for the righteous and the wicked, respectively. To understand the function of characters and their characterization, close attention is paid to the images and metaphors of psalms to highlight the way that these figures are characterized in psalms.

Parallel Lines

One of the most classically defined features of Hebrew poetry since the time of Lowth is that of parallelism.[48] While the identification and classification of parallel terms have in many cases become central to the poetic analysis of Hebrew psalms, it is only one of many ways that these figures are character-ized.[49] The use of parallel lines, whether by elaboration, apposition, or con-trast, is one of the most basic features of characterization in the psalms. As an example, lines where titles are directly paralleled in a way that a referential equivalence is intended can help group figures together, as here in Ps 32:

שִׂמְחוּ בַיהוָה וְגִילוּ צַדִּיקִים	11a	Rejoice in Yhwh and exult, righteous people,
וְהַרְנִינוּ כָּל־יִשְׁרֵי־לֵב:	11b	And shout for joy, all upright in heart.

Parallelism is structural but also a poetic device in its own right, as it contributes to meaning through the creative, rhythmic elaboration on themes through parallel lines.

Naming, Labeling, Identification

One of the features of the conventions of psalmic characterization is the simple tool of labeling and identification. Because the figures of the righteous and the wicked are labeled by terms that are not neutral, having a clearly positive or negative connotation, they are themselves instantly categorized within the context of the psalm. Other appellatives that are added continue to serve a characterizing function. The label of enemy is significant in relation to the wicked, and this labeling can occur as both an enemy of the righteous or of Yhwh (e.g., Ps 74). This is also a feature that is prominent in the use of parallelism where those identified as the righteous and the wicked are paralleled with other nominals referring to these same figures. First, there is the naming of characters. Unlike David, the righteous and the wicked do not have "names."[50] Names are also a kind of designation, though they have differing properties. Because the designations "righteous" and "wicked" refer to specific properties, they would be considered a more direct form of characterization.[51]

Identification, on the other hand, is also used to refer to the ways in which a character is reintroduced as discourse active.[52] This may come through the repetition of the same designation, though it could also refer to any character-istic that has been previously ascribed to the figure in question.

Identifying Participants in Psalms

The challenge presented above for interpreting the voices in the psalms is their identification as participants. A significant complication is the relationship of different characters as they appear across many psalms. A composite image (i.e., "characterization") of these figures can only be developed over time. They may receive a short statement with attributes that could be considered in the vein of characterization, but this cannot be developed fully outside of the context of the Psalter. The problem with participants receiving their characterizations in the context of the Psalter has been raised above in the evaluation of canonical approaches to the Psalter. They are limited in that they tend to conflate various data into a sort of synchronous composite that may not accurately draw from the range of examples for that character.

A further complication is the fluidity of person and referent in the Hebrew language. For example, is Yhwh still addressed when a third masculine singular (3ms) jussive follows a string of second masculine singular imperatives? Does the psalmist address themselves when using masculine pronouns or appellations in certain cases? While there is a semantic shift, it may not be a shift in address or referent.

The initial identification of participants must be done through the analysis of lexemes that can refer to individuals or groups. These include pronouns, names, other nominals (including participles functioning nominally), and embedded subjects or objects within verbs. Within the context of a psalm, there may be additional clues as to their identity, and whether or not they are considered semantically equivalent to other designations in the psalm.

I have used the language of figures and participants. The former refers to a semantic category, whereas the latter refers to a grammatical category. If participants are to be considered figures, they must have a demonstrable antecedent that functions as a person or in a person-like manner. Participants, as a grammatical category, can be any nominal which is part of the action of the psalm in some way (i.e., an agent or patient).

Association or Disassociation

As mentioned earlier, the "naming" of the righteous and the wicked instantly characterizes them in a good/bad binary. Though the righteous and the wicked are not always designated by those names, when one is compared with the other, or another kind of figure, the pattern in which they appear characterizes them based on those qualities that relate to them by association or are shown as an antithesis through disassociation. That is, the characteristics of the righteous—at least those that make them fall under the categorization of the righteous—are by disassociation not ascribed to the wicked.

One of the few elements common to all 150 psalms is some mention of God. Because many of the psalms are voiced as a prayer, the request for judgment against the wicked offers a clear judgment of the character of the wicked. However, the statement regarding the activities or perspective of God toward the wicked or the righteous has a particularly strong characterizing effect. Further, multiple characters relating to one another in consistent ways strengthen the consistent attribute of the characterization.[53] This will be true in psalms regarding how both God and the righteous or the psalmist speak of or act toward the wicked.

Predication

One of the basic features of character activity is simply the activities that are ascribed to them. What these figures do or do not do according to the psalm paints the clearest picture of their nature. This is often related to the images mentioned above, such as the wicked waiting to attack or hunting the righteous, but other activities, such as praise or cursing, that are more concrete also characterize these figures. One of the notable features is that there is comparatively little action ascribed to the righteous person directly. Uri Margolin elaborates that action must be cast into a broader setting in order for the information to be considered part of the characterization.[54] Not all actions necessarily signify a particular trait of the character, though it is an important way that characterization takes place in a discourse.

Role in Discourse

Another aspect of characterization relates to the causal relationships between these figures and the sequentiality of the discourse itself. This naturally relates to other aspects mentioned, such as predication or association/disassociation; however, it identifies specific ways in which the overall structure of the discourse is tied to the activities of a particular figure. For example, does one figure have the *role* of an antagonist or protagonist? These roles are discussed in relation to both the other figures in the poem and the overall discourse. This includes addressing the situation and the progression of the discourse.

Claudia Sticher identifies the two categories of participants in psalms: the "good" and the "bad," including in each analysis of a psalm a list of the designations for those figures.[55] Sticher's evaluation is somewhat simplistic, as it narrowly defines the conceptual world of the Psalter into strictly binary categories. The identification of the semantic functions of these terms is dependent more immediately on the context and the conceptual world of the individual psalm. The analysis below will form similar categories for designations, but with an additional focus on identifying other participants (whether they can clearly count within one category), including God himself.

Voicing and Quotation

A major feature of psalmic poetry that has been explored from various avenues in the history of interpretation is that of multivocality.[56] Jacqueline Vayntrub argues that the nature of Hebrew poetry as represented speech should be seen as a literary trope, rather than as an indicator of the background of the text based in so-called "orality."[57] She, in fact, suggests that "biblical poems are always in some way associated with the explicit or implicit speech of characters."[58] The rhetorical usage of quotation characterizes figures through the content of the words. Further, the activity of prayer is a voiced action, relating to both predication and to association with Yhwh. The psalmist, as the lyric "I" or the narrator, automatically serves the role of the authoritative voice.[59] This can also be considered under the category coined by Gérard Genette of "focalization," or point of view,[60] as is realized through voicing and quotation.

Drawing from the narratological distinction between narrator and character, Winko notes that only in some cases can a speaker be considered a character.[61] For the "I" to be considered a character, they must be constituted within the body of the poem itself as another character must be. In Margolin's articulation, they must have identifiable traits and participate in the discourse through some kind of predication. In the case of the psalms, a speaker of a poem may have a narrating function, or it may have a more intrinsic relationship to the structure of the poem as a unique participant in the poem. This is signaled in part by the use of first-person language in the psalm, which actualizes the speaker as an active participant in the discourse. When the "I" becomes a character, the character representations of self and of other figures are present in the discourse, all of which are characterizing factors.[62]

The identification of speakers and addressees is far from straightforward. For the purposes of this work, the focus will be on those specifically identified as speakers or as addressees explicitly in the text. Those addressed in the psalm itself may include God, the community, or the enemies. A designation of "general address" classifies those lines that do not have an explicit addressee, typically those lines that appear in the third person. This classification does not take into account the likelihood of multiple addressees. As poems that were most likely written to be performed orally, even those with an explicit addressee of God are also, by the performative nature of the psalms, addressed to the community, at least in the sense that it is likely an intended audience in addition to the divine audience. Because the focus of this work is on poetic conventions rather than reception or intended audience, I will only address those places where it is important for understanding the overall interpretation of the poem. It is the *telling* of the narrative itself that is important for this study, not the audience to whom it is told. As such, all psalms have a "general" address as their standard form. At the same time, psalms are sometimes addressed to others directly in certain instances rather than as a general audience. When imperatives are spoken generally, the audience is assumed to be the worshiping community.

Jacobson, writing on the rhetorical function of direct speech in the Psalter, notes that the most common category is quotations ascribed to the enemy.[63] While Jacobson does not focus on quotation as a feature of characterization per se, his work is indispensable for seeing the tendencies of how these figures are characterized. Jacobson finds that two general categories of enemy speech appear: first, those in which the enemy speaks an affront to God, and second, those in which the enemy speaks against the speaker.[64]

This feature of characterization characterizes not only the enemy but also God or the psalmist/righteous. Placing certain speech within the mouth of the enemy or the wicked highlights something that is untrue.[65] The function of the enemy's speech can endeavor to highlight the futility of such speech over against the patterns of the psalms wherein God will ultimately destroy the wicked, or they will be destroyed by their own devices. The same is true of the righteous. Though the speech of the wicked may not be "accurately" reported, it serves the function of highlighting the significance of the future reality of the righteous or the psalmist.

It can be challenging to determine the voice that is envisioned speaking in Hebrew psalms. However, multivocality as a liturgical phenomenon is less important for this work in understanding the role of the righteous and the wicked in interaction with God. Instead, when a figure is explicitly mentioned as speaking (i.e., a quotation from God or the enemies), these shifts are considered relevant for the characterization of these figures.

OUTLINE TO THE APPROACH TO
EVENT IN THE PSALMS

In order to be sensitive to the various ways in which characters can function in relationship to these features, I will utilize the following steps in the analysis of individual psalms. Each step builds on the previous one for a fuller understanding of the discourse to place the function of the righteous and the wicked properly within the whole psalm. The first step entails finding designations for individuals or groups, either through labels, pronouns, or embedded subjects in verbs. This includes determining if different labels refer to the same group or individual or to discrete participants. This will also involve identifying the voices of the psalm line by line through cataloging the person and number within the syntax of the Hebrew.[66] The question "Who is speaking and to whom?" is determinative for this stage of analysis. The direction of the voicing is not always discernible, and, if not, it is part of the general address of the poem. Voicing must be incorporated within a theory of character, yet it must not be the totality. In places where it is impossible to label or identify speakers, this must be noted. In many cases, the identification of a speaker (other than the "I" of the poem) or the addressee will be undefined. Participants, such as the voice of the psalmic speaker, are not necessarily considered characters unless they function meaningfully within the discourse of the poem. This does not pose a problem to understanding the poem in this approach, as it is part of the world of the poem.

The second step involves interpretation of the poem, especially the way that the logic of the poem creates meaning. This requires reading a psalm first in a linear fashion, from start to finish, as well as looking at shifts in temporal signifiers throughout the psalm. This step also includes a discussion of the processes of characterization present in the poem as part of the poem, that is, the actions of the figures within the psalm. The second step also pays attention to the discourse features of the psalm more broadly and thus focuses also on the "mediation" of the poem. The first step has already defined the participants in the poem, and this step will identify the way that characters fit within the overall meaning of the poem. The interpretation of poetic features in the psalms mentioned above is important for this step, as these features work together to inform the whole.

The third and final step will evaluate the function of the actions (or lack thereof) and the characters within the thrust of the larger poem. As with any poetic device, function is the most important to determine.[67] With the goal of understanding the psalmic imagination, this step asks the questions of how the characters relate to each other and what that relationship contributes to the overall message of the psalm. This includes an interaction with other poetic devices that are used to characterize these participants.

While these steps are determinative for the use of this model, the theory of character is also important to distinguish in this final stage. In the following chapter, the broad characterization of the righteous and the wicked in terms of stereotypical or conventional means is elaborated, drawing largely on the theory of characters developed above.

NOTES

1. Narratology, from which the theories of character are drawn, is itself a subset of poetics. See Jonathan Culler, *Literary Theory: A Very Short Introduction*, 2nd ed. (Oxford: Oxford University Press, 2011), 62; Adele Berlin, *Poetics and Interpretation of Biblical Narrative*, Bible and Literature Series 9 (Sheffield: Almond Press, 1983), 15.

2. For examples, see Fotis Jannidis ("Character," in *Handbook of Narratology*, ed. Peter Hühn et al., Narratologia 19 [Berlin: De Gruyer, 2009], 14), "a text- or media-based figure in a storyworld, usually human or humanlike"; Mieke Bal (*Narratology: Introduction to the Theory of Narrative*, 4th ed., trans. Christine van Boheemen [Toronto: University of Toronto Press, 2017], 104), "the anthropomorphic figures provided with specifying features the narrator tells us about"; Uri Margolin ("Character," in *The Cambridge Companion to Narrative*, ed. by David Herman, Cambridge Companions to Narrative [Cambridge: Cambridge University Press, 2007], 66), "any entity, individual or collective—normally human or human-like—introduced in a work of narrative fiction."

3. Uri Margolin, "Characters in Literary Narrative: Representation and Signification," *Semiotica* 106 (1995): 375.

4. See Sigrid Eder ("Storytelling in the Psalter? Chances and Limits of a Narrative Psalm Analysis—Shown Exemplarily in Psalm 64," *OTE* 32 [2019]: 349–353) for an example of figures in psalms functioning as characters.

5. Margolin, "Character"; Margolin, "Characters"; Uri Margolin, "The Doer and the Deed: Action as a Basis for Characterization in Narrative," *Poetics Today* 7 (1986): 205–225; James Phelan, "Character, Progression, and the Mimetic-Didactic Distinction," *Modern Philology* 84 (1987): 282–299; James Phelan, *Reading People, Reading Plots: Character, Progression, and the Interpretation of Narrative* (Chicago, IL: University of Chicago Press, 1989).

6. Aristotle, *Poetics*, ed. John Baxter and Patrick Atherton, trans. George Whalley (Montreal: McGill-Queen's University Press, 1997), §20, emphasis original.

7. Vladimir Propp, *Morphology of the Folktale*, ed. Louis A. Wagner, trans. Laurence Scott, 2nd ed., American Folklore Society Bibliographical and Special Series 9 (Austin, TX: University of Texas Press, 1968).

8. Fotis Jannidis, *Figur und Person: Beitrag zu einer historischen Narratologie*, Narratologia 3 (Berlin: De Gruyter, 2004), 2.

9. Algirdas Julien Greimas, *On Meaning: Selected Writings in Semiotic Theory*, trans. Paul J. Perron and Frank H. Collins, Theory and History of Literature 38 (Minneapolis, MN: University of Minnesota Press, 1987), 112.

10. Greimas, *On Meaning*, 107.

11. Seymour Chatman, *Story and Discourse: Narrative Structure in Fiction and Film* (Ithaca, NY: Cornell University Press, 1978), 110. Greimas (*On Meaning*, 116–119) does discuss thematic elements of figures, but that these are discursive rather than narrative elements, and treats them only secondarily as a reduction of elements of a discourse and functions to a theme.

12. Eder, Jens, Fotis Jannidis, and Ralf Schneider, "Characters in Fictional Worlds: An Introduction," in *Characters in Fictional Worlds: Understanding Imaginary Beings in Literature, Film, and Other Media*, ed. Jens Eder, Fotis Jannidis, and Ralf Schneider (Berlin: De Gruyter, 2010), 24.

13. Luis Alonso-Schökel, *Treinta Salmos: Poesía y Oración*, 2nd ed. (Madrid: Christiandad, 1986), 83; Prinsloo, "Psalm 5," 637; P. J. Botha, "The Junction of the Two Ways: The Structure and Theology of Psalm 1," *OTE* 4 (1991): 393.

14. Margolin, "Characters," 380.

15. Margolin, "Characters," 375–376.

16. Margolin, "Characters," 378.

17. Daniel Schwarz, "Character and Characterization: An Inquiry," *Journal of Narrative Technique* 19 (1989): 89–90.

18. Eder, Jannidis, and Schneider, "Characters," 11.

19. Jannidis, "Character," 23.

20. Eder, Jannidis, and Schneider, "Characters," 46.

21. Margolin, "Character," 70.

22. Margolin, "Character," 68.

23. Phelan, "Character," 284. Phelan is arguing against neo-Aristotelian scholars who see a clear distinction between the types of characters that are intended to reflect a person or a type of character that is intended to teach.

24. Phelan, "Character," 284–285.

25. Phelan's *Reading People* continues to be a valuable starting point for current research on character, as shown by the 2018 volume of *Style* (52, issues 1–2) devoted to the ongoing influence of this work.

26. Phelan, *Reading People*, 13.

27. Ralf Schneider, "Toward a Cognitive Theory of Literary Character: The Dynamics of Mental-Model Construction," *Style* 35 (2001): 607.

28. Jannidis, "Character," 18–19.

29. J. Mira Seo, *Exemplary Traits: Reading Characterization in Roman Poetry* (Oxford: Oxford University Press, 2013), 2.

30. Simone Winko, "On the Constitution of Characters in Poetry," in *Characters in Fictional Worlds: Understanding Imaginary Beings in Literature, Film, and Other Media*, ed. Jens Eder, Fotis Jannidis, and Ralf Schneider, Revisionen 3 (Berlin: De Gruyter, 2010), 228.

31. Winko, "Constitution," 209–212.

32. Chatman, *Story and Discourse*, 113.

33. Claudia Hillebrandt, "Figur und Person im Gedicht: Zum Stand der lyrikologischen Figurenforschung und zur Funktion von Figuren in lyrischen Gebilden," in *Lyrisches Ich, Textsubjekt, Sprecher?* vol. 1, *Grundfragen der Lyrikologie*, ed. Claudia Hillebrandt et al. (Berlin: De Gruyter, 2019), 157.

34. Eder, "Storytelling," 354.

35. Eder, Jannidis, and Schneider, "Characters," 30.

36. Eder, Jannidis, and Schneider, "Characters," 30.

37. Jannidis, "Character," 21.

38. Eder, Jannidis, and Schneider, "Characters," 31.

39. Jannidis, *Figur und Person*, 198.

40. The term "emplotment" is employed throughout Paul Ricoeur, *Narrative and Time*, vol. 1, trans. Kathleen McLaughlin and David Pellauer (Chicago, IL: University of Chicago Press, 1984), esp. 31–32, drawn from Aristotle's use of the term *muthos*. A recent volume of *Poetics Today* focused on the topic of emplotment. For "portrait" as a category for event in psalms, see Rebecca W. Poe Hays, *The Function of Story in the Hebrew Psalter* (Lanham, MD: Lexington Books, 2021), 17–20.

41. Jannidis, *Figur und Person*, 209.

42. Eder, Jannidis, and Schneider, "Characters," 30.

43. Brent A. Strawn, "Lyric Poetry," in *Dictionary of the Old Testament: Wisdom, Poetry & Writings*, ed. Tremper Longman and Peter Enns (Downers Grove, IL: IVP Academic, 2008), 438.

44. Berlin, "On Reading Biblical Poetry," 35.

45. E.g., Alison Ruth Gray, *Psalm 18 in Words and Pictures*, BibInt 127 (Leiden: Brill, 2014); Forti, *Like a Lone Bird*.

46. Brown, *Seeing the Psalms*, 10–12.

47. Gray, *Psalm 18*, 11.

48. See Watson, *Classical Hebrew Poetry*, 111–159; Alonso-Schökel, *Manual*, 48–63; Gillingham, *Poems and Psalms*, 69–88; Alter, *Art*, 1–28; Adele Berlin, *Dynamics of Biblical Parallelism*, 2nd ed. (Grand Rapids, MI: Eerdmans, 2008). Parallelism has become so synonymous with the study of Hebrew poetry that more than one work largely focuses on problematizing the category: Kugel, *Idea*, especially 1–58, 204–286; Dobbs-Allsopp, *On Biblical Poetry*, 24–57; Robert D. Holmstedt, "Hebrew Poetry and the Appositive Style: Parallelism, *Requiescat in pace*," *VT* 69 (2019): 617–648. The point in using parallelism as a category of characterization is to emphasize *one* feature of Hebrew poetry by which figures are identified or characterized.

49. Sigrid Eder, *Identifikationspotenziale in den Psalmen: Emotionen, Metaphern und Textdynamik in den Psalmen 30, 64, 90 und 147*, BBB 183 (Göttigen: V & R, 2018), 25.

50. It is likely that in many cases "David" in the body of psalms functions more like a designation referring to the monarchy than the name of a person (Pss 18:51; 89:21, 36, 50; 122:5; 132:17; 144:10). Other mentions of David in the psalms also speak of a Davidic covenant, though use the term to refer to David the person (Pss 78:70; 89:4; 132:10–11).

51. Eder, Jannidis, and Schneider, "Characters," 37.

52. Jannidis, "Character," 21.

53. Jonathan Culpepper, *Language and Characterisation: People in Plays and Other Texts*, Textual Explorations (2001; repr., London: Routledge, 2014), 172.

54. Margolin, "Doer," 206.

55. See, for example, Sticher, *Die Rettung*, 51–52.

56. See, as examples, Carleen Mandolfo, *God in the Dock: Dialogic Tension in the Psalms of Lament*, JSOTSup 357 (London: Sheffield Academic, 2002); Rolf A. Jacobson, *"Many Are Saying": The Function of Direct Discourse in the Hebrew Psalter*, JSOTSup 397 (London: T&T Clark, 2004); Meghan D. Musy, "Hearing Voices: Exploring Psalmic Multivocality as Lyric Poetry," PhD Dissertation (Hamilton: McMaster Divinity College, 2018); Suderman, "Dialogic Tension," 297–312; Catherine Petrany, *Pedagogy, Prayer, and Praise: The Wisdom of the Psalms and Psalter*, FAT 2.83 (Tübingen: Mohr Siebeck, 2015).

57. Vayntrub, *Beyond Orality*, 9–10.

58. Jacqueline Vayntrub, "Hearing the Voice of Biblical Poetry," *SEÅ* 86 (2021): 25.

59. Brown ("The Psalms and 'I': The Dialogical Self and the Disappearing Psalmist," in *Diachronic and Synchronic: Reading the Psalms in Real Time: Proceedings of the Baylor Symposium on the Book of Psalms*, ed. by Joel S. Burnett, W. H. Bellinger, Jr., and W. Dennis Tucker, LHBOTS 488 [New York: T&T Clark, 2007], 26–28) also states that within the text the psalmist is the "implied author." Brown differentiates this from the proposed speaker of the psalm. Because the "I" is the speaker or voice in many psalms, they are from a textual and rhetorical standpoint the implied author of the work; the words of the psalm are the words of the "I." Brown helpfully divides between the speaker of the psalm (in a textual sense) and the performer of the psalm in a liturgical sense (Brown, "Psalms and 'I,'" 34). At the same time, there is a blurred sense between the actual author and the implied author in Brown's essay. For example, Brown ("Psalms and 'I,'" 34) writes, "Liturgically, the psalmist reveals herself to be first and foremost a speech provider." Unless otherwise identified by context or direct speech, the identity of the "I" could be considered psalmist or speaker depending on the situation. Similarly, Samuel Terrien (*The Psalms: Strophic Structure and Theological Commentary*, Eerdmans Critical Commentary [Grand Rapids, MI: Eerdmans, 2003], 294) speaks of the psalmist's didactic voice. The psalmist's voice cannot neatly be distinguished from any other primary voice that could be called the "I" of the psalm. That is, the psalmic persona is not one or the other in the poem itself. Thus, the dialogic sense is nearly impossible to determine in many or most cases. Is there a dialogic movement between more than one first-person speaker in the psalms? Certainly, yes, though it cannot be stated that one voice is that of the *psalmist* and one the *performer* (so Brown, "Psalms and 'I,'" 43). Throughout the analysis chapters, I opt to use "speaker" instead of psalmist to identify the primary voice in the psalm.

60. Gérard Genette, *Narrative Discourse: An Essay in Method*, trans. Jane E. Lewin (1972; repr., Ithaca, NY: Cornell University Press, 1980), 189–194.

61. Winko, "Constitution," 226.

62. Culpepper, *Language and Characterisation*, 167–171.

63. Jacobson, *Many Are Saying*, 27.

64. Jacobson, *Many are Saying*, 27–59.

65. See Jacobson (*Many Are Saying*, 58–59), where the focus is on the enemy speech as a rhetorical feature for instruction.

66. Musy, "Hearing Voices," 35–36. This requires paying close attention to potential shifts in voicing, which may be signaled by a clear grammatical shift in speaker, a clear marker of direct speech, or a shift in pronominal referent.

67. Watson, *Classical Hebrew Poetry*, 20, 31–35.

Chapter 2

Semantics of צַדִּיק and רָשָׁע
in Biblical Hebrew

NOTES ON METHOD

Before moving to the analyses of these figures in the Old Testament and in psalms, this chapter focuses on the semantics of the terms צַדִּיק and רָשָׁע as foundational for understanding their usage in individual instances.[1] There are several challenges with defining the terms צַדִּיק and רָשָׁע. While there is not necessarily a direct relationship between the cognates of verb, adjective, or noun forms of צדק words, these are played off of each other in many cases in the Hebrew Bible, pointing to a connection in the meaning and function of the terms.[2] However, because of this relationship, the concept of righteousness is often explored in scholarship by focusing primarily on the definition of the two nouns צֶדֶק and צְדָקָה.[3] As a result, the assumption is that whatever significance these two nouns have, the adjective must describe the attributes that are in line with that conception.[4] At the same time, there exist concepts of "the righteous" and of "the wicked" that differ from the concepts of "righteousness" or "wickedness," however certain terms may be related.[5] Though these concepts are not themselves tied to a single term, in this study the focus is on the semantics and usage of the lexemes צַדִּיק and רָשָׁע.

A further complication regarding these words is that they appear more significantly in certain corpora than others, suggesting the possibility of corpus-specific usage.[6] There are commonalities due to their generally broad usage, but certain identifications or nuances appear more commonly in certain literary corpora, particularly in Psalms, Proverbs, and Job, as will be detailed in chapter 3. Therefore, we cannot come to a single meaning of these terms, nor do our common English translations do justice to the meaning of these adjectives in their contexts with the common glosses "righteous" or "wicked."

One final complication is that of method. Shemaryahu Talmon notes the difficulty in coming to a definitional understanding of terms used in biblical Hebrew due to the breadth of chronological data, the possibility of a variety of meanings, and the lack of systematic articulation in the Hebrew Bible; thus, we must define ancient Hebrew terms based on their usages and associations in individual contexts.[7] H. G. M. Williamson shares many of these complications and adds further the complications of limited data, issues deriving from manual transmission of texts, and the near impossibility of dating certain texts.[8] Though we cannot come to a perfect understanding of these Hebrew terms, I attempt to offer here a description of their uses derived from the individual uses of these terms. The description of meanings below is drawn in part from syntagmatics, that is, looking at the context of a single lexeme in each of its occurrences and in its relationship with other words to determine similarities and differences.[9] Due to the occurrence of these terms, the appearance of these terms in parallelism, noting in what ways words are compared or contrasted, is significant.[10]

Method in lexical semantics for Hebrew terms has been significantly influenced by cognitive linguistics in recent years.[11] The challenge of cognitive linguistics is the lack of access to the cognition of ancient Hebrew speakers. This contention is well recognized by scholars who employ a cognitive approach to lexical meaning;[12] however, the connection between cognition and meaning is much further removed for conceptual terms such as צַדִּיק and רָשָׁע than, for instance, those relating to daily life. In many cases, there is little that can be drawn from to determine meaning, and thus, a larger set of data helps to clarify the range of meanings. Below, I survey various uses of these terms in their literary context, analyzing the role in the sentence compared with other features, such as synonyms and antonyms or other related words or phrases.[13] Conceptions can be partly drawn from these contexts, though cannot fully define them. Because of the widespread usage of these terms, I have restricted the research to the Hebrew Bible. Further, I do not aim to be comprehensive in terms of concept, lexical field, or semantic frame, only to come to a clarification of the meaning of uses of these terms that relate to the thesis of this work. However, it is relevant that different contexts can provide a different nuance to the meaning. That is, what they have in common is not that they belong exclusively to a semantic field of covenant, relationship, or law, but that behavioral concerns are relevant in each of these—and other—domains. Through this application, the figures given the title צַדִּיק or רָשָׁע are defined not only by these terms, but by the context in which these terms appear.

DEFINITION OF צַדִּיק

Research on צדק Words

While the term צַדִּיק can be used in various semantic domains, צַדִּיק is usually related to one of two general trajectories: (1) properly behaved or (2) innocent in a matter. The proper behavior does not necessarily belong to the categories suggested by scholars based on research of these terms (or, commonly, word groups) throughout the Hebrew Bible, but rather depends on the context in which these activities are considered proper or correct. Hebrew cognates with the letters צדק are not the main basis on which to form an opinion regarding the definitions of the adjective צַדִּיק. At the same time, it is necessary to provide the background of the discussion as the root is often appealed to as determinative for the adjective's definition by scholars, as will be shown below. I do not consider the strength of individual arguments, seeing as this is not a discussion of the concept of righteousness but the terms צַדִּיק and רָשָׁע, though I discuss the trends of interpretation in broad strokes before looking at the instances of the term צַדִּיק in the Hebrew Bible. There are three common streams of interpreting the צדק root: (1) as a social or legal norm; (2) as a relational obligation; and (3) as a concept defining "world order."[14] These three can be found in many discussions of the concept of righteousness or the definitions of צדק words, particularly those found in dictionaries and encyclopedias of the Bible.[15]

Elizabeth Achtemeier is an example of a scholar who views righteousness as a relational concept.[16] She writes, as an example, "An act on the social plane is not righteous because it at the same time satisfies a demand of the law, though this of course often happened. It is righteous because it fulfills the demands of a social relationship. The relationship is always the determinative factor."[17] Achtemeier offers examples of Judah and Tamar (Gen 38:26) and David in his refusal to slay Saul (1 Sam 24:17; 26:23).[18] The definition is further developed by the large number of instances present especially in Proverbs, where the function of the language is not to define the terms but to make points about an established term. Ultimately, Achtemeier defines צַדִּיק as the one "who fulfilled the demands of the relationships in which he stood."[19] That is, Proverbs often presents characteristics that are praiseworthy of a righteous person with the outcomes of being a righteous person. Some of these outcomes include advantages for the community or for those in relationship with the righteous person.

This perspective helpfully focuses on the ramifications of relationships when the righteousness word group is used in relational texts and as part of a broader concept of righteousness connected to biblical theology. But it is not determinative of the usage of the term צַדִּיק. Achtemeier, and others who interpret righteousness in this way, routinely point to passages that have a specific concept of relationship in mind. This is a conflation between uses of the term in certain contexts (relationships between people, the function of the righteous within a community) and the other uses of the root, such as legal contexts, as will be discussed below. The nuance that the concept of righteousness, defined by the term, is a relational concept even in situations where a legal behavior is clearly suggested is neither necessary nor helpful; the law may be "meaningless outside the relationship, outside the covenant,"[20] but this does not mean that the צדק root must also be meaningless outside of a relational connotation. An act on the social plane may be considered צַדִּיק precisely because of its relationship to the law. This is not to say that the concept of righteousness is not a relational concept. However, when concepts are detailed, we find modern conceptions are definitive rather than ancient conceptions. Lyu is perhaps the best example of such a situation, citing only modern works in his definition of righteousness that is thoroughly relational, though he is one of the only scholars to explicitly clarify that his study is on the concept of righteousness rather than the language of the צדק root.[21] There are, of course, consequences relationally for behavior that is illegitimate. What Achtemeier has done is define all things in light of relationships in the Old Testament and subsumed terminology under that blanket. However, the concept of a relational obligation for the word צַדִּיק does not always fit.

One of the common uses of language related to "righteous" is in relation to the law or, more commonly, to judicial or court language.[22] Irons recently differentiates between two ideas of righteousness, one as a "relational concept" and the view which he defends, a "norm concept."[23] Irons defines this "norm concept" solely as an expression of the norms laid out in the law, and thus, expands beyond what the term "norm" means into a more formal legal context.[24] Irons appeals to the work of James Barr,[25] and yet commits a significant word fallacy by arguing that the word מִשְׁפָּט in frequent parallel with the words צֶדֶק and צְדָקָה determines the latter's formal, legal context. He writes, "The Hebrew word מִשְׁפָּט belongs to the same semantic domain as צֶדֶק/צְדָקָה and is in fact the closest word to being its synonym."[26] Irons offers no proof for this claim other than citing *TDOT*, which in the pages cited notes that the two terms are frequent parallels though concludes that the "two terms [מִשְׁפָּט] and [צֶדֶק], however, are not synonymous."[27] The use of these two terms in parallel offers some clarity as to their meaning, which is a basic syntagmatic principle, but does not presuppose a synonymic relationship as Irons suggests. Rather, the use of a lexicalized word pair, as Irons rightly suggests of these two terms, to determine the definition of one or the other terms does not embrace the formal function of the word pair *as* a word pair, but rather, seeks to illegitimately define one in every instance by its use as part of a common phrase. The relationship between the two words is well established, but it does not mean that they are directly parallel or true synonyms, nor even synonymous in the particular instances where both occur. Ultimately, while there are forensic or legal uses of the language of righteousness in the Old Testament, this is not necessarily or directly signaled through the parallel with the term מִשְׁפָּט.

The language of righteousness can have both relational and legal connotations. However, while Irons' adoption of the term "norm" appropriately draws on the behavioral connotation of the language of righteousness in the Old Testament, he defines "norms" by the law, something that is only connected to the term צֶדֶק in certain contexts.[28] The ramifications and uses of these terms in areas that relate to relational norms and legal norms can individually only be partly true, and in addition, together form still a smaller portion of the potential uses of the terms in other contexts, namely, that of the cult. This is more accurate, but still does not look at the complete possibility of usage. Proper behavior is dependent on and often defined by context, and thus, the passages each of the previous scholars point to rightly affirm their position simply because they relate to proper behavior in that particular context.

H. H. Schmid has argued that the language of righteousness belongs within the frame of creation, which undergirds all aspects of a biblical theology connected to the concept of kingship.[29] Schmid, apparently aware of James Barr's contributions, seeks to understand the צדק root in the HB in light of biblical theology.[30] For Schmid, creation is central to the concept of righteousness within the HB. He states that in wisdom and law, the nouns צֶדֶק and צְדָקָה along with the adjective צַדִּיק "play a dominant role," which is rooted in or connected to creation in the HB.[31] Through the use of ancient Near Eastern parallels, Schmid sees the concept of צדק as roughly equivalent to the Egyptian concept of *ma'at*.[32] To Schmid's credit, he views righteousness as operating in a wide range of domains, and thus, the "norm" or "standard" of world order is activated in different contexts.[33] Though he frames the different contexts in which the language of righteousness is used fairly, he still seeks to find an underlying principle that unites the concept, rather than acknowledging a range of meaning or contexts in which the language is appropriate. Further, the influence of the alien ancient concepts in this language—which does not contain any clear semantic overlap—is inherently problematic. Ultimately, Schmid articulates a view that includes righteousness as part of the ethics of creation, though the question remains as to whether the idea of conformity to creation is rightly understood, biblically or otherwise, as "righteousness."

Niehaus, evaluating Schmid's thesis, also defines the concept of righteousness as a "standard" that is related to creation, though with a different end.[34] Niehaus suffers from defining a term based on its most common or initial gloss, rather than appropriately reviewing its semantic domain. As

such, he defines the context for "standard" again based on theological categories, namely, with God's self as the standard by which righteousness is
measured.[35] Again, it is a move of biblical theology that cannot be sustained
through connection with the use of righteousness.

Even if the idea of a "standard" defines righteousness as a concept, or the
nouns צֶדֶק or צְדָקָה, this concept need not underlie the use of the adjective צַדִּיק.
There are further problems with extending a concept centered on a word or
root that appears with only moderate frequency outside of select corpora as
foundational for an ancient Israelite or biblical worldview. This is one of the
crucial distinctions between the concept of righteousness and the language of
righteousness. The language may be a signal of the concept, but the concept
does not necessarily come to influence the particular uses of terms. To understand the term צַדִּיק as a relational term stretches the evidence of its meaning
outside of its usage in a particular context. There may be a relational aspect
to צַדִּיק, but this is signaled less by the word itself than by the concepts that
are related to it in context.

Some of the confusion related to these terms stems from an understanding
of righteousness as an ontological rather than a situational designation. That is,
the identification of one as "righteous" is not in any way a theological claim to
this person's innocence before God unless this concept is explicitly signaled.
This is also further exacerbated by the confusion of roots. The verb צדק includes
the possible meanings of "be declared righteous, be justified, be vindicated."[36]
While one of several possibilities of the verb, the understanding of the concept
of righteousness in a legal sense appears to rely much more on the verb than
on its cognate forms. In a related way, Krašovec argues that "the dimensions
of God's righteousness are not expressed by abstract concepts but by semantic
fields within the literary structures of literary types and genres."[37] The same
assumption is operative here, though with particular reference to the terms צַדִּיק
and רָשָׁע as used to identify individuals. To clarify the possible meanings and
functions of the word in a variety of contexts, I turn to an analysis of the uses
of the word צַדִּיק in the Hebrew Bible. There is some overlap between examples
here and the examples in the section defining the word pair רָשָׁע and צַדִּיק,
though the emphasis is on where the term צַדִּיק appears on its own.

צַדִּיק in Context

The adjective צַדִּיק appears 206 times in the Hebrew Bible and functions
attributively, predicatively, and, most often, substantively. For this study, the
substantival uses are most relevant, yet often offer the least clarity in terms
of their meaning. As such, all uses will be considered here, though many
instances in Proverbs, Psalms, and Ecclesiastes are addressed in greater detail
in chapter 3.

Behavior

Basic to the first meaning of צַדִּיק is that it is related to proper behavior in some instances. Behavior is closely related to the other meanings of צַדִּיק (in some cases, specific behaviors, or in others, innocent of certain behaviors), though it is worth establishing this through specific examples where behavior is in view generally.

The clearest expression of צַדִּיק as a behavioral term can be found in Ezek 18:5, which begins by mentioning what the צַדִּיק "does" (עשׂה) and elaborates on the activities of the צַדִּיק with specific and concrete examples (Ezek 18:6–9). The ideas of interpersonal and legal activities are present, though the range of activities extends beyond any one context.[38] The purpose of this passage is not to provide a clear characterization of the צַדִּיק as a whole, but it shows that the boundaries of inclusion in that category are behavioral.

וְאִישׁ כִּי־יִהְיֶה צַדִּיק וְעָשָׂה מִשְׁפָּט וּצְדָקָה:	Ezek 18:5	"If a person that is a righteous person and does justice and righteousness,
אֶל־הֶהָרִים לֹא אָכָל וְעֵינָיו לֹא נָשָׂא אֶל־ גִּלּוּלֵי בֵּית יִשְׂרָאֵל וְאֶת־אֵשֶׁת רֵעֵהוּ לֹא טִמֵּא וְאֶל־אִשָּׁה נִדָּה לֹא יִקְרָב:	Ezek 18:6	They[39] do not eat at the mountains, they do not lift their eyes to the idols of the house of Israel, and they do not make the wife of their neighbor unclean, and they do not approach the woman of impurity,
וְאִישׁ לֹא יוֹנֶה חֲבֹלָתוֹ חוֹב יָשִׁיב גְּזֵלָה לֹא יִגְזֹל לַחְמוֹ לְרָעֵב יִתֵּן וְעֵירֹם יְכַסֶּה־בָּגֶד:	Ezek 18:7	And the person does not oppress, they return their debt, they do not rob goods, they give their bread to the hungry, and they cover the naked with a garment,
בַּנֶּשֶׁךְ לֹא־יִתֵּן וְתַרְבִּית לֹא יִקָּח מֵעָוֶל יָשִׁיב יָדוֹ מִשְׁפַּט אֱמֶת יַעֲשֶׂה בֵּין אִישׁ לְאִישׁ:	Ezek 18:8	They do not charge interest, they do not take usury, they offer their hand for justice, a fair judgment they execute between persons,
בְּחֻקּוֹתַי יְהַלֵּךְ וּמִשְׁפָּטַי שָׁמַר לַעֲשׂוֹת אֱמֶת צַדִּיק הוּא חָיֹה יִחְיֶה נְאֻם אֲדֹנָי יְהוִה:	Ezek 18:9	In my statutes they walk, and my judgments they keep in order to act faithfully; they are righteous, they will live"—an utterance of Lord Yhwh.

In the opposite sense, Ezek 3:20–21 focuses on the behavior of the צַדִּיק person shifting their identity; that is, they are no longer considered צַדִּיק if they sin.[40] Thus, while there is not a clear behavior in this case that makes them צַדִּיק, they no longer will receive that designation based on their behavior. Similarly, Zeph 3:5 shows that Yhwh is צַדִּיק related to his lack of negative behavior: "Yhwh is righteous in her midst, he does not do evil" (יְהוָה צַדִּיק בְּקִרְבָּהּ לֹא יַעֲשֶׂה עַוְלָה). Here again, the verb עשׂה relates to the activities of Yhwh defining him as צַדִּיק.

There are expressions of religious behavior that allow one to be considered צַדִּיק as well. In Mal 3:18, the צַדִּיק receives praise in relation to their actions toward Yhwh:

וְשַׁבְתֶּם וּרְאִיתֶם בֵּין צַדִּיק לְרָשָׁע בֵּין עֹבֵד אֱלֹהִים לַאֲשֶׁר לֹא עֲבָדֹו:	Mal 3:18	So you will return and discern between the righteous person and the wicked person, between the one who serves Yhwh and those who do not serve him.

In another clear example, Israel is referred to as גוֹי־צַדִּיק in Isa 26:2, further qualified as "the one who keeps faithfulness."[41]

פִּתְחוּ שְׁעָרִים וְיָבֹא גוֹי־צַדִּיק שֹׁמֵר אֱמֻנִים:	Isa 26:2	Open the gates, and the righteous nation will rise, the one who keeps faithfulness.

In other contexts, the verb שמר relates to behavior, such as the specific requirements to "keep" the covenant (Gen 17:9–10; Exod 19:5).[42] To "keep the way of Yhwh" (וְשָׁמְרוּ דֶּרֶךְ יְהוָה) is elaborated as "to do [עשׂה] righteousness and justice" in Gen 18:19. In Lev 22:31, the behavioral component becomes clear with the parallel of the verb עשׂה (cf. Lev 25:18):

וּשְׁמַרְתֶּם מִצְוֹתַי וַעֲשִׂיתֶם אֹתָם אֲנִי יְהוָה:	Lev 22:31	"You must keep my commandments and do them. I am Yhwh."

Similarly, requirements to observe festival obligations (Exod 12:17, 24, 25; Exod 34:18) also often use the verb שמר. Whether these obligations are "kept" depends on the behavior of the person, that is, whether they do the activities required. Based on these examples, then, Isa 26:2 fits a behavioral usage.

In one more example that is admittedly less clear, Noah is called an אִישׁ צַדִּיק, mentioned in apposition with "blameless" (תָּמִים), and as one who walked with God (Gen 6:9; cf. 7:1), which highlights moral innocence.[43] That Noah walks "with God," something said of Noah here and Enoch in Gen 5:22–24, highlights at least a general disposition in Noah's life. Further, in Gen 7:1, this grounds Yhwh's decision to let Noah and his family live.

The term צַדִּיק often connects with the idea of proper behavior in particular contexts or in regard to a particular matter, as will be shown more clearly below (e.g., 1 Sam 24:18; Isa 3:10; 8:20–29; Neh 9:33). The idea of behavior is present in many of the other uses of the term, sometimes where specific categories of behavior are in mind (fairness or justice below) and in the general designation for a good person (e.g., generosity in Ps 37:21, 26).

Fairness/Justice

One use of the term צַדִּיק that is also behavioral expresses the idea of fairness or justice in relation to a particular matter. In several examples, צַדִּיק is used this way to describe Yhwh and his actions.

הַצּוּר תָּמִים פָּעֳלוֹ	Deut 32:4	The rock, his actions are blameless,
כִּי כָל־דְּרָכָיו מִשְׁפָּט		For all his ways are just; A faithful god, and
אֵל אֱמוּנָה וְאֵין עָוֶל		without injustice,
צַדִּיק וְיָשָׁר הוּא:		Righteous and up`right is he.
צַדִּיק אַתָּה יְהוָה כִּי אָרִיב אֵלֶיךָ	Jer 12:1a	Righteous are you, Yhwh, for I will bring a lawsuit before you,
אַךְ מִשְׁפָּטִים אֲדַבֵּר אוֹתָךְ		Surely I will tell you justice.
יִגְמָר־נָא רַע רְשָׁעִים	Ps 7:10[44]	May the evil of the wicked people be brought to an end;
וּתְכוֹנֵן צַדִּיק		But you will establish the righteous person,
וּבֹחֵן לִבּוֹת וּכְלָיוֹת אֱלֹהִים צַדִּיק:		For the righteous God examines the hearts and kidneys.
צַדִּיק אַתָּה יְהוָה וְיָשָׁר מִשְׁפָּטֶיךָ	Ps 119:137	You are righteous, Yhwh, And upright are your judgments.

In each of these examples, either specific actions or general descriptions of Yhwh's judicial activity are highlighted through the use of צַדִּיק, emphasizing the correctness of these judgments in their context. The attribution of Yhwh as צַדִּיק is paralleled with his salvation in Isa 45:21, though it also appears in the broader context of a judicial scene.[45]

הַגִּידוּ וְהַגִּישׁוּ	Isa 45:21	Explain, and present,
אַף יִוָּעֲצוּ יַחְדָּו		Also let them take counsel together.
מִי הִשְׁמִיעַ זֹאת מִקֶּדֶם		Who made this known from ancient times?
מֵאָז הִגִּידָהּ		From that time, explained it?
הֲלוֹא אֲנִי יְהוָה		Was it not I, Yhwh?
וְאֵין עוֹד אֱלֹהִים מִבַּלְעָדַי		And not another god besides me,
אֵל־צַדִּיק וּמוֹשִׁיעַ		A righteous God, and a savior;
אַיִן זוּלָתִי:		There is none except me.

In a more specific example, Yhwh is also said to be צַדִּיק based on his specific action in judgment of the wicked in Ps 129:4. Thus, he is צַדִּיק in removing the wicked as a threat to the community.[46]

יְהוָה צַדִּיק	Ps	Yhwh is righteous,
קִצֵּץ עֲבוֹת רְשָׁעִים׃	129:4	He has cut the ropes of the wicked.

Yhwh is said to be צַדִּיק in Neh 9:8 because of his keeping of covenant, though rather than a covenantal term exclusively, it fits that his behavior was in keeping with the expected behavior.[47] Thus, while "faithfulness" is an idea that is accurately represented by this use, it is only because of the context. In Zeph 3:5, the description of God as צַדִּיק is paralleled specifically with his lack of doing "injustice." In the broader context, he is also praised for his justice:

יְהוָה צַדִּיק בְּקִרְבָּה	Zeph	Yhwh is righteous in her midst;
לֹא יַעֲשֶׂה עַוְלָה	3:5	He does not do injustice.
בַּבֹּקֶר בַּבֹּקֶר מִשְׁפָּטוֹ יִתֵּן		In every morning he offers his judgment,
לָאוֹר לֹא נֶעְדָּר		In the light, he is not missing,
וְלֹא־יוֹדֵעַ עַוָּל בֹּשֶׁת׃		And he does not know shame of injustice.

Fairness is also represented by צַדִּיק in Deut 4:8 as a description of the law.[48] It could also be used to describe Yhwh's activity as judge in Ps 7:12, though the grammar is not clear enough to make a definitive statement about the function of צַדִּיק in that clause.

The idea of fairness is also appropriate when the term צַדִּיק describes a royal figure. Though the meaning is not elaborated in the context, Zech 9:9 calls the triumphal Davidic king צַדִּיק. Based on the uses elsewhere of the term to describe a royal figure, Mark Boda argues that here it points to the righteousness and justice that the king will have.[49] Goswell, on the other hand, argues that the broader context of vv. 1–8 and the parallel with the verb ישׁע suggest that a military usage of the term is more appropriate in Zech 9:9, thus translating it as "victorious" (cf. Isa 45:21).[50] There are only two such places that scholars see this meaning of צַדִּיק, and neither fit the context better than the idea of justice. In other instances, it refers to a king's fair reign (2 Sam 23:3; Jer 23:5). Though the specific reasons for the description צַדִּיק are unclear in Jer 23:5, the "righteous branch" is a royal figure who accomplishes "justice and righteousness" (מִשְׁפָּט וּצְדָקָה).

In the Right

Still within the behavioral domain, צַדִּיק can refer to a person who is "in the right" in individual circumstances. In a comparative use of צַדִּיק in 1 Sam 24:18, Saul declares David to have been a comparatively greater צַדִּיק than himself (צַדִּיק אַתָּה מִמֶּנִּי). That is, David is "more righteous" than Saul because Saul has wronged David, and thus, David is measured by what he did and thus, is "in the right" by what he has done.

Another way that צַדִּיק is used of God relates to the guilty party confessing the appropriateness of God's behavior in a situation.[51] Lamentations 1:18 claims Yhwh as צַדִּיק, though here it is in the context of the speaker being in the wrong, and as the opposite, Yhwh is the one who is correct in the matter because of the speaker's sin.

צַדִּיק הוּא יְהוָה	Lam	Yhwh, he is righteous,
כִּי פִיהוּ מָרִיתִי	1:18a	For I rebelled against his command;

One could use the term "justified" in the matter, though because of the wide range and differing opinions in Christian theological usage of the concept of justification, the nuance of using this word to translate צַדִּיק becomes confused. Similarly, in Dan 9:14, Daniel calls Yhwh צַדִּיק for bringing judgment upon the Judeans, in contrast with the people who disobeyed. As such, Yhwh is צַדִּיק because of these actions in this particular situation.

וַיִּשְׁקֹד יְהוָה עַל־הָרָעָה וַיְבִיאֶהָ	Dan	So Yhwh kept watch regarding the calamity, and
עָלֵינוּ כִּי־צַדִּיק יְהוָה אֱלֹהֵינוּ	9:14b	he brought it upon us. For Yhwh our God is
עַל־כָּל־מַעֲשָׂיו אֲשֶׁר עָשָׂה		righteous according to all his works which he
וְלֹא שָׁמַעְנוּ בְּקֹלוֹ:		has done, but we did not listen to his voice.

In Neh 9:33, Yhwh is stated to be צַדִּיק in his judgment over against the people who have confessed their sinfulness. Thus, Yhwh's actions are צַדִּיק because they are deserved.

וְאַתָּה צַדִּיק עַל כָּל־הַבָּא עָלֵינוּ	Neh	Now you are righteous regarding all you have
כִּי־אֱמֶת עָשִׂיתָ וַאֲנַחְנוּ	9:33	brought upon us, for you acted with integrity,
הִרְשָׁעְנוּ:		but we, we have done wrong.

Finally, Yhwh is said to be צַדִּיק by the leaders of Judah and Israel in response to Yhwh's prophetic message through Shemaiah:

וּשְׁמַעְיָה הַנָּבִיא בָּא אֶל־רְחַבְעָם וְשָׂרֵי	2 Chr	And Shemaiah the prophet came to Rehoboam
יְהוּדָה אֲשֶׁר־נֶאֶסְפוּ אֶל־יְרוּשָׁלַם	12:5	and the princes of Judah who were gathered
מִפְּנֵי שִׁישָׁק וַיֹּאמֶר לָהֶם כֹּה־אָמַר		at Jerusalem from the presence of Shishak,
יְהוָה אַתֶּם עֲזַבְתֶּם אֹתִי וְאַף־אֲנִי		and he said to them, "This is what Yhwh
עָזַבְתִּי אֶתְכֶם בְּיַד־שִׁישָׁק:		says: 'You, you have forsaken me. So also, I,
		I have forsaken you.'"
וַיִּכָּנְעוּ שָׂרֵי־יִשְׂרָאֵל וְהַמֶּלֶךְ וַיֹּאמְרוּ	2 Chr	So the princes of Israel and the king humbled
צַדִּיק יְהוָה:	12:6	themselves and said, "Yhwh is righteous."

While it is stated elsewhere that Yhwh is צַדִּיק as a general category, the usage of the term here does not require this to be the case; rather, it is an expression of the fairness of Yhwh's dealing with the leaders—he has acted appropriately by forsaking the people in light of their having forsaken him. In each of these previous four examples, Yhwh's proper behavior for or against others is what grounds his receiving the title.[52]

In Ezra 9:15, Yhwh is said to be צַדִּיק, and many scholars see this as a gracious activity of leaving a remnant for Israel, interpreting the כִּי as causal.[53] Paul Byun, however, argues that the two instances of כִּי in the verse should be seen as concessive and thus, point rather to Yhwh's just decision rather than his graciousness.[54] In line with several other instances detailed here, Yhwh is considered צַדִּיק because of his punishment of others צַדִּיק.[55]

יְהוָה אֱלֹהֵי יִשְׂרָאֵל צַדִּיק אַתָּה כִּי־	Ezra	Yhwh, God of Israel, you are righteous, though
נִשְׁאַרְנוּ פְלֵיטָה כְּהַיּוֹם הַזֶּה הִנְנוּ	9:15	we have been left as a remnant this day. Here
לְפָנֶיךָ בְּאַשְׁמָתֵינוּ כִּי אֵין לַעֲמוֹד		we are before you in our guilt, for there are
לְפָנֶיךָ עַל־זֹאת:		none to stand before you on account of this.

Again, in each of these instances, we see that "in the right" is a meaning of the term צַדִּיק that relates to the appropriateness of behaviors, even those that have negative effects for those who are fairly judged.

Innocent of Wrongdoing

A common meaning of צַדִּיק that is distinct from that of active behavior is "innocent of wrongdoing" in a particular context. While the previous instances highlighted ways that someone has acted in a way that is proper, and thus, "in the right," they reveal when those who have *not* participated in an action are considered צַדִּיק. The idea of the צַדִּיק as "innocent of wrong-doing" in a matter appears in several instances, such as in Gen 20:4; Exod 23:7–8; 2 Kgs 10:9; Isa 5:23; 29:21. In Gen 20:4, צַדִּיק is used to describe the innocence of Gerar in protesting the wrongdoing of Abimelech taking Sarah as a wife. In Job 32:1, Job is described as "righteous in his own eyes" in the sense of "innocent" against the accusations of wrongdoing. The use in Exod 23:7–8 clearly points to the idea of the צַדִּיק—paralleled in v. 7 with נָקִי, "innocent"[56]—who is undeserving of death because they have not committed a crime, and here functions within a command to not promote injustice. This meaning extends to contexts where one being צַדִּיק is undeserving of death more generally (Lam 4:13; Gen 18:23–26; 20:4), as is further explored in the next section.

There are two instances in Amos where the term צַדִּיק parallels the language of poverty (Amos 2:6, 5:12).[57] Amos 2:6–8 should be understood as a list of seven sins against the people, who in one instance are the צַדִּיק who is sold for profit.[58] Both are used to emphasize that oppressing or denying justice to one who is צַדִּיק is wrong. In these instances, the term fits under the category of innocent of wrongdoing, but the emphasis is on their innocence pointing to the fact that they should not suffer.

Deuteronomy 16:19 depicts a prohibition against taking bribes, grounding the prohibition in the negative possibility of the words of צַדִּיקִם being twisted. In this case, there is no explicit positive articulation, other than the words are assumed to be trustworthy and reflect the ideals of justice that would other-wise be prevented by the bribe.

לֹא־תַטֶּה מִשְׁפָּט לֹא תַכִּיר פָּנִים וְלֹא־תִקַּח שֹׁחַד כִּי הַשֹּׁחַד יְעַוֵּר עֵינֵי חֲכָמִים וִיסַלֵּף דִּבְרֵי צַדִּיקִם:	Deut 16:19	Do not pervert justice; do not show partiality; and do not take a bribe, for the bribe blinds the eyes of the wise and twists the words of righteous people.

Isaiah 29:21 also includes צַדִּיק as one for whom justice is denied when lies take place in the gates.

In 1 Kgs 2:32, Solomon refers to the two men Joab killed, Abner and Amasa, as more righteous and good than he (צַדְּקִים וְטֹבִים מִמֶּנּוּ). In the context of the passage, the specific reasons for this comparison are not given, but the context suggests this is a way to elevate the severity of Joab's actions.

The idea of innocence will be further explored in the section comparing צַדִּיק and רָשָׁע as a word pair, though it is important that צַדִּיק, even on its own, often has a meaning that relates to innocence in a particular matter, rather than due to an abundance of moral good. Ellen F. Davis, speaking of Ps 37, suggests that one possible usage is that "righteous" can be a "technical term, denoting those who have legal rights, even if they are currently being violated."[59] So in the case of Ezek 23:45, where the "righteous men" (אֲנָשִׁים צַדִּיקִם) are mentioned as those who will judge those who have sinned, they may be designated by their innocence, rather than their fairness, although both are possible in that context.[60]

Deserving of Rescue or Blessing

A fairly common usage of צַדִּיק is to designate someone as innocent and thus undeserving of punishment, accusation, or attack. Hoffman writes that "the primary meaning of צדיק is first and foremost as a theoretical term, used primarily in the wisdom and psalm literatures, to refer to a person deserving of God's goodness."[61] While it is difficult to connect directly to word meaning, it is conceptually related and therefore part of the semantic category. The category that unfolds is that they are deserving of blessing or aid because of their identity as צַדִּיק. This could be the result of this identification from their behavior, though this is not usually directly stated.

This meaning is present in Abraham's dispute with God regarding the destruction of Sodom. Abraham counters God's plans to destroy the city (Gen 18:20–21) by asking, "will you truly sweep away the righteous person along with the wicked person?" (הַאַף תִּסְפֶּה צַדִּיק עִם־רָשָׁע, Gen 18:22). The remainder of the discourse sees Abraham continue to lower the number of צַדִּיקִים God would be willing to destroy undeservedly (Gen 18:23–33). In the instance of Gen 20:4 mentioned above, Abimelech asks if he should be killed even if צַדִּיק. A similar meaning can be found in prohibitions against injustice in legal cases (e.g., Exod 23:7), such as in the case of the innocent death of Ish-Bosheth in 2 Sam 4:11 (cf. 1 Kgs 2:32). In Ezek 3:20–21, the צַדִּיק who turns to sin will die, but the one who avoids sin will live (cf. Ezek 18:9, 20, 24, 26). The concept of being undeserving of suffering is also present in many of the instances mentioned in other sections of the definition of צַדִּיק.

General Description

The most common uses of צַדִּיק are substantive uses that refer to individuals or groups as a general description of a "good" person, that is, the "righteous one" or "righteous ones." Suzanna Millar suggests this person exhibits "holistic moral character."[62] Though in some cases the substantive use is applied to a particular person, for example, the servant of Yhwh in Isa 53:11, it is usually a general designation.[63] Even in this case, the term could easily be understood as one who is innocent and thus wrongly suffering or judged in the greater context of the song (see Isa 53:3–12 and the section "צַדִּיק and רָשָׁע as a word pair"). Otherwise, it is used either in contexts detailing the results of a particular situation or of the prototypical exemplary person. That is, when the term is used as an appellative description of a person, it can typically be understood as a general attribute that relates to proper behavior. Otherwise, the term can be used to designate one who is innocent. The context defines the specific behavior that constitutes this designation or if the idea of innocence in a matter is more appropriate. When the idea of innocence is relevant, it is usually in the context of unjust suffering that it appears.

Earlier studies frequently offer a religious idea of צַדִּיק as a "standing" before Yhwh. For example, von Rad writes, "A man was either [צַדִּיק] in the eyes of Jahweh or he was not."[64] This meaning imports biblical-theological categories, whereas many uses of the term in, for example, Proverbs and Psalms do not include the religious connotation suggested by von Rad.

The term צַדִּיק becomes a common title for a certain kind of person in a majority of uses in Proverbs (these are explored separately below). This kind of person is praiseworthy for their behavior. Many of these instances refer to the benefits of being one of the צַדִּיקִים (Prov 4:18; 11:28; 18:10 [sgl]), certain behaviors of the righteous (Prov 9:9; 10:21, 31; 13:22), or simply that being associated with the righteous person is encouraged (Prov 2:20; 4:18). In many of the above cases, the ramifications for the community of the righteous are highlighted (e.g., Prov 4:18; 9:9; 10:21). The connotations of one who benefits the community can emerge as a composite within a certain corpus, namely Proverbs, but this must not be definitional for the remainder of the uses of the term. This use will be further explored in the section defining the righteous and the wicked.

Olley suggests that the word "good" is possibly the most accurate modern English word that approximates the function of the adjective צַדִּיק as it describes a person with morally excellent attributes.[65] The meanings discussed for צַדִּיק do not neatly square with uses of "righteous" in English. In most English-speaking contexts, the term "righteous" belongs primarily to religious contexts, though it is otherwise uncommon.[66] This ultimately leads to inevitable misunderstanding whereby religious terminology from Hebrew or Greek in translation belongs solely in the religious terminology of the target language, and thus tends to reflect the theological significance given to that term within those faith communities. The new religious usage is determined by the religious context and thus read back into the term in the source language. While these complications may obfuscate the meaning of these terms in English, the categories of righteous and wicked are maintained for the sake of continuity with the translations of these terms in English. The צַדִּיק is often identified as such because of the wicked behavior of others, then, rather than their own good behavior. Their lack of wicked behavior is necessary for this designation, though it still highlights a passive designation. It is given not because of the good that they have done, but because the lot they receive is undeserved.

In conclusion, צַדִּיק is a term for one who behaves properly in a given context. This does not necessarily relate to obedience to the law, specific relational concepts, or to a world order, but is used in contexts where these concepts are present. The person who is considered צַדִּיק may behave rightly in light of the law, in light of relational obligations, and in light of a properly ordered world, though the language of righteousness in the Hebrew Bible does not embody these principles, nor does the Hebrew concept require them. There is, however, no set "standard" by which this behavior is measured. As such, Wenham's suggestion that צַדִּיק is "the most general term to describe good people" is accurate,[67] though the word itself can communicate other topics as well, even in the Psalms. How this is worked out in individual contexts, however, differs. In Proverbs, where the term צַדִּיק appears frequently, it relates to all these ideas *but is neither defined by them nor definitional for them.* That is, the usage of the term צַדִּיק is just as likely to characterize certain ideas than vice versa. Before turning to a clearer description of the functions of the two words together, the uses of רָשָׁע are addressed below.

DEFINITION OF רָשָׁע

The term רָשָׁע can, like the adjective צַדִּיק, often be understood as relating to behavior, in this case, improper behavior. In Proverbs or psalms scholarship, there are few attempts to define רָשָׁע apart from the word pair, even though the term appears more frequently than צַדִּיק in the Psalter. Indeed, it is noteworthy that many scholars do not spend time defining these terms in any way. Hoffman, in fact, states that "it is superfluous to define, being self-understood."[68] Here, however, the focus is exclusively on רָשָׁע before looking at the function and uses of the word pair of צַדִּיק and רָשָׁע together. The improper behavior also indicates one who is guilty or in the wrong, as well as one who is deserving of death or judgment. The specific behavior is often, though not always, mentioned in context.

There are several attributive uses of the term, though these do not add much in the way of the nuance of the meaning, and certainly do not fit neatly into a behavioral category. Unlike צַדִּיק, which rarely modifies a non-personal entity, רָשָׁע is sometimes used attributively of objects, such as the "wicked house" (Mic 6:10; Hab 3:13) and "wicked treasures" (Mic 6:10). However, other attributive uses describe people. Jeremiah 25:31 refers to "wicked flesh" that receives God's judgment. The attributive uses of the word to describe people could have a behavioral sense, though the contexts do not clarify this concept, modifying אָדָם (Job 20:29; 27:13; Prov 11:7), אִישׁ (Num 16:26 [pl]; 2 Sam

4:11 [pl]; Prov 21:29), מֹשֵׁל (Prov 28:15), נָשִׂיא (Ezek 21:30). Both Job 20:29 and 27:13 describe the (assumed) deserved judgment of the "wicked human."

Improperly Behaved

As with צַדִּיק, the meaning of רָשָׁע is most often related to improper behavior. This will be expounded in the further definitions below, though it is important here to show this general characteristic. In the most general sense, the attribution of רָשָׁע in specific contexts relates to behavior.[69] Thus, "The wicked people act wickedly" וְהִרְשִׁיעוּ רְשָׁעִים in Dan 12:10; while this refers to actions, it does not define those wicked behaviors (cf. 1 Sam 2:9).[70] Second Chronicles 19:2 refers to Ahab as רָשָׁע in judgment for Jehoshaphat helping Ahab.[71]

One way רָשָׁע is related to behavior is through the connection to the word עֶוֶל, used as a general expression for wrongdoing, and describes the behavior of the wicked in Ezek 3:20, 18:24, 26; 33:13, 15, 18.[72] Ezek 18:20 designates the person who is guilty of "sinning" as רָשָׁע. In Isa 13:11, Yhwh says he will judge the רָשָׁע for "their iniquity" (עֲוֺנָם).[73] Isa 53:9, one of the servant songs, the servant reaches the end of the רָשָׁע even though the servant did not participate in their activities of violence or illegitimate speech:[74]

וַיִּתֵּן אֶת־רְשָׁעִים קִבְרוֹ	Isa 53:9	He set his grave with the wicked people
וְאֶת־עָשִׁיר בְּמֹתָיו		And with the wealthy, his death,
עַל לֹא־חָמָס עָשָׂה		Though he did no violence
וְלֹא מִרְמָה בְּפִיו:		And there was no deceit in his mouth.

The activities of the רָשָׁע also indicate that they are deserving of penalty, either directly in a legal situation (Deut 25:1–2) or in general (Isa 3:11; 11:4; Ezek 3:18–19; Job 8:22).[75] In other contexts, the situation of the רָשָׁע is presented, either in their "end" or in their present situation: they will not have peace (Isa 48:22); they will be unable to escape (Job 10:3); they will be in pain (Job 15:20); they will not have understanding (Dan 12:10). The punishment the wicked receive often comes directly from God (Isa 13:11; 14:5; Jer 23:19; 25:31; 30:23; Zeph 1:3; Mal 3:21; Pss 3:8, 11:6; 75:11; 129:4; Job 9:22). Sometimes, they are defeated by their own devices (e.g., Prov 11:5). In Isa 11:3, they are killed by the root of Jesse (cf. 11:1). In Bildad's speech in Job 8:22, the emphasis is that the רָשָׁע contrasts with the innocent and that they will eventually be brought to justice or death. However, Job responds in Job 9:22, 24 that God destroys both the innocent and the רָשָׁע, and is unjust in letting the רָשָׁע rule. The question of the prosperity of the wicked also appears in many texts, which respond directly to this assumption of just retribution

(Jer 12:1; Job 21:7). In these contexts, their characterization as רָשָׁע makes them deserving of judgment. The behavioral nuance is also present in the following definitions.

Opponent or Violent Attacker

As a distinct subcategory of improper behavior, רָשָׁע is often used to designate an opponent. In 2 Sam 4:11, those who murder are called רְשָׁעִים. In several instances, they are those who lie in wait to harm others (e.g., Jer 5:26; Ps 119:95; Prov 24:15). In Psalms, as will be shown in greater detail below, they are sometimes generally those who oppose or attack others (Pss 10:2; 11:2; 17:9, 13; 37:12, 14, 32; 71:4; 140:5). In some cases, it is the opposition of speech (Ps 109:2) that defines the רָשָׁע. While this can relate to behavior generally, in these cases the רָשָׁע is a designation for someone who does wrong toward others.

Guilty Party

As a behavioral concept, the translation of "guilty" of a particular crime is appropriate, particularly where a legal context is mentioned.[76] Thus, Num 35:31 refers to the one who is "guilty of murder" רָשָׁע לָמוּת, for whom a bribe must not be taken. The guilty person who is not condemned in the situation in Num 35:31 is still designated by the term רָשָׁע in this context, even if they would not receive the judgment of death that is deserved due to the bribe. Similarly, Exod 23:1 commands against partnering with the רָשָׁע by being a false witness. The important emphasis here is that the legal declaration of "guilty" is not necessarily designated by the term רָשָׁע, but rather, guilty of wrongdoing and thus deserving of a punishment.

Psalm 109:7 is the only instance in the Psalms where the term רָשָׁע is not used substantively as the title of a person, and here it is paired with the verb שׁפט.

בְּהִשָּׁפְטוֹ יֵצֵא רָשָׁע	Ps 109:7	When they are judged, may they come out a guilty person,
וּתְפִלָּתוֹ תִּהְיֶה לַחֲטָאָה:		And may their prayer be as a sin.

While the verb שׁפט need not point exclusively to matters determined by a law court, there is a closer connection here than elsewhere in the Psalms. The verbal form רשׁע more clearly is used to refer to a guilty party in some kind of legal setting,[77] and thus it seems assumed on the basis of some contexts and on the usage of the verb form that a legal definition is primary. "Guilty" as a declaration is often the case in examples where both צַדִּיק and רָשָׁע appear together.

In the Wrong

More often than in legal cases, רָשָׁע refers to improper behavior regarding an individual matter. Exodus 9:27, as a first example, includes a description of the status of Pharaoh as רָשָׁע over against Yhwh as the צַדִּיק in the sense of "in the wrong" and "in the right" regarding a certain situation. In this instance, Pharaoh's refusal to let the Israelites leave to worship makes both Pharaoh and his people רְשָׁעִים, whereas Yhwh is צַדִּיק in sending the plague of hail.

וַיִּשְׁלַח פַּרְעֹה וַיִּקְרָא לְמֹשֶׁה וּלְאַהֲרֹן וַיֹּאמֶר אֲלֵהֶם חָטָאתִי הַפָּעַם יְהוָה הַצַּדִּיק וַאֲנִי וְעַמִּי הָרְשָׁעִים:	Exod 9:27	So Pharaoh sent and called Moses and Aaron, and said to them, "I have sinned in this occasion. Yhwh is the righteous one, and I and my people are the wicked ones."

This declaration came as a response to the plague of the hailstorm (Exod 9:22–26). The improper or proper behavior relating to a specific situation is also the case in Num 16:26, where those involved in the Korahite rebellion are called "wicked men" (הָאֲנָשִׁים הָרְשָׁעִים), pointing to their involvement as participants in the rebellion against authority. Similarly, in Exod 2:13, Moses addresses the רָשָׁע in the dispute between two Israelites, here pointing to the instigator or offending party:

וַיֵּצֵא בַּיּוֹם הַשֵּׁנִי וְהִנֵּה שְׁנֵי־ אֲנָשִׁים עִבְרִים נִצִּים וַיֹּאמֶר לָרָשָׁע לָמָּה תַכֶּה רֵעֶךָ:	Exod 2:13	So he [Moses] went out on that second day and, behold, two Hebrew men were fighting. He said to the offending ["wicked"] one, "Why did you strike your friend?"

In these cases, there may be legal implications of being רָשָׁע, but it is not strictly based on a law or judgment that one is identified with this adjective. Further, the definitions are not necessarily directly tied to relationships, though relationships are part of the context. Rather, it is the specific behavior in the situation. There are also interpersonal or relational ramifications, but these are not concepts that are necessarily tied to the meaning of the word in all contexts, only in the usage of the term in contexts where those concepts are present.

General Description for Bad Person

Most instances of the word רָשָׁע are substantive uses, as in most cases in Proverbs, Job, and Psalms. While this is a general description of a bad person, context often relates to some kind of outcome or activity to the רָשָׁע. In some cases, the improper behavior is described through the metaphor of hunting or attacking others (Jer 5:26). In Jer 5:25–29, Yhwh speaks of the punishment of the wicked people, who are first described in metaphor as hunting others, then defrauding others, and not judging fairly, and thus, it expanded beyond that one feature. More than actions, the behavioral context is heightened by the general deservedness of their judgment or destruction.

In some cases, there is no clear indication of what this person does to earn this title (Job 3:17; 24:6; 34:26).[78] In Job 10:3, it is simply the "counsel of the wicked people" (עֲצַת רְשָׁעִים) that is mentioned, though here it is also implied that Yhwh has not correctly judged them (cf. Job 22:18). In 1 Sam 2:9, in a sentence labeled as מָשָׁל, it simply states that "from wicked people wickedness goes out." Otherwise, the deserved death or judgment of the wicked is present, which from the broader uses of the word can be understood to stem from their behavior in an individual situation or in general.

The referent is not the same in all uses of either plural or singular instances of רָשָׁע. In some cases, the referent of רָשָׁע can be foreign nations (e.g., Ezek 7:21; Ps 9:18). However, there are times when רָשָׁע refers to wickedness within the people of God (e.g., Jer 5:26, Ps 55:4, cf. v. 12). Ezekiel 21:30 refers to Zedekiah as רָשָׁע.[79] In Ezek 7:21, the wicked are those who will be able to act in violence against the land, though it is not clear if this is foreign or domestic.

In a few cases, the possibility of repentance for רָשָׁע exists (Isa 55:7; Ezek 18:21–23). These instances emphasize the behavioral aspects of the term, as it is their behavior that makes them רָשָׁע, the turning from which will change their identification with that term. The possibility of repentance for the wicked is not mentioned explicitly in the psalms, even though repentance as a theme is covered significantly in the Psalter (e.g., Ps 32, 51). Even if there is a possibility of repentance implied by the identification or use of the term in some psalms, this does not change the function that the term has in general.

Deserving of Punishment

In many of the cases listed above, the רָשָׁע is one who is guilty of wrongdoing. However, even when there are instances of the word without a clear meaning of "guilty," the רָשָׁע is one who is deserving of punishment. Oftentimes, this is expressed through the future judgment of Yhwh (Isa 11:4; 13:11; Jer 25:31;

30:23; Pss 3:8; 9:6; 11:6; 92:8; 145:20; 146:9; 147:6). It is also explicit as a result of being one who is guilty. They should receive the punishment of death (Num 35:31) or other punishments (Deut 25:2). In other instances, their destruction is spoken of more generally (1 Sam 2:9; Pss 28:3; 37:17).

In contrast to those who are good or innocent—depending on the context—the wicked deserve death (e.g., 1 Sam 2:9; Ezek 3:18; 33:8), and they are not at peace (Isa 48:22; 57:20–21). Job's friends often affirm the eventual (Job 11:20; 18:5; 20:5, 29; 36:6) or supposed present consequences of the wicked (15:20). Job 20:4–29 is a detailed description of this end of the wicked. Eliphaz states that the "schemes of the wicked are kept from me" (Job 22:18). Elihu claims Job has too high a preoccupation with the wicked (Job 36:17).

Job, in contrast, sees that the wicked do not always receive this reward (see Job 21:7, 16). Job sees himself as unjustly given over to the wicked (Job 16:11). In Job 27:7–15, Job affirms this pattern of eventual destruction as well as that when that happens (רָשָׁע in vv. 7, 13), the righteous will benefit (Job 27:16–17). Even though Job does not see that the proper consequence has occurred, the meaning of רָשָׁע as one who is deserving of judgment is clear (see further the section on Job in chapter 3). In God's speeches in Job, the destruction of the wicked is affirmed (Job 38:13, 15), and God uses Job's lack of ability to punish the wicked as a contrast between God and Job in the rebuke speech (Job 40:12).

Whatever reason these figures are designated as רָשָׁע, the idea that they have done some kind of wrong and are therefore liable or deserving of judgment (in a court or by God) or of destruction more broadly is clear, and will be further clarified in the section and chapters below on the use of the word pair, the uses of these terms in specific books, and the analysis of psalms.

Summary

Because of the designation of the רָשָׁע as one characterized by their improper behavior in a general sense, the term can define those who behave improperly in the interpersonal sphere, the cultic sphere, as well as the geopolitical sphere. They can be the guilty party or the perpetrator of violence. In the case of foreign nations being identified as רָשָׁע, the wrongdoing is not dependent on the law, but primarily on the feature of antagonism against God's people. That is, the term becomes used as a reference to the enemy that is perceived to be in the wrong in their accusation or attack. This is the situation that we commonly find commonly in the psalms. Thus, as it has been used in the psalms, it is the term itself that can belong to the semantic domain of enmity. While this is primarily the case with international enemies, it is also the case with enemies of a more individual nature.

צַדִּיק AND רָשָׁע AS A WORD PAIR

The possible meanings of צַדִּיק and רָשָׁע provided in the previous two sections do not differ when they are used together, but it is central to this argument to show the semantic relationship between the two.[80] This section looks at instances where the two appear in direct contrast to show that the terms are considered as proper antonyms within the Hebrew language, and this antonymic relationship does not signal a particular sphere or semantic domain in which the terms operate. The argument here is that there are two uses of the contrast between these two figures: one where each figure represents those who behave properly/improperly in general, or where they indicate figures who are either wrong/innocent in relation to a specific matter.

Michael Fox notes that these two terms form "a conventional antithetical pair" in Proverbs,[81] and though not as commonly used in direct contrast, this is also the case in some psalms. For Hoffman, צַדִּיק "is most commonly defined by means of negative analogy: righteous is the opposite of wicked."[82] While the word pair is by far most common in Psalms and Proverbs, these two terms belong together within the conventions of the language of the Hebrew Bible more broadly. Including the Writings, the two terms appear together in eighty-one verses, forty-five of which are found in Proverbs.[83] Apart from these forty-five sayings in Proverbs where the two terms appear (see section on Proverbs below), the two terms appear within the same context in a total of forty-eight passages when broadened out to the level of a pericope or a section.[84]

Judicial Contrasts

Beyond the individual uses of the terms צַדִּיק and רָשָׁע in explicitly judicial contexts, they are also used together to describe the innocent or guilty party, respectively (Exod 23:7; 1 Kgs 8:32; Isa 5:23; 2 Chr 6:23). They appear together occasionally in legal contexts.[85] Deuteronomy 25:1 includes the adjectives צַדִּיק and רָשָׁע together in a judicial context with the meaning "innocent in the matter/innocent party" or "guilty in the matter/offending party," yet the judicial language is connected with the verbs רשע and צדק.

כִּי־יִהְיֶה רִיב בֵּין אֲנָשִׁים	Deut	If there is a legal dispute between people and they
וְנִגְּשׁוּ אֶל־הַמִּשְׁפָּט וּשְׁפָטוּם	25:1	go to the place of judgment and they judge
וְהִצְדִּיקוּ אֶת־הַצַּדִּיק		them, they shall declare the innocent one [צַדִּיק]
וְהִרְשִׁיעוּ אֶת־הָרָשָׁע:		innocent and declare the guilty one [רָשָׁע] guilty.

The sense of "in the right" or "in the wrong" in a certain context is more appropriate than a legal designation in many cases. Ecclesiastes 3:17 also includes the verb שׁפט, but the context is that both צַדִּיק and רָשָׁע will come under God's judgment.

אָמַרְתִּי אֲנִי בְּלִבִּי אֶת־הַצַּדִּיק וְאֶת־	Eccl	I, I said in my mind, "The righteous one and the
הָרָשָׁע יִשְׁפֹּט הָאֱלֹהִים כִּי־עֵת	3:17	wicked one God will judge, for there is a time
לְכָל־חֵפֶץ וְעַל כָּל־הַמַּעֲשֶׂה שָׁם:		for every desire and for everything done there."

As such, this is not a legal declaration, but it clarifies that צַדִּיק and רָשָׁע have those identities prior to judgment. In Hab 1:4, the concept perversion of justice appears in the same sentence as the terms צַדִּיק and רָשָׁע:

עַל־כֵּן תָּפוּג תּוֹרָה	Hab 1:4	Therefore, the law is powerless,
וְלֹא־יֵצֵא לָנֶצַח מִשְׁפָּט		And justice never goes forth;
כִּי רָשָׁע מַכְתִּיר אֶת־הַצַּדִּיק		For the wicked person surrounds the righteous person,
עַל־כֵּן יֵצֵא מִשְׁפָּט מְעֻקָּל:		Therefore, justice goes out twisted.

In this context, the two figures of the righteous and the wicked are not determined as "guilty" or "innocent," but rather the ability of the wicked to carry out violence against the righteous is itself a situation of injustice. Similarly, in Job 34:18, Elihu uses רָשָׁע in the sense of "guilty" in describing unjust practices, where nobles are called רָשָׁע unfairly.

Contrasting Behavior in General

Oftentimes assumed to function within a "moral" category,[86] the idea of behavior is articulated through both צַדִּיק and רָשָׁע.[87]

אִמְרוּ צַדִּיק כִּי־טוֹב	Isa 3:10	Say to the righteous person that it will be well,
כִּי־פְרִי מַעַלְלֵיהֶם יֹאכֵלוּ:		for the fruit of their deeds they will eat.
אוֹי לְרָשָׁע רָע	Isa 3:11	Woe to the wicked person—it will be bad,
כִּי־גְמוּל יָדָיו יֵעָשֶׂה לּוֹ:		For their recompense of their actions will be done to them.

Even when the verbal cognates are present, it is not always clearly a legal matter, but rather one of behavior.[88] The verb is connected to the adjective through the use of both together in single contexts, but one need not be determinative for or related to the other in contexts where they appear independently. Isaiah 3:10–11 includes only the context of behavior and emphasizes the relationship between the consequences of the actions of the righteous and the wicked, one theme that will be explored in the next section.

Guilty or Innocent Parties in a Particular Matter

In a related way, the terms צַדִּיק and רָשָׁע are often used to refer to the non-offending party or the offending party in a situation. In 2 Sam 4:11, David describes a situation where רְשָׁעִים kill the צַדִּיק, pointing to the guilty parties of Rechab and Baanah killing Ish-Bosheth unjustly in David's eyes (2 Sam 4:1–12). In Hab 1:13, the two terms are used in a comparative sense, potentially suggesting an idea of a comparative "grade" of being צַדִּיק.[89] These "grades" further clarify the contextual sense in that they both speak to how these individuals behave in a specific context. These uses of these terms point to the potential accusations of the wicked over against the righteous, a theme that appears throughout the Psalter (see also Isa 29:21). Thus, "innocent" or "not guilty" are possible glosses of צַדִּיק when the term refers to a particular situation, and in these cases, they are often contrasted with the "guilty" or "offending party" designated by רָשָׁע.

When not used in relation to the "right" or "wrong" party in a specific situation, the terms become a general designation of the character of individuals. This is the case in a majority of psalms and in Proverbs. As a first example, in the pericope of Abraham's request for God's staying of judgment of Sodom in Gen 18, the terms רָשָׁע and צַדִּיק are used in contrast for those in Sodom who are guilty of sinful behavior or not, describing those worthy or unworthy of destruction (Gen 18:23–25). The illegitimate behavior is explicitly referred to as sinful in 18:20 and 13:13. The judgment of the רָשָׁע and the reward of the צַדִּיק are assumed to be the result of their actions in many cases (2 Chr 6:23). In the same way, Isa 3:10–11 connects the reward of the צַדִּיק and רָשָׁע with their actions. The deed-consequence paradigm is not straightforward here, however. They are righteous or wicked because of what they do, and the results of their identity as righteous or wicked are either blessing or destruction, respectively.

Contrasting Ends

It is this distinction between the two, as two polar ends of a behavioral domain, that allows for their use as a literary device. The concepts that become associated with the words individually, but more properly the word pair, are significant. It is important to recognize that צַדִּיק and רָשָׁע are used as a word pair *both* as general designations for individuals or groups who behave properly/improperly *and* as those who are in the right/in the wrong in a matter. Rather, as part of the language and literature of the ancient Israelite and Judean people, the terms relate to uses elsewhere in the Hebrew Bible but are employed in distinctively psalmic ways.[90] Many have assumed that the presentation in Ps 1, and oftentimes Proverbs, is determinative for their usage elsewhere. The focus on semantics and poetics of these figures in individual contexts pushes against this, as will be shown in the analyses of chapter 4. צַדִּיק and רָשָׁע in psalms are an established antithetical pair, though the precise designation of these figures differs in different contexts.

In summary, the word pair itself maintains the usage of these terms in a variety of behavioral contexts. In some cases, they are used in legal or judicial contexts, but most often in poetic literature, they are used to describe overall character attributes. They are stable identities that are then used within a paradigm or as a literary device throughout the Old Testament. While context plays the most significant role in determining a word's usage, the context of psalmody also makes an important contribution to the meaning of the term for this work. It is not assumed that the "righteous" or "wicked" mean the same thing in every psalm, nor across canonical boundaries. In many cases, these figures fit within the conventions of the figural representations—that is, as something close to stock characters that appear in stock situations—at the core of the argument of this work, though not every mention of these adjectives is part of that conventional model.

The definitions of these terms do not, however, determine the identity of these individuals. It is the application of these terms in contexts that praise certain behaviors or certain outcomes that highlights relational or social behavior. There are many instances where the social outcomes of being righteous are emphasized (see below in chapter 3 for particular instances). In these instances, the behavioral aspect becomes definitional for who the righteous are and, as a result, what they do. In scholarship, the terms are often defined by the ideas that are associated with them rather than the specific nuance intended by their use.

NOTES

1. In this and future chapters, I use צַדִּיק and רָשָׁע rather than "righteous" and "wicked" to refer to these terms, whereas the latter two words appear in translation.

2. The adjective צַדִּיק is used alongside the noun צֶדֶק in Eccl 7:15; Ezek 3:20 (though see the critical apparatus in BHS) and the noun צְדָקָה in Jer 23:5; Ezek 18:5, 20, 24 (also adjective רָשָׁע, though not in direct comparison), 26; Ezek 33:12, 13, 18;

[תָּמִים] Prov 11:5. The adjective צַדִּיק is used alongside the verb צדק in 1 Kgs 8:32; 2 Chr 6:23 (and the noun צְדָקָה). The adjective רָשָׁע is used with the noun רֶשַׁע in 1 Sam 24:14; Ezek 18:20; Ezek 33:12; Mic 6:10; Ps 10:15; 94:21, 23; Prov 11:5. The adjective רָשָׁע is used with the verb רשׁע in 1 Kgs 8:32; Daniel 12:10. The adjective רָשָׁע is used with the verb צדק in Exod 23:7 (though here the adjective צַדִּיק also appears); Isa 5:23 (also includes צַדִּיק). The adjective רָשָׁע is used with the noun צֶדֶק in Isa 26:10. The adjective רָשָׁע is used with the noun צְדָקָה in Ezek 18:21; 33:19; Prov 11:18; Ps 11:7.

3. For example, J. J. Scullion, "Righteousness (OT)," in *Anchor Bible Dictionary*, ed. David Noel Freedman [New York: Doubleday, 1992], 5:727–735) who dedicates half of a page to צַדִּיק and nearly eight pages to discussion of the cognate nouns.

4. See, for example, Philip J. Nel, "Righteousness from the Perspective of the Wisdom Literature of the Old Testament," *OTE* 13 (2000): 320: "To be righteous entails the embodiment in a human being of all the qualities that will ensure the sustenance of all the prerequisites of an existence in harmony with the ideals of righteousness."

5. The phrase "concept of the righteous" is borrowed from Hauge, *Between Sheol and Temple*, 37.

6. The need to study צדק terms in individual uses for the concept of God's righteousness, see Krašovec, *God's Righteousness and Justice*, 1.

7. Shemaryahu Talmon, *Literary Motifs and Patterns in the Hebrew Bible: Collected Studies* (Winona Lake, IN: Eisenbrauns, 2013), 252.

8. H. G. M. Williamson, "Semantics and Lexicography: A Methodological Conundrum," in *Biblical Lexicology: Hebrew and Greek*, ed. Eberhard Bons, Jan Joosten, and Regine Hunziker-Rodewald, BZAW 443 (Berlin: De Gruyter, 2015), 328.

9. Williamson, "Semantics and Lexicography," 329.

10. See Krašovec, *God's Righteousness*, 23–25, 45–46.

11. See Marilyn Burton, *The Semantics of Glory: A Cognitive, Corpus-Based Approach to Hebrew Word Meaning*, SSN 68 (Leiden: Brill, 2017), 11–34; Kurtis Peters, *Hebrew Lexical Semantics and Daily Life in Ancient Israel: What's Cooking in Ancient Israel?* BibInt 146 (Leiden: Brill, 2016), 17–22.

12. Peters, *Hebrew Lexical Semantics*, 20; Stephen L. Shead, *Radical Frame Semantics and Biblical Hebrew: Exploring Lexical Semantics*, BibInt 108 (Leiden: Brill, 2011), 33–66.

13. For a similar method, see Sonja Noll, *The Semantics of Silence in Biblical Hebrew*, Studies in Semitic Languages and Linguistics 100 (Leiden: Brill, 2020), 5. On word relationships, see Burton, *Semantics of Glory*, 42–43.

14. John W. Olley, "'Righteousness'—Some Issues in Old Testament Translation into English," *Bible Translator* 38 (1987): 308.

15. For a helpful summary of linguistic criticisms applied to the theological dictionaries and earlier works on the concept of righteousness, see Mark A. Seifrid, "Righteousness Language in the Hebrew Scriptures and Early Judaism," in *The Complexities of Second Temple Judaism*, vol. 1, *Justification and Variegated Nomism*, ed. D. A. Carson, Peter T. O'Brien, and Mark A. Seifrid, Wissenschaftliche

Untersuchungen zum Neuen Testament 2.140 (Tübingen: Mohr Siebeck, 2001), 418–420. Also see the complexities regarding defining צדק words and concepts in Shead, *Radical Frame Semantics*, 53–54.

16. E. R. Achtemeier, "Righteousness in the OT," in *The Interpreter's Dictionary of the Bible*, ed. George Arthur Buttrick (Nashville, TN: Abingdon, 1962) 4:80–85. See also Gerhard von Rad, *The Theology of Israel's Historical Traditions*, vol. 1, *Old Testament Theology*, trans. D. M. G. Stalker (Louisville, KY: Westminster John Knox, 1962), 370–383.

17. Achtemeier, "Righteousness," 4:82.

18. Achtemeier, "Righteousness," 4:81.

19. Achtemeier, "Righteousness," 4:81. For others who view צַדִּיק as a relational term because of the concept of צֶדֶק or צְדָקָה, see Mowinckel, *Psalms*, 208–209; Kraus, *Theology*, 154–155; John Goldingay, *Psalms*, BCOTWP (Grand Rapids, MI: Baker, 2006–2008), 1:593; Ralph L. Smith, *Micah–Malachi*, WBC 32 (Nashville, TN: Thomas Nelson, 1984), 339; Nielsen, "Righteous and Wicked," 65. Charles Lee Irons ("Is 'Righteousness' a Relational Concept in the Hebrew Bible?" in *Reflections on Lexicography: Explorations in Ancient Syriac, Hebrew, and Greek Sources*, ed. Richard A. Taylor and Craig E. Morrison, Perspectives on Linguistics and Ancient Languages 4 [Piscataway, NJ: Gorgias, 2014], 137) includes a list of theological lexicons which appeal to this concept for "righteousness" in the OT more broadly.

20. Achtemeier, "Righteousness," 4:82.

21. Sun Myung Lyu, *Righteousness in the Book of Proverbs*, FAT 2.55 (Tübingen: Mohr Siebeck, 2012), 11–14.

22. E.g., N. T. Wright, "Righteousness," in *New Dictionary of Theology*, ed. Sinclair B. Ferguson, David F. Wright, and J. I. Packer (Downers Grove, IL: InterVarsity, 1988), 590.

23. Irons, "Righteousness," 136.

24. See, e.g., Irons, "Righteousness," 142–143.

25. Irons, "Righteousness," 135–137, 141.

26. Irons, "Righteousness," 141.

27. B. Johnson, "צָדַק," In *TDOT* 12:239-64.

28. As rightly pointed out in the instances mentioned by the scholars above, who see relationship as determinative.

29. This conception is followed by several scholars, e.g., Leo G. Perdue, *The Sword and the Stylus: An Introduction to Wisdom in the Age of Empires* (Grand Rapids, MI: Eerdmans, 2008), 102; Leo G. Perdue, "Cosmology and the Social Order of the Wisdom Tradition," in *The Sage in Israel and the Ancient Near East*, ed. John G. Gammie and Leo G. Perdue (Winona Lake, IN: Eisenbrauns, 1990), 458–459; Henning Graf Reventlow, "Righteousness as Order of the World: Some Remarks Towards a Program," in *Justice and Righteousness: Biblical Themes and Their Influence*, ed. Henning Graf Reventlow and Yair Hoffman, JSOTSup 137 (Sheffield: JSOT, 1992), 171–172.

30. See especially H. H. Schmid, *Gerechtigkeit als Weltordnung: Hintergrund und Geschichte der alttestamentlichen Gerechtigkeitsbegriffes*, Beiträge zur historischen Theologie 40 (Tübingen: Mohr Siebeck, 1968), 6, where in footnote 16 Schmid

acknowledges Barr's contribution (James Barr, *The Semantics of Biblical Language* [Oxford: Oxford University Press, 1961]) but suggests a greater significance on the root as significant for meaning. Schmid leaves to the reader whether he falls prey to the "root mania" Barr puts forward, which, to this reader, is something Schmid may be found guilty of.

31. H. H. Schmid, "Creation, Righteousness, and Salvation: 'Creation Theology' as the Broad Horizon of Biblical Theology," in *Creation in the Old Testament*, ed. Bernhard W. Anderson, Issues in Religion and Theology 6 (Philadelphia, PA: Fortress, 1984), 107–108.

32. Schmid, *Gerechtigkeit*, 46–61.

33. Schmid, *Gerechtigkeit*, 14.

34. Jeffrey J. Niehaus, "Righteousness and the Created Order: Appreciation and Critique of a Novel Idea," *JETS* 63 (2020): 235.

35. Niehaus, "Righteousness," 251–254.

36. *DCH*, 7:79.

37. Krašovec, *God's Righteousness*, 1.

38. Andrew Mein (*Ezekiel and the Ethics of Exile. Oxford Theological Monographs* [Oxford: Oxford University Press, 2001], 191) notes that these activities cover what was possible in the exile, relating to "moral activity, religion, sexuality, and social relations."

39. Heb 3ms, throughout Ezek 18.

40. Eccl 7:20 makes the connection between one who is צַדִּיק and sins. This will be explored further in Chapter 3.

41. Joseph Blenkinsopp (*Isaiah 1–39: A New Translation with Introduction and Commentary*, AB 19 [New York: Doubleday, 2000], 365) notes the moral context, though admits that the "moral dispositions listed here are less specific." Cf. Hab 2:4.

42. *DCH* 8:478, who cite direct parallels with עשׂה in Lev 18:4; Deut 4:6; Isa 56:1; and more broadly with עשׂה in Gen 18:19; Exod 31:16; Lev 18:5; 19:37; 20:8, 22; 22:31; 25:18; 26:3; Deut 7:11; 11:22; 13:19; 17:19; 19:9; 29:8; 1 Kgs 6:12; 9:4; 11:38; Jer 35:18; Ezek 11:20; 18:9, 19, 21; 20:19; 37:24; 43:11; Pss 103:18; 106:3; Neh 1:9; 1 Chr 29:19; 2 Chr 7:17.

43. Gordon J. Wenham, *Genesis 1–15*, WBC 1 (Waco, TX: Word, 1987), 169–170; Bill T. Arnold, *Genesis*, NCBC (Cambridge: Cambridge University Press, 2009), 98. Yair Hoffman (*A Blemished Perfection: The Book of Job in Context*, JSOTSup 213 [Sheffield: Sheffield Academic, 1996], 225) suggests this is the only concrete figure who receives this designation. For an in-depth look at the meaning of צַדִּיק in this passage, see Carol M. Kaminski, *Was Noah Good? Finding Favor in the Flood Narrative*, LHBOTS 563 (New York: T&T Cark, 2014), 139–168. Ultimately, Kaminski (*Noah*, 161–168) argues for a legal sense here based on the uses of צַדִּיק elsewhere in Genesis. Kaminski is focused far too much on defining the kind of context for usage, and thus, appeals to the broader theology of Genesis to further counter those who view צַדִּיק as covenantal (see Kaminski, *Noah*, 154–161), and by doing so, elaborates on the "context" of the designation through the word meaning beyond what is available in the immediate literary context. Cf. Ezek 28:15 for another use of תָּם with "way" language.

44. See chapter 5. Cf. Ps 7:9 for context.

45. See Joseph Blenkinsopp, *Isaiah 40–55: A New Translation with Introduction and Commentary*, AB 19A (New York: Doubleday, 2000), 261.

46. There are a few cases where there is no clear judicial sense in broader descriptions of Yhwh's character—rather than having a different meaning, the context does not give further clues as to the meaning of צַדִּיק in these contexts other than it refers to praiseworthy characteristics, especially in Psalms (Pss 11:7; 116:5; 145:17).

47. See Mark J. Boda (*Praying the Tradition: The Origin and Use of Tradition in Nehemiah 9*, BZAW 277 [Berlin: De Gruyter, 1999], 62–64) who, in connection with Ezek 18:9, shows that here and in Neh 9:33, the specific matter is related to the keeping of or breaking of the covenant.

48. Seifrid ("Righteousness Language," 430) notes this is the only time צַדִּיק describes a non-personal entity (inclusive of God).

49. Mark J. Boda, *The Book of Zechariah*, NICOT (Grand Rapids, MI: Eerdmans, 2016), 566.

50. Gregory Goswell, "A Theocratic Reading of Zechariah 9:9," *BBR* 26 (2016): 13. Isa 49:24 MT contains another mention of צַדִּיק, though there is extensive text-critical evidence for a reading עָרִיץ (so Blenkinsopp, *Isaiah 40–55*, 313–314). Brevard Childs (*Isaiah: A Commentary*, OTL [Louisville, KY: Westminster John Knox, 2001], 390) reads this use as "victor." Because of the contentious nature of this text, it is not included here. This is not done to deny the possibility of a meaning for the word that relates to victory, only that this usage is rare and, in all cases, including here, ambiguous.

51. Seifrid, "Righteousness Language," 429. Seifrid lists Exod 9:27; Lam 1:18; 2 Chr 12:1–6; Neh 9:33; and Dan 9:7. This also should be seen as the case in Ezra 9:15.

52. This is also likely the case in Isa 41:26 (John Goldingay and David Payne, *Isaiah 40–55*, ICC [New York: T&T Clark, 2006] 1:203), though 1QIsᵃ implies the noun צֶדֶק.

53. So, e.g., Michael W. Duggan, "Ezra 9:6–15: A Penitential Prayer within Its Literary Setting," in *The Origins of Penitential Prayer in Second Temple Judaism*, vol. 1, *Seeking the Favor of God*, ed. Mark J. Boda, Daniel K. Falk, and Rodney A. Werline, EJL 21 (Atlanta, GA: SBL, 2006), 168; Lisbeth S. Fried, *Ezra: A Commentary*, Critical Commentaries (Sheffield: Sheffield Phoenix, 2015), 376.

54. Paul Byun, "A Paradoxical Situation and God's Righteousness in Ezra 9:15," *ZAW* 131 (2019): 467–473.

55. However, in Ezra 9:13, Yhwh withholds the total punishment that would have been deserved.

56. See *DCH* 5:750.

57. Hemchand Gossai, "Ṣaddîq in Theological and Economic Perspectives," *SEÅ* 53 (1988): 10–13.

58. Carroll, *Book of Amos*, 165, 270.

59. Ellen F. Davis, *Scripture, Culture, and Agriculture: An Agrarian Reading of the Bible* (Cambridge: Cambridge University Press, 2009), 117.

60. Daniel Block, *The Book of Ezekiel: Chapters 1–24*, NICOT (Grand Rapids, MI: Eerdmans, 1997), 762.

61. Hoffman, *Blemished Perfection*, 225–226.

62. Suzanna R. Millar, *Genre and Openness in Proverbs 10:1–22:16*, AIL 39 (Atlanta, GA: SBL, 2020), 104. Paul Overland (*Proverbs*, Apollos Old Testament Commentary 15 [London: Apollos, 2022], 23) draws on this and uses the translation "moral" throughout his commentary. Scott ("Wise and Foolish," 160) notes that the forensic concept is largely absent in Prov 10–15, though he allows for some variation of meaning among uses in Proverbs.

63. It is also used as an eponym for Yhwh in Isa 24:16 and in Job 34:17. In the latter case, Elihu refers to Yhwh as צַדִּיק in his ruling in this context, as in David J. A. Clines, *Job 21–37*, WBC 18a (Nashville, TN: Thomas Nelson, 2006), 777; Samuel Balentine, *Job*, Smyth & Helwys Bible Commentary (Macon, GA: Smyth & Helwys, 2006), 571.

64. von Rad, *Theology*, 381. Followed by Scott, "Wise and Foolish," 161.

65. Olley, "Righteousness," 312.

66. Other colloquial uses include the negative designation "self-righteous," and, less commonly today, the use of "righteous" to mean something good or "cool."

67. Wenham, *Genesis 1–15*, 170.

68. Hoffman, *Blemished Perfection*, 228.

69. Because of this, Overland (*Proverbs*, 23) opts to use "guilty" throughout his commentary to avoid a more theological misunderstanding of the term.

70. On this usage relating to actions, see *DCH* 7:557. Cf. the usage of the *hiphil* of רשׁע in Dan 9:5.

71. Ralph W. Klein, *2 Chronicles: A Commentary*, ed. Paul D. Hanson, Hermeneia (Minneapolis, MN: Fortress, 2012), 268.

72. Mein, *Ezekiel*, 197.

73. See Hans Wildberger, *Isaiah 13–27*, trans. Thomas H. Trapp, CC (Minneapolis, MN: Fortress, 1997), 25–26.

74. For the parallel reading of the figures in Isa 53:9, see W. Creighton Marlowe, "The Wicked Wealthy in Isaiah 53:9," *Asbury Journal* 64 (2009): 71–72.

75. Daniel Y. Wu (*Honor, Shame, and Guilt: Social Scientific Approaches to the Book of Ezekiel*, BBRSup 14 [Winona Lake, IN: Eisenbrauns, 2016], 152) notes that for Ezekiel 3, the metaphor of direction is central to the activities or behavior.

76. See below in the section on צַדִּיק and רָשָׁע as a word pair for further examples of רָשָׁע as "guilty."

77. E.g., Exod 22:8; Isa 50:9; Ps 37:33; Job 8:29; 15:6; 34:17; 40:8.

78. Dominick S. Hernández ("'Evil' or 'Agitated': The Meaning of רְשָׁעִים in Job 3:17," in *Ve-'Ed Ya'aleh (Gen 2:6): Essays in Biblical and Ancient Near Eastern Studies Presented to Edward L. Greenstein*, vol. 2, ed. Peter Machinist et al. [Atlanta, GA: SBL: 2021], 791–800) suggests that the use in Job 3:17 does not make sense from the usual meaning of רָשָׁע in its context because "there is no other allusion to the issue of the righteous and the wicked in Job 3" (791), because there is no clear parallel function with רֹגֶז, and because of the use of the verb רשׁע in Job 34:29. He suggests that "agitated" is a better understanding of the term. However, the idea of the uneasy wicked fits perfectly with their characterization elsewhere.

79. Block, *Book of Ezekiel*, 689.

80. For an in-depth discussion and examples on the use of parallelism in determining semantic relationships, see Burton, *Semantics of Glory*, 43–117. Burton (*Semantics of Glory*, 49–50) lays out a method where word associations are used to develop overlapping terminology and rule out when a word falls outside of the synonymous relationship based on the context (or in this case, antonyms).

81. Michael V. Fox, *Proverbs 10–31*, AB 18b (New Haven, CT: Yale University Press, 2009), 494.

82. Hoffman, *Blemished Perfection*, 226.

83. Lance Hawley ("The Rhetoric of Condemnation in the Book of Job," *JBL* 139 (2020): 465, https://doi.org/10/15699/jbl.1393.2020.2) lists the following references for the contrast between righteous (he includes נָקִי) and wicked in Torah and Prophets: Gen 18:23, 25; Exod 9:27; 23:7; Deut 25:1; 2 Sam 4:11; 1 Kgs 8:32; Isa 5:23; 11:4; 26:10; Ezek 13:22; 18:20, 24, 27; 21:4; 33:12; Hab 1:4; and Mal 3:18. These, however, mention only the uses in parallel within the same verse.

84. Gen 18:22–33 (23–26, 38); Exod 9:13–35 (27); 23:1–9 (1, 7–8); Deut 25:1–3 (1–2); 1 Sam 24 (14, 18); 2 Sam 4 (11); 1 Kgs 8:22–53 (32); Isa 3:1–15 (10–11); 5:8–25 (v23); 26 (2, 7, 10); 53 (9, 11); 57 (1, 20–21); Ezek 3 (18, 19, 20, 21); 18 (5, 9, 20, 21, 23, 24, 26, 27); 21:6–12 (8, 9); 33 (8, 9, 11–15, 18, 19); Hab 1:1—2:5 (1:4, 13; 2:4); Mal 3:16–18 (v. 18, also 3:21); Pss 1 (1, 4–6); 7 (10, 12); 11 (2, 3, 5–7); 31 (18–19); 32 (10–11); 34 (16, 20, 22); 37 (10, 12, 14, 16–17, 20–21, 25, 28–30, 32, 34–35, 28–40); 55 (4, 23); 58 (4, 11, 12); 68 (3–4); 75 (5, 9, 11); 92 (8, 13); 94 (3, 13, 21); 97 (10, 11, 12); 112 (4, 6, 10); 119 (53, 61, 95, 110, 119, 137, 155); 129 (4, of Yhwh); 140 (5, 9, 14); 141 (5, 10); 145 (17, 20); 146 (8–9); Job 22 (18–19); 27 (7, 13, 17); 34 (17, 18, 26); 36 (6, 7, 17); Prov 2 (20, 22); Eccl 3:16–22 (17); 7:15–29 (15, 16, 20); 8:1–14 (10, 13, 14); 9:1–4 (1, 2); 2 Chr 6:12–42 (23).

85. Deut 25:1–2; 1 Kgs 8:32.

86. Both John Goldingay ("The Arrangement of Sayings in Proverbs 10–15," *JSOT* 61 (1994): 76) and Knut Heim (*Like Grapes of Gold Set in Silver: An Interpretation of Proverbial Clusters in Proverbs 10:1–22:16*, BZAW 273 [Berlin: De Gruyter, 2001], 80, 83, and *passim*) use "moral" to describe the צַדִּיק and רָשָׁע (and other related appellations) against "intellectual" titles in Prov 10–15, though with problematizing comments or quotation marks.

87. Scott ("Wise and Foolish," 161) suggests that this meaning extends from the judicial context through religious or cultic expectations. He presents this idea without argument, and as shown throughout this work, there are frequently various contexts in which the contrast between the terms arises.

88. 1 Kgs 8:47; Neh 9:33; 2 Chr 6:37; 20:35.

89. Cf. other comparative uses of צַדִּיק in 1 Sam 24:18 and 1 Kgs 2:32 noted above.

90. As argued in the introductory chapter and throughout this work, this does not mean that they are used in precisely the same way each time. Rather, this argument rests on the fact that scholars, as shown in the introduction, often employ usages more common to other books in the HB as determinative for the meaning and function of these figures in the psalms.

Chapter 3

The Contrast between the Righteous and the Wicked as a Literary Device

In the previous chapter, I discussed the lexical semantics of these two terms to provide the foundation of their meaning(s) in context. This chapter builds on this discussion of semantics to address the presence, distribution, and general features of the contrast between צַדִּיק and רָשָׁע in the Hebrew Bible, including the Psalms. Viewing these figures as distinct categories, and in their presentations in each passage and book, this chapter articulates the general uses of the word pair and thus establishes the literary pattern of the contrast between צַדִּיק and רָשָׁע. This chapter focuses on significant passages or books where the contrast between צַדִּיק and רָשָׁע is used as a literary device. I include only instances where these terms are used to designate human individuals or groups, rather than where the adjectives are used attributively, or where they refer to Yhwh or other specific figures.

While the righteous and the wicked frequently appear in a binary contrast,[1] Millar helpfully cautions that binary opposition is not equivalent to rigid binary thinking, allowing for the possibility that there is a literary strategy at play that is not exclusively representative of a dualistic worldview.[2] The previous chapter explored the meaning of these terms on their own and the meaning of the terms together from the perspective of semantics. Here, the particular uses and functions of the two are highlighted, including descriptions of their characterization and the general situations in which they are applied to the figures.

These examples allow for the language of צַדִּיק and רָשָׁע to be explored from more than one perspective, which, as has been already mentioned, is often in light of their function in the Book of Proverbs. While there are connections between differing corpora, it will be shown here that the function and use of these figures are different in various kinds of literature and even within individual books. There are a few stable traits that develop into a literary pattern that appears in Proverbs, Job, Ecclesiastes, Isaiah, Ezekiel, a few of the minor prophets, and, of course, the Psalms. However, the ways that these figures are used change depending on the context. There is not one "theme" of the righteous and the wicked, but a literary paradigm, to which several repeated themes are related through consistent usage, but several other themes are connected by context.

There are several attributes of the paradigm of צַדִּיק and רָשָׁע that are used in the HB. This begins with understanding their lexical meanings, explored in the chapter above. Since both terms operate on the level of behavior and function as opposites, both semantics and conventions work together in certain contexts to articulate certain ideas. As will be shown throughout, the righteous and the wicked paradigm is often used to describe the respective ends or fates of being one or the other figure. Many contexts state or imply that they deserve these respective ends. Other times the two terms are used to highlight particular behaviors. More commonly, however, as terms that are antithetical, they often have the function of relating information regarding the assumed opposition between the two. The sections below highlight these substantival uses within the word pair in various texts. As such, the functions and characterization within individual books are highlighted, beginning where the words occur most frequently.

PROVERBS

The two figures of צַדִּיק and רָשָׁע are contrasted most frequently in the Book of Proverbs. When discussion of these figures appears in scholarly literature, what results is commonly a simple portrait of these figures drawn from their descriptions throughout the Book of Proverbs.[3] That is, the descriptions of these figures are nearly always an accumulation of data rather than something that emerges from the terms' meanings or the functions of the contrast. Rarely are semantics appealed to, and if they are, it is almost entirely in reference to either the concept of righteousness or wickedness, respectively, rather than the meaning of the adjectives themselves.[4]

Even though the two terms appear in Proverbs more commonly than anywhere in the HB, and are the most common words in Prov 10–15, the "two types of people are neither defined nor concretely described in their actions or attributes in Proverbs."[5] As such, Christopher Ansberry refers to these figures as "one-dimensional without increasing in rotundity and profundity."[6] These statements represent both the significance of these figures for Proverbs and the challenges of understanding their meanings.

Some treatments of the righteous or wicked in Proverbs deal with them in relation to what is considered the "primary" characters in Proverbs: the wise and the foolish, חָכָם and כְּסִיל.[7] So prevalent are these figures and so close is their connection that Fox writes that "the core axiom of the book of Proverbs" is: "It is wise to be righteous and foolish to be wicked."[8] Many scholars consider that the wise/righteous and fool/wicked dichotomies refer to the same individuals, even if the words themselves have different meanings.[9] The term חָכָם appears forty-seven times in Proverbs, most often as a designation for an individual. This, however, is significantly lower than the sixty-six times צַדִּיק appears in Proverbs as a reference to an individual. כְּסִיל appears a similar forty-nine times. This is significantly lower than the seventy-eight instances of רָשָׁע in Proverbs. If these numbers offer any indication as to the importance of the צַדִּיק and רָשָׁע, it is worth viewing these figures on their own, even if mainly from a semantic perspective.

Heim has shown persuasively that in Proverbs, the חָכָם and צַדִּיק have differing semantic functions but may be coreferential of the same exemplary person.[10] While Heim makes the case that the righteous and the wise in Proverbs refer to the same person,[11] this is still only true in a paradigmatic sense. The wise are righteous and the wicked are foolish, and thus, they are semantically related. The function of each differs, however, even if both חָכָם and צַדִּיק, as examples, are praiseworthy figures and would have been considered part of the same community to an original audience. As a minor distinction, Clifford briefly notes that "divine retribution is a major interest with the opposition of the righteous and the wicked," though this is not the case with the wise and foolish.[12] The attributes being highlighted are different due to the differing semantic domains of both.

The figures צַדִּיק and רָשָׁע in Proverbs have also been explored from the perspective of virtue ethics. However, most of these recent approaches take into account the compositional structure and purpose of the Book of Proverbs. That is, the didactic purpose of individual Proverbs and the Book of Proverbs as a whole is itself highly suggestive for the function of the figures צַדִּיק and רָשָׁע. Thus, these terms are understood to have a distinctly pedagogical function in Proverbs.[13]

Two recent works have approached these figures as moral prototypes, adopting this concept from cognitive linguistics. Anne Stewart has noted that Proverbs develop a sort of prototypical individual, even with various appellations for the figures.[14] Part of the issue with utilizing cognitive science to understand this kind of literature is that prototypes, according to the theory from cognitive science, are necessarily experiential and culturally bound.[15] That is, while these figures may have functioned as moral prototypes in ancient Israel or Judah, they cannot be construed as moral prototypes absent from the cultural perspective. This is not to say that the language of prototypes is irrelevant, only that if moral prototypes are present, they are textualized from a cultural perspective that cannot be reflected fully in the texts. Within the didactic frame, the use of an idealized world in light of the prototypical figure of the "righteous" is part of the motivational purpose of

Proverbs.[16] Millar suggests that the "central, prototypical principle" of the righteous in Proverbs "is 'the righteous prosper.'"[17] If we applied a similar prototype theory to Psalms, we likely would come up with a different prototypical principle, such as "the righteous suffer" or "the righteous are at enmity with the wicked," as will be explored in the Psalms section below.

Westermann sees the contrast between the righteous and the wicked in Proverbs to be fixed within the structure of antithesis and under two categories of subjects: one where the actions of the two figures are contrasted and one where the fate of the two is contrasted.[18] Though Westermann's framework seeks to determine the relative dating of these concepts under the broader concept of "wisdom," Westermann has rightly highlighted that these two notions of ends and character can categorize a majority of instances of צַדִּיק and רָשָׁע in Proverbs.

The activities of the righteous are praised in at least twenty-three examples.[19] The way in which the activities are highlighted differs in specificity. In some cases, the general "way" of the righteous is highlighted (Prov 2:20; 4:18; 20:7). In other cases, the impact of these figures on other people is highlighted, including their concern for justice (Prov 12:5; 13:5; 21:15; 29:17), the poor (Prov 29:7), and the well-being of the community (Prov 11:10). One major theme that appears is the nourishing nature of the speech of the righteous (Prov 10:20, 21, 31, 32). Generosity also characterizes the righteous (Prov 21:26).

Similarly, the activities of the wicked are condemned, though not always in the sayings that highlights the activities of the righteous. The general way of the wicked is warned against in several instances (4:14, 19; 10:20; 11:18; 12:10, 26; 15:9; 18:3). The theme of violence also appears related to the wicked (10:6, 11). As with the righteous, the mouth or violent speech is highlighted in many of those examples (Prov 10:7, 11, 32; 15:28; 19:29), including explicit references to illegitimate speech (Prov 12:5, 6; 13:5). In a more general sense, the effect of the wicked against the community appears especially in later chapters (Prov 25:5; 28:12, 15, 28; 29:2, 12). Other actions ascribed to the wicked are receiving bribes (Prov 17:23). Proverbs 24:15–16 includes an example of both the ends and the activities of the wicked in light of their relation to the righteous:

אַל־תֶּאֱרֹב רָשָׁע לִנְוֵה צַדִּיק	Prov 24:15	Do not wait in ambush, wicked person, at the home of the righteous person;
אַל־תְּשַׁדֵּד רִבְצוֹ׃		do not destroy their resting place.
כִּי שֶׁבַע יִפּוֹל צַדִּיק וָקָם	Prov 24:16	For seven times a righteous person falls and rises,
וּרְשָׁעִים יִכָּשְׁלוּ בְרָעָה׃		but wicked people stumble into misery.

The second contrasting theme is that of the fate of the righteous and the wicked, which for the righteous means flourishing. This flourishing is often described in terms of security (Prov 10:5, 30), safety from trouble (11:9, 21; 12:7, 13, 21; 14:32; 24:26), or simply a general flourishing (10:3, 24, 28; 11:28; 12:12; 13:21, 25; 15:6). In a few cases, the flourishing of the righteous is grounded in the end of the wicked (Prov 12:7; 14:19; 28:28; 29:16). The internal quality of the righteous is rarely stated, though the external actions of singing and rejoicing are stated in Prov 29:6. Similarly, the community flourishes along with the righteous (Prov 29:2). In some proverbial sayings, religious benefits of being צַדִּיק are stated because of the relationship to God: Yhwh blesses the צַדִּיק (Prov 3:33); Yhwh will not allow the צַדִּיק to be hungry (Prov 10:3); Yhwh will hear the prayer of the righteous (Prov 15:29); and Yhwh is their safe place (Prov 18:10).[20]

The theme of the destruction of the wicked is clear in many cases in Proverbs. Occasionally, this explicitly mentions Yhwh (Prov 3:33; 10:3; 16:4), though in other cases it is mentioned generally (Prov 2:22; 10:16, 24, 25, 27, 28, 30; 11:7, 8, 23, 31; 12:7, 21; 13:9; 14:11; 15:6; 25:26) and sometimes in light of their activity (Prov 11:5; 14:32; 21:7). In Prov 21:12, it is the righteous who enact the active judgment of the wicked. Yhwh's rejection of the wicked shows up in a few cases that do not mention destruction (Prov 15:8, 9, 29; cf. 21:27). The result of being wicked is also described in material terms: they will be hungry (Prov 13:25). The self-destruction of the wicked falling to their own devices also appears numerous times (Prov 5:22; 11:5; 14:32; 21:7). The end of the wicked is sometimes subsumed under the righteous: the wicked will bow down to the righteous (Prov 14:19). In a rare counterexample, the question of the perceived flourishing of the wicked, something emphasized in Job, Ecclesiastes, and some psalms, appears in Prov 24:19–20.

The contrast between God's view toward the righteous and the wicked is highlighted in a few sayings (Prov 3:33; 10:3; 15:29; 17:15). Sometimes, however, the contrast between the two figures is more general. For example, the two are contrasted in the memory of the people after they die in Prov 10:7.

זֵכֶר צַדִּיק לִבְרָכָה	Prov	The memory of the righteous person is a blessing,
וְשֵׁם רְשָׁעִים יִרְקָב:	10:7	But the name of the wicked people will rot.

Throughout the Book of Proverbs, the two figures are contrasted in both behavior and end, and yet, there is no clear picture of what makes one righteous against what makes one wicked. More often than not, the emphasis is on *why* one should be righteous and not wicked, rather than on the activities that they participate in. Further, when activities are mentioned, it is difficult to tell if they are behaviors that are to be emulated by the readers or not, or if they are simply to help identify who might be considered one or the other.

This paradigm that is set forth is often referred to as the deed-consequence nexus, initially popularized by Klaus Koch in German as the *Tun-Ergehen Zusammenhang*.[21] Van Leeuwen suggests, I think rightly, that for Proverbs: "It is the long-term character and direction of a person or group (as 'righteous' or 'wicked') which determine life consequences and 'destiny.'"[22] It is not individual actions, nor is it a rigid system or a law, but the way of life that is at play.[23] Thus, the phrase "character-consequence" may be a more appropriate designation.[24]

The contrast between the two figures occurs in individual instances, but also at the level of the entire book of Proverbs. This leads to their broad characterization as figures within the Proverbs. These descriptions often stem from the assumptions about the definitions of these figures addressed in chapter 2. For example, Waltke summarizes their characterization in Proverbs this way: "The righteous . . . are willing to disadvantage themselves to advantage the community; the wicked are willing to disadvantage the community to advantage themselves."[25] While this is a somewhat simplistic summary of these terms, it represents in broad strokes the ways in which these figures function *related to the community*. They need not be defined by these concepts, but Waltke's summary is appropriate for the communal effect of these figures in general in Proverbs. However, this is not all instances of these figures in Proverbs, nor, as I shall show, are they appropriate for these figures in other books.

JOB

While the language of the righteous and the wicked is not present to the same extent as in psalms and Proverbs, the theme appears frequently in Job. Will Kynes has noted that some pre-modern categorizations of biblical books place Proverbs, Job, and Psalms together in the *sifrei emet*, the Book of Truth, which Kynes suggests, when read together, may reveal a greater emphasis on the righteous and the wicked than the three works of "wisdom" do.[26] This does not mean that the topic is absent from Ecclesiastes, however. Westermann suggests that while there is basic continuity of the theme between Proverbs, Job, and Ecclesiastes, a significant difference lies in the actual forms the contrast takes.[27] The theme of the end of the wicked is highlighted in Job over and above the actions of either the righteous or the wicked, and the fate of the righteous is questioned only secondarily.[28] Most distinctive, however, is that the theme is related through the speech of the friends to Job,[29] though also by Job himself, and is at least mentioned by God.

Abigail Pelham intimates that the categories of righteousness and wickedness are central to the worldviews of the characters in the Book of Job.[30] That is, the characters in Job use the righteous and the wicked to describe the world as it should or should not be, respectively.[31] Much like I argue that the righteous and the wicked have particular functions that relate to the world beyond merely identifying individuals or activities that are praiseworthy or otherwise, Pelham has suggested that the righteous and the wicked divide makes up a central part of the worldview of the characters in Job, with which they must wrestle when Job, one of the righteous, exists in situations that are part of the world of the wicked.[32] The struggle of the Book of Job relates to the situation in which a righteous person appears as a wicked person. If one considers the use of only the terms צַדִּיק and רָשָׁע, this is not necessarily the case, though it is true when relating to the broader concepts of righteous or wicked persons.

The term רָשָׁע appears in Job with much greater frequency than צַדִּיק.[33] However, Hoffman notes that, unlike in both Psalms and Proverbs, the use of צַדִּיק appears far less frequently than its synonyms in the Book of Job. The perspective of the Book of Job on the righteous and the wicked is more difficult to discern due to the multi-perspectival nature of the form of conversation between Job and his interlocutors.[34] It does not have a clearly unified perspective.[35] As such, the instances of the righteous and the wicked serve a variety of functions in Job.

The most common way the topic is addressed in scholarship is using the ostensibly simplistic viewpoint of Job's friends focused on a strict dualism.[36] Hawley writes that "Like Psalm 1, Job's friends assume that people fit one category or the other, viewing the world through a rigid, dichotomous lens."[37] However, the friends never explicitly call Job one of the wicked; they only call him to repent of sin.[38] Clines writes of Job 4:8–11, "Eliphaz does not for a moment mean to imply that Job is—or may perhaps be—in the company of the wicked."[39] Each of Job's accusers has at least one long discourse on the topic of wickedness (Job 15, 18, and 20), but even here they do not directly accuse Job of being one of the wicked.[40] Instead, the possibility that Job is רָשָׁע in general, rather than in a particular matter as is possible within the semantics of the term, is simply implied by the friends.

Newsom suggests that the speeches about wickedness by the friends of Job use tropes rather than reasoned argumentation.[41] Some of these tropes involve similar themes seen in Proverbs. There is the theme of the destruction of the wicked (Job 8:22 [Bildad]; 11:20 [Zophar]; 18:5 [Bildad]; 20:29 [Zophar]; 22:18–19 [Eliphaz]; 36:6 [Elihu]; 38:15), including a description of their situation in present terms (Job 15:20 [Eliphaz]). The temporary nature of wicked people's ostensible gain is emphasized by Zophar in Job 20:5. Elihu uses the terms רָשָׁע and צַדִּיק, but uses them differently than in the pattern of contrasting activities and ends except in Job 36:6–7, where the end of the righteous appear. In Job 36:17, Elihu rebukes Job for being overly obsessed with the judgment (דִּין) of the wicked.

God's speech in Job uses the language of the wicked in line with the judgment they receive. In God's rebuke, he asks twice if Job had the presence or power to judge the רָשָׁע (Job 38:13; 40:12), and once in an indicative statement about the future judgment of the (38:15) רָשָׁע. While the ideas of speech or other behaviors appear in relation to the righteous and the wicked in Job, only the end of the wicked is in view in God's speech.[42]

Job's use of the paradigm of the righteous and the wicked, or the two terms used independently but within the framework of behavior and reward, naturally differs from the friends. The indiscriminate judgment of the wicked and those who are innocent appears in Job 9:22–24. Job also sees that God has treated him as one of the wicked (Job 16:11). The צַדִּיק also does not receive their just position, as they are a "laughingstock" (שְׂחוֹק, Job 12:4). The flourishing of the wicked becomes a theme in Job's speech in Job 10:3; 21:7, 16–18. The question of flourishing is seen as its own theme, and yet conceptually it is part of the assumed end of the wicked. Job's viewpoint appears to shift in 24:18–25 and 27:7–23, where the destruction of the wicked is affirmed alongside the reward of the righteous (see esp. Job 27:13, 17).[43] Drawing on the theme often found in Psalms regarding the wicked waiting to attack the righteous, Aron Pinker argues that Job 27:18–19 describes the activity of the wicked hiding and preparing a trap.[44] Interestingly, the term צַדִּיק never is used by Job to declare himself innocent; this only occurs by implication. In conclusion, the character Job affirms the literary pattern of צַדִּיק and רָשָׁע, but argues that he is treated in a way that does not reflect the reality of blessing for the צַדִּיק and judgment for the רָשָׁע.

While it is outside the main thesis of this study, themes similar to that pattern of the righteous and the wicked paradigm appear throughout Job, even where the terms do not appear. Hawley contends that in Job's speeches, language that is commonly associated with the situation of the wicked is applied to himself as a way to describe his own situation, without admitting guilt.[45] Job regularly draws on the language that the friends use about the wicked to support his claims to innocence. For example, he describes his situation as being in terror and darkness in several places.[46] The theme of self-destruction of the wicked through traps appears in Job 18:7–12, part of Bildad's speech. However, God is referred to as the hunter of Job.[47] Fohrer, writing on the use of forms in Job, argues that both proverbial and psalmic forms of the righteous and the wicked paradigm influence Job.[48] Fohrer sees the functions rather flatly, simply as a didactic strategy.[49] The functions are intended to teach about the consequences of being one of the righteous and the wicked. However, the use of this pattern belongs to a larger rhetorical strategy used by each of the characters in Job in distinctive ways, all playing on the original themes of the connection between the behavior of the righteous and the wicked and their outcomes, and thus the situation of Job. The paradigm of the righteous and the wicked serves as ammunition in the fight regarding whether Job is innocent or not.

Overall, the use of the righteous and the wicked in Job contains the basic literary pattern of the contrast between the righteous and the wicked as those who are blessed or should be judged or destroyed. Rhetorically, the Joban discourse utilizes the descriptions of the wicked to highlight the struggle that Job faces, and while scholars disagree as to whether this is a subtle rebuke of Job, the images nonetheless form an important part of the worldview in question. Literary artistry or rhetorical intent aside, Job draws directly from the literary pattern established by the contrast between צַדִּיק and רָשָׁע. Yet, we find only small vignettes of the antagonism between the righteous and the wicked in Job that we find in Psalms. As we will see in other works, the use of these figures includes some stable concepts, namely the behavioral context and the possibility of their blessing or demise, respectively. At the same time, Job employs these in ways that are unique to the book.

ECCLESIASTES

It is well known that Ecclesiastes questions the validity of the righteous and the wicked paradigm as a source of theological determinism. However, the righteous and the wicked are only part of the larger discourse of the book. Ecclesiastes includes only seven instances of the term רָשָׁע in six verses, and similarly צַדִּיק also appears eight times in seven verses.[50] In all cases the two figures are directly contrasted in the immediate context within four distinct sections. Each use of the paradigm emphasizes the lack of continuity between the outcomes commonly associated with the righteous and the wicked and the inevitabilities of life—the deed-consequence or character-consequence nexus.

Qohelet uses the pattern of the righteous and the wicked to critique a formal deterministic worldview.[51] Stemming from Qohelet's observations about the world, the natural order of the character-consequence nexus is to Qohelet untenable.[52] In Eccl 3:17, Qohelet raises the question of the judgment of God, that both righteous and wicked will come under judgment as part of a larger discourse of the fate of humans.[53] The purpose of Eccl 3:17 regarding the eventual death of humans, good or bad, is evidenced by the continuation of the discussion in light of the death of animals in Eccl 3:18–21. While Qohelet is not focused on the righteous/wicked paradigm here, he undermines the surface-level assumption that fates can be controlled. The inevitability of death is true for both righteous and wicked, and yet, Qohelet does not undermine the basic assumption that the two categories exist. The question is only the fates that will befall them.

The pericope in Eccl 7:15–18 directly addresses the question of the deed-consequences nexus:

יֵשׁ צַדִּיק אֹבֵד בְּצִדְקוֹ וְיֵשׁ רָשָׁע מַאֲרִיךְ בְּרָעָתוֹ׃	Eccl 7:15b	There is a righteous person who dies in their righteousness and there is a wicked person who prolongs their days in their evil deeds.

The solution, Qohelet argues, is a sort of "moderation": "Do not be righteous excessively" (אַל־תְּהִי צַדִּיק הַרְבֵּה, Eccl 7:16). Part of the reason for this is offered later, that no one is thoroughly righteous (Eccl 7:20). In this case, the standard theme of the ends of being righteous is highlighted as a means of tearing down the excesses of striving after gain in light of the inevitabilities of the world. In the words of William Brown,

> Qoheleth attacks the causal nexus between righteousness and fortune, countering the extreme, albeit logical, conclusion that super righteousness will afford ultimate joy and fulfillment. Implicit is the recognition that all efforts that strive to fulfill the pure ideals of righteousness ultimately stem from the self-serving desire to reap ideal rewards, a matter of arrogant presumption. Yet to caution against consideration of the other extreme, Qoheleth immediately points out that wickedness will also result in early death [Eccl 7:17].[54]

The moderation, argues Brown, is not in some kind of faux righteousness or an a-little-of-this-a-little-of-that mentality, but because of the structure of the argument and the context of the book, the concept is related to the limited effect of striving for rewards that cannot be truly earned.[55] Qohelet plays on this theme rhetorically to display that the purpose of the language of the צַדִּיק is not a rule, but a general orientation to life.

Schwienhorst-Schönberger, on the other hand, argues that Eccl 7 shifts the meaning of the terms צַדִּיק and רָשָׁע, from contradictory terms forming a true binary to one where the wisdom acquired through the "fear of God" stands between the two poles of being excessively righteous or wicked.[56] He writes,

> The addressee is encouraged to adhere to justice, but not excessively. The meanings of the terms "just" and "wicked" have therefore subtly changed. The word "just" is now no longer synonymous with "morally good," as it was in traditional Wisdom, and "wicked" is no longer synonymous with "morally

corrupt." In Eccl 7:15–18 the two words describe a manner of conduct with a moral quality that must be determined.[57]

However, Schwienhorst-Schönberger reads these terms too rigidly, not paying attention to the contextual nature of the words. They still operate in binary opposition; only Qohelet mediates the extremity of this contrast, not the meaning of the words.

Ecclesiastes 8 also includes reflection on the theme of the end of the righteous and the wicked. Qohelet first appears to substantiate the view that the wicked will be destroyed (Eccl 8:10, 13), but then notes that the opposite of what is supposed to happen occurs:

יֶשׁ־הֶבֶל אֲשֶׁר נַעֲשָׂה עַל־הָאָרֶץ אֲשֶׁר יֵשׁ צַדִּיקִים אֲשֶׁר מַגִּיעַ אֲלֵהֶם כְּמַעֲשֵׂה הָרְשָׁעִים וְיֵשׁ רְשָׁעִים שֶׁמַּגִּיעַ אֲלֵהֶם כְּמַעֲשֵׂה הַצַּדִּיקִים אָמַרְתִּי שֶׁגַּם־זֶה הָבֶל׃	Eccl 8:14	There is an absurdity which can be observed on the earth: when there are righteous people whose situation that happens to them is in line with the deeds of the wicked people or there are wicked people whose situation happens to them in line with the deeds of the righteous people. I say, "This too is an absurdity."

The problem of the righteous and the wicked in Ecclesiastes is that "the righteous *should* be rewarded, the wicked punished," yet this is not the situation to which Qohelet bears witness.[58] Qohelet plays on the theme of the righteous and the wicked ends by declaring that both have the same end:

הַכֹּל כַּאֲשֶׁר לַכֹּל מִקְרֶה אֶחָד לַצַּדִּיק וְלָרָשָׁע לַטּוֹב וְלַטָּהוֹר וְלַטָּמֵא	Eccl 9:2a	There is one end for each and every one: for the righteous and the wicked, for the good and for the pure and for the unclean.

Here, affirming the general viewpoint espoused in Eccl 3:17, Qohelet shifts back to the topic that the end of each figure is the same. While the pattern of imminent destruction of the wicked appears throughout the OT, here, the broader end of death is mentioned. Early death or long life, poverty or wealth, are all indiscriminate of character in Qohelet's observation. The categories of righteous and wicked are maintained with stable boundaries for Qohelet, but the simplistic understanding of the pattern is questioned.

ISAIAH

There are a few instances of the contrast between the righteous and the wicked in Isaiah. In Isa 3:10–11, the wicked are not trapped by their own devices, but an expression of poetic justice still appears as an affirmation of the deed-consequence nexus:

אִמְרוּ צַדִּיק כִּי־טוֹב כִּי־פְרִי מַעַלְלֵיהֶם יֹאכֵלוּ׃	Isa 3:10	Say to the righteous person that it will be well, for the fruit of their deeds they will eat.
אוֹי לְרָשָׁע רָע כִּי־גְמוּל יָדָיו יֵעָשֶׂה לּוֹ׃	Isa 3:11	Woe to the wicked person—it will be bad, For their recompense of their hand will be done to them.

Those who are wicked in Isa 3:11 are to be identified with those in Isa 3:8–11. Thus, the righteous function here not as those who receive their own reward, but rather, as the recipients of the comfort that the wicked will receive their deserved destruction. The result of their character is a sort of reward—good or bad, respectively. The other example that is close to the standard righteous/wicked paradigm related to the actions and ends of each figure is Isa 26:7–10 and its pathway imagery, which is similar to Ps 1:5–6. Isaiah 5:23 uses another meaning of the two terms, focusing on the idea of "innocent" or "guilty" in a matter.[59]

In Isa 57:20–21, the situation of the wicked is used to emphasize the benefits of humility—in contrast, the wicked have no peace. Similarly, in Isa 48:22 Yhwh declares the same reality that "there is no peace for the wicked people," the only difference being the divine appellation.

אֵין שָׁלוֹם אָמַר יְהוָה לָרְשָׁעִים׃	Isa 48:22	"There is no peace," says Yhwh, "for the wicked people."
וְהָרְשָׁעִים כַּיָּם נִגְרָשׁ כִּי הַשְׁקֵט לֹא יוּכָל	Isa 57:20	So the wicked people are like the tossing sea that cannot be quiet.
וַיִּגְרְשׁוּ מֵימָיו רֶפֶשׁ וָטִיט׃		Its waters toss up gunk and mud.
אֵין שָׁלוֹם אָמַר אֱלֹהַי לָרְשָׁעִים׃	Isa 57:21	"There is no peace," says my God, "for the wicked people."

Being one of the wicked is cautioned against by using these admonitions. These examples exhibit the reality that is in line with the consequences or outcomes of being רָשָׁע. When the broader context of Isa 57 is considered, the latter two verses function in connection with the opening lines about the righteous.[60] The concern in Isa 57:1 and the following passage is rather on the fate of the righteous, as leadership fails to be concerned when the צַדִּיק dies. The focus is not on the behavior of the צַדִּיק, but on those who pay no mind to their demise. Here, instead of the deed-consequence pattern, the two are contrasted in their social consideration. In these cases, they display a clearer *present reality* than a future end, a theme that appears less frequently though still present in Proverbs, Job, and Ecclesiastes. While it does not fit perfectly within the deed-consequence nexus, the themes are still tacitly related because of the meaning of the terms.

EZEKIEL

Ezekiel contains the most significant amount of the language of the righteous and the wicked among the prophetic literature, with three sections devoted to these figures as a primary theme (Ezek 3:18–21; 18; 33:8–19). The most interesting contribution of the concept in Ezekiel is the possibility of repentance of the wicked.[61] In Ezek 3, the possibility of repentance for the wicked is laid out, with Yhwh warning Ezekiel that he would be held responsible for the death of the רָשָׁע if he did not share Yhwh's message with them (Ezek 3:16–19). The opposite idea is present, that the צַדִּיק may die if they turn to sin, again with the responsibility for their death upon Ezekiel should he not share the message of judgment (Ezek 3:20–21). The connection between character or action and their end is made evident in this context. A similar use of these terms appears in Ezek 13:22, where the false prophets are condemned for their deceptive communication, which discouraged the צַדִּיק and did not call the רָשָׁע to repentance (Ezek 13:17–23).

The righteous and the wicked are the central topics in Ezek 18:5–9, which is one of the clearest portraits of the righteous person in the Old Testament. The righteous person is detailed and described as one would live in line with their identity as a צַדִּיק (Ezek 18:9). The discussion continues as to whether the violent son would die (he would) or another faithful grandson of the righteous person (he would not). The passage states, "The sinning person is the one who will die" (Ezek 18:20). The difference in Ezek 18, when compared with much of the rest of the HB, is the focus on transgenerational retribution,[62] which comes down to the central question of whether the exile was theologically justified.[63] This perspective has made Ezek 18, along with Ezek 20, a scholarly crux for understanding the Book of Ezekiel and the relationship between corporate and individual responsibility.[64] The purpose of the righteous and the wicked paradigm in Ezek 18, then, is to demonstrate the level of individual responsibility or corporate responsibility.[65] Mein, however, argues that instead of this being a novel case, an abundance of legal language in Ezek

18 points to the judicial sense of this term being drawn on to articulate the concept of divine retribution.[66]

Ezekiel 18 continues with a repetition and reaffirmation of the theme found in Ezekiel of the possibility of repentance for the רָשָׁע and of turning to sin of the צַדִּיק, leading to the outcome of life for the רָשָׁע who repents (Ezek 18:21, 23, 27) or death for the צַדִּיק who becomes a sinner (Ezek 18:24, 26).

Ezekiel 33 continues the theme of the possibility of changing from identity as a רָשָׁע and leading to life or from a צַדִּיק and leading to death. The theme of Ezekiel's culpability in not calling the people to repentance found in Ezek 3:16–19 is reintroduced (Ezek 33:8–9), and the general principle of the possibility of changing one's perspective for good or ill is repeated emphatically with the call to repent (Ezek 33:11). The clearest articulation of Ezekiel's use of the righteous/wicked paradigm is Ezek 33:18–19:

בְּשׁוּב־צַדִּיק מִצִּדְקָתוֹ וְעָשָׂה עָוֶל וּמֵת בָּהֶם:	Ezek 33:18	When a righteous person turns from their righteousness and practices injustice, they will die in it.
וּבְשׁוּב רָשָׁע מֵרִשְׁעָתוֹ וְעָשָׂה מִשְׁפָּט וּצְדָקָה עֲלֵיהֶם הוּא יִחְיֶה:	Ezek 33:19	But when a wicked person turns from their wickedness and practices justice and righteousness, because of it they will live.

Throughout Ezekiel, then, the righteous/wicked paradigm is primarily used as a way to emphasize the possibility of changing orientation.[67] Ezekiel on the whole upholds a connection with the deed-consequence nexus,[68] even if the general context consistently emphasizes the element of repentance or change that is not present elsewhere (except Isa 55:7).

MINOR PROPHETS

There are relatively few mentions of צַדִּיק and רָשָׁע in the minor prophets, either together or alone.[69] Malachi 3:18–21 includes two mentions of the wicked, one of which is contrasted directly with the righteous. In Mal 3:18, the focus is on the ability to distinguish between the צַדִּיק and the רָשָׁע.[70] Malachi 3:18 explicitly connects the identity of the righteous and the wicked with whether or not they serve (עבד) God. The destruction of the wicked is described in Mal 3:21, though it is by the hands of those in the community. In this instance, it is difficult to determine the identity of the רְשָׁעִים, whether they are enemies within Israel or national enemies. In any case, the end of the wicked is clearly seen, which is based on the work of Yhwh though by the hand of the people.

Habakkuk includes three mentions of the wicked: Hab 1:4, 13, and 3:13. In 1:4, the two characters are mentioned in the context of lament, with the רָשָׁע serving as those who pervert justice and are at enmity with the צַדִּיק. In 1:13, the wicked also attack a righteous person, but it is not clear that these have a similar function as specific figures due to the comparative phrase at the end of the verse. Andersen suggests that because of the first-person language in Hab 1:4, the צַדִּיק functions like a righteous sufferer, similar to Job, though argues that the presence of the article suggests it is a specific person.[71] While offering a unique perspective, the enmity between the righteous and the wicked is present. In Hab 3:13, the wicked are said to be destroyed by Yhwh in Habakkuk's final prayer, using the phrase בֵּית רָשָׁע as in Mic 6:10. Habakkuk 2:4 includes one mention of the צַדִּיק, describing the lifestyle of the righteous rather than their end. In that context, the righteous person is contrasted with the enemy for whom a series of several "woes" are directed.

There are a few similarities between the presentation of the righteous and the wicked in the minor prophets and its presentation in the other prophetic literature. Most significantly, the majority of the uses of the paradigm take place in judgment oracles. However, the end of the righteous or wicked is not as clearly articulated, especially in contrast to the unique presentation in Ezekiel. Comparatively, the uses are somewhat less developed or directly related to the common use of the paradigm.

SUMMARY

This section has elaborated on the meaning and function of the righteous and the wicked across the HB. In the previous section, the word pair of צַדִּיק and רָשָׁע was shown to be related not only in meaning but also in uses in various contexts of the two terms together. This lays the foundation for the use of these terms as part of a theological or literary paradigm for which certain concepts or relatively stable characteristics are attached. The relationship between deed/character and consequence is present in many instances, but it is not comprehensive of the uses of the contrasts between the figures צַדִּיק and רָשָׁע. As explored in the previous chapter, the designation of either צַדִּיק or רָשָׁע is not solely "character" or "deed" in orientation. Particularly with צַדִּיק, the designation can simply be one who is innocent in a matter. Each context and each type of literature uses the titles for their own ends. Ezekiel's focus on repentance is far different than Proverb's use of the terms to highlight proper behavior related to the community. In the following section, the paradigm of the righteous and the wicked in the Psalms will be explored.

צַדִּיק AND רָשָׁע IN THE PSALTER

As I have argued, the צַדִּיק and רָשָׁע pattern in the OT often relates to the perceived consequences of the figures, though the way in which each book draws on these figures differs depending on the communicative goals. Proverbs, for instance, includes a straightforward contrast between the two figures based on their ends and activities. Job and Ecclesiastes, both in their own ways, argue against the validity of this pattern. In the prophetic literature, the pattern is clearly articulated, though the identity of the figures is more concrete than in each of the other books examined. While a majority of the non-psalmic uses of the righteous/wicked paradigm are directly related to the deed-consequence theme, this is somewhat evenly shared in Psalms with the usage of this paradigm as related to the concept of enmity. The point is that there is not a single theme, but multiple ways in which the terms are used.

Westermann seems to assume that the characterization of the righteous and the wicked in Psalms is roughly equivalent to that in Proverbs, suggesting that the two subjects of the deeds of the wicked and the fate of the wicked are highlighted.[72] However, as mentioned in the initial chapter, the deeds of the righteous are less commonly part of the stock presentation of that figure in the Psalms. Furthermore, the concept of violence and the context of enmity of the wicked are far more prevalent in Psalms than in Proverbs, even if the themes appear in both. This is influenced by the semantics of the term, where צַדִּיק in particular can relate either to moral goodness or to innocence in a particular matter. The assumption that the similarities between Psalms and Proverbs point to a single tradition from which the terms arise is logically flawed. As will be demonstrated more clearly below, while there is significant overlap between the presentation of these figures in Psalms and Proverbs, these presentations are not the same. Part of the difference comes from the structural differences, but also from the fact that the emphases are much different in the psalms.

In the end, the associations are tenuous and built on assumptions that derive from a particular mode of canonical inquiry that sees the Psalter as intentionally arranged to tell a single story. However, it is also true that the uses of the figures of the righteous and the wicked in one psalm may not be the same in others. Instead, the righteous and the wicked, while not exclusively determined by the relative Hebrew terms mentioned above, serve a particular function within texts. It is most important to separate out that the presentation in Ps 1 does not dictate the meaning and function of these terms in other psalms.

The term צַדִּיק appears in the context of רָשָׁע in individual psalms in the following cases: Pss 1:1, 4–6; 7:10,[73] 12;[74] 11:2, 3, 5, 6, 7;[75] 31:18–19; 32:10–11; 34:16, 20, 22; 37:10, 12, 14, 16, 17, 20, 21, 25, 28–30, 32, 34, 35, 38–40;

55:4, 23; 58:4, 11, 12; 68:3, 4; 75:5, 9, 11; 92:8, 13; 94:3, 13, 21; 97:10–12; 112:4,[76] 6, 10; 129:4;[77] 140:5, 9, 14; 141:5, 10;[78] 145:17,[79] 20; 146:8, 9. The term רָשָׁע appears without צַדִּיק in the psalms in the following cases: Pss 3:8; 9:6, 17, 18; 10:2–4, 13, 15; 12:9; 17:9, 13; 26:5; 28:3; 36:2, 12; 39:2; 50:16; 71:4; 73:3, 12; 82:2, 4; 91:8; 101:8; 104:35; 106:18; 109:2, 6, 7;[80] 119:53, 61, 95, 110, 119, 155;[81] 139:19; 147:6. The term צַדִּיק appears without רָשָׁע in the psalms in the following cases: Pss 5:13; 14:5; 33:1; 52:8; 64:11; 69:29; 72:7; 118:15, 20; 125:3;[82] 142:8.[83]

Structurally, it is common for these figures to appear as part of a psalmic refrain or conclusion, with either both figures present (e.g., Pss 1:5–6; 11:5–7; 32:10–11; 34:21–22; 58:10–11; 75:10; 97:10–12) or with only one figure present (צַדִּיק in Pss 5:13; 55:23–24; 64:11; 140:14; 142:8; רָשָׁע in Pss 101:8; 104:35; 112:10; 141:10). It is not a requirement that the figures appear at the end, though this feature is used within the structure of many psalms.

The remainder of this chapter focuses on themes and common topics that relate to the figures of the צַדִּיק and רָשָׁע.

Characterization of the Righteous and the Wicked in Psalms

This section highlights several distinctive features of the presentation of the righteous and the wicked in the psalms. The next chapter will analyze the way that these characters function within individual psalms, further highlighting the particular functions of the righteous and the wicked in contexts where both צַדִּיק and רָשָׁע appear in the same psalm. This section looks at all of the instances of these figures in psalms to develop the general pattern. This section differs from the previous sections in that it attempts to set up the next chapter more clearly, drawing on the research in other books and using it to articulate the relevant features rather than to describe their functions in the psalms. The conclusion will then highlight the particular functions to approach an understanding of the "identity" of the righteous and the wicked and their particular uses within the conventions of Hebrew Psalmody. I will evaluate these characteristics first in terms of the general descriptions of the character or the actions of the righteous and the wicked, and then in types of sayings used to describe these figures. This section is largely synthetic, building on general modes of presentation to create categories that are generally representative of the ways in which the figures appear in psalms.

One of the most noticeable features, and the feature through which this work is structured, is that of relationships between the righteous, the wicked, and Yhwh. The specific elements of the contrast or relationship between these figures depend on the context and can fall into several subcategories. This section is divided into three subsections: (1) characterization of the wicked; (2) characterization of the righteous; and (3) description of general situations.

Because conventional figures often serve roles that are related to others, part of the characterization relates to the situations in which they are presented. The characterization of the wicked is general throughout the psalms, and seldom does the characterization reflect the internal life of the wicked person.[84]

The Wicked

The descriptions of the wicked are often related to their counterparts. While the term רָשָׁע signals a semantic difference from other appellations, the enemies or antagonists of the psalms are characterized in generally similar ways. This incorporates the language of enmity with the language of the righteous and the wicked as seen in Proverbs. There are several similarities, but it is the context of enmity that is emphasized in psalms that does not show up elsewhere to the same degree.

The wicked receive more description of their activities than the righteous.[85] In all cases, the word refers in some way to an opposite or opponent of the psalmist, the needy, the righteous, or God. As those who are improperly behaved, there are several activities that are characteristic of רָשָׁע in psalms.

The Wicked as Those Who Speak Improperly

The first broad category of characterization comes from the way that the wicked speak. Illegitimate speech is one of the most distinctive characteristics of the wicked in the psalms.[86] The psalms often include indications of the antagonists as boastful or dishonest. They are first labeled as boastful or arrogant (Pss 12:3–5; 17:10; 20:3; 22:8–9; 31:19; 73:3; 75:5; 94:2–4; 140:5–8). Specific boasts of the enemies are also mentioned (Ps 13:5). Psalm 3 includes the request for judgment of the wicked's speech organs (3:8) following from the context of wicked speech earlier in the psalm (3:3). The antagonists are described as arrogant or boastful without the mention of רָשָׁע in other contexts (Ps 86:14). The arrogance of the wicked is also displayed by their behavior that is not related to speech (Ps 12:9). The arrogance is usually in direct opposition to the righteous or to the speaker, so often within the context of enmity.

The second form of illegitimate speech is that of dishonesty (Pss 5:7, 10; 27:12; 28:3; 31:18–19; 50:19; 58:4; 101:6, 8; 109:2; 140:10). Psalm 31:18–19 clearly calls for the silencing of the wicked, who are also referred to as both dishonest and arrogant in speech. The dishonest characterization of the antagonists appears also in contexts without the term רָשָׁע (Pss 38:13; 120:2–3). In some contexts, the speech is simply shown to be in direct opposition to the righteous (Pss 31:19; 89:51–52; 140:4–5), to the speaker (109:2), or, in less common instances, God (Ps 139:20). In an important contrast, Ps 15:2–4 mentions that the one who is allowed to enter God's tent speaks honestly (cf. 24:4). Similarly, the speaker claims to *lack* deceitful lips in Ps 17:1.

The wicked also speak improperly about God (Ps 10:13). The activities of the wicked also relate to their characterization as functionally atheistic (Pss 9:18; 10:4, 10:13; 22:8–9; 36:2; 55:20). This is also true of the "fool" in Ps 14:1. Psalm 119 naturally relates the identity of the wicked with reference to their negative attitude or relationship to the law (e.g., 119:53, 155). In Ps 50:16–23, God speaks directly to the wicked and questions their assumption of speaking God's laws due to the contrast with the wickedness they partici-pate in.

The Wicked as Violent

Throughout the Psalter, the wicked are described in great detail as those who perpetrate violence against the righteous and the poor. The most distinguishing feature of the presentation of the wicked in psalms is the term's connection with the language of enmity. They are almost exclusively described through their violent actions rather than other characteristics.[87] The term רָשָׁע appears in contexts of enmity in Pss 3, 7, 9, 10, 11, 17, 27, 94, and 140.

Partly due to the conventions of lament, the wicked are often shown to be those attacking the speaker either explicitly or implied by the context (Pss 3:1–2; 7:2–3; 13:5; 17:9, 11–14; 27:2; 31:5; 55:4; 71:4; 91:3; 94:21; 97:10; 119:61; 129:4[88]; 139:19; 140:5). The wicked also attack the poor (Pss 10:2, 8–9; 82:4). In other cases, the wicked are not described as participating but preparing for violence (Pss 7:13–17; 11:2; 12:9; 31:14). The violence of the wicked is also present in contexts where other figures are rescued from them (Ps 97:10).

The theme of the violence of the wicked continues with that of hunting the speaker, the poor, or the righteous (Ps 119:95). This includes language where the wicked are laying traps for the righteous or the speaker (Ps 119:110; 38:13). Often, this theme is used to emphasize the self-destruction of the wicked, with the wicked falling into their own traps (Ps 141:9–10).[89]

The violence of the wicked often relates to their greed (Ps 10:3; 17:14; 37:21).[90] They are also mentioned as perverting justice for gain by taking a bribe (Ps 26:10). The disparity between their flourishing and their activities, mentioned in some examples of the flourishing of the wicked, also appears a few times in psalms. This is a central theme in Ps 73 (Ps 73:3, 12) though it occurs elsewhere in the Psalter (Pss 82:2; 92:8). Psalm 92 admits that the wicked sometimes flourish but suggests it is only temporary (Ps 92:8).

In other words, the activities that most characterize the wicked are under-standably directly contrasted with the righteous. This is true in two senses:

(1) the wicked directly oppose the righteous through their acts of violence against them; and (2) the wicked are directly contrasted with the righteous based on their activities and speech.

These descriptions do not give a concrete picture of who the wicked are. They may be understood in terms of enemies generally, but the specific identification is far from clear.

The End of the Wicked

The end of the wicked is imagined or described in many psalms (Pss 9:4, 6–7, 18; 31:24; 50:16; 68:3; 75:9; 75:11; 92:8; 119:119; 129:4; 145:20; 146:9; 147:6). The negative characterization of the wicked correlates with the request for the end of the wicked (Pss 3:8–9; 5:11; 7:7, 10; 10:15; 17:13–14; 28:4; 31:18; 35:1–8; 104:35; 139:19; 140:9–12).

In some cases, the end of the wicked is actively accomplished by God. For example, the instances of רָשָׁע in Pss 145–147 follow a similar structure, with the first line (or several lines) emphasizing Yhwh's attitude toward different figures in the psalms using a participle followed by a single line stating Yhwh's actions toward the wicked.[91]

שׁוֹמֵר יְהוָה אֶת־כָּל־אֹהֲבָיו	Ps 145:20a	Yhwh keeps all those who love him,
וְאֵת כָּל־הָרְשָׁעִים יַשְׁמִיד:	20b	But all the wicked he destroys.
יְהוָה פֹּקֵחַ עִוְרִים	Ps 146:8a	Yhwh, giver of sight to the blind;
יְהוָה זֹקֵף כְּפוּפִים	8b	Yhwh, lifter of the bowed low;
יְהוָה אֹהֵב צַדִּיקִים:	8c	Yhwh, lover of the righteous ones;
יְהוָה שֹׁמֵר אֶת־גֵּרִים	Ps 146:9a	Yhwh, protector of the immigrant;
יָתוֹם וְאַלְמָנָה יְעוֹדֵד	9b	Orphan and widow, he upholds,
וְדֶרֶךְ רְשָׁעִים יְעַוֵּת:	9c	Yet the path of the wicked, he bends.
מְעוֹדֵד עֲנָוִים יְהוָה	Ps 147:6a	Yhwh upholds[92] the poor;
מַשְׁפִּיל רְשָׁעִים עֲדֵי־אָרֶץ:	6b	He brings the wicked people down to the earth.

God's active judgment of the wicked appears in a few other psalms (Pss 11:6; 75:11; 129:4), though more frequently as a request from the speaker for God to act against the wicked (Pss 17:8–9, 13; 40:15–16 ["them"]; 71:4; 139:19; 140:5; 141:10). The speaker also thanks God for the past protection from the wicked (Ps 18:4, 18–19). God's perspective toward the wicked is directly recorded in Pss 5:6; 11:5; 34:17.

The self-destruction of the wicked is a repeated theme (Pss 7:16–17; 9:16–17; 27:2; 106:18; 141:10). In other cases, the destruction of the wicked has no stated agent (Pss 1:4–6; 6:11; 20:9; 34:22; 37:38; 91:8; 94:14; 106:18; 119:155). In a few cases, it appears that either the speaker (Pss 18:38, 41–44;

101:8) or the righteous are responsible for the destruction of the wicked (Ps 58:11). In other cases, the righteous celebrate their victory over their enemies (Ps 52:8).

The Psalmic Speaker and the Wicked

The wicked are frequently characterized through the speaker's description or interaction with them. Beyond the descriptions of their actions or behavior, there is a continual request for the speaker to not be associated with them, either in general (Ps 26:5) or in their end (Ps 28:3).

The Righteous

The Righteous and Their Relationship with Yhwh

The description of the righteous in Psalms is often not specifically in relation to their behavior but most commonly in their relationship to Yhwh.[93] For example, Yhwh blesses the righteous (Ps 5:13), saves the righteous (Pss 34:20; 37:39), sustains the righteous (37:17), and will never let the righteous be moved (55:23). In a more general sense, Yhwh knows the way of the righteous (Ps 1:6), and his eyes are toward the righteous (Ps 34:16). God is simply stated to be "with the generation of the righteous" (Ps 14:5), which contrasts the negative situation of the enemies. The righteous are able to take refuge in Yhwh (Ps 64:11).[94] Similarly, the idea of protection is clear in Ps 5:13:

כִּי־אַתָּה תְּבָרֵךְ צַדִּיק יְהוָה	13a	For you, you will bless the righteous person, Yhwh.
כַּצִּנָּה רָצוֹן תַּעְטְרֶנּוּ:	13b	Like a shield of favor, you surround them.

The End of the Righteous

The typical "end" of the righteous is to be near God in some way (Ps 11:8), including entering through the gates of God (Ps 118:20). God is said to love the righteous (Ps 146:8). In other contexts, the presumed flourishing of the righteous is emphasized (Pss 52:8; 72:7;[95] 92:13). This includes the memory of their name (Ps 112:6).

The righteous are explicitly attacked by enemies in rare cases (Pss 37:12; 94:21), though the emphasis on salvation for the righteous also implies a situation from which they would need to be saved (Pss 34:20; 37:39). The victory of the righteous over the wicked is imagined in Ps 75:11, alluding specifically to the conflict between the two. The righteous are also sometimes the recipients of accusations rather than attacks (Ps 31:19).

Activities of the Righteous

The activities of the righteous are not often well defined. Of course, the semantics of the term צַדִּיק relate to right behavior in general or to innocence in a matter. The latter definition is often more relevant in psalms. The close connection between the characterization of the righteous and the pathway metaphor is present in only a few places (Ps 1:6). Because of the connection of the image of "way" as a behavioral metaphor,[96] the contrast becomes a contrast between approaches to life rather than specific actions.

The activity of the righteous is to worship God (Pss 64:11; 140:14), stated sometimes as an invitation (32:11; 33:1–3; 68:4), and in Ps 52:9 as part of the speech of the righteous. This is particularly true of the plural usage of the adjective (Pss 32:11; 33:1; 68:4; 97:12; 140:14; 142:8). Of particular note is the introduction of Ps 33:1:

רַנְּנוּ צַדִּיקִים בַּיהוָה	1a	Rejoice, you righteous people, in Yhwh;
לַיְשָׁרִים נָאוָה תְהִלָּה׃	1b	Praise is befitting for upright people.

This direct address presents a clear identity of the righteous as the community (also Ps 97:12).

The Righteous as a Community

The community of the righteous is also present in several psalms. The speaker emphasizes the benefit of being among the community of the righteous, though the speaker never explicitly self-designates as צַדִּיק (Pss 118:15). In Pss 141 and 142, the righteous are a community that the speaker is or wishes to be among (Pss 141:5; 142:8). The reference to a "congregation" of the righteous also appears in Ps 1:5, which would reference the beneficial nature of inclusion within that category.

The speaker always assumes a positive identification of the righteous in the psalms. The speaker specifically requests God to act on behalf of the righteous (Ps 7:9). There is an implicit connection several times between the speaker and the righteous (e.g., Ps 11:3). In many cases, this will be shown below to be the result of the speaker being persecuted unfairly by enemies, and therefore צַדִּיק in a particular matter.

The Righteous as Those in Need

The most common characterization of the righteous is as those who are in need of protection. William P. Brown writes, "In the Psalms, the 'righteous' are often cast as the most vulnerable."[97] As a result, this stems from the second meaning of צַדִּיק described in chapter 2, that these figures received this designation based on their unfair treatment. In the future-oriented description of the destruction of the wicked, the wicked are given the title "those who hate the righteous person" (Ps 34:22). In Ps 37:12 the "wicked person is planning against the righteous person," and these figures are paralleled with the "poor and needy" (Ps 37:14). The righteous are also attacked in Ps 94:21. The cases where false accusations are stated or implied against the righteous also fall under this categorization (e.g., Ps 31:19).

The focus of these figures as those in need does not relate to generally proper behavior as a general characterization. Instead, it is common in psalms that they are unfairly attacked or accused by others and thus are innocent sufferers.

Summary

The presentation of the figures of צַדִּיק and רָשָׁע in psalms is done in uniquely psalmic ways. The psalms do not adhere to the uses of these figures within particular "wisdom" uses or themes but expand them to the concerns of the psalmody. As such, the generic concerns come to bear even on the exclusive use of these terms in binary opposition. However, the designation or identity of the "righteous" often has implications relationally with Yhwh and against the wicked. The paradigm of retribution against the wicked and the eventual or supposed salvation of the righteous is clear regardless of which meaning of the word צַדִּיק is intended. Whether as the innocent who needs saving or the one who is properly behaved, the pattern is established that they are deserving of help from Yhwh. In a contrasting way, the wicked appear in a more consistent pattern of presentation as violent antagonists in psalms. In some cases, they are the "guilty," but primarily due to the activities described in the psalm itself. In terms of poetics, the righteous/wicked paradigm reveals a consistent situation where the "good guys" win in the end and the "bad guys" lose. The literary pattern that appears is not solely a deed- or character-consequence paradigm, but a paradigm of justice and fairness in the world.

CONCLUSION

There is no single direction of borrowing of these terms from other modes of literary production in Israel. Further, the themes and forms of these figures are not uniform throughout the Psalter. There are many influences that led to the understanding of these terms over time, and it is an assumption that the literary production of Psalms took place over several hundred years. The uses of the righteous/wicked paradigm are influenced by a variety of literary types and contexts, but it is important to note that the use of the terms is not simply a wisdom theme. Rather, in many of the contexts, the enmity that is present in prophetic literature is more clearly present.

While there are similarities between the presentations of צַדִּיק and רָשָׁע in Proverbs and in Psalms, there is enough that is distinct to merit studying the uses of these terms in their respective presentations. That is, the function of the righteous and the wicked goes beyond that of the comparative or antithetical form of Proverbs as they appear in psalms. Most significantly, they differ in that there is a greater emphasis on the צַדִּיק as one who is innocent rather than as one who is generally properly behaved. As will be explored in the following chapter, a focus on particular instances of the presentation of these figures will illuminate the ways in which meaning is presented and the functions of this pattern in specific instances.

NOTES

1. Samuel Balentine ("Proverbs," in *The Oxford Handbook of Wisdom and the Bible*, ed. Will Kynes [Oxford: Oxford University Press, 2021], 504, 510) notes how the divisions assume part of the logic of proverbs: that one cannot belong to both groups on either side of the contrast.

2. Millar, *Genre*, 109.

3. E.g., Leo G. Perdue, *Proverbs*, Interpretation (Louisville, KY: Westminster John Knox, 2012), 39–41; W. Creighton Marlowe, "Righteous People in Proverbs," in *Das heilige Herz der Tora: Festschrift fur Hendrik Koorevaar zu seinem 65. Geburtstag*, ed. by Siegbert Riecker and Julius Steinberg (Aachen: Shaker, 2011), 269–281; and with specific relation to retribution, Lennart Boström, "Retribution and Wisdom Literature," in *Interpreting Old Testament Wisdom Literature*, ed. David G. Firth and Lindsay Wilson (Downers Grove, IL: IVP Academic, 2017), 143.

4. E.g., the discussion of wealth and poverty in Lindsay Wilson, *Proverbs: An Introduction and Commentary*, TOTC 17 (Downers Grove, IL: IVP Academic, 2018), 26–28.

5. Ruth Scoralick, *Einzelspruch und Sammlung: Komposition im Buch der Sprichwörter Kapitel 10–15*, BZAW 232 (Berlin: De Gruyter, 1995), 30: "Die beiden Menschentypen werden in den Sprüchen weder definiert noch konkret in ihren Handlungen oder Eigenschaften beschrieben." Similarly, John W. Olley ("'Righteous' and Wealthy? The Description of the *ṣaddîq* in Wisdom Literature," *Colloquium* 22 [1990]: 39–40) observes that the actions and ends of the righteous in Proverbs 1–9 are vague, assuming that צַדִּיק primarily emphasizes the treatment of others. Cf.

Scott ("Wise and Foolish," 162): "Whereas the wise and the foolish are recognizable human beings in imaginable situations, the qualities and behavior of the righteous and the wicked are described in a curiously colorless fashion."

6. Christopher B. Ansberry, *Be Wise, My Son, and Make My Heart Glad: An Exploration of the Courtly Nature of the Book of Proverbs*, BZAW 42 (Berlin: De Gruyter, 2010), 75.

7. Kidner (*Proverbs*) includes a discussion of "subjects" in Proverbs yet neglects the general discussion of the righteous and the wicked altogether.

8. Fox, *Proverbs 10–31*, 510; similarly in Michael V. Fox, "What is the Book of Proverbs About?" in *Congress Volume: Cambridge, 1995*, ed. J. A. Emerton (Leiden: Brill, 1997), 158: "No one would deny that the righteous are wise and that it is wise to be righteous."

9. E.g., Waltke, *Book of Proverbs*, 93; Fox, *Proverbs 10–31*, 928; Perdue, *Proverbs*, 32, 161, 164; Scott, "Wise and Foolish," 160.

10. Heim, *Grapes of Gold*, 77–103.

11. See the conclusion in Heim, *Grapes of Gold*, 101–103.

12. Clifford, *Proverbs*, 22.

13. Lyu, *Righteousness*, 33–34.

14. Anne W. Stewart, *Poetic Ethics in Proverbs: Wisdom Literature and the Shaping of the Moral Self* (Cambridge: Cambridge University Press, 2016), 178.

15. Mark Johnson, *Moral Imagination: Implications of Cognitive Science for Ethics* (Chicago, IL: University of Chicago Press, 1994), 190–192.

16. Millar, *Genre*, 106.

17. Millar, *Genre*, 106.

18. Claus Westermann, *Roots of Wisdom: The Oldest Proverbs of Israel and Other Peoples*, trans. J. Daryl Charles (Louisville, KY: Westminster John Knox, 1995), 76.

19. Prov 2:20; 4:18; 9:9; 10:1, 16, 20, 21, 31, 32; 11:10, 23, 30, 5, 10, 26; 23:5; 15:28; 20:7; 21:12, 15, 26; 29:7, 27.

20. Schipper, *Proverbs 1–15*, 27, 29.

21. Klaus Koch, *Um das Prinzip der Vergeltung in Religion und Recht des Alten Testaments*, Wege der Forschung 125 (Darmstadt: Wissenschaftliche Buchgesellschaft, 1972).

22. Raymond C. Van Leeuwen, "Wealth and Poverty: System and Contradiction in Proverbs," *HS* 33 (1992): 27.

23. Craig Bartholomew and Ryan O'Dowd, *Old Testament Wisdom Literature: A Theological Introduction* (Downers Grove, IL: IVP Academic, 2011), 270–273.

24. Van Leeuwen, "Wealth," 27.

25. Waltke, *Book of Proverbs*, 97.

26. Will Kynes, *An Obituary for "Wisdom Literature": The Birth, Death, and Intertextual Reintegration of a Biblical Corpus* (Oxford: Oxford University Press, 2019), 223–224.

27. Westermann, *Roots of Wisdom*, 82.

28. Westermann, *Roots of Wisdom*, 82.

29. See Carol Newsom, *The Book of Job: A Contest of Moral Imaginations* (Oxford: Oxford University Press, 2009), 115–125; David J. A. Clines, "The

Arguments of Job's Three Friends," in *Art and Meaning: Rhetoric in Biblical Literature*, ed. David J. A. Clines, David M. Gunn, and Alan J. Hauser, JSOTSup 19 (Sheffield: JSOT, 1982), 201–203.

30. Abigail Pelham, *Contested Creations in the Book of Job: The-World-as-It-Ought-and-Ought-Not-to-Be*, BibInt 113 (Leiden: Brill, 2012), 42.

31. See Pelham, *Contested Creations*, 42–46 and *passim*.

32. Pelham, *Contested Creations*, 45.

33. צַדִּיק appears in Job 17:9; 22:19; 27:11; 32:1; 34:17; 36:7. רָשָׁע appears in Job 3:17; 8:22; 9:22, 24; 10:3; 11:20; 15:20; 16:11; 18:5; 20:5, 29; 21:7, 16, 17, 28; 22:18; 24:6; 27:7, 13; 34:18; 34:26; 36:6, 17; 38:13, 15; 40:12. Hoffman, however, notes that while the use of צַדִּיק appears far less frequently relative to רָשָׁע in Job than in Psalms or Proverbs, synonyms of צַדִּיק appear far more frequently (נָקִי, תָּם, יָשָׁר). The ratio of צַדִּיק to its synonyms in Psalms is 50:31, in Proverbs it is 65:27, yet in Job there are only 7:30 uses of צַדִּיק compared with its synonyms.

34. For a thorough discussion of words in the רשע and צדק and the perspectives and uses from individual speakers, see Renate Egger-Wenzel, *Von der Freiheit Gottes, anders zu sein: Die zentrale Rolle der Kaptiel 9 und 10 für das Ijobbuch*, FB 83 (Würzburg: Echter, 1998), 29–46, 76–91.

35. Newsom (*Book of Job*, 3–7) notes the complexity of finding a purpose behind the book as one of the major questions for Joban scholarship and thus leads to her polyphonic reading.

36. In contrast to an overly simplistic view of retribution in Job, see Joel S. Kaminsky, "Would You Impugn My Justice? A Nuanced Approach to the Hebrew Bible's Theology of Divine Recompense," *Interpretation* 69 (2015): 301–303.

37. Hawley, "Rhetoric," 465.

38. Hawley, "Rhetoric," 466.

39. David J. A. Clines, *Job 1–20*, WBC 17 (Dallas, TX: Word, 1989), 125; Clines, "Arguments," 201–203.

40. Hawley, "Rhetoric," 467.

41. See here Newsom, *Book of Job*, 115–125.

42. Hawley, "Rhetoric," 478.

43. Tremper Longman III, *Job*, BCOTWP (Grand Rapids, MI: Baker Academic, 2012), 38.

44. Aron Pinker, "The Wicked in Ambush (Job 27:18–19)," *BBR* 25 (2015): 307–309.

45. Hawley, "Rhetoric," 471. Hawley points to Job 6:3; 7:12; 23:15–17.

46. Hawley, "Rhetoric," 471. Hawley cites Job 15:21, 24; 18:11; and 20:25 for terror and 5:14; 15:22–23, 30; 18:5–6, 18; and 20:26 for darkness.

47. See Lance Hawley, *Metaphor Competition in the Book of Job*, Journal of Ancient Judaism Supplements 26 (Göttingen: Vandenhoeck & Ruprecht, 2018), 132–134.

48. Georg Fohrer, "Form und Funktion in der Hiobdichtung," *Zeitschrift der Deutschen Morgenländischen Gesellschaft* 109 (1959): 34. For a clear English summary of the argument, see Katharine J. Dell, *The Book of Job as Sceptical Literature*, BZAW 197 (Berlin: De Gruyter, 1991), 113.

49. Fohrer, "Form und Funktion," 35.

50. רָשָׁע appears in Eccl 3:17; 7:15; 8:10, 13, 14 (2x); 9:2. צַדִּיק appears in 3:17; 7:15, 16, 20; 8:14 (2x); 9:1, 2.

51. Loader, *Polar Structures*, 95, 100.

52. Craig Bartholomew, *Ecclesiastes*, BCOTWP (Grand Rapids, MI: Baker Academic, 2009), 117.

53. Seow, *Ecclesiastes*, 169.

54. William P. Brown, *Character in Crisis: A Fresh Approach to the Wisdom Literature of the Old Testament* (Grand Rapids, MI: Eerdmans, 1996), 141.

55. For a clearly laid-out structural argument with similar conclusions, see Loader, *Polar Structures*, 46–50.

56. Ludiger Schwienhorst-Schönberger, "Order: Wisdom, Retribution, and Skepticism," in *The Oxford Handbook of Wisdom in the Bible*, ed. Will Kynes (Oxford: Oxford University Press, 2021), 96.

57. Schwienhorst-Schönberger, "Order," 96.

58. Michael V. Fox, *Ecclesiastes*, JPS Bible Commentary (Philadelphia, PA: Jewish Publication Society, 2004), xxx.

59. The idea of "innocent" is also the case in the use of the term צַדִּיק in Isa 29:21 and 41:26.

60. Childs, *Isaiah*, 465.

61. Hawley ("Rhetoric," 465) suggests that while the idea of repentance for the wicked is only explicit in a few instances of prophetic literature, it is implicit because of the function of "wisdom teachings" to dissuade the listener from following the improper path.

62. Darr, Katheryn Pfisterer, "Proverb Performance and Transgenerational Retribution in Ezekiel 18," in *Ezekiel's Hierarchical World: Wrestling with a Tiered Reality*, ed. Stephen L. Cook and Corrine L. Patton, SBL Symposium Series 31 (Atlanta, GA: SBL, 2004), 200.

63. Jurrien Mol, *Collective and Individual Responsibility: A Description of Corporate Personality in Ezekiel 18 and 20*, SSN 53 (Leiden: Brill, 2009), 214.

64. As demonstrated throughout Jacqueline E. Lapsley, *Can These Bones Live? The Problem of the Moral Self in the Book of Ezekiel*, BZAW 301 (Berlin: de Gruyter, 2000), 18–41.

65. See Mol, *Collective and Individual Responsibility*, 223–227 for a rich discussion of the dynamics between individual and corporate responsibility in this passage.

66. Mein, *Ezekiel*, 184–186.

67. Ezekiel also simply names the enemies of the people as רָשָׁע (Ezek 7:21). Both terms are used twice in Ezek 21:8–9 as a sort of hendiadys, that both רָשָׁע and צַדִּיק will fall to the sword.

68. Ka Leung Wong, *The Idea of Retribution in the Book of Ezekiel*, VTSup 87 (Leiden: Brill, 2001), 30.

69. Uses of the terms that fall outside this discussion are: Hos 14:10, which mentions that the צַדִּיק will follow the law; and Amos 2:6 and 5:12, which mentioned earlier use of צַדִּיק in the sense of "innocent."

70. Mignon R. Jacobs, *The Books of Haggai and Malachi*, NICOT (Grand Rapids, MI: Eerdmans, 2017), 318.

71. Francis I. Andersen, *Habakkuk: A New Translation with Introduction and Commentary*, AB 25 (New York: Doubleday, 2001), 112, 122.

72. Westermann, *Roots of Wisdom*, 81–82.

73. In Ps 7:10, רָשָׁע and צַדִּיק appear as substantives in addition to one use of צַדִּיק as attributive of God.

74. In Ps 7:12, צַדִּיק is attributive, modifying שׁוֹפֵט, which is itself used predicatively of God.

75. In Ps 11:7, צַדִּיק is used predicatively of Yhwh.

76. In Ps 112:4, צַדִּיק is used predicatively of the person described in Ps 112.

77. צַדִּיק here is used predicatively of Yhwh.

78. Ps 141:4 includes a reference to the noun רֶשַׁע.

79. צַדִּיק here is used predicatively of Yhwh.

80. Ps 109:7 refers to judgment, not to a person.

81. Ps 119:137 contains a predicative use of צַדִּיק referring to Yhwh.

82. Ps 125:3 includes a reference to the noun רֶשַׁע.

83. Ps 116:5 uses צַדִּיק to refer to God.

84. Hermann Gunkel, "Psalm 1: An Interpretation," *The Biblical World* 21 (1903): 122.

85. Strangely, Stocks ("Voicing of Wisdom," 196) writes that in comparison with the wicked "there is notably less description of the wicked; they are identified principally as those who will suffer calamity." This simplification must also be drawn from the conclusion that the "righteous" are described in psalms that do not mention this title.

86. Sophie Ramond, "'Seek Peace and Pursue It' (Ps 34:15): A Call to Beleaguered Members of a Community," *JHS* 19 (2018): 3, DOI:10.5508/jhs.2019.v19.a; Gelander, Shamai. "The Language of the Wicked in the Psalms," *Proceedings of the World Congress of Jewish Studies* 10 (1989): 38.

87. In a comparative study, Anna Elise Zernecke ("Der Feind und die Hexe: Die Widersacher in mesopotamischen und biblischen Gebeten," *Die Welt des Orients* 49 [2019]: 112–115) has shown that while psalms and Akkadian prayers against sorcerers share several features, they differ in that the description of the antagonists is vague in psalms, whereas they serve particular and explicit roles in the Akkadian curse poems. In other ANE poetic texts, and even in other poetic texts of the Hebrew Bible, the enemies are often clearly defined.

88. Ps 129:4 refers to the speaker being saved by Yhwh from the עֲבוֹת רְשָׁעִים "cords of the wicked."

89. Pss 140 and 142 also include language referring to traps laid for the speaker.

90. In contrast, the generosity of the righteous is mentioned in Ps 37:21 and Ps 112:4; cf. Ps 15:5, which mentions the generosity of those who are able to dwell in Zion.

91. For notes on translation, see the relevant pages in the chapters below.

92. The only two instances of the verb עוד in *polel* forms are here and Ps 146:9, above. Alma Brodersen (*The End of the Psalter: Psalms 146–150 in the Masoretic*

Text, the Dead Sea Scrolls, and the Septuagint [2017; repr., Waco, TX: Baylor University Press, 2018], 183) notes the uniqueness of these terms as the most possible intertextual connection between these two psalms. However, she dismisses this as unlikely due to the verb appearing in other forms elsewhere. Additionally, Brodersen does not note the significant structural connections highlighted here. The likelihood or direction of quotation or allusion is not important for this discussion, but the similarities are striking.

93. While the wicked are also characterized by their relationship to Yhwh, their actions against the righteous or against others are described much more frequently.

94. Creach (*Yahweh as Refuge*) has demonstrated a connection between the language of refuge and the community, which he calls the righteous, throughout his work. However, this connection is made in relation to the concept of the righteous rather than the figures of the righteous.

95. In this case, the righteous flourish because of the earthly king.

96. While the righteous do not appear in Ps 119, the language of the pathway forms one of the central metaphorical reflections on the praise of those who follow Torah (see Brown, *Seeing the Psalms*, 34–35).

97. William P. Brown, *Deep Calls to Deep: The Psalms in Dialogue amid Disruption* (Nashville, TN: Abingdon, 2021), 295.

Chapter 4

The Righteous and the Wicked
in Individual Psalms

As the preceding chapter shows, the semantic possibilities for צַדִּיק are note-worthy in that there are two ways a person receives this designation. They are designated as צַדִּיק due to their general way of life or behavior, or because they are innocently wronged in a matter. The רָשָׁע also functions either as a general description or as in the wrong in a particular matter, typically as the opponent to either the righteous or the psalmist. When the two are contrasted, the theme or pattern of the eventual destruction of the wicked and the blessing or salvation of the righteous is assumed. In this chapter, I provide an analysis of all psalms with a contrast of צַדִּיק and רָשָׁע to show how the uses of these words and the literary pattern of their contrasting function within individual psalms, following the procedure laid out in chapter 1. Each analysis includes the text and translation, an interpretation that focuses on poetic features to elaborate the meaning of the psalm, and an explicit discussion of the function of the righteous and the wicked within the overall psalm.

PSALM 1

Text and Translation

אַשְׁרֵי־הָאִישׁ אֲשֶׁר לֹא הָלַךְ בַּעֲצַת רְשָׁעִים	1a	Fortunate[1] is the person who does not walk in the counsel of wicked people,
וּבְדֶרֶךְ חַטָּאִים לֹא עָמָד	1b	And in the path of sinners does not stand,
וּבְמוֹשַׁב לֵצִים לֹא יָשָׁב:	1c	And in the seat of scorners does not sit.
כִּי אִם בְּתוֹרַת יְהוָה חֶפְצוֹ	2a	But rather takes their[2] delight in Yhwh's instruction,[3]
וּבְתוֹרָתוֹ יֶהְגֶּה יוֹמָם וָלָיְלָה:	2b	And on his instruction meditates day and night.
וְהָיָה כְּעֵץ שָׁתוּל עַל־פַּלְגֵי מָיִם	3a	So they are like a tree planted along the streams of water
אֲשֶׁר פִּרְיוֹ יִתֵּן בְּעִתּוֹ	3b	Whose fruit matures in its season,
וְעָלֵהוּ לֹא־יִבּוֹל	3c	And whose foliage does not wither,
וְכֹל אֲשֶׁר־יַעֲשֶׂה יַצְלִיחַ:	3d	And all that they[4] do is made successful.
לֹא־כֵן הָרְשָׁעִים	4a	Not so wicked people,
כִּי אִם־כַּמֹּץ אֲשֶׁר־תִּדְּפֶנּוּ רוּחַ:	4b	Who are like chaff that the wind blows away.
עַל־כֵּן לֹא־יָקֻמוּ רְשָׁעִים בַּמִּשְׁפָּט	5a	Therefore, wicked people will not rise secure in judgment,[5]
וְחַטָּאִים בַּעֲדַת צַדִּיקִים:	5b	Nor sinners in the congregation of righteous people.
כִּי־יוֹדֵעַ יְהוָה דֶּרֶךְ צַדִּיקִים	6a	For Yhwh knows the path of righteous people
וְדֶרֶךְ רְשָׁעִים תֹּאבֵד:	6b	But the path of wicked people will die.

Interpretation

Psalm 1 is rather straightforward in its expression, causing many to suggest that this psalm is written in a didactic mode.[6] Psalm 1 is portraiture rather than a narrated event, though several brief moments are present in the psalm that contribute to the characterization of the figures present. Individual stanzas are not clearly demarcated in the psalm,[7] except for the shift in topic with the כִּי clause at the beginning of v. 2a from the description of who the person mentioned at the beginning is unlike to a positive description of their characteristics and the outcomes of their characterization (vv. 2a–3d). A second shift in focus occurs in v. 4a, where the end of the wicked comes into focus for vv. 4a–5b. A final verse that grounds the situation of both blessing of the righteous and destruction of the wicked concludes the psalm (v. 6a–6b), marked by another causal כִּי.[8]

Psalm 1 offers first a description of the person who is "fortunate"/אַשְׁרֵי (v. 1a), then describes those contrasted with them. The fortunate person is designated simply as "the person" (הָאִישׁ, v. 1a) who continues to be the subject of negated verbs in v. 1a–1c. As such, the portraiture begins by addressing what the אִישׁ does *not* do through three verbs and locations related to the activities of the antagonists in the psalm (v. 1a–1c). These depictions connect with the deservedness of their fortunate status. The wicked figures in Ps 1 are generally passive figures. They are implied to participate in the verbal actions which the אִישׁ does not do in v. 1a–1c, though even these activities are basic, everyday actions. This contributes to the positive characterization of the אִישׁ in contrast to those negative figures. The description of the activities of wicked people is only vaguely sketched as illegitimate due to the contrast with the אִישׁ in v. 1a and their characterization through the titles they receive. It is the nature of these antagonists' identity that characterizes their activity in the psalm, not vice versa.

The antagonists in the psalm are not direct enemies of the fortunate person, but those with whom the fortunate person and the righteous people are contrasted. They appear as the "wicked people" (רְשָׁעִים; vv. 1a, 4a, 5a, 6b), "sinners" (חַטָּאִים; vv. 1b, 5b), and "scorners" (לֵצִים, v. 1c). Though scholars have noted an intensification of the activities in v. 1a–1c and associated these with the identities of the figures mentioned as increasingly "bad,"[9] the context rather suggests that they are to be seen as figures within a general constellation of individuals whose lifestyle or "way" is not in line with that of Yhwh's instruction. The poetic intensification of the activities in v. 1a–1c is more in line with the verbal activity rather than the identification of the figure: the person of v. 1a does not "walk" (הָלַךְ, v. 1a), "stand" (עָמַד, v. 1b) or "sit" (יָשַׁב, v. 1c) with the respective figures.[10] Miller argues that these titles each refer to different characters based on the semantic differences between the terms.[11] Miller's argument is important for understanding the poetic function of these figures here; while they are not truly synonymous, they each refer to an individual iteration of those who can be considered to do the opposite of what the אִישׁ must do.[12]

Verses 2a–3b describe the activity of the אִישׁ through both concrete and metaphorical descriptions.[13] They remain the primary participant in vv. 2a–3d as the subject of verbs describing positive activities in v. 2a–2b, as the subject of the verbs in v. 3a–3c in a simile referring to the "tree" (עֵץ, v. 3a), and as the sole subject in v. 3d. Grammatically speaking, the verbs and pronouns with the tree as its grammatical subject,[14] as well as the relative pronoun אֲשֶׁר in

v. 3b, all refer back to this person. The term אַשְׁרֵי in other contexts is always followed by a positive affirmation, though here this affirmation is suspended until v. 2a–2b.[15] The positive description of the activities of this person focuses on their attention and delight in the instruction of Yhwh (vv. 2a–2b).

The first mention of Yhwh in the psalm defines the construct form of "instruction" (תּוֹרָה) in v. 2a. The instruction of Yhwh is the focus of the fortunate person's attention in v. 2a–2b, and this instruction, assumed to derive from Yhwh himself, is the source of this person's flourishing. The comparison between the אִישׁ and the verdant tree is a simile that characterizes this person. This simile is itself made of vignettes. Beat Weber notes that the image in v. 3a–3c moves from a "still image" (*Standbild*) of the tree to active images of the tree growing and producing fruit.[16] It focuses on the growth and flourishing of this person, which is connected to their activities in vv. 1a–2b.[17] The person, then, who does or does not do those things mentioned is like this tree *because* this is what they do or do not do. This contrast strengthens the positive relationship of the אִישׁ to Yhwh's instruction.

Following the description of what the אִישׁ is (not) like (vv. 1a–3d) is a description of the wicked people in vv. 4a–5b, characterized primarily by the end that awaits them. Unlike the אִישׁ in v. 2a–2b, their activities or behaviors are not clearly articulated.[18] The space dedicated to the description of the wicked is much shorter than that of the אִישׁ, which itself is a significant poetic device.[19] The strong contrast with the description of the flourishing-as-a-tree אִישׁ described in v. 3a–3d is grammatically striking with the terse, "Not so wicked people"/לֹא־כֵן הָרְשָׁעִים in v. 4a. This contrast is also visually striking with a second image, whereby the verdant, flourishing אִישׁ who delights in Torah is contrasted with the chaff that blows in the wind in v. 4b. The phonic similarity between the two terms "like a tree" (כְּעֵץ, v. 3a) and "like chaff" (כַּמֹּץ, v. 4b) further heightens this contrast.[20] The image of chaff blowing in the wind provides a brief but poignant event where the wicked disappear as quickly as chaff.[21]

The end of both righteous and wicked are described in more concrete terms in vv. 5a–6b. The description of the wicked people in vv. 4a–5b, 6b highlights their eventual situation through metaphor and as the subject of activities they cannot participate in. Specifically, they are unable to "rise" (יָקֻמוּ, v. 5a) in judgment nor among the congregation of the righteous (v. 5a–5b). Ultimately, in v. 6b, their "way" is said to conclude in death. At the same time, there is no one in the psalm who directly attacks them or is explicitly the cause of their downfall. The contrast with the future inability for the wicked or sinners to participate in the righteous community hearkens back to the refusal of the אִישׁ to participate with the wicked and sinners in v. 1a–1b ("scoffers" is not repeated). That is, in v. 1a–1b the person is commended not to associate with the antagonists, and in v. 5a it is the wicked who are not allowed to associate with the righteous ones.[22] This future-oriented end is part of the overall progression of the poem, serving as a temporal conclusion, specifically referring to the negative consequences that await those who are wicked. In the end, the wicked receive judgment and social isolation.

Verse 6a–6b emphasizes Yhwh's connection with the righteous people, here noting that "Yhwh knows the path of righteous people," in contrast with the path of the wicked people. This is only activity directly attributed to Yhwh in the psalm. The contrast of the two pathways expresses the nearness of Yhwh to the righteous people and the eventual death of the wicked people. The term דֶּרֶךְ is the central term to describe the "way" of life in the Old Testament.[23] Further, "way" metaphors are prevalent throughout the psalms.[24] In Ps 1, this metaphor encompasses both the lifestyle and the eventual end.[25] Abernethy suggests that the pathway metaphor of v. 6a–6b does not function primarily ethically, as it relates information about Yhwh's perspective on the circumstances of each figure—that is, it is about the ends of these figures and not their behavior.[26] At the conclusion of the psalm, the righteous are best described as receiving the benefits of Yhwh's concern and the wicked, in a step further than v. 5a–5b, are destined to have their own way perish. In v. 5b the figures are expressed as a "congregation of righteous people"/עֲדַת צַדִּיקִים. Whether or not this refers to a specific in-group historically is unimportant to the psalm itself. Rather, this phrase designates a group of those who behave properly contrasted clearly with those who will be destroyed. In v. 6a, the צַדִּיקִים, in this case designated only by this title, are those whose path Yhwh "knows."

Psalm 1 revolves around two general themes: (1) the expression of the activities of the אִישׁ, including what they avoid doing; and (2) the future-oriented judgment of the wicked. Brown points out that in Ps 1, the pathway metaphor emphasizes ethics and behavior, a way of life, whereas the metaphors relating to plant imagery focus on the "ends" of these figures.[27] Like in many psalms, the primary protagonist is not explicitly connected with the righteous, and even in this case, the connection between the אִישׁ and the righteous is only by association of the activities and the future realities. The movement of the poem begins with the vignette of the refusal of a person to participate in the activities of or associate with the wicked, sinners, and mockers and leads to the eventual destruction of the wicked. The final lines affirm the benefit of being one of the righteous as well as the ramifications of being identified as one of the wicked.

Function of צַדִּיק and רָשָׁע

The righteous and the wicked contrast is central to the structure of Ps 1, though primarily in the second half of the poem. This structure is utilized to highlight a didactic function about praiseworthy character in Ps 1. This emphasis is extended through the affirmation of the fortune of the righteous person through the rich botanical imagery and to the ephemeral nature of the wicked. The comparison between the two does not include specific actions, but rather, focuses on the ends of the two figures as the just reward for their way of life. In Christoph Levin's evaluation, there is little more than a simple comparison of the two figures.[28] The psalm uses the common pathway metaphor to discuss these contrasting "ways," which leads the figures to their eventual ends. Similarly, Gunkel sees the retribution principle in this psalm as basic and superficial.[29] Gunkel is correct that it is rather straightforward in its presentation, though the brevity of the psalm excludes much deeper reflection.

The situation of concrete activities is not shared with the person at the beginning of the psalm. That is, the person who is not like the wicked, sinners, or scorners *is* someone who delights in and meditates on Yhwh's teaching, and they are like a fruitful plant. The fact that the person is designated by a general noun is not itself entirely significant, though the function of the אַשְׁרֵי clause at the beginning of Ps 1 emphasizes the benefit of the reality behind the one described and their actions as worthy of emulating.[30]

The function of the אִישׁ is not the same as צַדִּיק, though scholarship often refers to the person in Ps 1 as the righteous.[31] James L. Mays, for instance, writes that "the psalm is designed to emphasize one thing as fundamental to the righteous—engagement with the law of the LORD."[32] The emphasis on the "engagement" with the teaching of Yhwh is centrally highlighted in the psalm. However, this not because the psalm somehow claims that אִישׁ is semantically or even functionally equivalent with the צַדִּיק. They can be properly understood as related from a thematic or conceptual lens, but they are not directly coreferential in the psalm. The righteous, as such, are not introduced until v. 5. Due to the connection between the person mentioned in 1a and the righteous people in 6a, the concept of the fortune of the righteous person is by association extended to the one who does not participate in the manner of the wicked, sinner, or scoffer. Jacobson notes that the use of the plural צַדִּיקִים here helps to distinguish these figures from the "bad" ones in the psalm, rather than to identify the אִישׁ of v. 1a directly with the righteous.[33] The instruction of Yhwh is thus to be loosely connected with the figures of the righteous people; however, this is only by association in this context. Rather than something that is definitional for the righteous person or righteous people in psalms, only because of the connection between the person at the beginning of the psalm and the righteous people at the end does the concept of Torah become associated with the righteous. The אִישׁ of v. 1a is related to, but not the same as, the צַדִּיקִים mentioned in vv. 5b and 6a. While both are contrasted with the רְשָׁעִים directly in vv. 1a and 4a (הָאִישׁ) or vv. 5a and 6b (צַדִּיקִים), they do not operate on the same semantic level. That is, it is the function of the description of the person (הָאִישׁ, v. 1a) to emphasize the benefit of following Yhwh's instruction. Further, the general term אִישׁ invites anyone to envision the pathway to becoming like the fortunate person described. The righteous are not used to make this emphasis in the psalm.

The righteous people contrast with the wicked people, who are noted for their ephemeral nature. That is, it is not the אִישׁ that is compared with the righteous, but the wicked who are contrasted with them. To make the jump that these are the same figures is only true on a conceptual level. They can be included together as those who are on one side of a binary, though they do not have the same semantic properties. Further, the singular and plural distinction is not insignificant. Now, the community of the righteous is likely made up of those who appear and behave as the אִישׁ does, which is why the conceptual connection is legitimate. However, the two terms serve different functions within the poem. At the same time, the conceptual and structural connection identifies the use of צַדִּיקִים in this context are those who display proper conduct or behavior, but only implicitly. This is most clear in the contrast with the negative figures throughout the psalm through the metaphorical use of "way" imagery.

Even if conflict between the righteous and the wicked is not present in the psalm, a kind of tension with the reality of the world exists as part of the world of the psalm, where the speaker must affirm the fortune of the person and the righteous people as well as the eventual destruction of the wicked. Because of its reflection on eventual destruction, the psalm reflects the basis of the understanding of the world as it ought not be. While the concept of conflict between these two characters is not explicitly mentioned, the nature of the contrasting—and implicitly deserved—ends highlights the distinction between these two figures beyond an ethical or deed-consequence perspective. As Kynes has written,

> whether final or not, as long as the judgment mentioned in Ps 1:5 is not immediate, it demonstrates that on closer consideration . . . the external tension the psalm has with other psalms in the Psalter may be internal as well. Despite its explicit declaration of retributive justice, it implicitly acknowledges exceptions to this rule. For some indefinite amount of time before their judgment, the wicked may prosper.[34]

Similarly, Brown notes that there is tension within the psalm regarding the possibility of "mortal threats made by bloodthirsty enemies" in reference to the end of the wicked in Ps 1.[35] While the character-consequence nexus is clearly present in this psalm, the function of the comparison between the righteous and the wicked highlights a structural feature of contrasting ways.

These ways are contrasted to emphasize or affirm the central tenets of the theme of the righteous and the wicked, that eventually the righteous will be rewarded and the wicked destroyed.

The activities presented in the psalm, namely the meditation on Torah, is praised alongside the rejection of activities and behaviors that are assumed or understood to be associated with the רָשָׁע and related figures. The wicked way is rejected through the contrast with the fortune received by the person who does not associate with them. The identity of the figures is not clear, and there is no implication that these are foreign enemies, but rather, others whose pathway may be followed if one is not forewarned (in this case by the speaker) not to associate with these figures.

In Ps 1, the designations צַדִּיקִים and רְשָׁעִים both are used as general designations of one who is properly or improperly behaved as a global attribute. The literary pattern of the contrast of the two figures draws on their use as antonyms and the eventual destruction of these figures, with the assumed situation that they deserve their respective ends.

PSALM 7

Text and Translation

שִׁגָּיוֹן לְדָוִד אֲשֶׁר־שָׁר לַיהוָה עַל־דִּבְרֵי־כוּשׁ בֶּן־יְמִינִי׃	1a	(Shiggaion. Davidic, which he sang to Yhwh concerning the words of Cush, the Benjamite.)
יְהוָה אֱלֹהַי בְּךָ חָסִיתִי	2a	Yhwh, my God, in you have I have taken refuge;
הוֹשִׁיעֵנִי מִכָּל־רֹדְפַי וְהַצִּילֵנִי׃	2b	Rescue me from all my pursuers and deliver me,
פֶּן־יִטְרֹף כְּאַרְיֵה נַפְשִׁי	3a	Lest he tears at my throat[36] like a lion,
פֹּרֵק וְאֵין מַצִּיל׃	3b	Tearing to shreds, with none to rescue.
יְהוָה אֱלֹהַי אִם־עָשִׂיתִי זֹאת	4a	Yhwh, my God, if I did this,
אִם־יֶשׁ־עָוֶל בְּכַפָּי׃	4b	If there is injustice in my palm,
אִם־גָּמַלְתִּי שׁוֹלְמִי רָע	5a	If I had repaid my companion with[37] evil,
וָאֲחַלְּצָה צוֹרְרִי רֵיקָם׃	5b	Then I would free[38] my adversary without condition;
יִרַדֹּף אוֹיֵב נַפְשִׁי וְיַשֵּׂג	6a	Then let the enemy of my being pursue and overtake,
וְיִרְמֹס לָאָרֶץ חַיָּי	6b	And trample my neck to the ground,[39]
וּכְבוֹדִי לֶעָפָר יַשְׁכֵּן סֶלָה׃	6c	And cause my glory to lay down in the dust. (*selah*)

(*Continued*)

קוּמָה יְהוָה בְּאַפֶּךָ	7a	Arise, Yhwh, in your anger,
הִנָּשֵׂא בְּעַבְרוֹת צוֹרְרָי	7b	Lift yourself against the fury of my adversaries,
וְעוּרָה אֵלַי מִשְׁפָּט צִוִּיתָ׃	7c	And rouse yourself, my God; you determined justice.
וַעֲדַת לְאֻמִּים תְּסוֹבְבֶךָּ	8a	So the congregation of peoples will gather around you,
וְעָלֶיהָ לַמָּרוֹם׃	8b	And you are[40] over them in the heights.
יְהוָה יָדִין עַמִּים שׁוּבָה	9a	Return,[41] Yhwh—may he judge the peoples—
שָׁפְטֵנִי יְהוָה כְּצִדְקִי	9b	Try me, Yhwh, according to my righteousness
וּכְתֻמִּי עָלָי׃	9c	And according to my innocence over me.[42]
יִגְמָר־נָא רַע רְשָׁעִים	10a	May the evil of the wicked people be brought to an end;
וּתְכוֹנֵן צַדִּיק	10b	But you will establish the righteous person,
וּבֹחֵן לִבּוֹת וּכְלָיוֹת אֱלֹהִים צַדִּיק׃	10c	For the righteous God examines[43] the hearts and kidneys.
מָגִנִּי עַל־אֱלֹהִים	11a	My shield is held by[44] God,
מוֹשִׁיעַ יִשְׁרֵי־לֵב׃	11b	The one who saves the upright in heart.
אֱלֹהִים שׁוֹפֵט צַדִּיק	12a	God is a righteous judge,[45]
וְאֵל זֹעֵם בְּכָל־יוֹם׃	12b	And God is indignant every day.
אִם־לֹא יָשׁוּב	13a	If he[46] does not return,
חַרְבּוֹ יִלְטוֹשׁ	13b	He[47] will sharpen his sword,
קַשְׁתּוֹ דָרַךְ וַיְכוֹנְנֶהָ׃	13c	He bent his bow, he made it ready.
וְלוֹ הֵכִין כְּלֵי־מָוֶת	14a	And makes ready for himself instruments of death,
חִצָּיו לְדֹלְקִים יִפְעָל׃	14b	He makes his arrows like flames.[48]
הִנֵּה יְחַבֶּל־אָוֶן	15a	Look! He is pregnant with iniquity,
וְהָרָה עָמָל	15b	And he has conceived misfortune,
וְיָלַד שָׁקֶר׃	15c	And he has given birth to lies.
בּוֹר כָּרָה וַיַּחְפְּרֵהוּ	16a	He dug a pit, he emptied it out
וַיִּפֹּל בְּשַׁחַת יִפְעָל׃	16b	And he fell into the hole he made.
יָשׁוּב עֲמָלוֹ בְרֹאשׁוֹ	17a	His misfortune will return upon his head,
וְעַל קָדְקֳדוֹ חֲמָסוֹ יֵרֵד׃	17b	And on his scalp his violence will descend.
אוֹדֶה יְהוָה כְּצִדְקוֹ	18a	I will thank Yhwh because of his righteousness,
וַאֲזַמְּרָה שֵׁם־יְהוָה עֶלְיוֹן׃	18b	And I will make music to the name of Yhwh Most High.

Interpretation

Psalm 7 focuses on the present threat against the speaker from which the
speaker requests Yhwh's aid (vv. 2a–6c). The final lines of declaration (v.
18a–18b) presuppose the possibility of God's future response to the speaker's
need. The entire psalm is voiced by the same speaker, though the psalm is
first addressed to Yhwh in vv. 2a–10b and a then continues with a general
address in vv. 10c–18b.[49] Thus, much of the psalm itself is a prayer to Yhwh.
The address to Yhwh includes several declarations of the speaker's own faithfulness (vv. 2a, 4a–6c, 9a–9c, 18a–18b) and several requests for Yhwh to act
(vv. 2b–3b, 7a–7c, 9a–9c).

The question of whether the speaker is deserving of threats from "my
pursuers" (רֹדְפַי, v. 2b), "my adversary" (צוֹרְרִי, v. 5b; plural, v. 7b), and "the
enemy of my being" (אוֹיֵב נַפְשִׁי, v. 6a) is present with the continual mention
of the speaker's innocence. In vv. 4a–5a, there are three conditional sentences
that refer back to the speaker's lack of participation in evil, though describing concrete events. They state emphatically that the speaker would accept
responsibility for the wrongs committed, had he committed them.[50] Through
this rhetorical structure, the speaker declares in no uncertain terms that if they
were not innocent, they would be fully deserving of the attacks against them
by the enemies.

The entire section of vv. 7a–12b focuses on God's justice.[51] It places Yhwh
as judge of the peoples, though in particular, of the speaker and the righteous
person. That is, the section highlights the deserved end of the wicked in
destruction (vv. 7a–7c, 10a) and of the righteous in salvation (vv. 9b–9c, 10b,
11a–12a), with the "congregation of the peoples" (עֲדַת לְאֻמִּים, v. 8a) and "the
peoples" (עַמִּים, v. 9a) serving as witnesses to Yhwh's justice (vv. 8a–9a).[52] As
part of this request, the speaker asks to be judged by Yhwh and found innocent (v. 9a–9c). God only serves as an active subject in v. 10b–10c in testing
the "righteous person" (צַדִּיק, v. 10b), who only appears here in the psalm.

The major crux of the psalm is the identity of the 3ms forms in vv.
13a–17b.[53] Verse 15a–15c is unambiguously considered to be a description
of the enemy,[54] and thus, vv. 16a–17b are rightly assumed to continue this
description. However, the subject ambiguity and lack of a clear disjunctive marker or indication of a shift in speaker leave vv. 13a–14b as either
descriptions of God or the wicked. Several argue that God is the most likely
subject as the nearest named figure and most recent verbal subject in v. 12b,
interpreting the preparations for battle in vv. 13b–14b to relate to Yhwh's
preparation for judgment.[55] The הִנֵּה would then function as the indicator of
a shift in speaker.[56] Others view the entire section to be a description of the
enemies' preparations due to the clear similarities in structure and content
with the later portions known to refer to the wicked.[57] There appears to be

an assumption that the subject of 13a must be the subject of the verbs and referent of pronouns in vv. 13b–14b.[58] Without an explicit shift, this is a generally fair assumption. However, a shift in speaker is noted by scholars in other locations between vv. 13a–17b as noted above. I argue that it is more likely that the first line of this section (v. 13a) has a different referent than that a shift occurs somewhere in the middle of a description that contains imagery within a shared semantic domain, that of preparation for battle.[59] As such, the אִם לֹא יָשׁוּב that grounds the unrealized situation described in vv. 14b–17b must be understood in order to clarify the remainder of the poem. Hossfeld argues that the conditional sense of the אִם לֹא best reflects the context of the psalm (so vv. 4b–5a), and thus, it is best to read the subject of this line as God, which refers back to the command of v. 9a, "Return, Yhwh," which also uses the verb שׁוּב.[60] However, Hossfeld further argues that the subject of each of the verbs in 13b–14b remains God, yet the antecedent of the pronominal suffixes in each line is the enemy.[61] A simpler solution, that builds on the evidence Hossfeld cites, is to take the subject of only v. 13a as Yhwh, and the remainder of the lines of 13b–17b to refer exclusively to the enemy.

God's anger (v. 12b) leads into the second conditional section of the psalm, that if Yhwh does not return—that is, to return and judge as in v. 9a—then the wicked will prepare for violence (vv. 13b–15c). The cause and effect in this event see the preparations for violence as the context for the eventual destruction of the wicked in vv. 16a–17b. There are thus two parts to the description, the first of which in vv. 13b–15c describes the situation of what would happen without God's judgment, and vv. 16a–17b describe their demise. Thus, the unreal situation shifts into the future-oriented situation of destruction of the wicked by their own devices. This description of the preparations for violence connects with the speaker's distress and moves toward the resolution that the speaker requests from Yhwh. Several vivid metaphors appear in v. 15a–15c, drawing on a blending of destruction and birthing metaphors.[62] The intensity of the preparations for violence is envisioned through the metaphor of the wicked giving birth to violence. This image draws on a natural consequence as much as intentional planning.

The psalm concludes with the speaker's declaration of praise to Yhwh in v. 18a–18b. As such, the structure implies that while the wicked enemies are destroyed by their own devices, their destruction is credited to Yhwh for acting in line with his righteousness (כְּצִדְקוֹ, v. 18a) because the conclusion is a declaration to praise Yhwh.[63] In this way, the praise of God is rooted in the attribute the speaker desires God to have in reference to their innocence in the matter at hand.[64]

The psalm then surrounds a present event of distress described as an undeserved attack from the wicked, which in the end will be resolved by the wicked's own folly and Yhwh's divine intervention. The psalm does not detail the reason for or specific content of the threat against the speaker other than to describe it in powerful, violent imagery.

Function of צַדִּיק and רָשָׁע

Both צַדִּיק and רָשָׁע are recipients of God's judgment in Ps 7. The righteous and the wicked appear together in v. 10a–10b, where their fates are directly contrasted. As such, the clear literary pattern that they deserve their respective ends is highlighted. In this context, the צַדִּיק is one who is wrongly treated, and thus, innocent in the matter. That is also true of the speaker, and this pattern is set in a request heightening the need for Yhwh to act in order to prove the pattern of salvation for the innocent and destruction of the wicked true.[65] As is typical in psalms, the speaker never claims the title צַדִּיק explicitly.[66] However, because God is the judge of the righteous, and the speaker requests God to judge them, they declare rhetorically their own innocence in the matter. The appearance of the declaration of innocence (v. 9b–9c) appearing immediately before the affirmation of salvation for the righteous (v. 10b) also confirms the association between the צַדִּיק and the speaker. In affirming this literary pattern, that each deserves their respective ends, the speaker further emphasizes the pattern they hope to be true in the matter at hand. The speaker is attacked, they believe innocently, so the literary pattern is used to emphasize that God is the one who must act to vindicate the speaker.

In v. 12a God is designated as צַדִּיק in light of his role as judge. In the context of the psalm, these declarations serve to affirm the general theology that the righteous are to be protected by Yhwh as well as to identify the speaker as one of the righteous by association, especially with the claim to innocence in v. 9b–9c. Were God to judge, the speaker will be considered צַדִּיק, and as such, underserving of the threat against them, and worthy of Yhwh's aid. In contrast, the רָשָׁע functions as the perpetrator of violence, and thus, deserving of the violent end that awaits them. Verses 13b–17b function, then, to further characterize this figure in both their violence and futility.

The descriptions of the righteous and the wicked in Ps 7 affirm the quality of Yhwh's judgments, and a clear theology of justice. More than in many psalms, Ps 7 articulates a theology of retribution or character-consequence nexus, a theology that unfolds as a reality in the psalm. The pattern is well known and drawn on in order to make an emphatic appeal for Yhwh to act in justice in that situation.

PSALM 11

Text and Translation

לַמְנַצֵּחַ לְדָוִד	1a	(To the leader. Davidic.)
בַּיהוָה חָסִיתִי	1b	In Yhwh I take refuge,
אֵיךְ תֹּאמְרוּ לְנַפְשִׁי	1c	How could you say the following to me:
נוּדִי הַרְכֶם צִפּוֹר:	1d	"Flee[67] from[68] your mountain, you 'bird.'
כִּי הִנֵּה הָרְשָׁעִים יִדְרְכוּן קֶשֶׁת	2a	For, look, the wicked people bend a bow,
כּוֹנְנוּ חִצָּם עַל־יֶתֶר	2b	They set their arrow on the string,
לִירוֹת בְּמוֹ־אֹפֶל לְיִשְׁרֵי־לֵב:	2c	To shoot in the darkness at the upright in heart"?
כִּי הַשָּׁתוֹת יֵהָרֵסוּן	3a	If[69] the foundations are torn down,
צַדִּיק מַה־פָּעָל:	3b	What can the righteous person do?
יְהוָה בְּהֵיכַל קָדְשׁוֹ	4a	Yhwh is in the temple of his holiness.
יְהוָה בַּשָּׁמַיִם כִּסְאוֹ	4b	Yhwh, his throne is in the heavens.
עֵינָיו יֶחֱזוּ	4c	His eyes will see,
עַפְעַפָּיו יִבְחֲנוּ בְּנֵי אָדָם:	4d	His pupils examine the children of humanity.
יְהוָה צַדִּיק יִבְחָן וְרָשָׁע	5a	Yhwh examines the righteous person—as well as the wicked person,
וְאֹהֵב חָמָס שָׂנְאָה נַפְשׁוֹ:	5b	And the one who loves violence, he[70] hates.
יַמְטֵר עַל־רְשָׁעִים פַּחִים	6a	He makes coals[71] rain on wicked people;
אֵשׁ וְגָפְרִית וְרוּחַ זִלְעָפוֹת	6b	Fire and sulphur and raging wind
מְנָת כּוֹסָם:	6c	Are the portion of their cup.
כִּי־צַדִּיק יְהוָה	7a	For Yhwh is righteous;
צְדָקוֹת אָהֵב	7b	He loves righteous deeds;
יָשָׁר יֶחֱזוּ פָנֵימוֹ:	7c	The upright person will see his face.

Interpretation

Psalm 11 begins with a declaration of Yhwh as the speaker's refuge (v. 1b). This serves as a precursor to a question directed to an unidentified 2mp "you." These figures appear first in v. 1c as those who question the speaker. This group of individuals are participants in the poem in that they are cited as giving advice to the speaker to flee, though they are not explicitly referenced again in the psalm; they voice the entirety of the quotation that begins with

v. 1d. The extent of the quotation, however, is unclear. Gerstenberger, who views these speakers as attackers of the speaker, sees the quotation including only v. 1d, due to the typically short quotations of enemies in psalms, and interprets the כִּי as deictic, which makes vv. 2–3 the content of a complaint.[72] Goldingay sees the quotation extending through v. 2, though he notes the option that it might end in v. 3.[73] Most scholars suggest the quotation continues through the end of v. 3, with the כִּי in vv. 2a and 3a functioning to introduce the reasons behind the suggestion for the speaker to run away.[74] Jacobson finds v. 3b unlikely to come from the voice of the speaker, and thus opts for a continuation of the direct speech of the questioners.[75] Verse 3b could be voiced by the speaker if the initial question in v. 1d refers to a call for the speaker to participate in battle. Because of the interpretation of the entire psalm put forward in the following section, I favor the quotation ending at v. 2c.

The psalm continues with a rhetorical question directed to the speaker by the community regarding the possibility of fleeing in vv. 1d–2b. I suggest that the use of "bird" (צִפּוֹר, v. 1b) is in this case pejorative, referring to the common theme of fleeing and avian imagery in the ancient Near East though used in a way to subvert the primary intention (cf. Ps 55:7).[76] The voices mock the speaker for fleeing to safety in the temple rather than warring against these "wicked people" (רְשָׁעִים, v. 2a) who prepare to attack the "upright in heart" (v. 2a–2c). This suggestion, however, would mean to flee from the safety of Yhwh. It suggests that the threat of the wicked can be dealt with through human means. Thus, the question of v. 3a–3b comes from the voice of the speaker and expresses the inability to enact real change due to fact that the "foundations" are already destroyed.[77] In the temporal world of the psalm, it represents a present reality to which the speaker cannot respond with any efficacy. The speaker's question is a rebuke against those who questioned the speaker, suggesting that to flee would be nothing more than an abandonment of Yhwh, and thus, of safety. If the speaker were to flee from the mountain (v. 1d) they would flee from Yhwh's refuge (v. 1b). The speaker is associated with the righteous through the reference to the term צַדִּיק in v. 3b and through the structure, wherein the title צַדִּיק refers back to the situation of attack that the questioners of the speaker address in 1d–2c.[78]

Verses 4a–7c function as a response to what the צַדִּיק ought to do even though they are unable to do anything about the current situation. This section highlights the physical location of Yhwh in heaven and on his throne (v. 4a–4b), a vantage point from which he can view all of humanity (v. 4c–4d). The situation views God in his temple acting as judge of the earth for the benefit of the righteous and the destruction of the wicked.[79] Here,

Yhwh "tests" (יִבְחָן) both righteous and wicked (vv. 4c–5a), and the psalm shows the results of his judgment on "wicked person" (רָשָׁע, v. 5a) and "the one who loves violence" (אֹהֵב חָמָס, v. 5b). Although both righteous and wicked receive God's examining (v. 5a), the result for the wicked is their destruction. As the heavenly judge (v. 4a–4d), God hates the violent (v. 5b) and he judges them through raining "coals" (פֶּחִים, v. 6a–6c). Through these raining coals the wicked receive their just due, the "portion of their cup" (v. 6c).[80] On the other hand, the future reward of seeing Yhwh's face is expressed with little imagery. The designation of Yhwh as צַדִּיק in v. 7a further associates the righteous person with Yhwh's characterization as a just judge.

The two moments of the psalm are voiced by different participants (the questioners and the speaker) and primarily focus on different figures (the wicked and Yhwh respectively). The psalm also shifts from an earthly focused to a heavenly focused setting. The destroyed foundations in v. 3a are thematically contrasted with the reality of Yhwh's heavenly temple which cannot be threatened (v. 4a–4b). When the quotation of the questioners is read to continue through v. 3b, their speech focuses on the problem, that the wicked prepare for to attack the righteous, hunting them with a bow. The speaker, on the other hand, focuses on Yhwh and his eventual salvation.

The problem established by the questioners becomes secondary to trust in Yhwh. In this psalm, the wicked appear to limit the freedom of the righteous, yet the speaker responds to this with confidence that Yhwh will act in judgment against the wicked and judge the righteous person fairly. Because of the mention that Yhwh judges the righteous and the wicked fairly, this further validates the decision of the speaker in their choice to remain in the temple, in the safe place of Yhwh's care. The speaker is aware of the consequences that await the wicked, and uses this to strongly advocate their position not to participate in military action against the wicked. Yhwh will fairly judge, and only the wicked—those who pose a problem for both the questioners and the speaker—will be condemned.

The final line of the psalm, v. 7c, repeats a word from the quotation in v. 2c, though with a slight difference.[81] Though the threat to the "upright in heart"/ יִשְׁרֵי־לֵב is mentioned by the questioners in v. 2c, the "upright" (יָשָׁר, v. 7c) are able to "see" Yhwh.[82] In context, this is the result of Yhwh's decisive action in v. 6a–6c rather than militaristic action. From a structural perspective, the conclusion of the upright in heart receiving nearness to Yhwh emphasizes the reasonableness of the speaker's refusal to war against the wicked. It is the presence of Yhwh, again, that makes the community safe.

In summary, Ps 11 emphasizes the idea that Yhwh is a safe refuge in times of distress. With the first line of the poem expressing the speaker taking refuge in Yhwh, the entire poem is set up as a way of affirming the protection of the righteous against the attacks of the wicked. The antagonism between the righteous and the wicked here is present, with the violent activities ascribed to the wicked employed to emphasize the difference between the groups. That Yhwh is a sage refuge is proven in the psalm through the description of Yhwh as a fair judge who eventually puts an end to the violent and protects those who would take refuge in him.

Function of צַדִּיק and רָשָׁע

Van Leeuwen believes that the contrast between the righteous and the wicked in v. 5a functions as a merism, citing Gen 18:23, 25 as support.[83] However, in this context, the righteous and the wicked appear explicitly elsewhere in the psalm with clear differentiation. Throughout the psalm, the two are contrasted, though both receive the universal testing by Yhwh. By design, the speaker is associated with the צַדִּיק and the יָשָׁר. The use of צַדִּיק in v. 3b, according to this interpretation, is a reference to the speaker or to others who are requested to aid in military efforts. While there is still no first-person reference to the speaker as the צַדִּיק in the psalms, here there is a loose connection with the speaker, as the response of the speaker includes the reference to the inability of the צַדִּיק to respond to the situation. This connection functions to emphasize that the righteous may be unable to ward off the threats of the wicked through military power—a theme also found in other psalms, such as well-known Ps 20:8 [7]. In this instance, the צַדִּיק is designated as one who is unjustly wronged in a military situation; they are "innocent" in that they should not be judged, but they are also unable to fight against these too-powerful threats of the enemy.

At the end of the psalm, Yhwh is identified as צַדִּיק, something that appears infrequently elsewhere in the Psalter (Pss 129:4; 145:17; cf. Lam 1:18). This connection functions to elaborate the close relationship between Yhwh and the righteous community due to the shared root צדק in the context as the object of Yhwh's affection. It is not only the relationship with the community that ensures the identity of one of the צַדִּיק, but that fidelity to Yhwh is part of the way these figures are identified. In light of the literary pattern of the contrast between the צַדִּיק and רָשָׁע, Ps 11 confirms that the safety of being one of the צַדִּיק comes from the help of Yhwh. God is on the side of the צַדִּיק, but this does not mean, in this case, military victory without Yhwh's protection.

PSALM 31

Text and Translation

לַמְנַצֵּחַ מִזְמוֹר לְדָוִד:	1a	(For the leader. A Davidic Psalm.)
בְּךָ יְהוָה חָסִיתִי	2a	In you, Yhwh, I take[84] refuge,
אַל־אֵבוֹשָׁה לְעוֹלָם	2b	Let me not be put to shame forever;
בְּצִדְקָתְךָ פַלְּטֵנִי:	2c	In your righteousness, rescue me.
הַטֵּה אֵלַי אָזְנְךָ	3a	Turn your ear toward me;
מְהֵרָה הַצִּילֵנִי	3b	Deliver me quickly.
הֱיֵה לִי לְצוּר־מָעוֹז	3c	Be my rock of refuge,
לְבֵית מְצוּדוֹת לְהוֹשִׁיעֵנִי:	3d	My fortress dwelling, to save me.
כִּי־סַלְעִי וּמְצוּדָתִי אָתָּה	4a	For you are my cliff and my fortress,
וּלְמַעַן שִׁמְךָ תַּנְחֵנִי וּתְנַהֲלֵנִי:	4b	So for the sake of your name, lead and guide me.[85]
תּוֹצִיאֵנִי מֵרֶשֶׁת זוּ טָמְנוּ לִי	5a	Get me out of the net which they hid for me,
כִּי־אַתָּה מָעוּזִּי:	5b	For you are my refuge.
בְּיָדְךָ אַפְקִיד רוּחִי	6a	In your hand I will give[86] my breath;
פָּדִיתָה אוֹתִי יְהוָה אֵל אֱמֶת:	6b	You saved me, Yhwh God of faithfulness.
שָׂנֵאתִי הַשֹּׁמְרִים הַבְלֵי־שָׁוְא	7a	I hate[87] the keepers of empty idols,
וַאֲנִי אֶל־יְהוָה בָּטָחְתִּי:	7b	And I—I trust in Yhwh.
אָגִילָה וְאֶשְׂמְחָה בְּחַסְדֶּךָ	8a	I will rejoice and be glad in your love
אֲשֶׁר רָאִיתָ אֶת־עָנְיִי	8b	Because[88] you see my affliction;
יָדַעְתָּ בְּצָרוֹת נַפְשִׁי:	8c	You know the distress my life is in.
וְלֹא הִסְגַּרְתַּנִי בְּיַד־אוֹיֵב	9a	And you have not delivered me into the hand of the enemy;
הֶעֱמַדְתָּ בַמֶּרְחָב רַגְלָי:	9b	You set my feet in the broad pasture.
חָנֵּנִי יְהוָה כִּי צַר־לִי	10a	Be gracious to me, Yhwh, because of my distress;
עָשְׁשָׁה בְכַעַס עֵינִי	10b	My eyes deteriorate with anger,
נַפְשִׁי וּבִטְנִי:	10c	My throat and my belly as well.[89]
כִּי כָלוּ בְיָגוֹן חַיַּי	11a	For my life is destroyed in grief,
וּשְׁנוֹתַי בַּאֲנָחָה	11b	And my years with sighing;
כָּשַׁל בַּעֲוֹנִי כֹחִי	11c	My strength wanes[90] because of my iniquity
וַעֲצָמַי עָשֵׁשׁוּ:	11d	And my bones deteriorate.
מִכָּל־צֹרְרַי	12a	Because of[91] all my adversaries
הָיִיתִי חֶרְפָּה וְלִשְׁכֵנַי מְאֹד	12b	I have become a disgrace even[92] to my neighbors
וּפַחַד לִמְיֻדָּעָי	12c	And a terror to my acquaintances;
רֹאַי בַּחוּץ נָדְדוּ מִמֶּנִּי:	12d	Those who see me in the street flee from me.
נִשְׁכַּחְתִּי כְּמֵת מִלֵּב	13a	I am forgotten, like one whose mind has died;
הָיִיתִי כִּכְלִי אֹבֵד:	13b	I have become like a destroyed container.
כִּי שָׁמַעְתִּי דִּבַּת רַבִּים	14a	For I hear the gossip of the many:
מָגוֹר מִסָּבִיב	14b	"Horror all around."
בְּהִוָּסְדָם יַחַד עָלַי	14c	When they are established as one against me
לָקַחַת נַפְשִׁי זָמָמוּ:	14d	They plan to take my life.

(Continued)

וַאֲנִי עָלֶיךָ בָטַחְתִּי יְהוָה	15a	But I, I trust you, Yhwh,
אָמַרְתִּי אֱלֹהַי אָתָּה׃	15b	I say "You are my God."
בְּיָדְךָ עִתֹּתָי	16a	My seasons are in your hand;
הַצִּילֵנִי מִיַּד־אוֹיְבַי וּמֵרֹדְפָי׃	16b	Deliver me from the hand of my enemies and from my pursuers.
הָאִירָה פָנֶיךָ עַל־עַבְדֶּךָ	17a	Shine your face toward your servant,
הוֹשִׁיעֵנִי בְחַסְדֶּךָ׃	17b	Save me in your mercy.
יְהוָה אַל־אֵבוֹשָׁה	18a	Yhwh, let me not be put to shame
כִּי קְרָאתִיךָ	18b	For I call to you.
יֵבֹשׁוּ רְשָׁעִים	18c	Let the wicked people be put to shame;
יִדְּמוּ לִשְׁאוֹל׃	18d	Let them be quiet in Sheol;
תֵּאָלַמְנָה שִׂפְתֵי שָׁקֶר	19a	Let lying lips be silent,
הַדֹּבְרוֹת עַל־צַדִּיק עָתָק	19b	Those who speak arrogantly against the righteous person
בְּגַאֲוָה וָבוּז׃	19c	In pride and contempt.
מָה רַב־טוּבְךָ	20a	How plentiful is your goodness,
אֲשֶׁר־צָפַנְתָּ לִּירֵאֶיךָ	20b	Which you treasure up for those who fear you,
פָּעַלְתָּ לַחֹסִים בָּךְ	20c	Which you make for those who take refuge in you
נֶגֶד בְּנֵי אָדָם׃	20d	Before the children of humanity.
תַּסְתִּירֵם בְּסֵתֶר פָּנֶיךָ	21a	You hide them in the hiding place of your presence
מֵרֻכְסֵי אִישׁ	21b	From the conspiracies of a person.
תִּצְפְּנֵם בְּסֻכָּה	21c	You hide them up in a shelter
מֵרִיב לְשֹׁנוֹת׃	21d	From the conflict of tongues.
בָּרוּךְ יְהוָה	22a	Blessed be Yhwh,
כִּי הִפְלִיא חַסְדּוֹ לִי	22b	For his mercy has been wonderful for me
בְּעִיר מָצוֹר׃	22c	In a besieged city.
וַאֲנִי אָמַרְתִּי בְחָפְזִי	23a	But I—I said, when I was alarmed,
נִגְרַזְתִּי מִנֶּגֶד עֵינֶיךָ	23b	"I am cut off[93] from before your eyes."
אָכֵן שָׁמַעְתָּ קוֹל תַּחֲנוּנַי	23c	Surely,[94] you heard to voice of my pleas
בְּשַׁוְּעִי אֵלֶיךָ׃	23d	When I cried to you for help.
אֶהֱבוּ אֶת־יְהוָה כָּל־חֲסִידָיו	24a	Love Yhwh, all his faithful ones.
אֱמוּנִים נֹצֵר יְהוָה	24b	The faithful people Yhwh preserves,
וּמְשַׁלֵּם עַל־יֶתֶר	24c	But he fully punishes the rest,
עֹשֵׂה גַאֲוָה׃	24d	The one who acts arrogantly.
חִזְקוּ וְיַאֲמֵץ לְבַבְכֶם	25a	Be strong and let your heart show courage,
כָּל־הַמְיַחֲלִים לַיהוָה׃	25b	All who wait for Yhwh.

Interpretation

Psalm 31 is a prayer in response to a situation from which the speaker requires direct intervention.[95] There are multiple problems that are stated: enemy attacks, sinfulness, and being forgotten and neglected. The request is mediated through an appeal to the speaker's commitment toward Yhwh as the grounds to impel Yhwh to act. Declarations of trust come in vv. 2a, 7b,

15a–15b, and 18b. As such, the speaker is self-characterized through their devotion to Yhwh, even in the nature of the mediated form of a prayer.

Psalm 31 begins with a call to Yhwh to rescue based on the speaker's declaration of making Yhwh their refuge, beginning with the emphatic "in you" (בְּךָ, v. 2a).[96] The initial phrase The requests in the ensuing section, vv. 2a–5b, focus on the need of the speaker to be rescued juxtaposed with declarations about Yhwh's character. The concept of refuge is constant throughout this request: "I take refuge" (חָסִיתִי, v. 2a); "rock of refuge" (צוּר־מָעוֹז, v. 3c); "fortress dwelling" (בֵית מְצוּדוֹת, v. 3d); "my cliff" (סַלְעִי, v. 4a); "my fortress" (מְצוּדָתִי, v. 4a); "my refuge" (מָעוּזִּי, v. 5b).[97] The declaration of Yhwh's nature, the faith of the speaker, and the speaker's need are all intertwined in vv. 2a–5b.

The setting of vv. 6a–9b uses exclusively QATAL verbs to speak of Yhwh's protection and past action. For the speaker, however, there is a shift between YIQTOL verbs with a cohortative sense (vv. 6a and 8a) and QATAL verbs (v. 7a–7b). The speaker thus uses both statements of a settled position (their attitudes toward Yhwh and toward their enemies) and the reality of what they will do to highlight the distress. Their perspective is sure, though their situation is one in which Yhwh needs to act. This shifts directly into a request to Yhwh.

A request begins in v. 10a with an imperative directed toward Yhwh,[98] followed by a lengthy description of the effects of distress (vv. 10b–14d). Verses 10b–10c and 11d describe the weariness from tears through the speaker's whole body: their eyes (v. 10b), throat (v. 10c), belly (v. 10c), and bones (v. 11d). This is also paired with the expressions of weakness in v. 11a–11c, though surprisingly, the reason for this struggle is "my iniquity" (v. 11c). The problem, then, that is given at this stage is the speaker's own sin, unlike the previous examples of the attack of the enemies, which returns in the following verse.

Verse 12a–12d offers a poignant image of the speaker's situation, where those who knew them previously reject them. Those who avoid the speaker become their attackers in v. 14d. Though the earlier section also dealt with the general situation of distress, vv. 10a–14d focus on the devastation dealt by the enemies of the speaker.[99] Verses 10b–14d could be understood as part of the prayer, but could also be considered to have a general address as there are no vocatives and the content differs from the earlier sections. The designation "the many" (רַבִּים, v. 14a) refers to another category of bystander.[100] However, in v. 14c–14d they turn to attack the speaker. This section evokes a sort of sympathy for the speaker. While their sinfulness was briefly mentioned, the situation they are in is dire, and they are now further isolated from others because of their enemies.

From this description, the speaker repeats the sentiment of vv. 2a and 7b, that they trust in Yhwh, using direct verbal echoes in v. 15a.[101] This declaration initiates a sequence of requests for Yhwh to act in two parts. First, the speaker asks for their own rescue (vv. 16a–18b). This is grounded again in declarations of the faithfulness of the speaker, with statements of entrusting their life to Yhwh (vv. 16a, 18b) and the self-designation of "your servant" (עַבְדֶּךָ, v. 17a), along with an appeal to Yhwh's lovingkindness (v. 17b). In this section, the request of v. 2b is repeated in v. 18a. Further, the phrase "my seasons are in your hands" expresses a similar sentiment as v. 6a.[102] Second, the speaker asks for the condemnation and destruction of the wicked enemies (vv. 18c–19c).[103] Both sides of the request have the same outcome for the speaker, though rhetorically one is a positive confirmation of the faithfulness of the speaker, and one is a condemnation of those who are deserving of judgment.

Verses 20a–22c belong to another section that speaks of Yhwh as a refuge, though this time referring to benefits for those who trust in Yhwh in the third person. Here, Yhwh saves "those who take refuge" in him (חֹסִים, v. 20c) from verbal attacks (v. 21b, 21d).[104] Though the speaker was not explicitly included in the description of Yhwh's action, the response is to praise Yhwh for Yhwh's mercy on the speaker's behalf, locating his action "in a besieged city" (בְּעִיר מָצוֹר, v. 22c). Again, a new situation appears which does not clearly relate to the situations previously mentioned, such as sinfulness, verbal attacks, or simple attacks from the enemy. At the same time, v. 23a–23d supplies a brief narration of Yhwh's past rescue of the speaker, where the speaker calls to Yhwh and Yhwh hears.

A shift is address in v. 24a calls the worshiping community to hope in God for their rescue. The call to praise affirms that those who are faithful to Yhwh receive Yhwh's faithful action toward them. This extends the context of distress from the individual speaker to the community at large. It also affirms that the one who behaves improperly will be destroyed (v. 24c–24d), as requested earlier in the psalm. The psalm, then, has a sort of narrative progression from the situation of distress to an eventual resolution in Yhwh's decisive action. This preludes a call to courage for the community in v. 25a–25b. Thus, the psalm concludes with an address to the community to hope in Yhwh that he will punish those who ought to be punished.

There are several repeated concepts that tie the psalm together. For instance, the speaker's situation is described in terms of whose "hand" the speaker is in: the hand of God in v. 6a, the hand of the enemy in v. 9a, and the hand of both enemies and God in v. 16a–16b.[105] Further, a focus on speech is present throughout the psalm. This is present in the threats from the antagonists in vv. 18c–19b, but it also appears with the reference to tongues (לְשֹׁנוֹת) in v. 21d. The request for Yhwh to act in these verses focus then on the silencing of those who speak illegitimately against the speaker. The problem in this section is primarily related to speech, rather than other images of the distress. The speech of the psalmic voice, on the other hand, is a theme throughout the psalm: the speaker consistently references their own vocal activity: "I say" (v. 15b), "I call" (v. 18b), "I said" (v. 23a), and "I cried" (v. 23d). These features serve to give the psalm a consistent pattern where the actions of the wicked are pitted against the speaker, and the speaker contrasts these figures with Yhwh.

Psalm 31 includes a wide range of images of distress. The general focus in the psalm is on detailed description of the distress itself to impel Yhwh to act, rather than on narrative progression. The end of the psalm focuses on motivating the community, emphasizing that Yhwh will act. This act is not something that has been fully realized in the psalm, and thus functions as an encouragement for the community to remain steadfast in their own crises.

Function of צַדִּיק and רָשָׁע

The contrast between צַדִּיק and רָשָׁע in Ps 31 functions to underscore the possibility of salvation in a present context of distress. The רְשָׁעִים are directly contrasted with the speaker in v. 18a–18d, where the shame that the speaker requests salvation from is asked to be brought upon the wicked person (v. 2b). The following verse continues to characterize the רְשָׁעִים for their speech, which explicitly identifies the צַדִּיק as the object of their derision, from which the righteous must be protected (v. 19a–19b). In these verses, the result of the destruction is the silence of the wicked. As such, the request emphasizes the significance of the wicked's speech as part of the problem for the speaker. In the contrast between the two figures, the idea that the רָשָׁע is in the wrong in a situation is more likely than as the figure who represents the activities that are generally condemnable. The צַדִּיק also does not here refer to the one who is prototypically properly behaved, nor should they be identified specifically with the worshiping community. Rather, they are those who are unjustly attacked by the wicked. They are, in this sense, semantically related to those who are innocent in a matter, and designated with this term because of the improper behavior of those who speak against them.

Only by implication is the speaker to be associated with the righteous person in v. 19b. That is, the threat of others directed toward the speaker is present throughout the psalm. These figures fit within the overall progression wherein the eventual destruction of the wicked and salvation of the righteous have not yet been actualized, and thus, the speaker must remind Yhwh of who he is and what he does. In terms of the literary pattern, the deservedness of the ends of these figures is clear and is used to persuade Yhwh to act. In the context of the whole psalm, however, this request is part of a sort of loose narrative that functions to encourage the community in their faithfulness to Yhwh. Psalm 31 is a psalm of the righteous and the wicked in medias res, and these figures function to heighten the present conflict described in the psalm.

PSALM 32

Text and Translation

לְדָוִד מַשְׂכִּיל	1a	(Davidic—Maskil)
אַשְׁרֵי נְשׂוּי־פֶּשַׁע	1b	Fortunate[106] is the person whose transgression is lifted,
כְּסוּי חֲטָאָה:	1c	The one whose sin is covered.
אַשְׁרֵי אָדָם לֹא יַחְשֹׁב יְהוָה לוֹ עָוֹן	2a	Fortunate is the person whose sin Yhwh does not consider,
וְאֵין בְּרוּחוֹ רְמִיָּה:	2b	And in their breath is no deceit.
כִּי־הֶחֱרַשְׁתִּי	3a	Yet[107] I was silent,
בָּלוּ עֲצָמָי בְּשַׁאֲגָתִי כָּל־הַיּוֹם:	3b	My bones were worn out from my groaning all day.
כִּי יוֹמָם וָלַיְלָה תִּכְבַּד עָלַי יָדֶךָ	4a	For day and night your hand was heavy upon me,
נֶהְפַּךְ לְשַׁדִּי בְּחַרְבֹנֵי קַיִץ סֶלָה:	4b	My moisture[108] was turned into the drought of the summer. (*selah*)
חַטָּאתִי אוֹדִיעֲךָ	5a	My sin I made known to you
וַעֲוֹנִי לֹא־כִסִּיתִי	5b	And my wrong I did not conceal.
אָמַרְתִּי אוֹדֶה עֲלֵי פְשָׁעַי לַיהוָה	5c	I said, "I will confess my transgression to Yhwh."
וְאַתָּה נָשָׂאתָ עֲוֹן חַטָּאתִי סֶלָה:	5d	And you,[109] you forgave the guilt of my sin. (*selah*)
עַל־זֹאת יִתְפַּלֵּל כָּל־חָסִיד אֵלֶיךָ לְעֵת מְצֹא	6a	Therefore, let all the faithful pray to you in a time you are found.[110]
רַק לְשֵׁטֶף מַיִם רַבִּים אֵלָיו לֹא יַגִּיעוּ:	6b	Surely[111] in the flood the many waters will not reach them.
אַתָּה סֵתֶר לִי	7a	You are my hiding place,
מִצַּר תִּצְּרֵנִי	7b	From distress you preserve me.
רָנֵּי פַלֵּט תְּסוֹבְבֵנִי סֶלָה:	7c	Songs of escape you place around me. (*selah*)
אַשְׂכִּילְךָ וְאוֹרְךָ	8a	"I will give you insight and I will teach you
בְּדֶרֶךְ־זוּ תֵלֵךְ	8b	In the way which you are to go;
אִיעֲצָה עָלֶיךָ עֵינִי:	8c	I will advise you;[112] my eyes are upon you.[113]

(Continued)

אַל־תִּהְיוּ כְּסוּס כְּפֶרֶד אֵין הָבִין	9a	Do not be like a horse or like a mule which have no understanding.
בְּמֶתֶג־וָרֶסֶן עֶדְיוֹ לִבְלוֹם	9b	Bridle and rein are its accessories to be restrained[114]
בַּל קְרֹב אֵלֶיךָ:	9c	So it does not approach you.
רַבִּים מַכְאוֹבִים לָרָשָׁע	10a	There are great pains for the wicked person,
וְהַבּוֹטֵחַ בַּיהוָה חֶסֶד יְסוֹבְבֶנּוּ:	10b	Yet lovingkindness will surround the one trusting in Yhwh."
שִׂמְחוּ בַיהוָה וְגִילוּ צַדִּיקִים	11a	Rejoice in Yhwh and exult, righteous people,
וְהַרְנִינוּ כָּל־יִשְׁרֵי־לֵב:	11b	And shout for joy all upright in heart.

Interpretation

Verses 1a–2c refer to a hypothetical person who is considered fortunate (אַשְׁרֵי) because they have been forgiven. This person is designated by several participle phrases: "the person whose transgression is lifted" (נְשׂוּי־פֶּשַׁע, v. 1b) and "the one whose sin is covered" (כְּסוּי חֲטָאָה, v. 1c).[115] This "person" is described to emphasize the situation of being forgiven, rather than any specific actions. Mignon R. Jacobs suggests that these first two verses represent "the experiential and temporally based center of the text."[116] The psalm largely focuses on the pattern of forgiveness, and thus the first two verses further serve an introductory function to the psalm in terms of its content.[117] While the change in circumstance as a result of the confession need not have been immediate in the occurrence of event spoken in the psalm,[118] it is implied through the structure. The section sets up the movement toward forgiveness.

Verses 3a–5d describe the situation of the unforgiven speaker, who is portrayed as in need and calling out to Yhwh.[119] This section begins with a contrast between the speaker's silence (הֶחֱרַשְׁתִּי, v. 3a) and groaning (שַׁאֲגָתִי, v. 3b).[120] The silence here speaks of the lack of confession, rather than an overall lack of utterance.[121] The silence is broken in v. 5a and 5c, where vocal words introduce the speaker's confession (ידע *hiphil*; אמר *qal*). Another central theme here is time. The speaker groans "all day" (v. 3b) and feels Yhwh's hand is upon them "day and night" (v. 4a), poetically heightening sin's effects. However, once confession occurs the immediate and emphatic response in the psalm is the forgiveness of sin by God in v. 5d, and so the fortune of the person mentioned in vv. 1b–2 then becomes the speaker's experience.[122]

Verse 6a begins with "therefore" (עַל־זֹאת) which then introduces a statement that the "faithful" should pray to Yhwh. Because of the speaker's testimony of forgiveness, the community is also offered the opportunity for forgiveness in this way.[123] Vignettes of need and rescue also appear in this section: a flood is kept from overtaking the faithful "the faithful" (חָסִיד, v. 6a–6b) and Yhwh is a safe place for the speaker in a general situation of distress (v. 7a–7c). The

vivid description promotes a sense of urgency.[124] These two moments serve
as a reiteration of the same concept presented earlier in v. 3a–5d, that Yhwh
protects those who are faithful, though without reference to a particular situation. The metaphor of waters as violence is fairly common in psalms,[125] so
here draws on conventional images of distress.

A major question is the identity of the speaker in vv. 8a–9c or 8a–10b.[126]
Several scholars see this quote spoken by Yhwh,[127] or by the psalmic speaker
in a didactic mode.[128] Hildebrandt argues that the possibility of intentional
ambiguity should be considered, which would highlight the significance of
the communal dynamics of forgiveness as clearing the way for the forgiven
sinner to function in line with God's teaching to the community.[129] In either
case, there is a shift in content and addressee to the second person from earlier
sections of the psalm.[130] However, because there is no clear shift in addressee
through v. 10b, it is best to assume that there is a single speaker for vv.
8a–10b, and because Yhwh is mentioned in the third person, it is most likely
to be the voice of the psalmic voice or another human speaker.

Verses 8a–10b is a speech directed to the audience, initiated through the
speaker's self-description of teaching others in v. 8a–8c. The teaching itself
uses the image of the horse being guided and controlled by bridle and bit,
compared with those who lack understanding (v. 9a–9c). The language in
this speech is unclear, though the mention of a lack of "understanding" of
the horse relates the content to knowledge. The conclusion that follows, then,
is an affirmation of the difficulties for the wicked and the benefits of being
"one trusting in Yhwh" (הַבּוֹטֵחַ בַּיהוָה, v. 10b). Verse 10a does not focus on the
actual end of the wicked, only that being one of the wicked results in "great
pains" (רַבִּים מַכְאוֹבִים, v. 10a).

The final lines of the psalm (v. 11a–11b) shift in addressee to call the community to worship Yhwh. The addressees are explicitly named "righteous
people" (צַדִּיקִים, v. 11a) and "upright in heart" (יִשְׁרֵי־לֵב, v. 11b). As a conclusion
to the psalm, it emphasizes the goodness of the pains of the wicked person and
the goodness of having Yhwh's חֶסֶד surrounding them. It is a call to worship
Yhwh because of these realities, as well as the reality of Yhwh's rescue of those
who are forgiven, as described in the first moments of the psalm.[131]

The psalm becomes a reflection on sin, forgiveness, Yhwh's rescue, the way
of knowledge, and worship of Yhwh. These features appear through a movement from distress to resolution, centered on forgiveness following confession.

Function of צַדִּיק and רָשָׁע

Both רָשָׁע and צַדִּיק appear as the prototypical figures of positive or negative character and behavior in Ps 32. The psalm emphasizes that sorrow

the wicked person will experience in v. 10a. The pains of the רָשָׁע also are highlighted in contrast with the fortunate person in vv. 1a–2b, structurally enveloping the psalm with the outcomes of a way of life both positively and negatively. In this case, the psalm affirms a sort of character-consequence nexus, with the contrasting behavior of the רָשָׁע being trust in Yhwh. They are implicitly characterized by their distrust, rather than their actions, and thus, trust in Yhwh is affirmed through the negative contrast in v. 10a–10b. They are secondarily contrasted with the righteous as well.

In v. 11a, the צַדִּיקִים are explicitly called to worship Yhwh. As such, their identity is clear as the worshiping community and those who are addressed by the speaker.[132] In this rare case, the designation goes beyond a prototypical figure to be identified directly with the audience (see also Ps 97:12). At the same time, it is not necessarily all who are addressed, but only those that can be considered among the צַדִּיקִים. As such, this function of the word does not indicate a person who is innocent in a matter or one who functions rhetorically as a generally properly behaved person, but as an identification of the community as those who are defined by the general orientation to Yhwh in worship. Further, because the wicked are noted by negative contrast in the previous verse for their lack of trust (v. 10a–10b), the contrast between the two only highlight the positive attributes of the righteous people: they trust in and worship Yhwh.

PSALM 34

לְדָוִד בְּשַׁנּוֹתוֹ אֶת־טַעְמוֹ לִפְנֵי אֲבִימֶלֶךְ וַיְגָרֲשֵׁהוּ וַיֵּלַךְ:	1a	(Davidic. When he changed his behavior in the presence of Abimelech and he sent him away so he left.)[133]
אֲבָרֲכָה אֶת־יְהוָה בְּכָל־עֵת	2a	I will bless Yhwh at all times;
תָּמִיד תְּהִלָּתוֹ בְּפִי:	2b	Continually his praise will be[134] in my mouth.
בַּיהוָה תִּתְהַלֵּל נַפְשִׁי	3a	In Yhwh my soul boasts,
יִשְׁמְעוּ עֲנָוִים וְיִשְׂמָחוּ:	3b	Let the poor hear and be glad.
גַּדְּלוּ לַיהוָה אִתִּי	4a	Magnify Yhwh with me,
וּנְרוֹמְמָה שְׁמוֹ יַחְדָּו:	4b	And exalt his name together.
דָּרַשְׁתִּי אֶת־יְהוָה וְעָנָנִי	5a	I searched[135] for Yhwh and he answered me,
וּמִכָּל־מְגוּרוֹתַי הִצִּילָנִי:	5b	And from all my fears he rescued me.

(Continued)

הִבִּיטוּ אֵלָיו וְנָהָרוּ	6a	They looked to him,[136] and they shone,
וּפְנֵיהֶם אַל־יֶחְפָּרוּ:	6b	And their faces were not confounded.
זֶה עָנִי קָרָא וַיהוָה שָׁמֵעַ	7a	This poor person called, and Yhwh heard,
וּמִכָּל־צָרוֹתָיו הוֹשִׁיעוֹ:	7b	Then from all their[137] distresses he saved them.
חֹנֶה מַלְאַךְ־יְהוָה	8a	The angel of Yhwh encamps
סָבִיב לִירֵאָיו וַיְחַלְּצֵם:	8b	Around[138] those who fear him and he delivers them.
טַעֲמוּ וּרְאוּ כִּי־טוֹב יְהוָה	9a	Taste and see[139] that Yhwh is good;
אַשְׁרֵי הַגֶּבֶר יֶחֱסֶה־בּוֹ:	9b	Fortunate is the person who seeks refuge in him.
יְראוּ אֶת־יְהוָה קְדֹשָׁיו	10a	Fear Yhwh, his holy ones,
כִּי־אֵין מַחְסוֹר לִירֵאָיו:	10b	For there is no lack for those who fear him.
כְּפִירִים רָשׁוּ וְרָעֵבוּ	11a	Young lions[140] are in need and are hungry,
וְדֹרְשֵׁי יְהוָה לֹא־יַחְסְרוּ כָל־טוֹב:	11b	But those who seek Yhwh will not lack anything good.
לְכוּ־בָנִים שִׁמְעוּ־לִי	12a	Come, children, listen to me,
יִרְאַת יְהוָה אֲלַמֶּדְכֶם:	12b	I will teach you fear of Yhwh.
מִי־הָאִישׁ הֶחָפֵץ חַיִּים	13a	Who is a person that desires life?
אֹהֵב יָמִים לִרְאוֹת טוֹב:	13b	One who loves days to be able to see goodness?
נְצֹר לְשׁוֹנְךָ מֵרָע	14a	Keep your tongue from evil
וּשְׂפָתֶיךָ מִדַּבֵּר מִרְמָה:	14b	And your lips from speaking[141] deceit,
סוּר מֵרָע וַעֲשֵׂה־טוֹב	15a	Turn aside from evil and do good,
בַּקֵּשׁ שָׁלוֹם וְרָדְפֵהוּ:	15b	Seek peace and pursue it.
עֵינֵי יְהוָה אֶל־צַדִּיקִים	16a	The eyes of Yhwh are toward righteous people
וְאָזְנָיו אֶל־שַׁוְעָתָם:	16b	And his ears toward their cry for help.
פְּנֵי יְהוָה בְּעֹשֵׂי רָע	17a	The face of Yhwh is against[142] those who do evil,
לְהַכְרִית מֵאֶרֶץ זִכְרָם:	17b	To cut from the earth their memory.
צָעֲקוּ וַיהוָה שָׁמֵעַ	18a	They[143] cry out and Yhwh hears,[144]
וּמִכָּל־צָרוֹתָם הִצִּילָם:	18b	And from all their distresses he saves them.
קָרוֹב יְהוָה לְנִשְׁבְּרֵי־לֵב	19a	Yhwh is near to those injured in heart,
וְאֶת־דַּכְּאֵי־רוּחַ יוֹשִׁיעַ:	19b	And the crushed in spirit he saves.[145]
רַבּוֹת רָעוֹת צַדִּיק	20a	Many are the problems of a righteous person,
וּמִכֻּלָּם יַצִּילֶנּוּ יְהוָה:	20b	But Yhwh saves them from all of them.
שֹׁמֵר כָּל־עַצְמוֹתָיו	21a	He protects all their bones;
אַחַת מֵהֵנָּה לֹא נִשְׁבָּרָה:	21b	Not one of them is broken.
תְּמוֹתֵת רָשָׁע רָעָה	22a	Calamity will kill the wicked person,
וְשֹׂנְאֵי צַדִּיק יֶאְשָׁמוּ:	22b	And those who hate the righteous person will be guilty.
פּוֹדֶה יְהוָה נֶפֶשׁ עֲבָדָיו	23a	Yhwh ransoms the life of his servants,
וְלֹא יֶאְשְׁמוּ כָּל־הַחֹסִים בּוֹ:	23b	And they will not be guilty, all those who seek refuge in him.

Text and Translation

Interpretation

Psalm 34 is presented as both a testimony and an exhortation to the community. The speaker calls the community directly to participate in several cases (vv. 4a–4b, 9a, 10a, 12a–12b, 14a–15b), particularly in sections where the speaker utilizes a didactic voice. Thematically, the psalm coheres around the emphasis that Yhwh will protect those whom he loves. Structurally, the psalm is an acrostic that is tied together with many repeated words or phrases.[146]

The opening lines of the psalm contains several distinct events. First, the speaker tells of their own praise of Yhwh and calls those in the community to worship with them (vv. 2a–4b).[147] Second, in v. 5a–5b, the speaker begins to retell a short and highly conventional vignette of Yhwh's rescue. Though there is a shift from first person to third, the speaker describes the turn in situation wherein the "poor man" sees Yhwh, which, as a result, leads to their "radiant" face (v. 6a–6b). Metaphorically the radiance of face represents the joyful status as recipients of Yhwh's help.[148] This story of rescue continues with the singular referent עָנִי in v. 7a–7c and the 3ms suffixes found there. Finally, v. 8a–8b speaks of the angel of Yhwh saving and protecting those who fear Yhwh. Thus, the speaker, the community, and the individual person who is in need are all described as recipients of Yhwh's rescue in vv. 5a–8b.

Moving from the stories of distress and salvation, vv. 9a–11b include a list of didactic statements about Yhwh's concern for those who trust him (vv. 9b, 10b–11b) interspersed with commands for the community to trust Yhwh (vv. 9a, 10a). Each explicit designations for the community include a modifier referring to Yhwh "his holy ones" (קְדֹשָׁיו, v. 10a), "those who fear him" (יְרֵאָיו, v. 10b), and "those who seek Yhwh" (דֹּרְשֵׁי יְהָה, v. 10b). The first instruction is to "taste" (טַעֲמוּ, v. 9a), and thus "see" the goodness of Yhwh. Vivian Johnson suggests that the verb טעם implies a "small sample," and thus suggests to the listeners to "try" God.[149] Luis Alonso-Schökel has argued that the outcome of the tasting as "good" (טוֹב) extends the food metaphor, as it can sometimes relate to the quality of what is consumed.[150] This is followed by a beatitude similar to Ps. 1, though using הַגֶּבֶר (v. 9b) instead of אִישׁ to describe the one who would be fortunate. The function is similar in that it invites anyone to experience Yhwh as their refuge. These invitations lead directly to the didactic speaker inviting the community to listen to the didactic speaker teach "fear of Yhwh" (יִרְאַת יְהוָה, vv. 12a–12b). This alludes back to the command to "fear Yhwh" (יְראוּ אֶת־יהוָה) in v. 10a. The audience is addressed as "children" (בָּנִים) in v. 12a, denoting a teaching relationship.[151] The content of this teaching is instigated by the rhetorical questions of v. 13a–13b, directed at "the person that desires life" (הָאִישׁ הֶחָפֵץ חַיִּים, v. 13a) and the "one who desires days" (אֹהֵב יָמִים, v. 13b). The remainder of the psalm continues the instruction from this speaker and includes both commands to the community and statements about Yhwh's actions or the situation of the righteous person.

Two lines of commands address activities that the audience should refrain from doing or do (vv. 14a–15b). Verse 14a–14b focuses on the rejection of illegitimate speech. Verse 15a–15b includes more general instructions, first to reject "evil" (רָע) and rather "do good" and to attempt to accomplish peace. Leon Liebreich suggests that the activities in vv. 14a–15b are implicitly those of the righteous.[152] While from a poetic standpoint they are commended to the community directly, the mention of the righteous in the following line creates a connection that does implicitly define the behaviors of the righteous based on these lines. Significantly, it is both innocence (refraining from evil) and virtue (practicing goodness and seeking peace) that are to define the community, and by proximity and structural connection, the righteous. A description of Yhwh's activities on behalf of the righteous and against the wicked begins in v. 16a until the end of the psalm in v. 23b, from the perspective of Yhwh's throne room. Yhwh's perspective toward righteous and wicked are expressed through metaphors of Yhwh's face in vv. 16a–17a: Yhwh's eyes and ears pay attention to the needs of the righteous people (צַדִּיקִים, v. 16a) and his face is against the wicked people and their actions. The antagonists are simply labeled by the vague description of "those who do evil" (עֹשֵׂי רָע, v. 17a). They are also those whom Yhwh acts against in v. 17b. The description of the one in need, on the other hand, is vivid: they are "those injured in heart" (נִשְׁבְּרֵי־לֵב, v. 19a) and "crushed in spirit" (דַּכְּאֵי־רוּחַ, v. 19b), while their physical bodies remain unharmed (v. 21a–21b).[153] In these cases, those in need are designated as "righteous person" (צַדִּיק, vv. 20a, 22b). In v. 22b, they appear only as a passive participant of the hatred of the antagonists. Yhwh's actions on behalf of the righteous person appear throughout this final section of the psalm. An unexpected contrast follows the description of calamity with the reference to guilt in vv. 22b and 23b. In v. 22b, this calamity refers to the state of wicked. In v. 23b, the final line of the psalm surprisingly makes the lack of taking refuge in Yhwh the core of guilt. The community are here referred to as "his servants" (עֲבָדָיו, v. 23a), and "those who seek refuge in him" (הַחֹסִים בּוֹ, v. 23b).

The psalm is an alphabetic acrostic, though it is missing a ו-line and concludes with a פ-line (v. 23a).[154] Thus, some shifts in person are influenced by this form, where choice is somewhat restricted. At the same time, the psalm as a whole focuses on the testimony of Yhwh's actions toward the speaker and the resultant calls to praise or faithful living that the speaker offers to the community. These shifts in voicing from general to direct address highlight the significance of the situation that the speaker records for the community.

Function of צַדִּיק and רָשָׁע

The righteous and the wicked play a major role in the overall meaning of Ps 34. Notably, one sees both innocence and proper behavior as definitional of the righteous. Christine Brown Jones rightly suggests that the צַדִּיק in Ps 34 represents both the faithful community and those who are in need of God, semantically equivalent to the "poor" in psalms, connected by their experiences of fear.[155] They are those in need (vv. 16b, 20a, 22b) and, in their need, they cry out to Yhwh (v. 18a). Sophie Ramond notes a clear shift from titles related to poverty to that of the righteous halfway through Ps 34.[156] Interestingly, the term צַדִּיק appears only halfway through the psalm (vv. 16a [pl], 20a, 22b).[157] The psalm clearly affirms the basic tenet of Yhwh's attitude of benevolence toward the צַדִּיק in vv. 16a and 20a. In the context of the direct didactic speech of vv. 14a–15b, the affirmation of Yhwh's concern for the צַדִּיקִים in v. 16a–16b may work to highlight the desirability of pursuing the traits highlighted in the psalm. That is, the righteous are not only characterized as those in need who can expect Yhwh's aid but also that, implicitly, they are characterized both by their innocence and prototypical goodness.

The צַדִּיק is also mentioned in v. 22b, though as the object of the wicked person's hate. In parallel to the singular "wicked person" (רָשָׁע, v. 22a), the antagonists are described as "those who hate the righteous person" (שֹׂנְאֵי צַדִּיק, v. 22b), which directly affirms the context of conflict between these two figures. The characterization of the wicked is unambiguously against the righteous.[158] Verse 22a–22b affirms the eventual destruction of the wicked. This comes immediately after the affirmation of Yhwh's protection of the צַדִּיק in the midst of their "many problems." While Yhwh acts against those who attack the poor in v. 17a, Yhwh is not the agent of the wicked's demise in v. 22a—rather, they are struck by "calamity." This is also specifically connected with the idea of the wicked person, whose guilt is characterized in part by the hatred of the righteous person. As such, רָשָׁע in Ps 34 functions clearly as an antagonist. They are against those who are undeserving of violence, and through their actions, the opposite of those who are faithful. Throughout the psalm, the righteous are the recipients of a plurality of distresses (e.g., vv.

7b, 18b, 20b), yet the end of the wicked is emphasized through this single statement of their end.[159]

Psalm 34 includes a clear articulation of the basic literary pattern, rooted to the meaning of the words, that the צַדִּיק are seen and heard by Yhwh, and thus, he will rescue them. In the context of the event between testimony and command, the mention of the righteous highlights the possibility for past and present situations to be resolved through Yhwh's actions. The repeated mention of "all" the afflictions for the righteous emphasize Yhwh's attitude and perspective toward them—Yhwh will save them.[160] This is especially clear with the mention of the righteous person's problems, and the affirmation that Yhwh will save them in vv. 20a–21b. Both meanings of the word צַדִּיק, either as one innocent, and thus righteous because they suffer without cause, or as one who is generally properly behaved are possible here. In both cases, the affirmation of the theme that Yhwh is for the righteous and against their opposites, or their attackers, is plain.

Through the rhetorical ploy of the didactic voice, the presentation of the צַדִּיק and רָשָׁע would be expected to function as a way to teach ethical behavior. However, this is not the case—at least, not directly. Rather, the speaker teaches behavior that is desirable through direct commands and through devices. At the same time, in the section of vv. 16a–22b, the צַדִּיק are those in need. Framed this way, it is not their behavior that makes them such, but rather, it is an affirmation of the literary pattern that operates to define the צַדִּיק as also relating to proper behavior. Primarily, however, the righteous is described as "injured in heart" and "crushed in spirit" (v. 19a–19b). Because they innocently suffer, Yhwh listens to their cries (vv. 17a, 18b). Ultimately, Yhwh saves them from their many problems (v. 20a–20b). The contrast of the righteous and the wicked in the psalm, then, offers comfort, whereas other features in Ps 34 offer instruction as to ethics.

In summary, Ps 34 affirms the general contrast between the righteous and the wicked based on the way that Yhwh acts toward them. The wicked are characterized only vaguely for the antagonism toward the righteous or the speaker, though this is made clearer through the characterization of the righteous person as one who is in need. The righteous and the wicked thus function together in the psalm to emphasize Yhwh's faithfulness toward those who call out to him in their need. Further, the contrast between צַדִּיק and רָשָׁע functions to make a similar statement on two levels: Yhwh will save both those who are faithful and those who are unjustly persecuted.

PSALM 37

Text and Translation

לְדָוִד	1a	(Davidic.)
אַל־תִּתְחַר בַּמְּרֵעִים	1b	Do not be angry about those who are bad,
אַל־תְּקַנֵּא בְּעֹשֵׂי עַוְלָה:	1c	Do not be jealous about those who do wrong,
כִּי כֶחָצִיר מְהֵרָה יִמָּלוּ	2a	For like grass they will dry up quickly,
וּכְיֶרֶק דֶּשֶׁא יִבּוֹלוּן:	2b	And as green shoots of grass they will wither.
בְּטַח בַּיהוָה וַעֲשֵׂה־טוֹב	3a	Trust in Yhwh and thus do good,[161]
שְׁכָן־אֶרֶץ וּרְעֵה אֱמוּנָה:	3b	Dwell in the land and graze on faithfulness,[162]
וְהִתְעַנַּג עַל־יְהוָה	4a	Delight yourself in Yhwh,[163]
וְיִתֶּן־לְךָ מִשְׁאֲלֹת לִבֶּךָ:	4b	And he will give[164] to you your mind's desires.
גּוֹל עַל־יְהוָה דַּרְכֶּךָ	5a	Entrust your path to Yhwh,
וּבְטַח עָלָיו וְהוּא יַעֲשֶׂה:	5b	And trust in him, and he, he will act,
וְהוֹצִיא כָאוֹר צִדְקֶךָ	6a	And he will bring out your righteousness as light,
וּמִשְׁפָּטֶךָ כַּצָּהֳרָיִם:	6b	And your justice like midday.[165]
דּוֹם לַיהוָה וְהִתְחוֹלֵל לוֹ	7a	Be still before Yhwh and wait for him;
אַל־תִּתְחַר בְּמַצְלִיחַ דַּרְכּוֹ	7b	Do not be angry about the one whose path is prosperous,
בְּאִישׁ עֹשֶׂה מְזִמּוֹת:	7c	About a person who carries out schemes.
הֶרֶף מֵאַף וַעֲזֹב חֵמָה	8a	Let go of anger and forsake ire,
אַל־תִּתְחַר אַךְ־לְהָרֵעַ:	8b	Do not be angry, it will surely lead to evil,
כִּי־מְרֵעִים יִכָּרֵתוּן	9a	For those who are evil will be cut off.
וְקֹוֵי יְהוָה	9b	But those who hope in Yhwh,
הֵמָּה יִירְשׁוּ־אָרֶץ:	9c	They, they will inherit the land.
וְעוֹד מְעַט וְאֵין רָשָׁע	10a	But still, just a little longer[166] and there will be no wicked person;
וְהִתְבּוֹנַנְתָּ עַל־מְקוֹמוֹ וְאֵינֶנּוּ:	10b	You will look around their place and they will not be there.
וַעֲנָוִים יִירְשׁוּ־אָרֶץ	11a	But the poor will inherit the land,
וְהִתְעַנְּגוּ עַל־רֹב שָׁלוֹם:	11b	And they will take pleasure in an abundance of peace.
זֹמֵם רָשָׁע לַצַּדִּיק	12a	The wicked person is planning against the righteous person
וְחֹרֵק עָלָיו שִׁנָּיו:	12b	And gnashes their teeth against them.
אֲדֹנָי יִשְׂחַק־לוֹ	13a	The Lord laughs at them,
כִּי־רָאָה כִּי־יָבֹא יוֹמוֹ:	13b	For he sees that their day will come.
חֶרֶב פָּתְחוּ רְשָׁעִים	14a	The wicked people have drawn a sword,
וְדָרְכוּ קַשְׁתָּם	14b	And they readied their bow
לְהַפִּיל עָנִי וְאֶבְיוֹן	14c	To throw down the poor and needy,
לִטְבוֹחַ יִשְׁרֵי־דָרֶךְ:	14d	To slaughter those who are upright in their way.
חַרְבָּם תָּבוֹא בְלִבָּם	15a	Their sword will enter into their heart,
וְקַשְּׁתוֹתָם תִּשָּׁבַרְנָה:	15b	And their bows will be broken.
טוֹב־מְעַט לַצַּדִּיק	16a	The little of the righteous person is better
מֵהֲמוֹן רְשָׁעִים רַבִּים:	16b	Than the abundance of many wicked people.

(Continued)

כִּי זְרוֹעוֹת רְשָׁעִים תִּשָּׁבַרְנָה	17a	For the arms of wicked people will be broken
וְסוֹמֵךְ צַדִּיקִים יְהוָה׃	17b	And righteous people Yhwh sustains.
יוֹדֵעַ יְהוָה יְמֵי תְמִימִם	18a	Yhwh knows the days of the blameless,
וְנַחֲלָתָם לְעוֹלָם תִּהְיֶה׃	18b	And their inheritance will be everlasting;
לֹא־יֵבֹשׁוּ בְּעֵת רָעָה	19a	They will not be ashamed in terrible times ,
וּבִימֵי רְעָבוֹן יִשְׂבָּעוּ׃	19b	And in the days of hunger they will have their fill.
כִּי רְשָׁעִים יֹאבֵדוּ	20a	But wicked people will perish,
וְאֹיְבֵי יְהוָה כִּיקַר כָּרִים	20b	And the enemies of Yhwh, like the valuable parts of rams,[167]
כָּלוּ בֶעָשָׁן כָּלוּ׃	20c	They are consumed in smoke;[168] they are consumed.
לֹוֶה רָשָׁע וְלֹא יְשַׁלֵּם	21a	The wicked person borrows and does not repay,
וְצַדִּיק חוֹנֵן וְנוֹתֵן׃	21b	But the righteous person is gracious and giving.
כִּי מְבֹרָכָיו יִירְשׁוּ אָרֶץ	22a	For those who are blessed by them will inherit the land,
וּמְקֻלָּלָיו יִכָּרֵתוּ׃	22b	But those who are cursed by them will be cut off.
מֵיְהוָה מִצְעֲדֵי־גֶבֶר כּוֹנָנוּ	23a	By Yhwh a person's steps are established,
וְדַרְכּוֹ יֶחְפָּץ׃	23b	And he delights in their way.
כִּי־יִפֹּל לֹא־יוּטָל	24a	For[169] if they fall, they will not be thrown down,
כִּי־יְהוָה סוֹמֵךְ יָדוֹ׃	24b	Because Yhwh supports their hand.
נַעַר הָיִיתִי גַּם־זָקַנְתִּי	25a	I was a youth, now I am old,
וְלֹא־רָאִיתִי צַדִּיק נֶעֱזָב	25b	And I have never seen a righteous person be abandoned,
וְזַרְעוֹ מְבַקֶּשׁ־לָחֶם׃	25c	Nor their offspring searching for bread.
כָּל־הַיּוֹם חוֹנֵן וּמַלְוֶה	26a	All the day, being gracious and lending,
וְזַרְעוֹ לִבְרָכָה׃	26b	And their offspring are a blessing.
סוּר מֵרָע וַעֲשֵׂה־טוֹב	27a	Turn aside from evil and thus do good,[170]
וּשְׁכֹן לְעוֹלָם׃	27b	And live for a long time.
כִּי יְהוָה אֹהֵב מִשְׁפָּט	28a	For Yhwh loves justice
וְלֹא־יַעֲזֹב אֶת־חֲסִידָיו	28b	And he does not forsake his faithful ones;
לְעוֹלָם נִשְׁמָרוּ	28c	They are protected forever.[171]
וְזֶרַע רְשָׁעִים נִכְרָת׃	28d	But the offspring of wicked people are cut off.
צַדִּיקִים יִירְשׁוּ־אָרֶץ	29a	Righteous people will inherit the land,
וְיִשְׁכְּנוּ לָעַד עָלֶיהָ׃	29b	And they will dwell in it in perpetuity.
פִּי־צַדִּיק יֶהְגֶּה חָכְמָה	30a	The mouth of the righteous person utters wisdom,
וּלְשׁוֹנוֹ תְּדַבֵּר מִשְׁפָּט׃	30b	And their tongue declares justice.
תּוֹרַת אֱלֹהָיו בְּלִבּוֹ	31a	The teaching of their God is in their heart
לֹא תִמְעַד אֲשֻׁרָיו׃	31b	And their steps will not give way.
צוֹפֶה רָשָׁע לַצַּדִּיק	32a	The wicked person lies in ambush of the righteous person
וּמְבַקֵּשׁ לַהֲמִיתוֹ׃	32b	And seeks to destroy them.
יְהוָה לֹא־יַעַזְבֶנּוּ בְיָדוֹ	33a	Yhwh will not forsake them into their hand
וְלֹא יַרְשִׁיעֶנּוּ בְּהִשָּׁפְטוֹ׃	33b	And will not condemn them when he judges them.
קַוֵּה אֶל־יְהוָה וּשְׁמֹר דַּרְכּוֹ	34a	Hope for Yhwh and keep his way
וִירוֹמִמְךָ לָרֶשֶׁת אָרֶץ	34b	And he will raise you to inherit the land.
בְּהִכָּרֵת רְשָׁעִים תִּרְאֶה׃	34c	When the wicked people are cut off, you will see.[172]
רָאִיתִי רָשָׁע עָרִיץ	35a	I saw a wicked person, a ruthless person,[173]
וּמִתְעָרֶה כְּאֶזְרָח רַעֲנָן׃	35b	And they were as one spreading themselves out like a flourishing tree.

(Continued)

וַיַּעֲבֹר וְהִנֵּה אֵינֶנּוּ	36a	Then they[174] passed on, and look, they were no longer there;
וָאֲבַקְשֵׁהוּ וְלֹא נִמְצָא:	36b	So I searched for them, but they were not found.
שְׁמָר־תָּם וּרְאֵה יָשָׁר	37a	Observe the decent and watch the upright,
כִּי־אַחֲרִית לְאִישׁ שָׁלוֹם:	37b	For the end of such a person is peace.
וּפֹשְׁעִים נִשְׁמְדוּ יַחְדָּו	38a	But those who rebel will be exterminated together;
אַחֲרִית רְשָׁעִים נִכְרָתָה:	38b	The end of the wicked people will be cut off.
וּתְשׁוּעַת צַדִּיקִים מֵיְהוָה	39a	And the salvation of the righteous people is from Yhwh,
מָעוּזָּם בְּעֵת צָרָה:	39b	Their refuge in times of distress.
וַיַּעְזְרֵם יְהוָה וַיְפַלְּטֵם	40a	And Yhwh helps them and he rescues them,
יְפַלְּטֵם מֵרְשָׁעִים	40b	He rescues them from the wicked people,
וְיוֹשִׁיעֵם כִּי־חָסוּ בוֹ:	40c	And he saves them because they seek refuge in him.

Interpretation

Psalm 37 is a reflection on the realities of the righteous and the wicked in the psalmic voice, which offers an encouragement toward faithful living and hope in God.[175] This is related to multiple themes while largely focusing on an encouragement to trust in Yhwh and to anticipate the eventual destruction of the wicked people. The shifts of voice throughout Ps 37 are unpredictable and frequently refer to earlier parts in the psalm. There are several 2ms imperatives with the psalm generally addressed to the community.[176] This is interspersed with longer descriptions of the righteous, the wicked, and Yhwh in third person with a general address. Because this address appears throughout, and because the content of didactic speech does not change, the same prototypical 2ms addressee remains throughout the psalm. Shifts from plural and singular forms of צַדִּיק appear constantly as well. Due to a lack of clear shift in content or direction, it should be assumed that there is a single speaker for Ps 37. As such, the entire psalm is also spoken directly to the community in a didactic mode. The speaker of the psalm also appears as an explicit participant throughout through the use of a few first-person verbs and pronouns (v. 25a–25b, 35a, 36b). While it is unusual in psalms for the speaker to make an explicit self-reference beyond describing their activities of devotion, the psalmic voice self-characterizes as an elder, which apparently functions to substantiate the speaker's claims (v. 25a–25b).[177]

The psalm frequently discusses both positive and negative figures. The group of antagonists are characterized by their ephemerality through mention of their eventual destruction (vv. 2a–2b, 9a, 10a–10b, 15a–15a–15b, 17a, 20a–20c), their ostensible prosperity (vv. 7b, 16b), their violence (vv. 7c,[178] 12a–12b, 13b–14d, 32a–32b), and their unjust gain (v. 21a).[179] Their activities are against the righteous (vv. 12b, 40b) and the poor and needy (v. 14b–14d), and they are noted as those who receive the scorn of Yhwh (v. 13a). Though the end of the wicked is mentioned without agent throughout the psalm, Yhwh is at least implied as the agent through the parallel of Yhwh's salvation of the righteous person, including saving them directly from wicked people (v. 40b).

Because the positive group of figures are prevalent throughout the psalm and relate to consistent themes, they should be associated together with צַדִּיק, which is the most common designation in Ps 37 (צַדִּיק; vv. 12a, 16a, 17b [pl], 21b, 25b, 29a [pl], 30a, 32a, 39a [pl]). They receive the designations: "those who hope in Yhwh" (וְקֹוֵי יְהוָה, v. 9b), "those who are upright in their way" (יִשְׁרֵי־דָרֶךְ, v. 14d), "his faithful ones" (חֲסִידָיו, v. 27b).[180] The figures of the "poor" (עֲנָוִים, v. 11a), "poor and needy" (עָנִי וְאֶבְיוֹן, v. 14c) are also considered the recipients of the attacks of the wicked, and are further paralleled in v. 14c–14d with those who would be considered among the righteous. Though the semantic function of these designations differs, they should be considered coreferential in this psalm as designations for those in need of Yhwh's help.[181] This becomes clearer with the range of figures that are said to be inheritors of the earth (vv. 9b, 11a, 22a, 29a).

With the repeated theme of the land (vv. 3b, 9c, 11a, 22a, 29a–29b, 34b; cf. v. 18b), the psalm also becomes, as Brueggemann has concisely stated, "an instruction about how to keep the land and how to use the land."[182] The repeated phrase of who will inherit the earth (יִירְשׁוּ־אָרֶץ) appears with five distinct subjects: "those who hope in Yhwh" (וְקֹוֵי יְהוָה, v. 9b), "the poor" (עֲנָוִים, v. 11a), "those who are blessed by them" (מְבֹרָכָיו, v. 22a), "righteous people" (צַדִּיקִים, v. 29a), and finally "you" (v. 34b). A similar declaration is given to the community in 34b, "And he will raise you to inherit the land," וִירוֹמִמְךָ לָרֶשֶׁת אָרֶץ, which is again connected with those who hope for Yhwh, only in this case with the verb קוה (*piel*) in imperative form.

The first section of the psalm includes the highest number of imperative forms as well as focuses on the addressee's view toward the wicked and how to live faithfully (vv. 1b–11b).[183] The imperatives in vv. 1b–c, 7b, and 8a–8b all relate to having the right attitude toward the wicked.[184] These imperatives shift with other directives to be faithful to Yhwh (vv. 3a, 4a, 5a, 7a). The reasons for these directives—both those regarding an attitude toward the wicked and those with positive actions toward Yhwh—are rooted in affirmations of the finite nature of the wicked (vv. 2a–2b, 9a, 10a–10b) and the blessing for those who act rightly toward Yhwh (vv. 3b, 4b, 5b–6b, 9b–9c). These two reasons are addressed using similar imagery in vv. 2a–3b, where imminence of the destruction of the wicked is implied in v. 2a–2b with the imagery of fading grasses.[185] This is then contrasted with the imagery of grazing in v. 3b.[186] With the language of poverty throughout, Ellen Davis suggests this metaphor emphasizes the "concreteness of the psalmist's vision, offered to people whose food supply is in jeopardy."[187] This section focuses on setting up the attractiveness of trusting Yhwh over against the ostensible gains of the wicked, rooted in the eventual destruction of the wicked and the positive benefits for those who trust in Yhwh.

The second section of the psalm focuses on the salvation of those who are attacked by the wicked (vv. 12a–22b). There are many scenes within the poem that describe the wicked's preparations for violence (vv. 12a–12b, 14a–14d). This is characterized as futile due to the immediate mention of their eventual destruction (vv. 13a–14b). The wicked are further characterized as those God laughs at (v. 13a). This description follows the wicked's threat by gnashing teeth (v. 12b). Through both images the wicked are characterized as violent and as frivolous in light of Yhwh's strength. The basis of Yhwh's laughter is the eventual destruction of the wicked (v. 13a). This eventual destruction appears throughout the section (vv. 13a–13b, 15a–15b, 17a–17b, 20a–20c, 22b). The self-destruction of the wicked is also highlighted: they prepare their sword in v. 14a, which is the instrument of their self-destruction in v. 15a. This is contrasted with Yhwh's protection of the faithful, though in indicative statements, unlike the previous section (vv. 17b–18b, 22a). The section also includes a short statement about the activities of the רָשָׁע and צַדִּיק, contrasting their respective greed or generosity (v. 21a–21b).[188] The antecedent of the 3ms pronoun suffixes in v. 22a–22b is difficult to determine. They could refer to God or as the righteous person, though because the צַדִּיק is the nearest subject, these more likely speak of the righteous figure than of Yhwh. The entire section continues to contrast the faithful with the wicked, and here emphasizes the destruction of the wicked without reference to what the addressee should do. Verses 16–26 also contain a dense cluster of economic terms.[189]

In vv. 23a–33b, the focus shifts to Yhwh's activities toward the righteous. The most common theme here is the positive consequences for the faithful from Yhwh (vv. 24a–24b, 25b–25c, 28a–28c, 29a–29b, 33a–33b). Verse 24a–24b offers a sort of summary of the call to the community, which includes waiting for Yhwh and acting in a manner corresponding with his ideals.[190] Verse 25a–25c includes the speaker's lifelong observations of never seeing significant ill befall the righteous person. Verse 26a speaks again of the righteous person's generosity. The activities of the righteous are again described in vv. 31a–32b, regarding wisdom, justice, and following the teaching of God.[191] Though v. 32 appears to emphasize moral obligations for the צַדִּיק, the following verse mentions that Yhwh will not find them guilty when he judges.[192] There are two imperatives directed to the community in v. 27a, though a third functions as a consequence to the first two, if those who are addressed turn from evil to do good (סוּר מֵרָע וַעֲשֵׂה־טוֹב, v. 27a), they will live (וּשְׁכֹן לְעוֹלָם, v. 27b).[193] These commands and consequences are rooted in Yhwh's character, and his protection of the faithful community (v. 28a–28c). Finally, this section includes short statements regarding the end of the wicked

(v. 28d) or a description of their violence (v. 32a–32b). In this section, several vignettes further characterize these figures, rooted in both present actions and future rewards.

Verses 34a–40c serve as a conclusion to the psalm, reiterating many of the themes mentioned earlier. The focus shifts largely to the end of the wicked again, much like vv. 12a–22b. The section begins with an imperative to hope in Yhwh with the result of inheriting the land (v. 34a–34b), and also includes a later command to learn by watching the good (v. 37a–37b). The descriptions of the wicked focuses here largely on their end (vv. 34c, 36a–36b, 38a–38b), though they also mention their ostensible luxury (v. 35a–35b). Verses 35a–35b include a brief event of the rise and downfall of the wicked through the metaphor of a tree. The wicked appear again in v. 40b as those from whom Yhwh saves the righteous (v. 40b). Yhwh's salvation of the righteous figures is the main point of the final two verses which express this end in terms of those who take refuge in Yhwh (vv. 39b, 40c). As the conclusion, then, this affirmation of salvation highlights the identity of the righteous figures as those who need salvation.

The central focus of the psalm is the salvation of the righteous individual by Yhwh. This takes place through the destruction of the wicked (e.g., v. 28a). The salvation of the righteous is described at the end of the psalm as well (vv. 39a–40c). Here, the idea of trust or refuge in Yhwh becomes the grounds of his rescue in v. 40a–40c.

The overall discourse functions as a reflection of several, overlapping themes regarding the relationship between the righteous, the wicked, and God, all from a didactive voice. The self-characterization of the speaker as an older person (v. 25a) highlights the effect of teaching those in the community through a lived experience. The psalm moves between the possible jealousy of the wicked, the admonition away from this path through the description of the activities of wicked and righteous, and of the eventual ends of both figures. Each of these themes receives focus in a large portion of the psalm, all of which highlight the faithfulness of Yhwh and his salvation of those who follow the faithful path. As a clear synopsis of the psalm, Cheung writes that the goal of the writer is "to encourage the dispirited righteous to remain hopefully faithful" in adversity.[194]

Function of צַדִּיק and רָשָׁע

The contrast between the righteous and the wicked in Ps 37 give a structure to the entire psalm. The figures of righteous and wicked are so intertwined with the whole of Ps 37 that it is difficult to establish discrete functions. The specific meaning of the terms—especially of צַדִּיק also shifts throughout the psalm.[195] Because of this feature, the psalm itself plays off of the possible meanings of the term, much like in Ps 34. At the same time, the entire psalm affirms the logic of the eventual destruction of the wicked. The רָשָׁע is explicitly the antagonist of the צַדִּיק in vv. 12a and 32b. In 40b, the רְשָׁעִים are those from whom Yhwh saves the righteous people.

In an uncommon presentation for psalms, the righteous are described in terms of their explicit activities (vv. 21a–21b, 30a–30b). This function of describing concrete positive activities, combined with the eventual destruction of wicked and blessing of the righteous, highlights certain actions that define who the righteous are and what they do. Due to these descriptions and the prevalence of detail regarding other aspects of the righteous, Ps 37 becomes the clearest "portrait" of the righteous in the Psalter.

Due to the central focus on justice combined with the number of imperative forms directed at the community, Scott C. Jones argues that the purpose of Ps 37 is not to philosophize about world order so much as call the community—whom he emphasizes as the "poor"—to action.[196] While Jones creates an unnecessary distinction between philosophy and action, the function of the righteous figure in Ps 37 would support the general claim that the psalm serves as a call to be, believe, and behave in a certain way. It also calls the community to hope. The function of the wicked in the psalm does not serve, as the righteous does, to define certain activities or behaviors. Rather, they are understood as those who stand against the righteous writ large. As such, the psalm articulates a theology in which the righteous flourish even in light of the present flourishing of the wicked. The hope comes with the strong affirmation of the eventual destruction of the wicked and the striking ways in which Yhwh's attitude toward them is portrayed. The twin affirmation of the blessing of the righteous and destruction of the wicked comes together to make a statement about the relationship of the righteous people to the land. Because the wicked are removed from the land and the righteous inherit it, the righteous can have their well-being without the threat of removal or destruction.[197]

In sum, the function of the righteous and the wicked provide the background of the entire psalm. These two figures structure the psalm thematically—on top of the acrostic form—and highlight the theology of the character-consequence nexus in ways that also define certain behaviors associated with the character of being righteous. It is a psalm that decries violence against the community and affirms a continual hope in Yhwh as exhibited both through belief and action. In a contrast to several other psalms in this study, the function of the righteous and the wicked also encourages particular aspects of faithful living apart from commitments to trust in Yhwh, though these are also clearly present.

PSALM 55

Text and Translation

לַמְנַצֵּחַ בִּנְגִינֹת מַשְׂכִּיל לְדָוִד:	1a	(To the leader. On stringed instruments. A Maskil. Davidic.)
הַאֲזִינָה אֱלֹהִים תְּפִלָּתִי	2a	Hear, God, my prayer,
וְאַל־תִּתְעַלַּם מִתְּחִנָּתִי:	2b	And do not hide yourself[198] from my plea.
הַקְשִׁיבָה לִּי וַעֲנֵנִי	3a	Be attentive to me and answer me;
אָרִיד בְּשִׂיחִי וְאָהִימָה:	3b	I am restless in my complaint, and I am disquieted
מִקּוֹל אוֹיֵב	4a	Because[199] of the voice of the enemy,
מִפְּנֵי עָקַת רָשָׁע	4b	Because of[200] the pressure[201] of the wicked person.
כִּי־יָמִיטוּ עָלַי אָוֶן	4c	For they drop misfortune on me,
וּבְאַף יִשְׂטְמוּנִי:	4d	And in anger they harass me.[202]
לִבִּי יָחִיל בְּקִרְבִּי	5a	My heart writhes[203] within me
וְאֵימוֹת מָוֶת נָפְלוּ עָלָי:	5b	And deadly terrors fall upon me.
יִרְאָה וָרַעַד יָבֹא בִי	6a	Fear and trembling come upon me,
וַתְּכַסֵּנִי פַּלָּצוּת:	6b	And horror covered me.
וָאֹמַר מִי־יִתֶּן־לִי אֵבֶר כַּיּוֹנָה	7a	But I said, "Who will give me wings like a dove?"
אָעוּפָה וְאֶשְׁכֹּנָה:	7b	I want to fly away and be at rest.
הִנֵּה אַרְחִיק נְדֹד	8a	Behold, I would remove myself by flapping,[204]
אָלִין בַּמִּדְבָּר סֶלָה:	8b	I would stay in the wilderness. (*selah*)
אָחִישָׁה מִפְלָט לִי	9a	I would rush to my safe place,
מֵרוּחַ סֹעָה מִסָּעַר:	9b	From the rushing wind, from the storm.
בַּלַּע אֲדֹנָי פַּלַּג לְשׁוֹנָם	10a	Stir up confusion, Lord, split their tongue,
כִּי־רָאִיתִי חָמָס וְרִיב בָּעִיר:	10b	For I see[205] violence and conflict in the city;
יוֹמָם וָלַיְלָה יְסוֹבְבֻהָ עַל־חוֹמֹתֶיהָ	11a	Day and night they surround it, around its walls,
וְאָוֶן וְעָמָל בְּקִרְבָּהּ:	11b	And misfortune and trouble are inside it.
הַוּוֹת בְּקִרְבָּהּ	12a	Destruction is inside it,
וְלֹא־יָמִישׁ מֵרְחֹבָהּ תֹּךְ וּמִרְמָה:	12b	Oppression and treachery do not leave its city square,
כִּי לֹא־אוֹיֵב יְחָרְפֵנִי וְאֶשָּׂא	13a	Yet[206] an enemy does not taunt me—then I could accept that;
לֹא־מְשַׂנְאִי עָלַי הִגְדִּיל	13b	It is not one who hates me that has acted mightily against me—
וְאֶסָּתֵר מִמֶּנּוּ:	13c	then I could hide from him.
וְאַתָּה אֱנוֹשׁ כְּעֶרְכִּי	14a	But you, someone just like me,
אַלּוּפִי וּמְיֻדָּעִי:	14b	My companion and my friend,
אֲשֶׁר יַחְדָּו נַמְתִּיק סוֹד	15a	We who used to have sweet counsel together;
בְּבֵית אֱלֹהִים	15b	In the house of God
נְהַלֵּךְ בְּרָגֶשׁ:	15c	We would walk among the throng.

(*Continued*)

יַשִּׁי מָוֶת עָלֵימוֹ	16a	Let death deceive[207] them,[208]
יֵרְדוּ שְׁאוֹל חַיִּים	16b	Let them go down to Sheol alive,
כִּי־רָעוֹת בִּמְגוּרָם בְּקִרְבָּם׃	16c	Because evil is lodging inside them.
אֲנִי אֶל־אֱלֹהִים אֶקְרָא	17a	I, upon God I call,[209]
וַיהוָה יוֹשִׁיעֵנִי׃	17b	And Yhwh will save me.
עֶרֶב וָבֹקֶר וְצָהֳרַיִם	18a	Evening, morning, and noon
אָשִׂיחָה וְאֶהֱמֶה	18b	I complain and I groan,
וַיִּשְׁמַע קוֹלִי׃	18c	And he heard my voice.
פָּדָה בְשָׁלוֹם נַפְשִׁי מִקְּרָב־לִי	19a	He redeemed my life in peace from the fight against me,
כִּי־בְרַבִּים הָיוּ עִמָּדִי׃	19b	For many are with me.[210]
יִשְׁמַע אֵל וְיַעֲנֵם	20a	God will hear and answer them,
וְיֹשֵׁב קֶדֶם סֶלָה	20b	And he is enthroned of old.[211] (*selah*)
אֲשֶׁר אֵין חֲלִיפוֹת לָמוֹ	20c	There is no change for them,
וְלֹא יָרְאוּ אֱלֹהִים׃	20d	And they do not fear God.
שָׁלַח יָדָיו בִּשְׁלֹמָיו	21a	They sent their hand against the ones at peace with them,
חִלֵּל בְּרִיתוֹ׃	21b	They defiled their covenant.
חָלְקוּ מַחְמָאֹת פִּיו	22a	Their speech was soft like butter,[212]
וּקֲרָב־לִבּוֹ	22b	But a battle was in their heart.
רַכּוּ דְבָרָיו מִשֶּׁמֶן	22c	Their words were smooth like oil,
וְהֵמָּה פְתִחוֹת׃	22d	But they were drawn swords.
הַשְׁלֵךְ עַל־יְהוָה יְהָבְךָ	23a	Cast off your burden onto Yhwh
וְהוּא יְכַלְכְּלֶךָ	23b	And he will support you,
לֹא־יִתֵּן לְעוֹלָם מוֹט לַצַּדִּיק׃	23c	He will never allow the righteous person to slip.
וְאַתָּה אֱלֹהִים תּוֹרִדֵם לִבְאֵר שַׁחַת	24a	But you, God, you bring them down to the pit of destruction.
אַנְשֵׁי דָמִים וּמִרְמָה לֹא־יֶחֱצוּ יְמֵיהֶם	24b	Men of blood and treachery will not divide their days.[213]
וַאֲנִי אֶבְטַח־בָּךְ׃	24c	But I, I will trust in you.

Interpretation

Because of numerous text-critical and form critical-issues, interpreting Ps 55 has been considered a "daunting" task.[214] Viewed as a unity, however, Ps 55 is a prayer for God to help the speaker. While much of the psalm does not have an explicit addressee, the content and structure of the psalm suggest that Yhwh is addressed at least through v. 10b, though most likely until v. 12c, in v. 19a–19b, and in vv. 23a–24c. Psalm 55 divides neatly into four stanzas: vv. 2a–9b, vv. 10a–16c, vv. 17a–22d, and the concluding vv. 23a–24c.[215] There are a number of repetitions in the psalm that bring the psalm together. It is bookended by both the mention of God in vv. 2a and 24a as well the forms of the verb מוט in vv. 4c and 23c.[216] The related terms "complaint" (שִׂיחַ) and "groan" (שִׂיחַ) in v. 3a are repeated as verbs in v. 18a.[217]

The psalm begins with the scene of a request to Yhwh. The psalmic speaker increasingly trusts God as the poem progresses because they are afforded comfort.[218] With the psalm presented as a prayer, with direct address to Yhwh in vv. 2a–3a, 10a, 19a, 24a–24c, the described situation is central. The enemies of the speaker are described in stereotypical language that makes them appear as national or foreign enemies in the beginning of the psalm (vv. 4a–4b, 5b, 6b). The distress of the speaker focuses on the harassment of the wicked person, such that the speaker wishes to escape (vv. 7a–9b). Throughout the psalm, the antagonists receive the designations "enemy" (אוֹיֵב, v. 4a), "wicked person" (רָשָׁע, v. 4b), and "men of blood and treachery" (אַנְשֵׁי דָמִים וּמִרְמָה, v. 24b).[219] The implication that these are enemies in a physical sense is emphasized in vv. 11a–12b, which imagines a scene of a city that is under siege. Up until this point in the psalm, the general event is that of the speaker calling to Yhwh for help in light of the described threat of the enemies.

Only at v. 13a does the situation of the psalm begin to be redefined, where identity of the antagonist is revealed as "my companion and my friend" (אַלּוּפִי וּמְיֻדָּעִי, v. 14b).[220] In the present structure of the poem, these figures are coreferential, even if the terms in the first part of the poem appear similar to military enemies. The "false friend" character is the focus of vv. 13a–16c, 20c–22d, 24a. It is an acquaintance from whom the speaker needs rescue. The antagonist is addressed beginning in v. 14a, with a 2ms pronoun "but you" (וְאַתָּה) situating the addressee in v. 14b. With the increase of the significance of betrayal, the speaker hearkens back to a previous time where they and the former friend participated together in the community and in worship of Yhwh. Thus, vv. 14a–15c describes pertinent background information of the events that occur in the remainder of the psalm.

The next section shifts back to the prayer with a request for the wicked to be destroyed (v. 16a–16c).[221] The section continues to describe the speaker's present distress (vv. 17a–19b), though does not contain a specific request. Instead, the speaker mentions their activities of calling out to God (vv. 17a, 18a–18b) and confidence that God will act (vv. 17b, 18c–19b).[222] The focus on the speaker's perspective contrasts clearly from that of the false friend, particularly from the context of vv. 15a–15c where the focus is on the religious expression of both speaker and friend alike. The self-characterization with the emphatic אֲנִי in v. 17a highlights the speaker's own fidelity in contrast with the friend, which implicitly characterizes this figure as rejecting Yhwh. The situation of rejection from the former friend also contrasts in the affirmation of trust from the speaker, which emphasizes that they are not isolated from God nor from community.

The description of the antagonist resumes in vv. 20c–22d. This continues to provide the portraiture for their former friend turned enemy through their actions. This is described in terms of defiling a covenant (v. 21b), the content of which is unclear.[223] ThereThey are directly characterized as well. They are inherently violent, though have impressive speech (v. 22a, 22c).[224] While their behavior appears congenial, it is ultimately unmasked in the speaker's clarification of intention and violence.

The final section of the poem turns to address the community and affirms the theme that God will provide for those who trust in him (vv. 23a–24c). Verse 23a–23b is addressed directly to the audience through 2ms verbal imperatives and suffixes, though the address should continue through v. 23c.[225] It is God who brings the enemies "down to the pit" (v. 24a). This includes the forward-looking expressions of Yhwh's protection of the righteous and the destruction of those who are against the righteous addressed directly to God.

In summary, Ps 55 focuses on a situation wherein the speaker is attacked by someone who was once a friend. This is mediated through the prayer of the speaker, whose distress is reported to Yhwh. Several scenes in Ps 55 focus on the portraiture of the false friend. The event that lies behind the shift from friendship to enmity is not explicitly defined, though the result is central to the psalm. Finally, the psalm concludes with a call to action for the community and the affirmation that in a future-oriented reality, Yhwh will both care for the righteous and destroy those "men of blood and treachery." In the very final line, the speaker's prayer is resolved as they speak to commit their trust to Yhwh.

Function of צַדִּיק and רָשָׁע

The רָשָׁע is explicitly mentioned as the antagonist of the speaker in v. 4b, where it is paralleled with "enemy"/אוֹיֵב in v. 4a. In the context of the psalm, the enemy is clarified to be "someone just like me/My companion and friend" (v. 14a–14b). The contrasting perspectives on the on the enemy paint a chaotic picture of the distress of the speaker.[226] This phenomenon is not unique to Ps 55,[227] though it is perhaps the most explicit and surprising example. The deceitfulness of the antagonists' speech is mentioned in vv. 22a–33d. The צַדִּיק is mentioned in v. 23c. Semantically, the affirmation of God not allowing the צַדִּיק to slip in v. 23c is an expansion of v. 23b, equating the identity of the 2ms suffix with the צַדִּיק. The function of these two lines together establishes the validity of the of directive line of v. 23a. The affirmation of the protection of the righteous in v. 23c and the destruction of the enemies in 24a–24b ground the conclusion of the speaker's trust in Yhwh.[228]

Yhwh protects the צַדִּיק in the psalm, fitting the typical pattern. In this case, the צַדִּיק are those who suffer wrongly at the hands of their former friend. Thus, it is not their general behavior, but their innocence in a matter that define them as such. The רָשָׁע is not directly contrasted with the צַדִּיק in this context, though within the broader psalm it is a designation for those who persecute the speaker unfairly. The contrast between these figures affirms that the innocent person will be protected by Yhwh. It gives hope to the one who is wronged by a companion by emphasizing that Yhwh is truly on the side of the innocent.

PSALM 58

Text and Translation

לַמְנַצֵּחַ אַל־תַּשְׁחֵת לְדָוִד מִכְתָּם:	1a	(For the leader. Do not destroy. Davidic. A Miktam.)
הַאֻמְנָם אֵלֶם צֶדֶק תְּדַבֵּרוּן	2a	Do you truly speak the silence[229] of righteousness?
מֵישָׁרִים תִּשְׁפְּטוּ בְּנֵי אָדָם:	2b	Do you judge the children of humanity with fairness?
אַף־בְּלֵב עוֹלֹת תִּפְעָלוּן	3a	Indeed—with a mind of iniquity you work,
בָּאָרֶץ חֲמַס יְדֵיכֶם תְּפַלֵּסוּן:	3b	In the land of violence you watch your hands.
זֹרוּ רְשָׁעִים מֵרָחֶם	4a	Wicked people are estranged from the womb,
תָּעוּ מִבֶּטֶן דֹּבְרֵי כָזָב:	4b	They wander from the belly, speaking falsehood.[230]
חֲמַת־לָמוֹ כִּדְמוּת חֲמַת־נָחָשׁ	5a	Their venom is like the venom of a snake,
כְּמוֹ־פֶתֶן חֵרֵשׁ יַאְטֵם אָזְנוֹ:	5b	Like a deaf viper that shuts its ear
אֲשֶׁר לֹא־יִשְׁמַע לְקוֹל מְלַחֲשִׁים	6a	Which does not listen to the voice of charmers,
חוֹבֵר חֲבָרִים מְחֻכָּם:	6b	The one who casts spells well.
אֱלֹהִים הֲרָס־שִׁנֵּימוֹ בְּפִימוֹ	7a	God, break their teeth in their mouth,
מַלְתְּעוֹת כְּפִירִים נְתֹץ יְהוָה:	7b	The jaws of the young lions, Yhwh, crush.
יִמָּאֲסוּ כְמוֹ־מַיִם יִתְהַלְּכוּ־לָמוֹ	8a	Let them be rejected like water running down.
יִדְרֹךְ חִצָּיו[231] כְּמוֹ יִתְמֹלָלוּ:	8b	They[232] bend their bows,[233] their arrows are like they are useless.[234]
כְּמוֹ שַׁבְּלוּל תֶּמֶס יַהֲלֹךְ	9a	Like a snail[235] melting as it goes,
נֵפֶל אֵשֶׁת בַּל־חָזוּ שָׁמֶשׁ:	9b	A stillborn child of a woman[236] that does not see the sun.
בְּטֶרֶם יָבִינוּ סִּירֹתֵיכֶם אָטָד	10a	Before your thorns are aware of the branch,[237]
כְּמוֹ־חַי כְּמוֹ־חָרוֹן יִשְׂעָרֶנּוּ:	10b	Whether alive or whether burned, may he sweep them away.
יִשְׂמַח צַדִּיק כִּי־חָזָה נָקָם	11a	The righteous person will rejoice for they will have seen vengeance;
פְּעָמָיו יִרְחַץ בְּדַם הָרָשָׁע:	11b	They will wash their feet in the blood of the wicked person.
וְיֹאמַר אָדָם אַךְ־פְּרִי לַצַּדִּיק	12a	And a person will say "Surely this is the fruit of the righteous person;
אַךְ יֵשׁ־אֱלֹהִים שֹׁפְטִים בָּאָרֶץ:	12b	Surely there is a God judging the earth."

Interpretation

Psalm 58 focuses almost exclusively on the characterization of the wicked people using highly expressive language. However, the initial lines of the psalm are spoken to a group of people who do not fulfill their proper duties of judgment (vv. 2a–3b). The addressee of verses 2a–3b is unclear, though it is spoken in direct address to a group of people through 2mp verbs.

As rejected in the translation section, many suggest on the basis of reading אֵלִים as a form of "gods" and that this a direct address, as in Pss 82:1 or 97:7.[238] It is the position here that the addressee is not explicitly defined. Due to the description of the wicked people following the questioning of the justice of these figures, they are taken to be some kind of human judge or leader responsible for protecting others. This sets up the situation of the result of these figures' inability to judge fairly. Their lack of justice comes from their "mind" (לֵב, v. 3a) and their hands (יְדֵיכֶם, v. 3b), which function to introduce their lack of concern in their internal and external world.[239]

The psalm shifts from addressing these judges to a description of the result of their inaction by depicting the wicked people are like.[240] This description characterize these "wicked people" (רְשָׁעִים, v. 4a) as being "estranged" and "speaking falsehood" from birth (v. 4a–4b). They then receive the first of four animal images.[241] The first compares the wicked to a snake (vv. 5a–6b), describing these figures in terms of their illegitimate speech with the comparison to venom,[242] and as those who do not listen.[243] As such, both mouth and ears are mentioned that poetically relate to their wicked activity through the metaphor of the snake.

In v. 7a, the psalm moves to a request for Yhwh to destroy the antagonists (vv. 7a–10b). God is directly addressed in v. 7a–7b with two imperatives and, with jussive verbs, the address to God continues from vv. 7a–10b. The multiplicity of images provides vignettes of destruction that combine to create a powerful request of a single hoped-for event: the death of the wicked person. The speaker requests for the teeth of an unidentified third person masculine plural subject, most likely the wicked, to be broken (cf. Ps 3:8). While earlier verses describe them as a snake, the image shifts here to that of lions (כְּפִיר, v. 7b). In quick succession, the end of the wicked are described as drying water (v. 8a), those whose weapons are useless (v. 8b), a melting snail (v. 9a), a miscarried child (v. 9b), and as one being swept away (v. 10a–10b). An underlying conflict is clear by the context and the content of the psalm, although the nature of or actors in that conflict are not defined.

This request comes to fruition in vv. 11a–12b in the aftermath of the destruction of the wicked. The "righteous person" (צַדִּיק) appears in vv. 11a and 12a, where they rejoice in their enemies' destruction and bathe in the blood of the "wicked person" (רָשָׁע, v. 11b). The final event in the poem is the speech of the eyewitness to these events, designated simply as the "person" (אָדָם, v. 12a), who states that this situation—that of the death of the wicked and the righteous flaunting their victory—is proof of a God who judges the earth. In this case, God judges against the wicked and for the righteous.

The psalm, in summary, focuses largely on vivid metaphorical descriptions of the wicked's character through the wish for their destruction, and the imagined joy of the righteous when that destruction takes place. The psalm moves from the call to illegitimate judges, to the reality that exists because these judges have not performed their duties, to the request for God to act, and finally to the situation for the righteous person that will result when God acts. The final moment of the poem sees a bystander giving an eyewitness account to the theological reality behind the psalm, that God acts on behalf of the righteous.

Function of צַדִּיק and רָשָׁע

While the textual difficulties in Ps 58 make some lines impossible to interpret confidently, the functions of the righteous and the wicked are clear. First, a broad description of the wicked appears in vv. 4a–6c. As is common in the psalms, the connection between illegitimate speech and the identity of the wicked is made in v. 4b. The final two verses describe what may be one of the most violent descriptions of the victory of the righteous over the wicked in the Psalter. The psalm affirms the eventual destruction of the wicked person. The blessing of the righteous person, however, is not interpreted generally or in some sense nearness to God as is often the case in psalms where the request is made for God to act. Instead, the reward, explicitly the "fruit of the righteous person" (פְּרִי לַצַּדִּיק, v. 12a), is: "The righteous person will rejoice for they see vengeance/They will wash their feet in the blood of the wicked person" (v. 11a–11b). Declaring the death of the wicked as "fruit" of the righteous person is itself striking. The metaphor of fruit often hearkens to reward for behavior.[244] To put it in plainer terms, the death of the wicked is the reward of the righteous and the thing for which the righteous will rejoice. Only the results of God's actions are praised in this psalm, and not God himself. Further, it is the witness who comes closest to praising God in Ps 58 through the affirmation that "there is a God judging the earth" (v. 12b) because the wicked are destroyed.

Seybold suggests that the "fruit" of the righteous in this psalm clearly articulates the wisdom theme of whether the righteous receive their due reward.[245] In this case, it is given to the righteous to see the wicked condemned because God has judged fairly (unlike those illegitimate judges addressed at the outset of the poem). Due to the judicial context, it would be appropriate to view the צַדִּיק as one who is innocent in the psalm. Jerome Creach has stated that the outcome of being one of the righteous has religious implications.[246] The destiny of the righteous is their just reward of victory over their adversaries. It is not because they are those who are rightly behaved that they receive this reward. Situated in judicial language, it is Yhwh's salvation for those who are unjustly attacked that allows the צַדִּיק to enjoy the end of the wicked. It is not that they receive their just reward for proper behavior.[247] Rather, it is that justice has been served because they were not deserving of the attacks of the wicked who allowed to reign free.

PSALM 68

Text and Translation

לַמְנַצֵּחַ לְדָוִד מִזְמוֹר שִׁיר׃	1a	(To the choirmaster. Davidic. A psalm. A song.)[248]
יָקוּם אֱלֹהִים	2a	God arises;[249]
יָפוּצוּ אוֹיְבָיו	2b	His enemies are scattered,
וְיָנוּסוּ מְשַׂנְאָיו מִפָּנָיו׃	2c	And those who hate him flee from his presence.
כְּהִנְדֹּף עָשָׁן תִּנְדֹּף	3a	Like smoke that is driven away, you drive off;[250]
כְּהִמֵּס דּוֹנַג מִפְּנֵי־אֵשׁ	3b	Like wax melting from being near[251] fire
יֹאבְדוּ רְשָׁעִים מִפְּנֵי אֱלֹהִים׃	3c	The wicked people perish from being near God.
וְצַדִּיקִים יִשְׂמְחוּ	4a	But the righteous people will be glad;
יַעַלְצוּ לִפְנֵי אֱלֹהִים	4b	They will exult in the presence of Yhwh,
וְיָשִׂישׂוּ בְשִׂמְחָה׃	4c	And they will rejoice with joy.
שִׁירוּ לֵאלֹהִים	5a	Sing to God
זַמְּרוּ שְׁמוֹ	5b	Praise his name
סֹלּוּ לָרֹכֵב בָּעֲרָבוֹת	5c	Raise up worship to the rider of the clouds,[252]
בְּיָהּ שְׁמוֹ	5d	In Yh, his name,[253]
וְעִלְזוּ לְפָנָיו׃	5e	And exult before him.
אֲבִי יְתוֹמִים וְדַיַּן אַלְמָנוֹת	6a	A father of orphans and a defender of widows,
אֱלֹהִים בִּמְעוֹן קָדְשׁוֹ׃	6b	God is in the abode of his holiness.
אֱלֹהִים מוֹשִׁיב יְחִידִים בַּיְתָה	7a	God resettles the isolated in a household,
מוֹצִיא אֲסִירִים בַּכּוֹשָׁרוֹת	7b	Leads out the imprisoned into fortune,
אַךְ סוֹרְרִים שָׁכְנוּ צְחִיחָה׃	7c	Though the rebellious inhabit a parched land.
אֱלֹהִים בְּצֵאתְךָ לִפְנֵי עַמֶּךָ	8a	God, when you went out before your people,
בְּצַעְדְּךָ בִישִׁימוֹן סֶלָה׃	8b	When you marched in the desert, (*selah*)
אֶרֶץ רָעָשָׁה אַף־שָׁמַיִם נָטְפוּ	9a	The earth quaked, even the skies dripped,
מִפְּנֵי אֱלֹהִים זֶה סִינַי	9b	Because of the presence of God—this is Sinai[254]—
מִפְּנֵי אֱלֹהִים אֱלֹהֵי יִשְׂרָאֵל׃	9c	Because of the presence of God, the God of Israel.

(Continued)

גֶּשֶׁם נְדָבוֹת תָּנִיף אֱלֹהִים	10a	You caused generous rains to fall, God,
נַחֲלָתְךָ וְנִלְאָה אַתָּה כוֹנַנְתָּהּ:	10b	Your inheritance, it was weary; you aided it.
חַיָּתְךָ יָשְׁבוּ־בָהּ	11a	Your beings dwelled in it,
תָּכִין בְּטוֹבָתְךָ לֶעָנִי אֱלֹהִים:	11b	You aided, in your goodness, the poor, God.
אֲדֹנָי יִתֶּן־אֹמֶר	12a	The Lord utters a word;
הַמְבַשְּׂרוֹת צָבָא רָב:	12b	The women who announce news are a large army.
מַלְכֵי צְבָאוֹת יִדֹּדוּן יִדֹּדוּן	13a	Kings of armies they flee, they flee;
וּנְוַת־בַּיִת תְּחַלֵּק שָׁלָל:	13b	The beauties[255] of the house divide the spoil.
אִם־תִּשְׁכְּבוּן בֵּין שְׁפַתָּיִם	14a	If you lie down among the sheepfolds,[256]
כַּנְפֵי יוֹנָה נֶחְפָּה בַכֶּסֶף	14b	The wings of a dove are covered in silver,
וְאֶבְרוֹתֶיהָ בִּירַקְרַק חָרוּץ:	14c	And its feathers in the yellow of gold.
בְּפָרֵשׂ שַׁדַּי מְלָכִים בָּהּ	15a	When the almighty scattered kings on it,
תַּשְׁלֵג בְּצַלְמוֹן:	15b	It snowed on Zalmon.
הַר־אֱלֹהִים הַר־בָּשָׁן	16a	O mountain of God, O mountain of Bashan,
הַר גַּבְנֻנִּים הַר־בָּשָׁן:	16b	O mountain of many peaks,[257] O mountain of Bashan.
לָמָּה תְּרַצְּדוּן הָרִים גַּבְנֻנִּים	17a	Why do you look on with envy,[258] many peaked-mountains,
הָהָר חָמַד אֱלֹהִים לְשִׁבְתּוֹ	17b	At the mountain God desires as his dwelling?
אַף־יְהוָה יִשְׁכֹּן לָנֶצַח:	17c	Surely Yhwh will inhabit it forever.
רֶכֶב אֱלֹהִים רִבֹּתַיִם	18a	The chariots of God are twenty thousand, thousands repeating[259]
אַלְפֵי שִׁנְאָן		
אֲדֹנָי בָם סִינַי בַּקֹּדֶשׁ:	18b	The Lord is among them, at Sinai in the sanctuary.
עָלִיתָ לַמָּרוֹם	19a	You went to the heights,
שָׁבִיתָ שֶּׁבִי	19b	You took captive prisoners,
לָקַחְתָּ מַתָּנוֹת בָּאָדָם	19c	You took gifts from[260] men,
וְאַף סוֹרְרִים	19d	Even the rebellious,
לִשְׁכֹּן יָהּ אֱלֹהִים:	19e	For Yh, God, to dwell.[261]
בָּרוּךְ אֲדֹנָי	20a	Blessed be the Lord;
יוֹם יוֹם יַעֲמָס־לָנוּ	20b	Daily he carries burdens for us,
הָאֵל יְשׁוּעָתֵנוּ סֶלָה:	20c	God our salvation. (selah)
הָאֵל לָנוּ אֵל לְמוֹשָׁעוֹת	21a	Our God is God of deliverances,
וְלֵיהוִה אֲדֹנָי לַמָּוֶת תּוֹצָאוֹת:	21b	And to Lord Yhwh belongs escape from death.
אַךְ־אֱלֹהִים יִמְחַץ רֹאשׁ אֹיְבָיו	22a	Surely God will crush the head of his enemies,
קָדְקֹד שֵׂעָר מִתְהַלֵּךְ בַּאֲשָׁמָיו:	22b	The hairy scalp of the one who walks in his guilt.
אָמַר אֲדֹנָי מִבָּשָׁן אָשִׁיב	23a	The Lord says, "From Bashan,[262] I will bring back,
אָשִׁיב מִמְּצֻלוֹת יָם:	23b	I will bring back from the depths of the sea,
לְמַעַן תִּמְחַץ רַגְלְךָ בְּדָם	24a	In order that your foot will stomp in blood;
לְשׁוֹן כְּלָבֶיךָ מֵאֹיְבִים מִנֵּהוּ:	24b	The tongues of your dogs have their share[263] of enemies."
רָאוּ הֲלִיכוֹתֶיךָ אֱלֹהִים	25a	They see your processions, God,
הֲלִיכוֹת אֵלִי מַלְכִּי בַקֹּדֶשׁ:	25b	The procession of God, my king, in the sanctuary.
קִדְּמוּ שָׁרִים אַחַר נֹגְנִים	26a	The singers went out front, the instrumentalists after;
בְּתוֹךְ עֲלָמוֹת תּוֹפֵפוֹת:	26b	Amongst them, young women playing tambourines.

(Continued)

בְּמַקְהֵלוֹת בָּרְכוּ אֱלֹהִים	27a	Bless God in the assemblies,
יְהוָה מִמְּקוֹר יִשְׂרָאֵל׃	27b	Yhwh from the spring of Israel.
שָׁם בִּנְיָמִן צָעִיר רֹדֵם	28a	There is Benjamin, the youngest, ruling them,
שָׂרֵי יְהוּדָה רִגְמָתָם	28b	The princes of Judah their crowd,[264]
שָׂרֵי זְבֻלוּן שָׂרֵי נַפְתָּלִי׃	28c	The princes of Zebulun, the princes of Naphtali.
צִוָּה אֱלֹהֶיךָ עֻזֶּךָ	29a	Your God commanded your strength
עוּזָּה אֱלֹהִים זוּ פָּעַלְתָּ לָּנוּ׃	29b	Be mighty, God, with what you do for us.
מֵהֵיכָלֶךָ עַל־יְרוּשָׁלָ͏ִם	30a	From[265] your temple over Jerusalem,
לְךָ יוֹבִילוּ מְלָכִים שָׁי׃	30b	To you kings will bring gifts.
גְּעַר חַיַּת קָנֶה	31a	Rebuke the animals of the reeds:
עֲדַת אַבִּירִים בְּעֶגְלֵי עַמִּים	31b	The herd of bulls among the calves of the people,
מִתְרַפֵּס בְּרַצֵּי־כָסֶף	31c	Those who trample pieces[266] of silver.
בִּזַּר עַמִּים קְרָבוֹת יֶחְפָּצוּ׃	31d	Scatter[267] the peoples, they take pleasure in battles.
יֶאֱתָיוּ חַשְׁמַנִּים מִנִּי מִצְרָיִם	32a	Envoys[268] will come from[269] Egypt,
כּוּשׁ תָּרִיץ יָדָיו לֵאלֹהִים׃	32b	Cush will stretch out their[270] hands to God.
מַמְלְכוֹת הָאָרֶץ שִׁירוּ לֵאלֹהִים	33a	Kingdoms of the earth, sing to God;
זַמְּרוּ אֲדֹנָי סֶלָה׃	33b	Make music to the Lord, (*selah*)
לָרֹכֵב בִּשְׁמֵי שְׁמֵי־קֶדֶם	34a	To the one who rides in the heavens,[271] the heavens of the East[272]
הֵן יִתֵּן בְּקוֹלוֹ קוֹל עֹז׃	34b	See, he utters his voice, a voice of strength.[273]
תְּנוּ עֹז לֵאלֹהִים	35a	Ascribe strength to God,
עַל־יִשְׂרָאֵל גַּאֲוָתוֹ	35b	His pride is over Israel,
וְעֻזּוֹ בַּשְּׁחָקִים׃	35c	And his strength is in the skies.
נוֹרָא אֱלֹהִים מִמִּקְדָּשֶׁיךָ	36a	God is feared from your sanctuary,
אֵל יִשְׂרָאֵל הוּא נֹתֵן עֹז וְתַעֲצֻמוֹת לָעָם	36b	The God of Israel, he gives strength and might to the people.
בָּרוּךְ אֱלֹהִים׃	36c	Blessed be God.

Interpretation

Due to numerous challenges in reconstructing the texts, the interpretation of Ps 68 can only be seen in broad strokes or in places where the language itself is clear. The psalm often shifts in content and address. There are several general themes that are present in the psalm that relate to the meaning of the psalm: (1) Yhwh's destruction of the enemies; (2) Yhwh's relationship to geographic locations, particularly mountains;[274] and (3) the praise of Yhwh by various groups. Further, the psalm imagines the reign of God and the results of a victory over his enemies. Though the interpretation of the psalm is diffi-cult, the individual stanzas or strophes are fairly consistently divided in schol-arship.[275] The broad strokes of movement suggested by Beth Tanner helpfully establish the general settings of the psalm: "God moves from the sanctuaries of old . . . via a great procession . . . to the temple in Jerusalem."[276] Thus, former holy mountain sites are forsaken for a permanent dwelling. There are four places mentioned where God resides or is present: Sinai, Bashan, Jerusalem, and the heavens. All mountains and places that are the heights belong to God, and Bashan is representative of them. Ultimately, Ps 68 emphasizes that God's temple and sanctuary is at Jerusalem (v. 30c; cf. vv. 6b, 25b, 36a).

Todd Scacewater argues explicitly that Ps 68 should be read as a narrative, with vv. 1–19 representing past events of God's actions in leading "Israel from Egypt, through the wilderness, into Canaan, and finally to the heights of Mount Zion in Jerusalem," and with vv. 20–36 describing future events.[277] Methodologically, Scacewater finds verbal echoes elsewhere in the OT to determine the narrative setting for the various stanzas of the poem. For example, vv. 8–11 are seen to narrate God's leading Israel in the wilderness,[278] though hardly any sentence can be even indirectly connected.[279] As another example, verbal echoes to several passages from Judg 4–5 in vv. 12–15 suggest to Scacewater that the narrative event in mind is the defeat of Sisera.[280] Goldingay has noted that lack of concrete place names in Ps 68, unlike those in Judg 5:4–5, deny a specific situation as the background to the psalm.[281] If borrowing has occurred in Ps 68, it neither indicates nor implies a narrative setting. The poetry is rather unclear, and determining meaning in this way skews the function of the poetry itself.

Seen through the lens of God's activities, the groups of people can be divided as those who receive the benefits from Yhwh and those who receive his judgment. Yhwh's judgment is pictured in language that implies a military defeat: enemies flee from Yhwh (vv. 2b–2c, 12a, 15a), they die (vv. 3a–3c, 22a–22b), are captured (v. 19b), and Yhwh takes or receives gifts from them (v. 19c–19d, 30b, 32a–32b). The words of Yhwh are part of Yhwh's power over the enemies (vv. 12a, 34b; cf. the direct speech in vv. 23a–24b). In contrast, for those Yhwh helps he provides nourishing rain (vv. 10a–11b), elevates their position (vv. 6a–7b), accomplishes salvation for them (vv. 20b–21a), allows them to participate in the victory (v. 24a–24b), and gives them strength (v. 36b).

The psalm begins with Yhwh's theophany in vv. 2a–4c.[282] Here, "God arises" (v. 2a) against "enemies" (אוֹיְבָיו, v. 2b) and "those who hate him" (מְשַׂנְאָיו, v. 2c), which leads to enemies fleeing and the wicked people (רְשָׁעִים, v. 3c) being destroyed (vv. 2b–3b), and the righteous people worshiping (צַדִּיקִים, v. 4a–4c). The צַדִּיקִים in v. 4a are the 3mp verbal subjects in v. 4a–4c. Verse 2 shares language with Num 10:35 suggesting a literary relationship.[283] This section initiates the defeat of the enemies that occurs throughout the psalm.

The introduction of Yhwh's defeat moves into a call to praise directed at the community in v. 5a–5e.[284] God is here referred to as the "rider of the clouds" (רֹכֵב בָּעֲרָבוֹת, v. 5c). Both directives toward praise (v. 27a) and the appellative of Yhwh as a "rider" (v. 34a) are repeated later in the psalm.

Yhwh acts here on behalf of the disadvantaged (vv. 6a, 7a–7c),[285] and these verses are no longer addressed to the community directly. The first mention of Yhwh's dwelling, the "abode of his holiness," appears here, which most likely applies to the Zion temple.

The section of vv. 8a–11b provides a picture of Yhwh blessing his people through a combination of military and meteorological imagery. Due to the direct address to God in vv. 8a–8b and 10a–11b, all of vv. 8a–11b should be understood as directed to God. Verses 8a–11b begin with allusions to the wilderness wanderings (v. 8a–8b) and at least a loose description of the Sinai event (cf. Judg 5:4–5). These events are also tied with Yhwh's activity on behalf of the disadvantaged, as mentioned in v. 11b. This section refers to the groups Yhwh saves as "your [God's] people" (עַמְּךָ, v. 8a), "your [God's] inheritance" (נַחֲלָתְךָ, v. 10b), "your [God's] beings" (חַיָּתְךָ, v. 11a), and "the poor" (עָנִי, v. 11b). While the first two verses describe a situation reminiscent of the wilderness wanderings, the rain motif is more general.[286] The rain for Yhwh's people also contrasts the situation of the enemies of Yhwh in v. 7c. It is also possible that the section describes not the exodus event nor wilderness wanderings, but the image of God fighting on behalf of his people. The themes of the movement of God, the destruction of enemies, and the resultant blessing for his people are thus all connected in these verses. The "desert" instead (v. 8b), then, highlights the place where God's nourishing rains come as a metaphor of restoration. That this took place at Sinai expresses a connection with the place where God has acted from in the past.

Verses 12a–15b describe the effects of Yhwh's victory. God's "word" (אֹמֶר), disseminated through the pronouncement of "the women" (הַמְבַשְּׂרוֹת, v. 12b),[287] is the cause of the enemies' retreat (v. 13a, v. 15a). The repeated word "hosts/armies" (צְבָאוֹת) in vv. 12b and 13a contrasts the power of God's word with military might. It is this "large army" of women that announce God's word, presumably, that then reap the spoils from God's defeat of his enemies (v. 12b). The meaning or function of v. 14a–14c is unclear. The words are all relatively straightforward, but the semantic and grammatical relationship between them is not. Verse 14a in particular does not clearly relate to v. 14b–14c, and is addressed to unidentified 2mp participants. The final description of the snow on Zalmon is unimportant to the overall progression of the poem (v. 15b), though may describe a geographical or temporal setting. In this section, we have the results of a defeat through Yhwh's word, which is announced by women and cause the enemies again to flee the presence of Yhwh in defeat.

Due to the continuation of the 2ms directed speech initiated in v. 17a, I take each of the titles in v. 16a–16b to be vocatives,[288] and thus, vv. 16a–17c address the personified mountain of Bashan.[289] The locations mentioned do not require a specific physical location for this section of the psalm to make sense.[290] Though these could be mountains which claim some tie to non-Yahwistic cult,[291] the overall motif in the psalm of Yhwh's presence throughout a number of locations suggest that Bashan, too, is a mountain of God. It is, however, not *the* mountain of God in which Yhwh has chosen to dwell permanently. While this interpretation has the benefit of the language of movement throughout the psalm, including the mentions of Sinai as a place of God, in any case the point is clear: Zion is preferred to Bashan. In terms of the movement of God, Bashan is more of a touch point on the way toward the temple, and need not have been a place Yhwh dwelled.

In v. 20a, a declaration of praise initiates an expression of God's concern for the 1cp subject in vv. 20b–21a. The reward for the community in this section is expressed in two ways: first in Yhwh's salvation (vv. 20b–21b) and second in the destruction of the enemies (vv. 22a–24b). The titles for God given here are fitting of the content: "God our salvation" (הָאֵל יְשׁוּעָתֵנוּ, v. 20c) and "God of deliverances" (לְמוֹשָׁעוֹת אֵל, v. 21a). Those God acts against here are "his enemies" (אֹיְבָיו, v. 22a), "one who walks in his guilt" (מִתְהַלֵּךְ בַּאֲשָׁמָיו, v. 22b), and "enemies" (אֹיְבִים, v. 24b). The direct quotation from God in vv. 23a–24b does not include a grammatical object for the repeated verb אָשִׁיב. The context does not indicate who this is in particular, though they are at least those categorized as against the enemies due to their participation in their violent actions against the vulnerable. In the broader section, the enemies are brought so that those who were not present in the battle will enact vengeance through the gruesome activities of violent kicking and feeding the enemies to dogs (v. 24a–24b).[292] This figure, allowed to participate in the punishment of the enemies, designated by the 2ms suffixes in v. 24a–24b, is also the recipient of God's beneficent action. The location "from Bashan" (מִבָּשָׁן, v. 23a) could locate either the place from which Yhwh will bring the enemies or the place of Yhwh's speech. Though the former is the typical interpretation, both options locate Yhwh's defeat of enemies in Bashan, as mentioned earlier.

Following the moment of God's call to the undefined referent to attack the enemies, the speaker envisions a procession. It is described in vv. 25a–26b, with further references to those who are part of the procession in v. 28a–28c, including "singers" (שָׁרִים, v. 26a), "instrumentalists" (נֹגְנִים, v. 26a), and "young women" (עֲלָמוֹת, v. 26b). Several participants from the tribes of Israel also appear, specifically Benjamin, presumably to refer to the leader by metonymy, and the "princes" of Judah, Zebulun, and Naphtali. There is no clear reason for the tribes or figures mentioned here.[293] Verse 27a–27b punctuates this parade with a call to praise directed toward the community. This section displays as a sort of victory procession in the context of the rest of the psalm, but focuses on the actual substance of the parade.

Verses 29a–32b shifts the focus to the temple in Jerusalem. An unidentified 2ms subject appears in v. 29a, though vv. 29b–31d all contain Yhwh as the addressee through 2ms forms throughout. Here, "kings" (מְלָכִים, v. 30b), "envoys" (חַשְׁמַנִּים, v. 32a), "Cush" (כּוּשׁ, v. 32b), and "kingdoms of the earth" (מַמְלְכוֹת הָאָרֶץ, v. 33a) shift from fleeing God (v. 13a), to drawing close to God by bringing gifts (vv. 30b, 32a–32b). Gifts were taken by Yhwh in v. 19a–19d, though here they are offered. God is also called in v. 31a–31d to act against animals and peoples as a display of his power,[294] though the significance of v. 31a–31c is unclear.

Verses 33a–36c continue the theme of the peoples honoring Yhwh, though the content shifts from offering physical gifts to offering praise. Verse 33a–33b is explicitly addressed to "kingdoms of the earth" (מַמְלְכוֹת הָאָרֶץ, v. 33a), with imperatives continued through v. 35c. The doxology in this concluding section corresponds to the opening of the psalm, and thus frames the entirety in praise.[295] There are two important repetitions from earlier in the psalm: the imperative forms directing praise (vv. 5a–5c, 33a–33b) and God referred to as "one who rides" (vv. 5c, 34a), though here he is "the one who rides in the heavens" (רֹכֵב בִּשְׁמֵי [construct], v. 34a). God is located in these final verses primarily in the heavens (vv. 34a–34b, 35a).

The psalm is not a linear retelling of any historical events, though there are several allusions to passages outside of the Psalms. Rather, it is a classical psalmic expression of God's reign and his defeat of his enemies. This defeat has implications for the righteous, for Israel, and for the world. The only clear progression of the psalm leads from the scattering of the enemies earlier in the psalm to the gathering of these enemies in Jerusalem to honor God through gift giving and praise. The psalm also deals with the question of holy places, establishing Zion as the place of God's dwelling while affirming that God has acted throughout the world: the desert, the mountains of Bashan, the heavens, the waters, and among all nations and peoples.

Function of צַדִּיק and רָשָׁע

The basic literary pattern of the contrast between the righteous and the wicked is utilized to introduce the psalm. The instrument of God's destruction of the wicked and blessing of the righteous in Ps 68 is the same: God's own presence. The function of the righteous and the wicked in the introduction serves as a short form of the paradigm of those considered righteous or wicked: the former are blessed, and the latter are destroyed. Semantically, the צַדִּיקִים are not directly identified as those who are innocent in a matter, though because their praise is offered in response to the defeat of the enemies, there is at least an implicit sense in which they are threatened. At the same time, they worship Yhwh, both because that is what the righteous do and because their enemies are defeated. Here, they are to be understood primarily as the worshiping community and as those who receive Yhwh's beneficent action.

Though the figures of the righteous do not appear at the end of the psalm, Fokkelman connects the first section which contrasts the righteous and the wicked with the elevation of the community as those who are enabled to praise through Yhwh's defeat of the enemy in the final section.[296] However, the defeat of the enemy is less explicit than God's ruling over the world. That is, the major focus is not God's active defeat of the enemies, present primarily in v. 22a–22b, but the effect of God's reign.

The distinctive presence of the righteous and the wicked at the beginning of the psalm, as well as the parallels with Ps 1 and Ps 97, have led some to believe that vv. 2a–4c were added later.[297] The combination of this motif with the language from Num 10:35 and the ark account bring the presence of Yhwh and the destruction of the wicked into clear connection.[298]

Scacewater notes that the mention of the destruction of the wicked in v. 3c is the only part of the first narrative (vv. 1–19) that is clearly imperfective in meaning.[299] The affirmation that the righteous praise Yhwh because of his presence is then connected with the repeated refrains for the community to praise God. As in a majority of the psalms, it is not the activities of the righteous and the wicked that are emphasized, but rather the community identity. Those who are wicked will be destroyed; in this case, they are the enemies of the nation. Those who are righteous will worship because they are saved by Yhwh's power. This salvation is presented as a continual reality associated with the mountain of Sinai. The connection of the Sinai tradition with the contrast between the righteous and the wicked focuses the identity of Israel as the community of those who have been Yhwh's choice and his presence.

The placement of the distinction between the righteous and the wicked at the beginning of the psalm is a shift from the more usual placement at the conclusion (see chapter 3). Stylistically, this sets the subject matter for the psalm as the righteous and the wicked more than reinterpreting the themes present at the end. God's presence is extended throughout time and space with the affirmation that God blesses the righteous and judges the wicked. Connecting with the rest of the psalm, this introduction informs the universality of this theme. It is not only those who are righteous or wicked within Israel that will receive these just outcomes. All the world, in all places, will experience God's power. His blessing or conquering presence that the righteous and the wicked receive in vv. 2a–4c does not exist only in the temple at Zion, but throughout the whole earth.

PSALM 75

Text and Translation

לַמְנַצֵּחַ אַל־תַּשְׁחֵת מִזְמוֹר לְאָסָף שִׁיר:	1a	(To the choir director. Do not destroy. A psalm of Asaph. A song.)
הוֹדִינוּ לְךָ אֱלֹהִים הוֹדִינוּ	2a	We thank you, God, we thank you.
וְקָרוֹב שְׁמֶךָ סִפְּרוּ נִפְלְאוֹתֶיךָ:	2b	And near is your name. They recount your wonders.
כִּי אֶקַּח מוֹעֵד	3a	"When[300] I seize the appointed time,
אֲנִי מֵישָׁרִים אֶשְׁפֹּט:	3b	I, with integrity, I will judge.
נְמֹגִים אֶרֶץ וְכָל־יֹשְׁבֶיהָ	4a	The earth and all its inhabitants tremble.[301]
אָנֹכִי תִכַּנְתִּי עַמּוּדֶיהָ סֶּלָה:	4b	I set up its pillar." (*selah*)
אָמַרְתִּי לַהוֹלְלִים אַל־תָּהֹלּוּ	5a	I said to the boasters, "Do not boast,"
וְלָרְשָׁעִים אַל־תָּרִימוּ קָרֶן:	5b	And to the wicked people, "Do not lift a horn.
אַל־תָּרִימוּ לַמָּרוֹם קַרְנְכֶם	6a	Do not lift your horn high
תְּדַבְּרוּ בְצַוָּאר עָתָק:	6b	nor[302] speak with arrogance of neck."
כִּי לֹא מִמּוֹצָא וּמִמַּעֲרָב	7a	For not from the east nor from the west,
וְלֹא מִמִּדְבַּר הָרִים:	7b	and not from the wilderness will lifting occur.[303]
כִּי־אֱלֹהִים שֹׁפֵט	8a	For God judges
זֶה יַשְׁפִּיל וְזֶה יָרִים:	8b	Who[304] he brings low and who he lifts up.
כִּי כוֹס בְּיַד־יְהוָה	9a	For a cup is in Yhwh's hand,
וְיַיִן חָמַר מָלֵא מֶסֶךְ	9b	and wine foaming—a full mixture.
וַיַּגֵּר מִזֶּה אַךְ־שְׁמָרֶיהָ יִמְצוּ יִשְׁתּוּ	9c	He pours sweet wine.[305] Surely its dregs they will drain;
כֹּל רִשְׁעֵי־אָרֶץ:	9d	All the wicked people of the earth will drink.
וַאֲנִי אַגִּיד לְעֹלָם	10a	But I, I will declare forever;
אֲזַמְּרָה לֵאלֹהֵי יַעֲקֹב:	10b	I will sing to the God of Jacob.
וְכָל־קַרְנֵי רְשָׁעִים אֲגַדֵּעַ	11a	"And all the horns of the wicked people I will cut off;
תְּרוֹמַמְנָה קַרְנוֹת צַדִּיק:	11b	But the horns of the righteous person will be lifted."

Interpretation

The greatest challenge in interpreting Ps 75 is the delineation of speaker. The voice of God clearly begins in v. 3a, but there is disagreement as to whether it ends at v. 4b,[306] or if it extends through v. 6b.[307] First-person language is primary in all four verses, but this is not a clear indication of speaker, as elsewhere both God and psalmic speaker speak in the first person. Tanner argues that the speaker's voice appears again in v. 5a–5b based on the evidence of the *selah* and the speech indicator "I said," implying a shift back to the speaker.[308] The reasons for the speech in v. 6a is offered in v. 7a, and suggests a continuity of thought with the previous verses. Thus, I take the first divine speech to end in v. 4a.

The second question of shift in voice is whether God resumes speaking in v. 11a,[309] or if the voice of the psalmic speaker continues.[310] Both vv. 10a–10b and 11a–11b use first-person speech, but v. 10a–10b clearly comes from the voice of the speaker as a declaration to praise God. While there is a first-person active verb describing the action to be taken against the wicked, the blessing that the righteous receive uses a passive verb signifying the righteous's horn being raised by some other agent. Many other psalms with divine speech include the deity speaking of the surety of the future action to be taken.[311] While the commonality of this feature in divine speech is not irrefutable evidence, it seems more likely that God would be the one who would judge the wicked by cutting off their horns. Based on this discussion, I argue that the breakdown of speakers of the psalm are thus: the collective "we" (v. 2a–2b); God (vv. 3a–4b); the speaker (vv. 5a–10b); and God (v. 11a–11b).

The activity of judgment is set up in God's speech in vv. 3a–4b and concludes in v. 11b when the future action of cutting off or raising of horns is mentioned. God speaks of preparing to judge in his first speech and speaks of the substance of his judgment in the second speech. God does not participate in any actions outside of his speech. However, v. 3a mentions the context of Yhwh's judgment and the "appointed time." Verse 4a continues with a statement describing the "earth and all its inhabitants" (אֶרֶץ וְכָל־יֹשְׁבֶיהָ) trembling as witnesses to God's act. The psalm continues with imagery of the world as a building, with God having the ability to establish it, characterizing God as powerful over the entirety of the world.[312]

Verses 5a–9d significantly contribute to the animosity between the speaker and the antagonists. First, the self-quoted speech of the speaker to the "boasters" (הוֹלְלִים, v. 5a) simply commands them not to boast (v. 5a). Building upon the concept of illegitimate speech, the "wicked people" (רְשָׁעִים, vv. 5b, 11a) are commanded not to lift their "horns" (v. 5b–6b). While Hossfeld and Zenger suggest that the speaker(s) "count themselves in the group of the righteous and the poor,"[313] they never directly identify with the righteous and the poor, only against the wicked and the boaster.

The imagery of horns mentioned in vv. 5b–6a recurs in v. 11a–1b. Many commentators highlight the intended "point" of the metaphor of horns in psalms or, more generally, in the ancient Near East horns, represent "symbols of strength and power."[314] Keel includes a slightly more nuanced description, noting that "horns are widely used as a symbol of power in the ancient near

East," pointing to iconography of bulls attacking people and of leaders who are depicted with horns.[315] On the other hand, Margit Süring suggests that in this passage, horns are used as a metaphor emphasizing arrogance.[316] This may offer a reading in context, but does not appear to stem from the metaphor itself. The most up-to-date description of the horn metaphor comes from a recent work on New Testament Christology by Gregory Lanier, where the conceptual metaphors that appear in Old Testament quotations in Luke are analyzed in both the Septuagint and Masoretic Text (LXX and MT).[317] Lanier notes that within the Hebrew conceptual metaphor there is a close connection between the concept of horn and status, such as an animal lifting its head would have an increased position or power.[318] In other instances, the conceptual metaphor draws specifically on imagery describing an attack against an enemy.[319] Arrogance is present in the context of Ps 75, but the sense of a threat or exertion of power is the most important aspect of the metaphor of the horn in vv. 5a–6b. Here the speaker makes a claim against the wicked not to consider themselves more powerful than they are in threatening the speaker.

Verses 7a–9d provide the basis for the speaker's speech and point both backward and forward in the psalm to God's activity of judgment. Verse 7a–7b emphasizes a worldwide context, as is implied in v. 4a. The spatial merism east and west suggests a totality, and the use of the wilderness provides another cardinal point from which no "lifting"—that is, elevation of status—will come (v. 7a–7b). Verse 8a–8b supplies a summary statement of the activity of God's judgment, with an antithetical pair of those who will be humbled and those who will be raised up. The antagonism present in the psalm thus far suggests that this may implicitly refer to the two groups of speaker/righteous and boaster/wicked. In v. 9a–9d, the "wicked of the earth" (רִשְׁעֵי־אָרֶץ, v. 9d) become the clear object of God's judgment through the imagery of forced drink. The imagined judgment involves Yhwh serving mixed wine to the wicked. Mixtures of wine may have been somewhat common in the ancient world,[320] though the direct connection of the imagery to judgment is not clear.[321] Perhaps it is intended to emphasize that the wicked drink only the dregs, what is undesirable, or that the totality of the mixed drink God has prepared is consumed.[322] Whether there is an explicit connection between the metaphorical use of wine with judgment is unclear, but the vivid imagery painted of God pouring out wine of judgment that will ultimately be consumed by the wicked is unmistakable. The wicked receive their due from God.

Verse 10a–10b shifts in tone and stands apart from the rest of the psalm. The disjunctive וַאֲנִי marks an unambiguous shift in speaker, and what follows is a declaration of the speaker to praise Yhwh. The speaker celebrates the judgment that they will receive by celebrating God in this context.

God speaks again in v. 11a–11b and refers to both the "righteous person" (צַדִּיק, v. 11b) and the "wicked people" (רְשָׁעִים, v. 11a). This speech is similar to other instances where these characters are mentioned together only at the end of the psalm. In this case, the unique contribution is that the summary is given in the divine voice. They both receive the judgment from God, yet in a clear antithetical saying, the wicked receive the judgment of having their horn removed.[323] The righteous, on the other hand, receive the judgment of having their horn lifted.[324] Again, the "lifting" of the horn is in view, but it becomes more powerful when heard through the voice of God. That the horn of the wicked is cut off shows that God removes the ability for the wicked to threaten the righteous/the speaker, as suggested by the use of the metaphor above in vv. 5a–6b. The passive verb of the lifting of the righteous horn is striking. It is not the righteous who lift their horn, but it is lifted up by some other agent, by implication God. If the metaphor earlier in vv. 5a–6b and in the first line of v. 11a–11b describes the removal of that threat, the passive verb may suggest that a different nuance of the common horn metaphor is at play here. A further nuance in the difference between the lifting of the horns for the righteous and the wicked is that the horns of the righteous appear with a feminine ending (קַרְנוֹת) whereas the horns of the wicked appear with masculine ending (קַרְנֵי). The difference between the two words is not likely accidental.[325] Within the context of the lifting of the righteous's horn, an intentional shift in gender of the horns to show that the nature of horns that are lifted differs again from those of the wicked that are removed. In this case, it is not a lifting in military might and threat, but in status.

Jacobson suggests that the function of the speech from God in Ps 75 is to admonish the community to obey.[326] Yet if this were the case, it would be likely to find language that relates to following God's commands or refer-ence to ethical ideals—both are absent from this psalm. While there may be ethical implications of identifying with the righteous and the wicked, there is nothing in the psalm that even describes their general activity, other than that the speaker is opposed to the wicked and God will judge them. The structure of the psalm is largely mediated through the psalmic speaker's voice, though the voice of God and of the self-quotation of the speaker figure significantly in the presentation of the wicked in particular.

Function of צַדִּיק and רָשָׁע

The vague descriptions of the righteous and the wicked are part of the natural presentation of these two participants in the psalms. They are not described primarily by what they do. Instead, they are presented simply as those who fall under the judgment of God, and as such, draw on the common literary pattern. God is the main actor in this psalm, but mainly in future referring events. The functions of the righteous and the wicked within the psalm are closely connected to the psalm as a whole. Their conflict provides a loose backbone to the structure of the psalm. The conflict between the two and the judgment of God for both is a means by which the poem progresses—though this is not a narrative, sequential progression. This progression is determined by an underlying conflict between the righteous and the wicked. The judgment reveals an implicit notion of animosity between the speaker—grouped with the righteous in the psalm through the speaker's speech against the boasters and the wicked—and the group of antagonists. The wicked are clearly described throughout by their violence and illegitimate speech. While it cannot be certain, it is implied that these words function to speak against the righteous.

The judgment of both righteous and wicked also emphasizes a future where the wicked are condemned and the innocent shown to be victorious. Though semantically it is not clear that צַדִּיק refers to one who is generally properly behaved or one who is innocent in a matter, the distinction between the two figures at the end of psalm highlights that their position will be elevated when God judges the wicked. That is, the pattern that God rescues the צַדִּיק is clear here. This offers comfort to the community as the final affirmation of the psalm; it is not praise that concludes Ps 75 (though it is certainly present in vv. 2a–2b and 10a–10b), but an articulation that an end of the wicked is coming and this will result in a new reality for the צַדִּיק.

PSALM 92

Text and Translation

מִזְמוֹר שִׁיר לְיוֹם הַשַּׁבָּת:	1a	(A psalm. A song. For the sabbath day.)
טוֹב לְהֹדוֹת לַיהוָה	2a	It is good to give thanks to Yhwh,
וּלְזַמֵּר לְשִׁמְךָ עֶלְיוֹן:	2b	And to sing of the name of the Most High,
לְהַגִּיד בַּבֹּקֶר חַסְדֶּךָ	3a	To recount your loving kindness in the morning
וֶאֱמוּנָתְךָ בַּלֵּילוֹת:	3b	And your faithfulness at night,
עֲלֵי־עָשׂוֹר וַעֲלֵי־נָבֶל	4a	On ten strings and on the harp,
עֲלֵי הִגָּיוֹן בְּכִנּוֹר:	4b	With music from the lyre.
כִּי שִׂמַּחְתַּנִי יְהוָה בְּפָעֳלֶךָ	5a	For you have brought me happiness, Yhwh, by your actions;
בְּמַעֲשֵׂי יָדֶיךָ אֲרַנֵּן:	5b	About the deeds of your hands, I rejoice loudly.
מַה־גָּדְלוּ מַעֲשֶׂיךָ יְהוָה	6a	How[327] great are your deeds, Yhwh,
מְאֹד עָמְקוּ מַחְשְׁבֹתֶיךָ:	6b	Your thoughts are exceedingly deep.
אִישׁ־בַּעַר לֹא יֵדָע	7a	A foolish person does not know,
וּכְסִיל לֹא־יָבִין אֶת־זֹאת:	7b	And a fool does not understand this:

(Continued)

בִּפְרֹחַ רְשָׁעִים כְּמוֹ עֵשֶׂב	8a	When wicked people flourish like grass,
וַיָּצִיצוּ כָּל־פֹּעֲלֵי אָוֶן	8b	And all the doers of evil blossom,[328]
לְהִשָּׁמְדָם עֲדֵי־עַד:	8c	They will[329] be destroyed[330] forever.
וְאַתָּה מָרוֹם לְעֹלָם יְהוָה:	9a	But you are exalted forever, Yhwh.
כִּי הִנֵּה אֹיְבֶיךָ יְהוָה	10a	For, behold, your enemies, Yhwh,
כִּי־הִנֵּה אֹיְבֶיךָ יֹאבֵדוּ	10b	For, behold, your enemies perish,
יִתְפָּרְדוּ כָּל־פֹּעֲלֵי אָוֶן:	10c	All the doers of evil will be scattered.
וַתָּרֶם כִּרְאֵים קַרְנִי	11a	You lifted my horn like an ox,
בַּלֹּתִי בְּשֶׁמֶן רַעֲנָן:	11b	I am prepared[331] in luxuriant oils.
וַתַּבֵּט עֵינִי בְּשׁוּרָי	12a	Now my eye looks for those watching me,
בַּקָּמִים עָלַי מְרֵעִים תִּשְׁמַעְנָה אָזְנָי:	12b	Those who rise against me, hostile people, my ears will hear.
צַדִּיק כַּתָּמָר יִפְרָח	13a	A righteous person will flourish like a date palm;
כְּאֶרֶז בַּלְּבָנוֹן יִשְׂגֶּה:	13b	Like a cedar in Lebanon, they will grow;
שְׁתוּלִים בְּבֵית יְהוָה	14a	Planted in the house of Yhwh,
בְּחַצְרוֹת אֱלֹהֵינוּ יַפְרִיחוּ:	14b	In the courts of our God they will flourish.
עוֹד יְנוּבוּן בְּשֵׂיבָה	15a	Still, they prosper at an old age;
דְּשֵׁנִים וְרַעֲנַנִּים יִהְיוּ:	15b	They will be productive and lush,
לְהַגִּיד כִּי־יָשָׁר יְהוָה צוּרִי	16a	To declare that Yhwh my rock is upright,
וְלֹא־עַוְלָתָה[332] בּוֹ:	16b	And there is no injustice in him.

Interpretation

Psalm 92 characterizes the righteous, the wicked, and Yhwh. The psalm begins with the portraiture and praise of Yhwh, focusing on his praise-worthiness through the day (vv. 2a–3b) and through music (v. 4a–4b). Verse 2a–2b could be considered to have a general address, though with the parallel verbal structure of the infinitives construct in vv. 2a–3a, where v. 3a shifts to referring to Yhwh with a 2ms pronoun suffix, it should be understood as address to Yhwh. It moves speaker's description of Yhwh's previous actions on their behalf, and the reality that this has created for them (vv. 5a–6b).[333] It emphasizes both Yhwh's actions and the nature of Yhwh, notably, the depth of his thought, pointing to the inaccessibility of Yhwh's thoughts (cf. Isa 55:5–7).[334]

In contrast to the character of Yhwh, the figures of the fool and the wicked appear together in vv. 7a–8c, which emphasizes the folly of wickedness because of the eventual destruction that will befall the wicked (v. 8a–8c).[335] The antagonists of the psalm are referred to here as "wicked people" (רְשָׁעִים, v. 8a) and "doers of evil" (פֹּעֲלֵי אָוֶן; v. 8b; also v. 10c). A group of others that are related, though not coreferential, with these figures are the "foolish person" (אִישׁ־בַּעַר, v. 7a) and the "fool" (כְּסִיל, v. 7b). As such, the foolishness characterizes the actions of the wicked as well. Tucker argues that the infinitive construct in v. 8c is best to be read in a modal sense, which would here imply that the "flourishing of the wicked *necessarily* ends with their destruction."[336] The eventual destruction of these figures resumes in v. 10a–10c, in contrast to Yhwh's permanent exaltation (v. 9a). Here they are described twice as "your enemies" (אֹיְבֶיךָ; v. 10a, 10b) in speech directed toward Yhwh.[337] The imagined reality of Yhwh's perpetual glory stands in contrast from the situation of the wicked.[338] The wicked and Yhwh are further contrast in several images. Mention of Yhwh's "thoughts" (מַחְשְׁבֹת, v. 6b) is contrasted with the foolish person's lack of understanding in v. 7a–7b. Then in v. 8c, the wicked are destroyed forever (עֲדֵי־עַד), which is then contrasted with Yhwh's being exalted "forever" (עֹלָם) in v. 9a.

The next transition focuses on the description of the speaker, as one who has been established by Yhwh in victory (v. 11a–11b).[339] The speaker describes their own activities in v. 12a–12b as seeing or hearing the enemies, designated as "those watching me" (שׁוּרָי, vv. 12a); "those who rise against me" (קָמִים עָלַי, v. 12b); and "hostile people" (מְרֵעִים, v. 12b). In vv. 13a–15b, the "righteous person" (צַדִּיק, v. 13a), is compared to a tree planted in the temple of Yhwh. This metaphor emphasizes both the speaker's location and their fruitfulness.[340] The stability of the righteous as a tree and ephemerality of the wicked as grass is based on the fact that God provides this order to the world.[341] Though the description remains on the righteous person, in vv. 14a–15b these descriptions shift to 3mp forms. As such it is extended from the individual to all who fit this description. The community is invited into this vision through the use of the designation "our God" (אֱלֹהֵינוּ, v. 14b).

The final verse (v. 16a–16b) resumes the grammatical strategy of the opening lines (vv. 2a–3b) of using an infinitive construct to emphasize the praiseworthiness of Yhwh. The term "my rock" (צוּרִי, v. 16a) also refers to Yhwh in metaphor. The psalm, then, is mediated through the pattern of a call to praise, of showing the worthiness of Yhwh grounded in the realities of the righteous person found within the body of the psalm.

There are four major topics in Ps 92, found in the different sections: first, the praiseworthiness of Yhwh; second, the description of the fool and enemy of Yhwh; third, the salvation of the speaker; fourth, the description of the righteous person. The psalm includes a number of contrasts between the wicked and God, and the righteous and God.

Function of צַדִּיק and רָשָׁע

Psalm 92 displays a clear antithesis between the righteous and the wicked. In one sense, the structural contrast between the righteous and the wicked in Ps 92 is a way to emphasize the justice of God as it affirms the literary pattern that the righteous will be rewarded and the wicked punished.[342] The productivity and prosperity of the righteous person are related to the concept of being placed within the temple of Yhwh. As such, the ephemerality of the wicked person, described through the botanical metaphor of grass, is contrasted with that of the enduring nature of the righteous person. The ends of both figures are affirmed through the psalm through these metaphors.

The contrasts between the righteous and the wicked in Ps 92, with the exception of v. 11a, all relate to botanical metaphors.[343] In v. 8a the wicked people flourish (פרח) like grass, whereas in v. 13a it is the righteous person who flourishes (פרח) as a date palm.[344] The verb "flourish" (פרח) is also repeated in v. 14b in 3mp (*hiphil*), whereas it occurred in a 3ms form in v. 13a (*qal*). Nava Cohen reveals the significance of the botanical images and their function as they relate to the characterization of the wicked and righteous ends.[345] Cohen sees four "axes" of these metaphors—stature, power, quantitative, and temporal—upon which the wicked fall to the negative side and the righteous fall to the positive side.[346] The rich imagery then serves to heighten this contrast in more than one way.

The placement of the destruction of the wicked in light of the foolishness of other figures creates a sort of confirmation of the self-evidence of the eventual destruction of the wicked. In the context of the enemy language of the psalm, the wicked and righteous affirm that God is just in light of the threats against those who are righteous. In Ps 92, the צַדִּיק is best understood as the one who is generally properly behaved, and this is associated with religious activities in terms of their location of flourishing. Unlike in many other cases in this study, the צַדִּיק is never threatened by an enemy in Ps 92, only in context by the reality of their ostensible life (though see Pss 1 and 112). The focus is instead on teaching the desirability of being associated with Yhwh because of the rewards that come from being one of the צַדִּיק rooted in the presence of God.

PSALM 94

Text and Translation

אֵל־נְקָמוֹת יְהוָה	1a	Yhwh, God of vengeance,
אֵל נְקָמוֹת הוֹפִיעַ:	1b	God of vengeance, shine forth.
הִנָּשֵׂא שֹׁפֵט הָאָרֶץ	2a	Rise up, one who judges the earth,
הָשֵׁב גְּמוּל עַל־גֵּאִים:	2b	Give back what is owed to the proud.
עַד־מָתַי רְשָׁעִים יְהוָה	3a	How long will wicked people, Yhwh,
עַד־מָתַי רְשָׁעִים יַעֲלֹזוּ:	3b	How long will wicked people be proud?[347]
יַבִּיעוּ יְדַבְּרוּ עָתָק	4a	They spout, they speak arrogantly;
יִתְאַמְּרוּ כָּל־פֹּעֲלֵי אָוֶן:	4b	All doers of evil speak about themselves.[348]
עַמְּךָ יְהוָה יְדַכְּאוּ	5a	Your people, Yhwh, they crush,
וְנַחֲלָתְךָ יְעַנּוּ:	5b	And they afflict your inheritance.
אַלְמָנָה וְגֵר יַהֲרֹגוּ	6a	Widow and immigrant, they slay,
וִיתוֹמִים יְרַצֵּחוּ:	6b	And orphans, they murder;
וַיֹּאמְרוּ לֹא יִרְאֶה־יָּהּ	7a	They say,[349] "Yh does not see,
וְלֹא־יָבִין אֱלֹהֵי יַעֲקֹב:	7b	And the God of Jacob does not pay attention."

(Continued)

בִּינוּ בֹּעֲרִים בָּעָם	8a	Pay attention, those among the people who are foolish,
וּכְסִילִים מָתַי תַּשְׂכִּילוּ׃	8b	And fools, when will you be wise?
הֲנֹטַע אֹזֶן הֲלֹא יִשְׁמָע	9a	Will the one who planted the ear not hear?
אִם־יֹצֵר עַיִן הֲלֹא יַבִּיט׃	9b	Will the one who fashioned the eye not look?
הֲיֹסֵר גּוֹיִם הֲלֹא יוֹכִיחַ	10a	Will the one who disciplines nations not rebuke,[350]
הַמְלַמֵּד אָדָם דָּעַת׃	10b	The one who teaches humanity knowledge?
יְהוָה יֹדֵעַ מַחְשְׁבוֹת אָדָם	11a	Yhwh knows the thoughts of humanity,
כִּי־הֵמָּה הָבֶל׃	11b	That they are fleeting.
אַשְׁרֵי הַגֶּבֶר אֲשֶׁר־תְּיַסְּרֶנּוּ יָּהּ	12a	Fortunate[351] is the person whom you discipline, Yh,
וּמִתּוֹרָתְךָ תְלַמְּדֶנּוּ׃	12b	And whom you teach out of your instruction,
לְהַשְׁקִיט לוֹ מִימֵי רָע	13a	In order to give respite for them[352] from the days of evil,
עַד יִכָּרֶה לָרָשָׁע שָׁחַת׃	13b	Until a pit is dug for the wicked person.
כִּי לֹא־יִטֹּשׁ יְהוָה עַמּוֹ	14a	For Yhwh will not leave his people;
וְנַחֲלָתוֹ לֹא יַעֲזֹב׃	14b	And he will not forsake his inheritance,
כִּי־עַד־צֶדֶק יָשׁוּב מִשְׁפָּט	15a	Until righteousness[353] is returned in justice
וְאַחֲרָיו כָּל־יִשְׁרֵי־לֵב׃	15b	And the upright in heart pursue it.[354]
מִי־יָקוּם לִי עִם־מְרֵעִים	16a	Who will rise up for me against those who do harm?
מִי־יִתְיַצֵּב לִי עִם־פֹּעֲלֵי אָוֶן׃	16b	Who stands for me against the doers of evil?
לוּלֵי יְהוָה עֶזְרָתָה לִּי	17a	If[355] Yhwh were not my help,
כִּמְעַט שָׁכְנָה דוּמָה נַפְשִׁי׃	17b	My life would quickly have dwelled in silence;
אִם־אָמַרְתִּי מָטָה רַגְלִי	18a	If I said, "My foot slips,"
חַסְדְּךָ יְהוָה יִסְעָדֵנִי׃	18b	Your lovingkindness would hold me up.
בְּרֹב שַׂרְעַפַּי בְּקִרְבִּי	19a	When disquieting thoughts are abundant within me,
תַּנְחוּמֶיךָ יְשַׁעַשְׁעוּ נַפְשִׁי׃	19b	Your consolation will delight my soul.
הַיְחָבְרְךָ כִּסֵּא הַוּוֹת	20a	Can the throne of destruction join you?
יֹצֵר עָמָל עֲלֵי־חֹק׃	20b	One who crafts misfortune for me with a statute?
יָגוֹדּוּ עַל־נֶפֶשׁ צַדִּיק	21a	They band together against the life of the righteous person,
וְדָם נָקִי יַרְשִׁיעוּ׃	21b	And the blood of the innocent person they condemn,
וַיְהִי יְהוָה לִי לְמִשְׂגָּב	22a	But Yhwh has been my stronghold.
וֵאלֹהַי לְצוּר מַחְסִי׃	22b	And my God is the rock of my shelter.
וַיָּשֶׁב עֲלֵיהֶם אֶת־אוֹנָם	23a	He turned their iniquity against them,
וּבְרָעָתָם יַצְמִיתֵם	23b	And with their evil he will destroy them;
יַצְמִיתֵם יְהוָה אֱלֹהֵינוּ׃	23c	Yhwh our God will destroy them.

Interpretation

Psalm 94 includes situations of both conflict and resolution. Hossfeld highlights the constant shift in the psalm "between crisis and relief from crisis"
throughout the psalm.[356] Even with switching perspective and a nonlinear
timeline, there are several distinct scenes that emerge.

The first part of Ps 94 is a request for God to act, grounded in the description of the activities of the wicked people (vv. 1a–7b). The titles given to God provide the tone of the request: "God of vengeance" (אֵל נְקָמוֹת; v. 1a, 1b) and "one who judges the earth" (שֹׁפֵט הָאָרֶץ, v. 2a). This prayer requesting God to act characterizes the enemies of the speaker, describing their various attitudes and activities, focusing both on the arrogance (vv. 2b, 3b, 4a–4b, and the speech of v. 7a–7b) and their violence toward others (vv. 5a–6b). The antagonists are referred to as "the proud" (גֵּאִים, v. 2b), "wicked people" (רְשָׁעִים, v. 3a, 3b), and "doers of evil" (פֹּעֲלֵי אָוֶן; vv. 4b; also v. 16b). These figures do violence against "your people" (עַמְּךָ, v. 5a), "your inheritance" (נַחֲלָתְךָ, v. 5b), "widow" (אַלְמָנָה, v. 6a), "immigrant" (גֵר, v. 6a), "orphans" (יְתוֹמִים, v. 6b), and later, the "righteous person" (צַדִּיק, v. 21a) and the "innocent person" (נָקִי, v. 21b). They are quoted in v. 7a–7b, which is embedded in a speech to Yhwh by the speaker. This quotation focuses on their perspective of Yhwh. The repetition of the verb בִּין in vv. 7b and 8a creates a contrast between the words and the ostensible viewpoint of the wicked. The speaker implicitly criticizes the wicked who believe God does not "pay attention" by warning the fools to "pay attention" to the realities of God.

The next section shifts the direct address to these antagonists (vv. 8a–11b), called here "those among the people who are foolish" (בֹּעֲרִים בָּעָם, v. 8a) and "fools" (כְּסִילִים, v. 8b).[357] In this psalm the speech includes a description of past action that connects with the possible actions of Yhwh in the future, spoken through a series of rhetorical questions. Rather than didactic speech, this address serves to highlight God's justice against those who oppress others.[358] Through the imagery of the senses, the speaker makes an emphatic claim regarding Yhwh's perception of injustice.[359] The conclusion of this section contrasts the question regarding Yhwh as "one who teaches humanity knowledge" (v. 10b) with the affirmation that Yhwh knows humanity, in a way that highlights the ephemerality of human beings and establishes the right way to live.

This affirmation of knowledge underscores the macarism in v. 12a–12b, which focuses on the fortune that arrives through Yhwh's instruction of the eventual situation of justice (vv. 12a–15b).[360] Through the use of an infinitive construct in v. 13a, the instruction results in eventual "respite" for those whom Yhwh instructs.[361] Verse 13a–13b displays a specific event that will allow the "days of evil" to conclude: the destruction of the wicked (v. 13b). This section, then, affirms that Yhwh's actions will bring about the resolution of the conflict described earlier in the psalm. It does not bring the situation to its conclusion, but only affirms that the justice required to protect the community will be enacted in the future by Yhwh when he judges the antagonists.[362]

Verse 16a–16b raises rhetorical questions addressing "who" will act on behalf of the speaker against their attackers (v. 16a–16b). While these questions ask about future-oriented aid, the psalm shifts to focus on the event of

Yhwh's past and present action to help the speaker. Verses 17a–18b express a hypothetical situation regarding what would have happened if God had acted in the past. The speaker uses this rhetorical strategy to remind Yhwh that in the past his faithfulness has established the present reality and states that the speaker will be comforted by Yhwh when fears arise again (v. 19a–19b). Thus, Yhwh's present activity serves as a comfort for the speaker.

A second set of rhetorical questions are offered in v. 20a–20b, shifting the focus back to the antagonists in the psalm. Here the specific identity of those the antagonists attack is the righteous person, which is paralleled with the "innocent" (v. 21a–21b). The conflict in the psalm returns briefly before shifting back to Yhwh's benevolent activity toward the speaker (vv. 22a–23b). Blending two themes that appear elsewhere in the psalms,[363] Yhwh uses the antagonist's own "evil" as the tool of his active judgment in the concluding verse (v. 23a–23c). Yhwh, called "God of vengeance" in v. 1a–1b, fulfills this title in the final verses of the psalm, which promises that Yhwh will destroy the wicked, who are designated only by 3mp pronouns in v. 23a–23c.

The psalm is centered predominantly on the conflict the speaker is in and on the Yhwh's protection of the community. The progression of the psalm never moves beyond the present situation in the narrated time, but it does speak of both the past and future actions of Yhwh, contending that Yhwh will once again act in line with his character and previous actions. In terms of mediation, the psalm is both prayer and instruction.[364] It is presented as speech both for and about Yhwh in light of distress.

Function of צַדִּיק and רָשָׁע

The term רָשָׁע appears three times in Ps 94 (vv. 3a [pl], 3b [pl], 13b) and צַדִּיק once (v. 21a). The first two mentions of the רְשָׁעִים are those who speak arrogantly (vv. 3a–4b), and as the psalm progresses, those who attack Yhwh's people and the innocent (vv. 5a–7b). Their arrogance allows them to perpetuate violence without believing in consequences. However, the consequence in the psalm is made clear through the destruction of the wicked. Verse 13b affirms that the רָשָׁע will eventually be destroyed, using the language of a "pit" (שַׁחַת) to describe their end. It functions to emphasize that while the wicked will be destroyed, the discipline and teaching of Yhwh will sustain the faithful person until (עַד) that end is reached (vv. 12a–13b).

The antagonists in the latter part of the psalm are explicitly those that attack the righteous person (v. 21a). Because of this, and the clear parallel with נָקִי in v. 21b, the semantic function of צַדִּיק here is as one who is unjustly wronged or innocent in the matter. In this case, it is the arrogant or illegitimate speech and the violence of the wicked against which they are innocent.

At the broader level, it is the whole community of faithful people of Yhwh who are innocently righteous as recipients of attacks (vv. 4a–6b). By association, the speaker can be included among the righteous in that both speaker and righteous need a defense against their opponents (v. 16a–16b). The speaker, thus, speaks on behalf of the community and the righteous who are attacked by the wicked.

The specific identity of the accusers is not clear; they could be antagonists internal or external to the community.[365] Neumann sees the division between the righteous and the wicked to reflect a division within Israel that surrounds piety.[366] However, it is not clear from the psalm's context that this would be the case. In the psalm, the function of the righteous and the wicked serve to highlight the injustice of the situation of those who are righteous being attacked and the future reality that those who are unfairly persecuted will receive justice through Yhwh's actions, as the speaker has experienced in the past. The articulation that Yhwh will enact justice for the righteous and against the wicked makes clear for the community that they can trust Yhwh as their safe place (v. 22a–22b). The final affirmation is that God repurposes the evil of the wicked as the tool of their judgment (v. 23a–23c).

PSALM 97

Text and Translation

יְהוָה מָלָךְ	1a	Yhwh reigns.
תָּגֵל הָאָרֶץ	1b	The earth cheers,
יִשְׂמְחוּ אִיִּים רַבִּים׃	1c	The many coastlines[367] rejoice.
עָנָן וַעֲרָפֶל סְבִיבָיו	2a	Cloud and fog are surrounding him,
צֶדֶק וּמִשְׁפָּט מְכוֹן כִּסְאוֹ׃	2b	Righteousness and justice are the foundation of his throne.
אֵשׁ לְפָנָיו תֵּלֵךְ	3a	Fire goes before him
וּתְלַהֵט סָבִיב צָרָיו׃	3b	And burns all around[368] his adversaries.
הֵאִירוּ בְרָקָיו תֵּבֵל	4a	His lightning illuminates the world;
רָאֲתָה וַתָּחֵל הָאָרֶץ׃	4b	The earth sees and writhes.
הָרִים כַּדּוֹנַג נָמַסּוּ מִלִּפְנֵי יְהוָה	5a	The mountains melt like wax from Yhwh's presence;
מִלִּפְנֵי אֲדוֹן כָּל־הָאָרֶץ׃	5b	By the presence of the Lord, the entire earth.
הִגִּידוּ הַשָּׁמַיִם צִדְקוֹ	6a	The heavens announce his righteousness,
וְרָאוּ כָל־הָעַמִּים כְּבוֹדוֹ׃	6b	And all the peoples see his glory.

(Continued)

יֵבֹ֣שׁוּ כָּל־עֹ֣בְדֵי פֶ֭סֶל	7a	All those who serve images will be ashamed,
הַמִּֽתְהַלְלִ֣ים בָּאֱלִילִ֑ים	7b	Those who boast in worthless idols.
הִשְׁתַּחֲווּ־ל֝וֹ כָּל־אֱלֹהִֽים׃	7c	All gods bow down[369] to him.
שָׁמְעָ֤ה וַתִּשְׂמַ֨ח ׀ צִיּ֗וֹן	8a	Zion hears and rejoices,
וַתָּגֵ֗לְנָה בְּנ֣וֹת יְהוּדָ֑ה	8b	And the daughters of Judah celebrate,
לְמַ֖עַן מִשְׁפָּטֶ֣יךָ יְהוָֽה׃	8c	Because of your judgments, Yhwh.
כִּֽי־אַתָּ֤ה יְהוָ֗ה עֶלְי֥וֹן עַל־כָּל־הָאָ֑רֶץ	9a	For you, Yhwh most high, are over all the earth;
מְאֹ֥ד נַ֝עֲלֵ֗יתָ עַל־כָּל־אֱלֹהִֽים׃	9b	You are greatly exalted above all gods.
אֹהֲבֵ֣י יְ֭הוָה שִׂנְא֫וּ רָ֥ע	10a	Those who love Yhwh, hate evil.
שֹׁ֭מֵר נַפְשׁ֣וֹת חֲסִידָ֑יו	10b	He protects the life of his faithful ones;
מִיַּ֥ד רְ֝שָׁעִ֗ים יַצִּילֵֽם׃	10c	From the hand of wicked people, he delivers them.
א֖וֹר זָרֻ֣עַ לַצַּדִּ֑יק	11a	Light is sown[370] for the righteous person,
וּֽלְיִשְׁרֵי־לֵ֥ב שִׂמְחָֽה׃	11b	And joy for the upright in heart.
שִׂמְח֣וּ צַ֭דִּיקִים בַּֽיהוָ֑ה	12a	Rejoice in Yhwh, righteous people,
וְ֝הוֹד֗וּ לְזֵ֣כֶר קָדְשֽׁוֹ׃	12b	And give thanks for the memory of his holiness.

Interpretation

The psalm focuses on the reign of Yhwh, and takes place in a three-part structure: (1) the theophany in vv. 1a–6b; (2) responses to the theophany in vv. 7a–9b; and (3) the effect of Yhwh's rule in the present in vv. 9a–12b.[371] The primary event described is itself the theophany,[372] the reign of Yhwh or the situation where Yhwh is enthroned, but with no introduction. As E. N. Ortlund states, "it looks … as if Yahweh appears out of nowhere."[373] While the meaning of the initial event depends partly on the understanding of the verb מלך as "reigns," or as Mowinckel famously argued, "has become king,"[374] the description of the event surrounding the reality of Yhwh's reign (new or established) is highly evocative. For the most part, the participants in this section of the poem are nonhuman, typically inanimate, subjects: "the earth" (הָאָרֶץ, vv. 1b, 4b, 5b), "coastlines" (אִיִּים, v. 1c), and "heavens" (הַשָּׁמַיִם, v. 6a), and yet they all participate in the worship of Yhwh.[375] The human subjects are Yhwh's adversaries in v. 3b, though it is not clear if human or nonhuman enemies are intended here. In any case, it is God who defeats the enemies without any reference to human agents.[376] In the final line of the first movement of the poem, v. 6b, all peoples are mentioned as witnesses to the glory of Yhwh, that is, to Yhwh's defeat of his enemies.[377]

The psalm shifts in v. 7a to the future-oriented and hoped-for salvation. It begins with a pronouncement of judgment on "those who serve images" (עֹבְדֵי פֶסֶל, v. 7a) and "those who boast in worthless idols" (הַמִּתְהַלְלִים בָּאֱלִילִים, v. 7b). Later, the psalm mentions that the "gods" will bow to Yhwh (v. 7c; cf. these figures' reappearance in v. 9b).[378] These verses describe the results of what happens to those who oppose Yhwh. In v. 8a, the positive affirmation of being witness to the revelation of Yhwh's glory is that Zion and the "daughters of Judah" celebrate Yhwh's מִשְׁפָּט. Yhwh is directly praised in vv. 8c–9b. This leads into a command to the community of God, and renewed affirmation of Yhwh's concern for the protection and deliverance of his people. The community of the faithful people are designated as "those who love Yhwh" (אֹהֲבֵי יְהוָה, v. 10a), "his faithful ones" (חֲסִידָיו, v. 10b), "righteous person" (צַדִּיק, v. 11a), and "righteous people" (צַדִּיקִים, v. 12a). In v. 11a–11b, the outcome of Yhwh's action is noted for its benefit of the righteous people. The "light" (אוֹר) in v. 11a evokes the illumination of fire in vv. 3a–4b, and the command to rejoice in v. 12a repeats the verb (שׂמח) from vv. 1c and 8a. With these connections, both the reign of Yhwh and his concern for his people are the grounds for praise in v. 11a–11b. The final two lines are a call to worship grounded directly in the work of Yhwh on behalf of the righteous.

In summary, the psalm describes a single event: the theophany of Yhwh. It is presented in three different movements: first, the description of the actual event and the corresponding response from the inanimate and animate figures; second, the response of this theophany for Yhwh's antagonists and for the community; and finally, the human response in light of this reality.

Function of צַדִּיק and רָשָׁע

The single mention of the רְשָׁעִים in Ps 97 is in the phrase "hand of the wicked people" (v. 10c) from which Yhwh rescues his faithful people (חֲסִידָיו) in v. 10b–10c. This clearly shows the wicked as the enemies of Yhwh's people, the function of which is to highlight not behavior but the status as enemies of the righteous person. The righteous person is the recipient of Yhwh's care in v. 11a. Because of the content and flow of the psalm, it is parallel to "his faithful ones" (חֲסִידָיו, v. 10b) and to "the upright in heart" (יִשְׁרֵי-לֵב, v. 11b) here functioning as near synonyms. These are members of the worshiping community who receive Yhwh's protection against the wicked. As an antithesis to v. 10c, the light of salvation shone from Yhwh is in content related to the deliverance from the wicked as an enactment of Yhwh's justice.[379] In the final line, the worshiping community are addressed as צַדִּיקִים with two lines of 2mp imperatives to worship Yhwh. The direct attribution of the identity of the צַדִּיקִים to the community here is significant, and functions to affirm the protection the community will receive from Yhwh as well as an encouragement to the community to participate in the praise of Yhwh (see also Ps 34:23).

Semantically, the use of צַדִּיק in Ps 97 can relate to either innocence in a matter or to the general attribute of being morally upright. More accurately, the righteous here are representative of those who praise because God has protected them. As the conclusion, they function to highlight that those who are צַדִּיק will be saved (v. 11a), and that the proper response is to worship

(v. 12a). Ultimately, the faithful people are regarded as the primary beneficiaries of Yhwh's reign over the whole world, one that can move mountains and cause even inanimate objects to give voice to the praise of Yhwh.

PSALM 112

Text and Translation

הַלְלוּ יָהּ	1a	Hallelujah![380]
אַשְׁרֵי־אִישׁ יָרֵא אֶת־יְהֹוָה	1b	Fortunate is the person who fears Yhwh,
בְּמִצְוֹתָיו חָפֵץ מְאֹד:	1c	Who delights greatly in his commandments.
גִּבּוֹר בָּאָרֶץ יִהְיֶה זַרְעוֹ	2a	Their[381] offspring will be mighty in the land.
דּוֹר יְשָׁרִים יְבֹרָךְ:	2b	The generation of the upright people will be blessed.
הוֹן־וָעֹשֶׁר בְּבֵיתוֹ	3a	Goods and riches will be in their house,
וְצִדְקָתוֹ עֹמֶדֶת לָעַד:	3b	And their righteousness stands perpetually.
זָרַח בַּחֹשֶׁךְ אוֹר לַיְשָׁרִים	4a	Light emerges in the darkness for the upright people,
חַנּוּן וְרַחוּם וְצַדִּיק:	4b	The gracious, compassionate, and righteous.
טוֹב־אִישׁ חוֹנֵן וּמַלְוֶה	5a	It is good for a person who is gracious and lends;
יְכַלְכֵּל דְּבָרָיו בְּמִשְׁפָּט:	5b	They will maintain just speech.
כִּי־לְעוֹלָם לֹא־יִמּוֹט	6a	For[382] they will not ever be moved,
לְזֵכֶר עוֹלָם יִהְיֶה צַדִּיק:	6b	The righteous person will ever be remembered.
מִשְּׁמוּעָה רָעָה לֹא יִירָא	7a	From calamitous news, they will not be afraid,
נָכוֹן לִבּוֹ בָּטֻחַ בַּיהֹוָה:	7b	Their heart is filled with trust in Yhwh.
סָמוּךְ לִבּוֹ לֹא יִירָא	8a	Their heart is upheld, they will not be afraid,
עַד אֲשֶׁר־יִרְאֶה בְצָרָיו:	8b	Even[383] when they look upon their adversaries.
פִּזַּר נָתַן לָאֶבְיוֹנִים	9a	They distribute widely, they give to the poor,
צִדְקָתוֹ עֹמֶדֶת לָעַד	9b	Their righteousness stands perpetually,
קַרְנוֹ תָּרוּם בְּכָבוֹד:	9c	Their horn will be high in glory.
רָשָׁע יִרְאֶה וְכָעָס	10a	A wicked person will see and become angry;
שִׁנָּיו יַחֲרֹק וְנָמָס	10b	They will grind their teeth and fade away.
תַּאֲוַת רְשָׁעִים תֹּאבֵד:	10c	The desires of the wicked people will perish.

Interpretation

The entirety of Ps 112 appears as a third-person portraiture of a commendable person, including both their character attributes and the description of the reality that they live because of their identity. It begins, following the title, with הַלְלוּ יָהּ, serving as an introduction to the poem. The psalm predominantly focuses on the identity and description of the person first designated as "the person who fears Yhwh" (אִישׁ יָרֵא אֶת־יְהֹוָה, v. 1b) who are the antecedent of the verbs and 3ms throughout the psalm except for v. 10a–10c. Yhwh is only mentioned twice in the poem (vv. 1b, 7b) by name and once with a 3ms pronoun suffix (v. 1b), all as objects of the righteous person's attention. The righteous are also referred to as "upright people" (יְשָׁרִים, v. 4a), and "righteous person" (צַדִּיק, v. 6b). The poem is presented through an alphabetic acrostic.

The psalm begins with the beatitude "fortunate" (אַשְׁרֵי, v. 1b), commending the fear of Yhwh. It proceeds to describe the rich rewards and general attributes of this figure. The first two verses (vv. 1a–2b) can be seen as a general description of their blessing, bookended by the two semantically similar terms אַשְׁרֵי and יְבֹרָךְ.[384] The verses that follow elaborate on this with more concrete examples. While the characters in the psalm are active, there is little conflict in the broader situation of the description of the commendable person. Only general situations of blessing are described, such as the state of the community who are impacted by this person's behavior. The attributes include concrete descriptions of their character and behavior (vv. 1b–1c, 4b, 5a–5b, 7b, 9a) as well as the realities of being that person for themselves (vv. 2a, 3a–3b, 4a, 6a–8b, 9b–9c) and for others (vv. 2a–2b, 5a, 9a).[385] Their beneficiaries include "their offspring" (זַרְעוֹ, v. 2a), "the generation of the upright people" (דּוֹר יְשָׁרִים, v. 2b), and "the poor" (אֶבְיוֹנִים, v. 9a).[386] Schaefer has noted that the attitudes or conduct alternate, which functions to show how the way one lives life is directly related to rewards that follow.[387] Many of these are overlapping in both blessing and activity, such as the theme of generosity mentioned twice in the psalm (vv. 5a, 9a). The ultimate result of their character is their triumph over against their enemies (v. 9c).[388]

Their positive activities described throughout are contrasted with those of the wicked in the conclusion of the psalm (v. 10a–10c), where the wicked person is said to have been witness to what the fortunate person has done. The antagonists are designated both as "wicked person" (רָשָׁע, v. 10a) and "wicked people" (רְשָׁעִים, v. 10c). In this section, the figure is also contrasted with the wicked: the righteous person "will see" (יִרְאֶה) the downfall of "their adversaries" (צָרָיו) in v. 8b, while the wicked person "will see" the prosperity of the righteous person in v. 10a.[389] What stirs the anger of the wicked could either be all that the righteous person does, their apparent blessings, or simply that they are elevated. The imagery of gnashing teeth appears elsewhere in the psalms to describe fury against a person.[390]

The psalm itself is not complex, and thus, there is little to elaborate on in terms of its meaning and function. It presents an ideal through description of how the hearers may live.[391] The description of the fortunate person takes up a majority of the psalm, with a short conclusion relating to the wicked figure at the end, by which all of the features of the fortunate person are contrasted.

Function of צַדִּיק and רָשָׁע

The entirety of Ps 112 is a description of a faithful person, though the term צַדִּיק is used as a referent to this person only in v. 6b. In this case, the meaning of the term clearly relates to one who displays proper behavior in general. The entire psalm, then, functions as a description of a person who would also be considered צַדִּיק, even though the term is mentioned only in a single line. In terms of its function, it only supports the broader thesis of the psalm regarding the fear of Yhwh and the general behaviors that are recommended. Even in this psalm where the positive features of the righteous are highlighted, the result for the רָשָׁע at the end is that their "desires" pass away. The function of this conclusion is to offer the counterpoint to the fortunate person, as their opposite. They witness the blessing, are jealous, and ultimately, are doomed to perish. As the conclusion, it highlights the futility of the wicked way against the blessing of the righteous person.

PSALM 140

Text and Translation

לַמְנַצֵּחַ מִזְמוֹר לְדָוִד׃	1a	(To the director. A psalm. Davidic)
חַלְּצֵנִי יְהוָה מֵאָדָם רָע	2a	Rescue me, Yhwh, from an evil person;
מֵאִישׁ חֲמָסִים תִּנְצְרֵנִי׃	2b	From a violent person, protect me.
אֲשֶׁר חָשְׁבוּ רָעוֹת בְּלֵב	3a	Those who devise evil in their minds,
כָּל־יוֹם יָגוּרוּ מִלְחָמוֹת׃	3b	Every day[392] they threaten war.
שָׁנֲנוּ לְשׁוֹנָם כְּמוֹ־נָחָשׁ	4a	They sharpen their tongues like a snake,
חֲמַת עַכְשׁוּב תַּחַת שְׂפָתֵימוֹ סֶלָה׃	4b	The poison of vipers is behind their lips. (*selah*)[393]
שָׁמְרֵנִי יְהוָה מִידֵי רָשָׁע	5a	Protect me, Yhwh, from the hands of a wicked person;
מֵאִישׁ חֲמָסִים תִּנְצְרֵנִי	5b	From a person of violence, you will preserve me,
אֲשֶׁר חָשְׁבוּ לִדְחוֹת פְּעָמָי׃	5c	Those who plan to knock me off balance.[394]
טָמְנוּ־גֵאִים פַּח לִי	6a	The proud hid a trap for me,
וַחֲבָלִים פָּרְשׂוּ רֶשֶׁת לְיַד־מַעְגָּל	6b	They spread ropes, a net on the side of the road,
מֹקְשִׁים שָׁתוּ־לִי סֶלָה׃	6c	Snares they have set for me. (*selah*)
אָמַרְתִּי לַיהוָה אֵלִי אָתָּה	7a	I say[395] to Yhwh "You are my God."
הַאֲזִינָה יְהוָה קוֹל תַּחֲנוּנָי׃	7b	Yhwh, listen to the sound of my request.
יְהוִה אֲדֹנָי עֹז יְשׁוּעָתִי	8a	Yhwh, my Lord, strength of my salvation,
סַכֹּתָה לְרֹאשִׁי בְּיוֹם נָשֶׁק׃	8b	You protected my head on the day of fighting.
אַל־תִּתֵּן יְהוָה מַאֲוַיֵּי רָשָׁע	9a	Do not grant, Yhwh, the desires of the wicked person;
זְמָמוֹ אַל־תָּפֵק יָרוּמוּ סֶלָה׃	9b	Do not accommodate their[396] plan, or they will be proud. (*selah*)

(Continued)

רֹאשׁ מְסִבָּי	10a	The heads[397] of those surrounding me,
עֲמַל שְׂפָתֵימוֹ יְכַסּוּמוֹ׃	10b	Let the misfortune of their lips cover them.[398]
יִמּוֹטוּ עֲלֵיהֶם גֶּחָלִים	11a	May burning coals fall[399] on them,
בָּאֵשׁ יַפִּלֵם	11b	May he cast them into the fire,
בְּמַהֲמֹרוֹת בַּל־יָקוּמוּ׃	11c	May they not be able to escape deep pits.
אִישׁ לָשׁוֹן בַּל־יִכּוֹן בָּאָרֶץ	12a	May a chattering person not last in the land,
אִישׁ־חָמָס רָע יְצוּדֶנּוּ לְמַדְחֵפֹת׃	12b	A person of violence, may calamity hunt him into a cage.[400]
יָדַעְתִּ כִּי־יַעֲשֶׂה יְהוָה דִּין עָנִי	13a	I know[401] that Yhwh makes rulings for the poor,
מִשְׁפַּט אֶבְיֹנִים׃	13b	Judgments for the needy.
אַךְ צַדִּיקִים יוֹדוּ לִשְׁמֶךָ	14a	Surely righteous people will laud your name;
יֵשְׁבוּ יְשָׁרִים אֶת־פָּנֶיךָ׃	14b	Upright people will dwell in your presence.

Interpretation

The primary situation described in the poem is that of the distress of the speaker that is caused directly by the antagonists in the psalm.[402] The psalm is mediated as a prayer, spoken in the first person, with many requests to Yhwh.[403] The content of the psalm focuses on the description of the attacks of the wicked. The antagonists in Ps 140 are designated by "relatively common expressions in a rich vocabulary of hostility."[404] They receive the designations "evil person" (אָדָם רָע, v. 2a) "violent person" (אִישׁ חֲמָסִים, vv. 2b, 5b, 12b [sgl]), "wicked person" (רָשָׁע, vv. 5a, 9a), "the proud" (גֵּאִים, v. 6a) "those surrounding me" (מְסִבָּי, v. 10a), and "chattering person" (אִישׁ לָשׁוֹן, v. 12a).

The psalm begins with a clear complaint about the activities of the speaker's enemies and multiple requests to Yhwh to "rescue" (v. 2a), "protect" (vv. 2b, 5a), and "preserve" (v. 5b) the speaker.[405] These are contrasted with descriptions of the activities of these wicked, which relate to planning evil (vv. 3a–4b, 5c–6c). The attack of the wicked against the speaker is described using various images. Hauge points out that there are three distinct motifs related to the enemies in Ps 140: war, hunting, and speech.[406] The violent activity in v. 4a–4b blends the components of speech (tongue and lips) with the language of violence. Speech organs are referenced elsewhere in the psalm: lips appear again in v. 10b: "let the misfortune of their lips cover them" and a reference to the tongue appears (לָשׁוֹן, v. 12a, translated above in the construct "chattering person"). The use of the snake allusion in v. 4a–4b relates to other uses of the concept of snake venom, which connect the wicked person to the concept of foolish behavior based on the analogy of the illegitimate speech of the wicked or the fool in Proverbs.[407]

The speaker continues to make requests to Yhwh throughout the psalm, yet in v. 7a the emphasis, through the self-quotation introduced by "I say" (אָמַרְתִּי), is on the speaker's commitment to Yhwh. The speaker then reminds Yhwh to listen and offers statements regarding their connection with Yhwh and Yhwh's past action on their behalf (v. 7b–8b). What follows is a long list of requests for Yhwh to judge the wicked, first directly through imperatives (v. 9a–9b) then indirectly through jussive forms (vv. 10a–12b). These requests specifically address the judgment which the speaker wishes for the wicked. While there are no actions explicitly ascribed to Yhwh in the psalm, the mediation of the psalm as a prayer suggests that these judgments are to be expected to be actions coming from Yhwh.

Two verses of affirmations conclude the psalm. First, in v. 13a–13b, the speaker declares their confidence in Yhwh to enact justice for the poor and needy. The needy in this psalm need not refer to the righteous, though there is a connection between the two. Rather than a precise identification of the two groups, the connection is in how God relates to both groups. The psalm provides an assurance that Yhwh will act on behalf of those in need, and that the righteous will participate in the praise of Yhwh. In this case, the "needy" (עָנִי, v. 13a) and the "poor" (אֶבְיֹנִים, v. 13b) become those who are enabled to praise as the "righteous people" (צַדִּיקִים, v. 14a) and the "upright people" (יְשָׁרִים, v. 14b). The parallel between the two bicola and is further clarified by the conventions of praise following salvation. Those who were in need later worship Yhwh and are in his presence. The use of the righteous at the end does not automatically suggest that the speaker sees him or herself as one of the righteous. The association is closely related, but the use of the word itself in the third person (as is always the case) is suggestive of the overall use of this figure in the psalms. It is an intentional rhetorical strategy that implicitly connects the speaker with the righteous, along with the clear reference to the wicked attacking the speaker, in association with the righteous without actually saying as much. The actions ascribed to the righteous are future-oriented, giving the possibility of praising as resulting from the possibility of God's future-oriented activity. That is, this psalm sets up nicely the paradigm that God's actions *enable* the righteous to worship; it is not only grounds of praise but also essential to the very nature of praise.

Function of צַדִּיק and רָשָׁע

The contrast between the righteous and the wicked is one of the main features in Ps 140. Within the context of the psalm as a cry for help,[408] the righteous and the wicked underscores the eventual salvation of the righteous. At the same time, the only occurrence of the צַדִּיקִים explicitly takes place at the end, in summary form. Here, they function as the worshiping community (cf. Pss 32:11; 68:4, 97:12; 140:14; 142:8). The wicked are the primary topic of the psalm, focusing largely on the violent nature of their character and activities. This emotive description functions within the appeal to Yhwh to act. The description of the wicked people includes many elements common elsewhere: the intensity of violence, the mention of speech organs and illegitimate speech, hunting imagery. This conventional language is compounded to include many of these common elements in quick succession, heightening the intensity of the speaker's need. The declaration at the end of the psalm is twofold: first, v. 13a–13b affirms Yhwh's beneficent action on behalf of those who need help, in this case, through the work of judging on their behalf; second, the future reality that results from Yhwh's decisive action is declared: the righteous people will praise Yhwh and the upright people are able to dwell in the presence of God. The outcome of Yhwh's salvation, then, is the praise of the people. Thus, the identity of "poor" and "needy" are not always such, as they are transformed into the righteous and the upright people through their praise enabled by God's judgment on their behalf. In the overall progression of the psalm, the speaker's expression of need is resolved in the praise of the righteous, and as such, it appears that the speaker claims association within this group, if only in the future.[409]

Here, there is a sort of blending of the two uses of צַדִּיקִים. They are those who innocently suffer harm,[410] but they are also those who are identified as the worshiping community. The function of the righteous, then, affirms the future blessing of these figures and the ability to praise, following the clear destruction of the wicked for the wrong they have done. Salvation for the innocent is inherent to the meaning of these words, and the result is that those who are rescued will praise. Paralleled with the עָנִי and אֶבְיֹנִים, the צַדִּיקִים in Ps 140 should be understood as those in need, and thus, the salvation of Yhwh enables their praise. The function here also defines worship as what is right.[411]

PSALM 141

Text and Translation

מִזְמוֹר לְדָוִד	1a	(A psalm. Davidic.)
יְהוָה קְרָאתִיךָ חוּשָׁה לִּי	1b	Yhwh, I call to you, come quickly to me;
הַאֲזִינָה קוֹלִי בְּקָרְאִי־לָךְ:	1c	Listen to my voice when I call to you.
תִּכּוֹן תְּפִלָּתִי קְטֹרֶת לְפָנֶיךָ	2a	My prayer is permanently in your presence like incense,[412]
מַשְׂאַת כַּפַּי מִנְחַת־עָרֶב:	2b	A gift[413] from my hand, an evening offering.
שִׁיתָה יְהוָה שָׁמְרָה לְפִי	3a	Set a guard, Yhwh, over my mouth,
נִצְּרָה עַל־דַּל שְׂפָתָי:	3b	Keep watch over the door to my lips.
אַל־תַּט־לִבִּי לְדָבָר רָע	4a	Do not give my heart over to an evil thing
לְהִתְעוֹלֵל עֲלִלוֹת בְּרֶשַׁע	4b	To take part[414] in wicked deeds
אֶת־אִישִׁים פֹּעֲלֵי־אָוֶן	4c	With men who are evildoers,
וּבַל־אֶלְחַם בְּמַנְעַמֵּיהֶם:	4d	That I would not eat of their delicacies.

(*Continued*)

יְהֶלְמֵנִי־צַדִּיק חֶסֶד וְיוֹכִיחֵנִי	5a	May a righteous person strike me[415] with kindness and rebuke me.
שֶׁמֶן רֹאשׁ אַל־יָנִי רֹאשִׁי	5b	Do not let my head[416] be deprived of oil;[417]
כִּי־עוֹד וּתְפִלָּתִי בְּרָעוֹתֵיהֶם:	5c	Indeed[418] then[419] my prayer will still be against their, evil deeds.
נִשְׁמְטוּ בִידֵי־סֶלַע שֹׁפְטֵיהֶם	6a	Their judges are thrown down from the cliffs
וְשָׁמְעוּ אֲמָרַי כִּי נָעֵמוּ:	6b	And they hear my words, for they are lovely.
כְּמוֹ פֹלֵחַ וּבֹקֵעַ בָּאָרֶץ	7a	As with the plowing and breaking up of the earth,
נִפְזְרוּ עֲצָמֵינוּ לְפִי שְׁאוֹל:	7b	Our bones will be scattered at the entrance to Sheol.
כִּי אֵלֶיךָ יְהוִה אֲדֹנָי עֵינָי	8a	But my eyes are toward you, Lord Yhwh,
בְּכָה חָסִיתִי אַל־תְּעַר נַפְשִׁי:	8b	I take refuge in you; do not leave my life unprotected.
שָׁמְרֵנִי מִידֵי פַח יָקְשׁוּ לִי	9a	Keep me from the jaws[420] of the trap they have laid for me
וּמֹקְשׁוֹת פֹּעֲלֵי אָוֶן:	9b	And from the snares of the evildoers.
יִפְּלוּ בְמַכְמֹרָיו רְשָׁעִים	10a	May the wicked people fall into their[421] traps
יַחַד אָנֹכִי עַד־אֶעֱבוֹר:	10b	Though I am unscathed[422] while I pass by.

Interpretation

Psalm 141 is voiced entirely in the first person and directly addressed to Yhwh as a prayer. The psalm is characteristically vague, including a combination of several images for distress. The speaker describes their actions of prayer in vv. 1a–2b. The speaker uses the image of the prayer acting as incense before God (v. 2a–2b). The use of the terminology relating to continuity of the prayer may be an allusion to the continual burning of incense in the temple (Exod 30:8). According to some scholars, the burning of incense indicates that the one praying lives far away from Jerusalem, thus limiting the access to the temple.[423] However, if the incense alluded to here refers to the continual incense, the image is one of nearness to Yhwh, as the incense was burned at the altar, not the temple in general.[424] It describes not the geography but the nature of the prayer; it is always present before Yhwh.

The psalm is set in the context of needing the speaker needing aid from Yhwh (v. 1b–1c). However, this takes an interesting turn in vv. 3a–4d, where words typically used of protection from enemies are employed specifically to protect the speaker from partaking in wicked speech. In v. 3b it is not the threat of the illegitimate speech of the wicked that the speaker requests help, but rather, the potential threat of the speaker's own improper speech. As with a majority of specific situations proposed for the poem, there is little in the poem to suggest this much. Only v. 3 includes mention of speech, and v. 4 mentions wicked deeds and even eating with evildoers (פֹּעֲלֵי אָוֶן; v. 4c; also v. 9b) as problematic.

Verse 5a ascribes an action to the "righteous person" (צַדִּיק, v. 5a) which at first sounds to more likely to be of the wicked. The speaker speaks in a modal request for the righteous person to "strike" (הלם) the speaker,[425] yet the weapon is creatively interpreted as a "kindness" (חֶסֶד). Holt believes that this makes the righteous a group of peers,[426] though this is only by implication not direct association. In the context of the potential situation of the speaker participating in the activities of the wicked, the rebuke of the righteous is a welcome reward.

Verse 6a–6b includes a vivid picture of the end of "their judges," with the 3mp antecedent presumably in reference to the wicked or evildoers. As such, they are part of a group of antagonists but not coreferential to the wicked or evildoers.[427] This short picture imagines these figures being flung from the sides of a rock. Verse 7a–7b creates an image of plowing and relates it to death. It seems that here the focus is on the fleetingness of human life, though this is not clear. The use of the 1cp pronominal suffix in v. 7b may suggest that the community is in view in addition to the speaker, thus declaring not simply the fleetingness of the wicked (whose judgment is likely to be understood alongside that of their leaders), but of all humanity. The identity of this collective remains unclear.

The result in the context of the psalm suggests the possibility of Yhwh's intervention, but at the closing, only safe return is mentioned (v. 8a–8b). The psalm may imply that safety is due to Yhwh's answer, or the hoped-for result of the prayer of the speaker, but Yhwh's actions are not directly mentioned at the end of the psalm. The psalm concludes with a request for Yhwh to protect the speaker from the traps set up by the "evildoers" (פֹּעֲלֵי אָוֶן, v. 9b) and "wicked people" (רְשָׁעִים, v. 10a). In the context of the psalm, the trap may be interpreted as the attempt for the wicked to coerce the speaker to participate in wicked activities. In the end, it is the request for poetic justice, that the traps serve only to hurt those who laid them while the speaker walks by without harm (vv. 9a–10b).

The psalm is a spoken prayer. It is vaguely defined distress, but it also includes the possibility of error on the part of the speaker. At the same time, the whole context suggests the need of the speaker for Yhwh's aid to both protect and save.

Function of צַדִּיק and רָשָׁע

The function of the righteous and the wicked in Ps 141 is marked by a creative reuse of these figures. In the first place, it is the speaker who is at risk of taking part in wickedness. This is thwarted only by the righteous person committing violence against the speaker in striking them. As such, in this instance, the צַדִּיק is part of the community. The righteous person knows the appropriate action to take in rebuking the speaker. The righteous person interacts directly with the speaker in an imagined hypothetical future situation.

The threat of those antagonists for the speaker is that they will influence the speaker to participate in improper activities. The common activities of the wicked that relate to speech and the activities of the righteous that relate to praise clarify the conflict here. Speech commonly defines the group with whom one is associated. The wicked show up in the end of the psalm, and are the focus of vv. 9a–10b. The "evildoers" (פֹּעֲלֵי אָוֶן) are paralleled with the wicked here, and because of the similarity of activities are to be understood as the same figures. The speaker here request for the wicked to receive poetic justice for their attempts to entrap the speaker. The speaker is safe in contrast to the wicked, who meet their end. Yhwh is not the direct actor mentioned for either the end of safety for the speaker or that of the destruction for the wicked. The literary pattern of the destruction of the wicked is clear here, though it does not fit the situation of the צַדִּיק earlier.

The righteous and the wicked, then, in Ps 141 stand in a creative role reversal whereby the possibility of being associated with the wicked becomes stronger than many psalms assume. The "strike" the speaker hopes the righteous offers in loving kindness provides the necessary reproof for the speaker to avoid being associated with the wicked. In the concluding verses, then, the speaker can request for the wicked to be destroyed in order that the speaker might remain out of the reach of the violence against them.

PSALM 146

Text and Translation

הַלְלוּ־יָהּ	1a	Hallelujah!
הַלְלִי נַפְשִׁי אֶת־יְהוָה:	1b	Self,[428] praise Yhwh.
אֲהַלְלָה יְהוָה בְּחַיָּי	2a	I will praise Yhwh throughout my life;
אֲזַמְּרָה לֵאלֹהַי בְּעוֹדִי:	2b	I will sing to my God for the duration of my lifetime.
אַל־תִּבְטְחוּ בִנְדִיבִים	3a	Do not trust in leaders,
בְּבֶן־אָדָם שֶׁאֵין לוֹ תְשׁוּעָה:	3b	In a human[429] with whom there is no rescue.
תֵּצֵא רוּחוֹ יָשֻׁב לְאַדְמָתוֹ	4a	His breath[430] departs, he returns to the earth;[431]
בַּיּוֹם הַהוּא אָבְדוּ עֶשְׁתֹּנֹתָיו:	4b	On that day his thoughts vanish.
אַשְׁרֵי שֶׁאֵל יַעֲקֹב בְּעֶזְרוֹ	5a	Fortunate are those whose help is the God of Jacob,
שִׂבְרוֹ עַל־יְהוָה אֱלֹהָיו:	5b	Whose hope is in Yhwh their God,
עֹשֶׂה שָׁמַיִם וָאָרֶץ	6a	Maker of skies and land,
אֶת־הַיָּם וְאֶת־כָּל־אֲשֶׁר־בָּם	6b	The sea and everything in them,
הַשֹּׁמֵר אֱמֶת לְעוֹלָם:	6c	Keeper of faithfulness forever,

(Continued)

עֹשֶׂה מִשְׁפָּט לָעֲשׁוּקִים	7a	Bringer of justice for the oppressed,
נֹתֵן לֶחֶם לָרְעֵבִים	7b	Giver of food to the hungry,
יְהוָה מַתִּיר אֲסוּרִים:	7c	Yhwh, liberator[432] of the imprisoned,
יְהוָה פֹּקֵחַ עִוְרִים	8a	Yhwh, giver of sight to the blind,
יְהוָה זֹקֵף כְּפוּפִים	8b	Yhwh, lifter of the bowed low,
יְהוָה אֹהֵב צַדִּיקִים:	8c	Yhwh, lover of the righteous ones,
יְהוָה שֹׁמֵר אֶת־גֵּרִים	9a	Yhwh, protector of the immigrant,
יָתוֹם וְאַלְמָנָה יְעוֹדֵד	9b	Orphan and widow, he sustains,
וְדֶרֶךְ רְשָׁעִים יְעַוֵּת:	9c	Yet the path of the wicked, he bends.
יִמְלֹךְ יְהוָה לְעוֹלָם	10a	Yhwh reigns forever,
אֱלֹהַיִךְ צִיּוֹן לְדֹר וָדֹר	10b	Your God, Zion, for generations.
הַלְלוּ־יָהּ:	10c	Hallelujah!

Interpretation

On the whole, Psalm 146 is presented as a declaration to praise Yhwh and a portraiture of Yhwh through his concern and action toward people.[433] The structure of the psalm is framed with the 2mp imperative הַלְלוּ־יָהּ and includes four parts.[434] Further, it is bookended by two vocatives, first to the self (נֶפֶשׁ, v. 1b) and in the final lines to Zion (v. 10b), as well as a shift from first-person address to second person.[435] Though Zion is the explicit vocative addressee, the community is intended to be addressed.[436] Psalm 146 includes several vague vignettes of Yhwh's protection of several figures in light of the limitation of humanity.

Verses 3a–4b focus on the human leader, who will be contrasted with Yhwh as divine ruler.[437] These latter figures are designated by the titles "leaders" (נְדִיבִים, v. 3a) and "human" (בֶּן־אָדָם, v. 3b). It is unclear whether the second term modifies the first, implying that those who are in power are mortal, or if the second term broadens the warning to all of humanity.[438] It is more likely to be an expansion with the repetition of the בְּ to designate both. In any case, these figures are powerless against the eventualities of life or the judgment of God. Verse 3a–3b involves a description of the lack of ability of leaders to save, though it is mediated through the exhortation of the speaker to the community. As a reason not to trust in leaders, there is an implication that the audience may need rescue. Verse 4a–4b focuses on the end of life of the leader. While there is little specificity as to how or when the leader dies, it is clear that the death of this person is in view. It is possible that vv. 3a–4b depict a single event. The reference to "that day"/הַהוּא in v. 4b could refer back to the day in which no rescue arrived, though more likely it refers to the day of his death. As for many psalms, this is only speculation and no firm connection between the lines can be made other than v. 3a–3b intimates the lack of ability and v. 4a–4b clarifies part of that lack of ability, noting that death is the end of all people (leaders included). These leaders, as the antagonists of the psalm, are related to the רְשָׁעִים in v. 9c as both represent groups who meet their end in the psalm.[439] However, there is no clear connection between the "wicked" and the leaders in these verses and they should not be seen as coreferential.[440] The context of the psalm may imply a connection between the wicked and the leaders, but it is not clearly stated.

Verse 5a–5b continues the exhortative tone, using the beatitude אַשְׁרֵי.[441] This beatitude highlights not so much an explicit action, as is often the case with the word אַשְׁרֵי, but rather describes a situation of a fortunate reality for the community.[442] The lack of ability for leaders to rescue is thus directly contrasted with Yhwh as being the "help" and "hope" for those who are considered fortunate (v. 5a–5b). This implicit call to trust in Yhwh sets up the movement from the vignette of the leader to the vignette of Yhwh.

Verses 6a–9c characterize Yhwh through participles describing Yhwh's character attributes in a litany of activities. Yhwh's character is described in terms of his actions and the recipients of his actions. First, he is creator (v. 6a–6b). Then he is one who is concerned with those in need (vv. 6c–9b). Tucker argues that the statement of Yhwh as creator before the list of Yhwh's concerns for humanity signifies that Yhwh is "the one with power who is capable of creating life anew for those in need."[443] Each line contains a single description of an activity that combines with the others to display a broad, working characterization of Yhwh through the actions ascribed to him by the speaker. Most of the activities in vv. 7a–9c do not provide concrete images. Ballhorn notes that of the figures in vv. 7a–9b, only the צַדִּיקִים is a group to which "one can consciously affiliate oneself," unlike, for example, the needy.[444] However, based on the research in chapter 2, the meaning of the term here can fit clearly with those who are unjustly persecuted. While this may be simplistic in reality, the psalm presents a world wherein the entire group of those Yhwh cares for in vv. 7a–9b are defined by their need and that the need is met by Yhwh. That is, the oppressed receive justice, the blind sight, the bowed low are raised,[445] the imprisoned are freed, and so on. If the problem of the status of the individual is met through Yhwh's actions, then what is the issue solved by Yhwh's love (אהב) of the צַדִּיקִים?[446] Or, put differently, what is threat to which the solution is Yhwh's love? In other contexts, Yhwh's love for people can often result in concrete action on their behalf (Isa 43:4; 48:14; Jer 31:3; Hos 11:1; 2 Chr 2:10; 9:8). Likewise here, paralleled with the actions of Yhwh toward the other figures, Yhwh's outlook toward and his protection of the righteous is shown through his love for them.

The final twist in the psalm succinctly emphasizes the end of the wicked in contrast with those for whom the care of Yhwh is directed. Here, Yhwh "bends" (עות, v. 9c) the way of the wicked, which puns "sustains" (עוד, v. 9b).[447]

In v. 10a–10b, the eternal reign of Yhwh concludes the psalm, which contrasts the ephemerality of the rulers described in vv. 3a–4b.

In summary, the psalm focuses on the portraiture of Yhwh through his
concern for those in need and his actions against the wicked people. The
entire poem is mediated through the speaker's retelling of what is perceived
to be true about leaders and about God, established at the beginning in the
declaration to praise Yhwh.

Function of צַדִּיק and רָשָׁע

Like in many other instances, the righteous and the wicked only appear in
a sort of final summary form. Because the righteous and the wicked are
not immediately contrasted, many commentators have suggested that v. 8c
should be relocated to immediately precede v. 9c. Kraus suggests that "the
singer thinks of himself [*sic*] as among the צַדִּיקִים, who have placed their
hope entirely on Yahweh."[448] However, there is nothing in the psalm to suggest this much. Kraus appears to assume that because these figures are listed,
they must have some relationship. However, the fact that the term צַדִּיקִים is
dislocated from direct contrast with the wicked and is among five lines that
focus on various groups that receive the care of Yhwh that maintain the same
structure suggests that a direct connection is not in mind here, at least not any
more than one of the other groups. The destruction of the wicked *is* contrasted
with the fortune of the righteous, though not directly.

In this psalm, the righteous is only one of several mentioned groups that are
contrasted with the wicked. John Kselman points to a chiastic structure in vv.
8c–9c, wherein the righteous in 8c and wicked in 9c are contrasted in structurally inverted lines.[449] Each line of the list in vv. 7a–9a has the same structure
of Yhwh+participle+object, with the object as a personal figure or group. The
pattern changes in v. 9b, and thus, there is a clear grammatical parallelism
between v. 9b and 9c, which suggests they be read together. Alma Brodersen
counters that this conclusion is based an assumed connection between the
two figures צַדִּיק and רָשָׁע, and that the structure of the list of figures is self-
contained.[450] Brodersen's view precludes the possibility of overlapping structural markers in Hebrew poetry. Even if the chiastic structure proposed by
Kselman does not derive from intention, it is a poignant contrast as it is presented; a classic word pair is separated by other words that provide a window
into the workings of Yhwh's activity. While not intrinsically coreferential,
there is potential for a sort of dual-enrollment as righteous or, for example,
immigrant. Though this is not the case for each of these situations, those who
are identified by their needful situation because of the wicked receive the
affirmation that Yhwh will provide the solution for their problem as well as
provide the solution to the reason for their problem in bending the way of the

wicked, that is, to make that wicked way ineffectual. At the same time, all of these figures are contrasted with the wicked, who receive Yhwh's judgment. Semantically, this conclusion cannot function as an antithesis to each of these figures, though it is clear that the wicked stand apart as those judged by Yhwh whereas the remainder of the figures in the psalm are helped by him.

Gerstenberger suggests that the use of the term צַדִּיקִים differs from those in the remainder of the list, as the term "does not specify any kind of deprivation, only those that are 'the beloved partners of Yahweh.'"[451] He further argues that the slight change in structure may point to later addition. This may be possible, but it appears that in the context of the psalm, the righteous are to be counted among the remainder of those who are in need, either from their poverty or disability. Rooted in the uses and meaning of the word, the צַדִּיק can also be one who is wrongly suffering (see chapter 2), especially under the hand of another. In this case, the "righteous" fit plainly in this list. As we have seen in the remainder of the psalms, the righteous are often considered so by their acknowledgment of need of Yhwh's care. Further, throughout the psalms, the righteous are in need because of their persecution from others. Thus, the use of the righteous and the wicked in Ps 146 functions to highlight Yhwh's justice for the oppressed. It is not simply their devotion or the status as "beloved partners of Yahweh" that they are considered in this list of other figures. By nature of being part of this category, they are essentially those in need of help.

The righteous and the wicked function in Ps 146 to display the power of God.[452] He both saves the needy and judges the wicked, and as such, has the power to do so. Drawing on this literary pattern, the hoped-for reality becomes clear. The activities of Yhwh ground the ability for the community (vv. 1a and 10c) and for the speaker (vv. 1b–2b) to praise Yhwh. The function of the righteous and the wicked in Ps 146 highlights that Yhwh is consistent in character and activity. He is just and powerful to defend those who need defending and to judge those who should receive judgment. The contrast between the wicked and the whole host of other figures highlights the far-reaching implications of the wicked as a literary device, and yet also affirms that Yhwh can address them all, even overthrowing those wicked rulers who oppress others.

SUMMARY

This chapter has analyzed the eighteen psalms which mention both צַדִּיק and רָשָׁע. The analyses highlight the ways in which the literary pattern of the contrast between the two figures as well as the eventual destruction of the wicked function on the level of the discourse. As conventional resources within the literary mode of psalmody, each psalm employs the rigid contrast between the two to clear poetic effect. The above interpretations focused on the meaning of the terms צַדִּיק and רָשָׁע, including their plural forms, in context, emphasizing the way their usage influenced which meaning of the term is most likely. Following this, I demonstrated the way the contrast functioned as part of the overall psalm.

In Ps 1, the terms function to underscore the desirability of Torah by concluding with the end of the wicked and righteous as affirmations of the way of the fortunate person of Ps 1:1. In Ps 7, the צַדִּיק and רָשָׁע function to articulate a theology of justice against those that threaten the community. In Ps 11, the literary pattern affirms that Yhwh is a safe refuge as the one who judges the רָשָׁע, and that the צַדִּיק cannot bring the end of the wicked about on their own without Yhwh's help. In Ps 31, the speaker uses the literary pattern to impel Yhwh to act by reminding him of the deserved ends, and thus, siding themselves with the צַדִּיק. In Ps 32, the literary pattern functions to emphasize that the righteous way is worth following, and this is exemplified through trust in Yhwh and participating in worship of him. In Ps 34 the pattern functions to offer hope to his community to trust in Yhwh's faithfulness and to emphasize right living. In Ps 37, the whole range of attributes of both figures are drawn on to emphasize that the faithful will inherit the land and to speak against the present violence that keeps them from experiencing this. In Ps 55, the function of these figures emphasizes that the pattern of what is right or wrong extends into the community life. In Ps 58, the function of the figures offers hope to a community who are wrongly threatened by imagining that justice will prevail. In Ps 68, the figures, placed at the outset, introduce that Yhwh's justice—of judging both צַדִּיק and רָשָׁע rightly—is a reality in the entire world. In Ps 75, the contrast between the figures offers hope that the end of the wicked will bring about a change in reality for innocent sufferers from in need to triumphant. In Ps 92, the contrast highlights the desirability of being one of the righteous, with its access to long life and nearness to God. In Ps 94, the function of the contrast affirms that those who are unfairly persecuted will be protected by Yhwh, and justice against their opponents will be accomplished. In Ps 97, the contrast is set in God's reign over the world, and that those who are in need are the beneficiaries of his powerful action. In Ps 112, the two figures are used to define faithful living and commend it to the audience. In Ps 140, the contrast between the figures functions to identify that those who worship Yhwh will be rescued by him, with Yhwh's judgment against the wicked. In Ps 141, the pattern emerges that the צַדִּיק may become like the רָשָׁע, and thus, impels Yhwh to act as he must in the community. Finally, in Ps 146, these figures function to display a rightly ordered world where God offers those in need exactly what they need, and in so doing overthrows the wicked and displays his power and praiseworthiness.

While Psalm 1 has continued to have an undue influence on the interpretation of these figures throughout the psalms in scholarship, this chapter has shown that even within the first Book of the Psalter there are different meanings to the term צַדִּיק. A literary pattern appears, but a singular message or "theology" of these figures does not emerge from the evidence in the psalms themselves. These psalm analyses have supported the thesis that the contrast between these figures function as part of the stock imagery of psalms with both consistency and variation in their presentations. In particular, the meaning of צַדִּיק has been shown to include both the concepts of innocence and moral uprightness. A majority of the uses of צַדִּיק in the psalms analyzed relate to the meaning of innocent in a matter rather than to the meaning of an individual who properly behaved. In many cases, the צַדִּיק does not display any characteristics of those who function as a general description of the morally upright, though there is a sense where that meaning could be drawn from the individual contexts of some psalms. While these individual meanings differ, the literary pattern of the destruction of the רָשָׁע and the rescue or blessing of the צַדִּיק has been highlighted in each section.

NOTES

1. While most often translated "blessed" (Tremper Longman III, *Psalms: An Introduction and Commentary*, TOTC [Downers Grove, IL: InterVarsity2014], 56–57) or "happy" (DeClaissé-Walford, Jacobson, and Tanner, *Book of Psalms*, 59; Kraus, *Psalm 1–59*, 112; Robert Alter, *The Book of Psalms: A Translation with Commentary* (New York: W. W. Norton, 2007), 3; Walter Brueggemann and William H. Bellinger, Jr., *Psalms*, NCBC (New York: Cambridge University Press, 2014), 27; Gerstenberger, *Psalms, Part 1*, 40). Brown (*Seeing the Psalms*, 55, endnote on 231) translates as "fortunate" to show the "good fortune" that await the person in Ps 1; similarly, Goldingay (*Psalms*, 1:79). I follow this translation as it separates more religious contexts of the use of "blessed" in modern North American English and the primarily internal aspects of the term "happy."

2. Heb 3ms.

3. The word תּוֹרָה is translated in various ways by scholars depending largely on what they believe this term refers to here and in v. 2b. Here I follow DeClaissé-Walford, Jacobson, and Tanner (*Book of Psalms*, 61), who point out the weakness of the term "law" as unhelpfully legalistic in contemporary religious contexts. Those that see this term as referring specifically to the Pentateuch (e.g., Michael LeFebvre, "'On His Law He Meditates': What is Psalm 1 Introducing?" *JSOT* 40 [2016]: 443; P. J. Botha, "Intertextuality and the Interpretation of Psalm 1," *OTE* 18 (2005): 503–520; Whybray, *Reading*, 39) are most likely correct, pointing to the simplest solution to the meaning of this term. Others, especially those employing a canonical approach, see the term referring to the Psalter itself as a new Torah (e.g., Brevard

Childs, *Introduction to the Old Testament as Scripture* [Philadelphia, PA: Fortress, 1979], 513; Gerald H. Wilson, *The Editing of the Hebrew Psalter*, SBLDS 76 [Chico, CA: Scholars, 1985], 206) point to a possible function of Ps 1 in the Psalter rather than internal evidence that תּוֹרָה in this context refers to anything other than Yhwh's teaching. It is perhaps most important that the construct form of the word designates this instruction as from Yhwh. Because of the connection to the temple made through the use of language that connects Zion to a garden paradise (see Jerome F. D. Creach, "Like a Tree Planted by the Temple Stream: The Portrait of the Righteous in Psalm 1:3," *CBQ* 61 [1999]: 36–43), it is meaningful to broaden the term to "instruction" to include that which comes from Yhwh directly. In this case, it is not the Psalter but the instruction of behavior commensurate to Yhwh's blessing of those who are identified with the righteous and the eventual destruction of the wicked.

    4. Heb 3ms.

    5. Craigie (*Psalms 1–50*, 58, emphasis original) suggests that "in judgment" should be understood as "in the *place* of judgment," pointing to Deut 25:1. While he argues that this implies an eschatological judgment, this should be understood as those who will in an undefined future time receive judgment and be declared as those at fault. Thus, the metaphor expresses that the wicked are unable to "rise" in light of the judgment received.

    6. Gerstenberger, *Psalms, Part 1*, 42.

    7. Even with a psalm of six verses, numerous proposals for structure have been put forward. C. John Collins ("Psalm 1: Structure and Rhetoric," *Presbyterion* 31 [2005]: 38) lists eight distinct proposals; there are at least twenty-two different options for structure when dividing further into the structuring of cola, as shown in P. van der Lugt, *Psalms 90–150 and Psalm 1*, vol. 3, *Cantos and Strophes in Biblical Hebrew Poetry*, OTS 63 (Leiden: Brill, 2014), 581.

    8. The particle כִּי in v. 6a introduces "the reason . . . for what is said in vv. 1–5" (*BHRG* §40.29.2.(2).(b).)

    9. So Goldingay, *Psalms*, 1:82; Longman, *Psalms*, 56.

    10. Hans-Joachim Kraus, *Psalms 1–59*, CC, trans. Hilton C. Oswald (Minneapolis, MN: Augsburg, 1988), 115.

    11. Miller, "Bad Guys," 427.

    12. P. J. Botha ("Junction of the Two Ways," 393) writes that it can be assumed that these refer to the same group, though it is better to say they refer to the same category of figures.

    13. For connections between these verses and Josh 1:8 see Creach, "Like a Tree," 35; Robert L. Cole, "An Integrated Reading of Psalms 1 and 2," *JSOT* 98 (2002): 78–79; and Luis Alonso-Schökel and Cecilia Carniti, *Salmos: Traducción, introducciones y comentario* (Estella: Verbo Divino, 1993), 1:134.

    14. Mitchell Dahood, *Psalms*, AB (Garden City, NY: Doubleday, 1966–1970), 1:4.

    15. Yehoshua Gitay, "Psalm 1 and the Rhetoric of Religious Argumentation," in *Literary Structures and Rhetorical Strategies in the Hebrew Bible*, ed. by L. J. de Regt, J. de Waard, and Jan P. Fokkelman (Assen: Van Gorcum, 1996), 234. For example, Pss 2:12; 40:5; 146:5. Aaron D. Rubin ("The Form and Meaning of Hebrew

'*ašrê*," *VT* 60 (2010): 370) states that the term is exclusive to poetic texts; however, 1 Kgs 10:8, 2 Chr 9:7, and Dan 12:12 the term appears in direct speech. Negative affirmations also appear in Ps 40:5 and Isa 56:2, though in both instances these follow after an initial positive affirmation.

16. Beat Weber, "'Dann wird er sein wie ein Baum . . . ' (Psalm 1,3): Zu den Sprachbildern von Psalm 1," *OTE* 23 (2010): 414.

17. See Brown, *Seeing the Psalms*, 58.

18. Weber, "Sprachbildern," 421.

19. Weber, "Sprachbildern," 421.

20. Botha, "Intertextuality," 506.

21. Weber ("Sprachbildern," 421–422) highlights several features related to this image, including, importantly, that chaff is necessarily a plurality (chaff is never single) and that contrasts the worthless part of agricultural products against the valuable part. Weber does not make the connection between fruit and chaff here.

22. Alonso-Schökel and Carniti, *Salmos*, 1:137.

23. Bernd U. Schipper, *The Hermeneutics of Torah: Proverbs 2, Deuteronomy, and the Composition of Proverbs 1–9*, AIL 43 (Atlanta, GA: SBL, 2021), 48–49; Zehnder, *Wegmetaphorik*, 294–296.

24. Brown, *Seeing the Psalms*, 31–53; Andrew T. Abernethy, "'Right Paths' and/ or 'Paths of Righteousness'? Examining Psalm 23.3b within the Psalter," *JSOT* 39 (2015): 305–309. For the extension of the conceptual metaphor LIFE IS A JOURNEY and psalms see Alec Basson, "The Path Image Schema as Underlying Structure for the Metaphor Moral Life is a Journey in Psalm 25," *OTE* 24 (2011): 22–24 and Kartje, *Wisdom Epistemology*, 77–79.

25. Brown, *Seeing the Psalms*, 34–35.

26. Abernethy, "Right Paths," 305.

27. Brown, *Seeing the Psalms*, 57.

28. Levin, "Gebetbuch" 361.

29. Gunkel, "Psalm 1," 123.

30. Waldemar Janzen, "'*ašrê* in the Old Testament," *Harvard Theological Review* 58 (1965): 217–218.

31. For example, Kraus, *Psalms 1–59*, 116; Frank-Lothar Hossfeld and Erich Zenger, *Die Psalmen I: Psalm 1–50*, Die Neue Echter Bibel 29 (Würzburg: Echter, 1993), 46; Brown, *Seeing the Psalms*, 56; Weber, "Sprachbildern," 413; Botha, "Intertextuality," 506. DeClaissé-Walford, Jacobson, and Tanner (*Book of Psalms*, 60) still refer to the אִישׁ of Ps 1 as "righteous," while also noting that the term צַדִּיק does not appear until much later in the psalm. Goldingay (*Psalms*, 1:82), however does make this distinction, though implies this person is included as one of the righteous people and later (1:85) speaks of the "faithful"—his translation for צַדִּיק—as the subject of the imagery of the tree.

32. Mays, *Psalms*, 40–41.

33. DeClaissé-Walford, Jacobson, and Tanner, *Book of Psalms*, 62.

34. Will Kynes, *My Psalm Has Turned into Weeping: Job's Dialogue with the Psalms*, BZAW 437 (Berlin: De Gruyter, 2012), 159. Kynes is here referring to other

psalms that question a rigid retribution principle. Cf. Goldingay, *Psalms*, 1:85, who also sees the subtle possibility threat to the way of life in Ps 1.

35. Brown, *Seeing the Psalms*, 57.

36. On the basis of hunting imagery and the mention of "neck" in v. 6b, it is best to read נֶפֶשׁ here as a representation of the physical body part (Brown, *Seeing the Psalms*, 136; Norbert Lohfink, "Ps 7,2–6—vom Löwen gejagt," in *Die Freude an Gott, unsere Kraft: Festschrift für Otto Bernhard Knoch zum 65. Geburtstag*, ed. Johannes Joachim Degenhardt and Otto Bernhard Knoch [Stuttgart: Katholisches Bibelwerk, 1991], 62).

37. There is no preposition in Hebrew, though here it is supplied to indicate that the content of repayment is רַע itself. See e.g., 1 Sam 24:18, Isa 3:9, Prov 3:30 for the verb גמל with the sense of "repay" and the object רַע.

38. Commentators (Kraus, *Psalms 1–59*, 166) and translations follow the LXX in reading the WAYYIQTOL וָאֲלַחֲצָה, "plundered" or "oppressed" here. I do not accept this reading for two reasons. First, as Goldingay (*Psalms*, 1:142) notes, the verb חלץ never has the meaning of "to plunder." Second, the shift in verbal form is important. The ו attached to the verb could signal the apodosis of the conditional phrases insti-gated by the אם in vv. 4a–5a (see *IBHS* §34.5.2 for cohortative as apodosis). While the long הָ ending could simply be a "paragogic" *heh*, the verb could also be repointed as a cohortative by changing the initial to , as done here. It is more likely that this refers to what the speaker ought to do if they had indeed improperly dealt with their companion.

39. Lohfink ("Ps 7," 65) sees the leonine imagery extending through v. 6, and thus this is an expression of a lion holding down the speaker as its prey.

40. Supplied in context with the 2ms suffix in the preceding line.

41. The imperative has been brought from the end of 8b to the beginning of 9a. See esp. Ps 6:5, cf. Pss 80:15, 90:13. Vivian L. Johnson (*David in Distress: His Portrait Through the Historical Psalms*, LHBOTS 505 (New York: T&T Clark, 2009), 132) reads שָׁבָה, though this is unnecessary based on the reconstruction here.

42. Some (Leslie C. Allen, *Psalms 101-150*, 2nd ed, WBC 21 (Waco, TX: Word, 1983), 97–98; Jacob Leveen, "The Textual Problems of Psalm VII," *VT* 16 [1996]: 441), suggest repointing to עֵלִי, "Most High." Others (Kraus, *Psalms 1–59*, 167; Gert Kwakkel, *According to My Righteousness: Upright Behaviour as Grounds for Deliverance in Psalms 7, 17, 18, 26 and 44*, OTS 46 [Leiden: Brill, 2002], 26) note that emendation is unnecessary, as the preposition highlights the significance of the innocence resting on the speaker like a weight.

43. DeClaissé-Walford, Jacobson, and Tanner (*Book of Psalms*, 112) read the participle as a vocative title, "examiner," and while possible, this reading does not account for the ו at the beginning of the line.

44. The usage of the preposition here appears to have the sense of Yhwh wearing the shield to protect the upright in heart. See Kwakkel, *According to My Righteous-ness*, 48.

45. It is traditional (LXX, English translations) to read the participle here as sub-stantive instead of verbal, though Kraus (*Psalms 1–59*, 167) translates this verbally. Both are grammatically possible and have conceptual precedent earlier in the psalm,

though the substantive use seems most likely given the pattern of parallelism (so Kwakkel, *According to My Righteousness*, 28).

46. See Kevin Foth, "A Solution to the Subject(s) of Psalm 7:13–14," *VT* 74 (2024), 594–602, https:/doi/org/10.1163/15685330-bja10140, for a detailed argument for taking Yhwh as the subject of this line, summarized below.

47. As argued below, this refers to the enemy.

48. Woodenly "burning ones."

49. A shift in speaker at v. 9a is not required (against Mandolfo, *God in the Dock*, 37).

50. Terrien, *Psalms*, 120.

51. Erik Aurelius ("Davids Unschuld: Die Hofgeschichte und Psalm 7," in *Gott und Mensch im Dialog: Fetschrift für Otto Kaiser zum 80. Geburtstag*, ed. by Markus Witte, BZAW 345 [Berlin: De Gruyter, 2004], 407) sees a break instead at v. 11, though on the basis of parallels with other psalms' structures.

52. Kwakkel, *According to My Righteousness*, 41–42; Davida Charney, "Maintaining Innocence Before a Divine Hearer: Deliberative Rhetoric in Psalm 22, Psalm 17, and Psalm 7," *BibInt* 21 (2013): 60.

53. The argument here is drawn from Foth, "Solution."

54. DeClaissé-Walford, Jacobson, and Tanner, *Book of Psalms*, 116.

55. Hossfeld and Zenger, *Die Psalmen I*, 74; DeClaissé-Walford, Jacobson, and Tanner, *Book of Psalms*, 116–117; Robert L. Hubbard, "Dynamistic and Legal Processes in Psalm 7," *ZAW* 94 (1982): 269; Kwakkel, *According to My Righteousness*, 49–51; Johnson, *David in Distress*, 132.

56. Goldingay, *Psalms 1–41*, 143. Marianne Grohmann ("Ambivalent Images of Birth in Psalm vii 15," *VT* 55 [2005]: 440), however, highlights that הִנֵּה in this context precedes a vivid image, and thus, is used in line with the common function to call attention to a visual description. See also T. Muraoka, *Emphatic Words and Structures in Biblical Hebrew* (Jerusalem: Magnes Press, 1985), 137–140.

57. Kraus, *Psalms 1–59*, 168, 174; Bernd Janowski, "JHWH der Richter—ein rettender Gott," *JBTh* 9 (1994): 60; Bellinger, *Psalmody*, 52.

58. Broyles (*Psalms*, NIBC (Peabody, MA: Hendrickson, 1999), 70) lists all options for referents in v. 13a and 13b *except* the position followed forward in this section.

59. The assumption of parallel structures or lines is a strong limiting factor in interpreting this referent.

60. Hossfeld and Zenger, *Die Psalmen I*, 74.

61. Hossfeld and Zenger, *Die Psalmen I*, 74.

62. For an analysis of the interaction between these metaphors see Grohmann, "Ambivalent Images," 445–457.

63. Bellinger, *Psalmody*, 52.

64. Charney ("Maintaining Innocence," 61) argues that this emphasizes the ambiguity of who is at fault, the speaker or the enemies, and this is thus decided by how Yhwh acts. However, in the broader context of the psalm, the enemies are in the wrong as those who will be judged by their actions and fall into their own traps.

65. Federico G. Villanueva (*The 'Uncertainty of a Hearing': A Study of the Sudden Change of Mood in the Psalms of Lament*, VTSup 121 [Leiden: Brill, 2008], 147) further notes that the request for judgment against the wicked is done through jussive, whereas the request to establish the righteous is more emphatic through an imperative.

66. Von Rad (*Theology*, 381), however, incorrectly states that the psalmist claims the title here, as in Pss 17:1–5, 18:22–24, and 26:1–6. Brueggemann and Bellinger, *Psalms*, 56 refer to the speaker as "the righteous" in Ps 7.

67. Reading *qere*. For a review of the textual history of this variant see Sumner, "Reanalysis," 79–80.

68. Sumner ("Reanalysis," 83), on the basis of the usage of the verb elsewhere and the interpretation in 4Q Catena A, argues that it is most likely that the mountain here is the point of departure, rather than the destination.

69. For כִּי as protasis of a conditional, see *BHRG* §40.29.1.

70. נַפְשׁוֹ here refers to the person of Yhwh (Goldingay, *Psalms*, 1:192).

71. Some (e.g., Kraus, *Psalms 1–59*, 201) suggest that, following the Targums, this should be rendered as "coal" (פֶּחָם) instead of "bird traps" (פַּחִים). Because of the context and use of the avian imagery, it is possibly a genuine pun, wherein the speaker declares that disobedience in taking an active role in violence would result in falling into a bird trap. Because of the ironic use of the term "bird," the line, if understood as a genuine pun, would underscore the negative result were the speaker to flee from the safety of Yhwh's refuge.

72. Gerstenberger, *Psalms, Part 1*, 77.

73. Goldingay, *Psalms*, 1:190–191.

74. Kraus, *Psalms 1–59*, 201; DeClaissé-Walford, Jacobson, and Tanner, *Book of Psalms*, 148.

75. DeClaissé-Walford, Jacobson, and Tanner, *Book of Psalms*, 148; Dahood, *Psalms*, 1:69.

76. This theme appears clearly in Jer 48:28; Ezek 7:16. See Cat Quine, "The Bird and the Mountains: A Note on Psalm 11," *VT* 67 (2017): 470–479. 474–475, and Sumner, "Reanalysis," 80–82, for inscription evidence.

77. Goldingay (*Psalms*, 191) interprets these foundations metaphorically, though because of the context of fleeing from attack it is much more likely to be literal.

78. Some have questioned whether the reference to צַדִּיק in vv. 3b and 5a could refer to Yhwh rather than a person, though especially in 5a it does not make syntactic sense with the ו before the would-be object of the verb (Paul R. Raabe, "Deliberate Ambiguity in the Psalter," *JBL* 110 (1991): 222–223).

79. Terrien, *Psalms*, 149.

80. Cf. Ps 75:9. "Cup" imagery is not uncommon metaphorical language of judgment, particularly in prophetic literature (e.g., Isa 51:17, 22; Hab 2:16).

81. Goldingay (*Psalms*, 1:188) suggests that these figures in v. 7c relate to the speakers of vv. 1d–2c, implying that the psalmist should flee to safety. It is rather more likely that they are viewed generally as the community or as a rhetorical feature functioning as a representative voice of an idea to which the speaker responds. The

encouragement at the end about the upright people (v. 7c) does not identify them with the questioners at the beginning in any way. Instead, it emphasizes the possibility for the community to trust in Yhwh rather than in the psalmist or in the possibility of fleeing.

82. Hossfeld and Zenger (*Die Psalmen*, 89) note a pun of חזה here (to see) and חסה in v. 1b, which form an envelope structure around the psalm. The verb חזה also appears as an action of Yhwh toward humanity—expanded to both righteous and wicked—in v. 4c (Konrad Schaefer, *Psalms*, Berit Olam [Collegeville, MN: Liturgical Press, 2001], 28).

83. Van Leeuwen, "Theology," 70.

84. The QATAL throughout Ps 31 is translated as a gnomic perfect due to the overall context of a request (Goldingay, *Psalms*, 1:441). The claim could be represented in past tense, though present in English is preferred to indicate the situation in the psalm.

85. Hossfeld and Zenger (*Die Psalmen I*, 196) argues that the YIQTOL forms in vv. 4–5 represent an intense plea.

86. Megan I. J. Daffern ("The Semantic Field of 'Remembering' in the Psalms," *JSOT* 41 [2016]: 95) notes this is the only time פקד is found in the psalms with a human subject.

87. The LXX, Syriac, Vulgate, and one MT manuscript display a 2ms form here. While this would make for a simpler reading, Kraus (*Psalms 1–59*, 360) is incorrect that the 2ms would be required for the וַאֲנִי to make sense. Further, there is no need for the ו + pronoun to have a disjunctive sense; it is rather broadly emphatic on the more important activity of praise of Yhwh (see *IBHS* §16.3.1b).

88. For the use of אֲשֶׁר to introduce a cause, see *BHRG* §36.3.1.1(5)(d).

89. "As well" absent in Hebrew. DeClaissé-Walford, Jacobson, and Tanner (*Book of Psalms*, 302) suggests all of the nouns in v. 10a–10b are single subjects of the verb עָשֵׁשׁ from v. 10b. This is an example of "vertical parallelism," wherein the second line depends grammatically on the first (see David Toshio Tsumura, "Vertical Grammar of Parallelism in Hebrew Poetry," *JBL* 128 [2009]: 174–189).

90. Woodenly, "Stumbles."

91. Goldingay (*Psalms*, 1:435) suggests on the basis of parallelism that מִן here should mean "before" in the sense of in the witness of the enemies. However, given the context of the illegitimate speech against the speaker (vv. 14a–14b, 19a–19b, 21d) the source of the social alienation appears to have been those set against the speaker.

92. Though some see the מְאֹד here as out of place (e.g., Kraus, *Psalms 1–59*, 360; Craigie, *Psalms 1–50*, 258), the word can function to express a degree (DeClaissé-Walford, Jacobson, and Tanner, *Book of Psalms*, 302; cf. *IBHS* §11.2.12.c).

93. As traditionally translated from the MT, which is unclear. In context, the failure of Yhwh to see the speaker appears most likely, so "cut off" is retained (see Craigie, *Psalms 1–50*, 258).

94. See Tamar Zewi, *Parenthesis in Biblical Hebrew*, Studies in Semitic Languages and Linguistics 50 (Leiden: Brill, 2007), 139–141 for a discussion of אָכֵן as an affirmation.

95. Schaefer (*Psalms*, 76) places the psalm in two "movements" (divided in v. 10a, as below) yet shows how each of the sections overlap in content. In light of this, it is best to view the psalm as responding to one situation. Goldingay (*Psalms*, 1:437), however, notes that the conventional language in the psalm is indeterminate.

96. Megan I. J. Daffern, "Imagining Prayer: Deepening Awareness of Audiences in the Psalms," in *Psalms and the Use of the Critical Imagination: Essays in Honour of Professor Susan Gillingham*, ed. Katherine E. Southwood and Holly Morse, LHBOTS 710 (London: T&T Clark, 2022), 88.

97. See Alec Basson, "'You are my Rock and Fortress': Refuge Metaphors in Psalm 31; A Perspective from Cognitive Metaphor Theory," *Acta Theologica* 2 (2005): 11–14, for a discussion of the refuge language from a cognitive linguistic perspective, which highlights the nature of Yhwh as one who provides security and protection; Basson lists only צוּר, חסה, and מָעוּז. Creach (*Yahweh as Refuge*, 25–31) provides a fuller list of terminology relating to refuge, mentioning terms here as related through context (34). Cf. the idea of "rock" as refuge in Brown, *Seeing the Psalms*, 19.

98. Kraus, *Psalms 1–59*, 360.

99. Léo Laberge ("A Literary Analysis of Psalm 31," *Église et théologie* 16 [1985]: 159) notes that this section divides neatly on content.

100. This term as a substantive is used to designate enemies of the speaker in Pss 3:2–3; 56:3, though also have a more neutral nuance, e.g., Pss 71:7, 109:30.

101. The וַאֲנִי in v. 15a can serve as a clear discourse marker indicating a shift in focus. See *BHRG* §36.1.1.3.

102. Schaefer, *Psalms*, 77.

103. Verses 18c–19c should still be seen as addressed to Yhwh, though in third person, and the YIQTOL verbs understood as jussives.

104. The "children of humanity" (בְּנֵי אָדָם, v. 20d) are also ambiguous; they could either designate the antagonists or humanity in general. In the context, the rewards of Yhwh's refuge are shown "before" the children of humanity, and thus, serve as witnesses to the blessing of the community.

105. Luis Alonso-Schökel, "En la mano de Dios (Salmo 31)," *Estudios Biblicos* 56 (1998): 406.

106. See note on Ps 1:1.

107. Many scholars translate the כִּי here as introducing a temporal clause (DeClaissé-Walford, Jacobson, and Tanner, *Book of Psalms*, 306; Craigie, *Psalms 1–50*, 263; Hossfeld and Zenger, *Die Psalmen I*, 201; Kraus, *Psalms 1–59*, 366; Goldingay, *Psalms*, 1:451). I opt for a concessive sense as a means to highlight the progression from the effects of sin to forgiveness (see *BHRG* §40.29.1.(1).d).

108. Kraus (*Psalms 1–59*, 367) argues a better reading of this would be לְשֹׁנִי, "my tongue." Contextually this makes good sense, though there are no texts that support this reading. Goldingay (*Psalms*, 1:451) acknowledges that the definition of the word is unclear. In any case, the emphasis is on something turning dry is clear, thus, my translation retains the idea of moisture as central. If the word does refer to a cake, the metaphor implies movement from enjoyable to eat to dry and unpalatable.

109. An emphatic pronoun (McCann, *Theological Introduction*, 109).

110. This meaning of רַק מָצָא is an interpretive *crux* for the psalm. The function of the verb מצא is explored here, in the following note the entire phrase. Some interpret מצא as "to reach" (Simon Chi-Chung Cheung, *Wisdom Intoned: A Reappraisal of the Genre 'Wisdom Psalms'*, LHBOTS 613 (London: Bloomsbury, 2015), 139; Dahood, *Psalms*, 1:193), though thematically the idea of "finding" God in witnessing his events unfold is present here. For other uses of מצא with God as the object, see Deut 4:29; Jer 29:13–14; Job 23:3. This meaning has support in the LXX.

111. Some emend מָצָא רַק to מצוק shifting the topic to a time of "distress" (DeClaissé-Walford, Jacobson, and Tanner, *Book of Psalms*, 307; Craigie, *Psalms 1–50*, 264). Kraus (*Psalms 1–59*, 367), admitting the difficulty, removes רַק in his translation, though shifts the object to a second person pronoun. My tentative solution is to read רַק with the following line, following Cheung, *Wisdom Intoned*, 140 in interpreting it as a modal adverb. On the emphatic use, see of *BHRG* §40.41.(2) and Muraoka, *Emphatic Words*, 131. See examples in Gen 20:11, Deut 4:6; 1 Kgs 21:25; 2 Chr 28:10.

112. The "you" is supplied from context as part of the list of ways the speaker will aid the addressee.

113. Following Goldingay, *Psalms*, 1:452 in interpreting this as a verbless clause (also Kraus, *Psalms 1–59*, 367).

114. Line 9b is unclear. See DeClaissé-Walford, Jacobson, and Tanner, *Book of Psalms*, 307 for a brief summary of suggestions for these lines. I have attempted to retain equine imagery in the translation following from possibilities of meaning. Though the translation is uncertain, the connection between wisdom and equestrian imagery is retained.

115. For the meaning of the metaphors as forgiveness in Ps 32 see Jože Krašovec, *Reward, Punishment, and Forgiveness: The Thinking and Beliefs of Ancient Israel in the Light of Greek and Modern Views*, VTSup 78 (Leiden: Brill, 1999), 594–595.

116. Mignon R. Jacobs, "Sin, Silence, Suffering, and Confession in the Conceptual Landscape of Psalm 32," in *Text and Community: Essays in Memory of Bruce M. Metzger*, vol. 2, ed. J. Harold Ellens (Sheffield: Sheffield Phoenix, 2007), 15.

117. Though some scholars have seen the experience of healing from sickness as the "lyric moment" or *Sitz im Leben* of the psalm, the idea of forgiveness is clearly present in the psalm whereas language of illness is not (Stephanus D. Snyman, "Psalm 32: Structure, Genre, Intent and Liturgical use," in *Psalms and Liturgy*, ed. Dirk J. Human and Cas J. A. Vos, JSOTSup 410 [London: T&T Clark, 2004], 164).

118. Jacobson, *Many are Saying*, 64.

119. Kraus (*Psalms 1–59*, 370) uses the term "narration" to describe these scenes.

120. Alter, *Book of Psalms*, 111.

121. Kraus, *Psalms 1–59*, 369; Craigie, *Psalms 1–59*, 267.

122. Snyman, "Psalm 32," 166.

123. Kraus, *Psalms 1–59*, 370.

124. Cheung, *Wisdom Intoned*, 138.

125. See Pss 18:5, 17; 69:2–3, 16; 124:4.

126. Jacobson (*Many Are Saying*, 82) does not consider this psalm because of the ambiguity of speech.

127. Kraus, *Psalms 1–59*, 257; Dahood, *Psalms*, 1:196.

128. Snyman, "Psalm 32," 165; Mandolfo, *God in the Dock*, 101; Longman, *Psalms*, 165.

129. Samuel Hildebrandt, "Whose Voice is Heard? Speaker Ambiguity in the Psalms," *CBQ* 82 (2020): 207–208.

130. Beth Tanner (DeClaissé-Walford, Jacobson, and Tanner, *Book of Psalms*, 309) writes that part of the effect of the shift to 2ms forms precludes the inclusion of the "they" mentioned in vv. 6–7.

131. Goldingay, *Psalms*, 1:460.

132. A similar call is given in Ps 33:1, which has caused some to see a single psalm composition, as is evident in a few Masoretic manuscripts.

133. Discussion of the superscriptions falls outside of this book, but it is worth noting that the longer superscription of Ps 34 has attracted significant discussion of the relationship between the superscription and 1 Samuel. See Christopher R. Seitz, "Psalm 34: Redaction, Inner-Biblical Exegesis and the Longer Psalm Superscriptions—'Mistake' Making and Theological Significance," in *The Bible As Christian Scripture: The Work of Brevard S. Childs*, ed. Christopher R. Seitz and Kent Harold Richards, Biblical Scholarship in North America 25 (Atlanta, GA: SBL, 2013), 279–298; Raymond Apple, "Psalm 34—Does the Heading Fit?" *JBQ* 46 (2018): 97–103; Johnson, *David in Distress*, 69–76; P. J. Botha, "Annotated History—The Implications of Reading Psalm 34 in Conjunction with 1 Samuel 21–26 and Vice Versa," *OTE* 21 (2008): 593–617; Kent Harold Richards, "Psalm 34," *Interpretation* 40 (1986): 177–180; Patrick W. Skehan, "A Note on Psalm 34:1," *CBQ* 14 (1952): 226.

134. Translating the tense of the verbless clause in light of the previous finite verb in v. 2a.

135. Benjamin Giffone ("A 'Perfect' Poem: The Use of the QATAL Verbal Form in the Biblical Acrostics," *HS* 51 [2010]: 65) sees the QATAL verbs here as part of a narrative section, and thus, past referring.

136. Commentators (Kraus, *Psalms 1–59*, 382; Craigie, *Psalms 1–50*, 277; DeClaissé-Walford, Jacobson, and Tanner, *Book of Psalms*, 322; Hossfeld and Zenger, *Psalmen I*, 212; Brown, *Deep Calls to Deep*, 346) generally follow the Greek and Vulgate in supplying a 2mp imperative here. Goldingay (*Psalms*, 1:480) instead maintains the MT, while noting that "both apply to other worshippers the message of the testimony." Because there is little change in meaning, the MT is retained.

137. Heb 3ms for both plural pronouns in this verse.

138. סָבִיב functions adverbially here. See *BHRG* §39.18.a–c.

139. Dahood (*Psalms*, 1:206) replaces the verb ראה with ירא following Prov 23:31 with the meaning "to drink." This expands the metaphor of eating with drinking, though the verb ראה does not need to be modified in this phrase.

140. See the development of this metaphor in J. J. M. Roberts, "The Young Lions of Psalm 34,11," *Bib* 54 (1973): 265–267. The LXX adopts πλούσιοι here.

141. The prefixed מִן functions as "separative" here (so *IBHS* §66.2.2b.16).

142. See *BHRG* §39.6.(1).(iii).

143. LXX adds οἱ δίκαιοι.

144. Because these QATAL verbs appear in a section of non-finite verbs and verbless clauses, since they follow from the verb עָשָׂ֫ה which here offers a continuous aspect, Giffone ("A 'Perfect' Poem," 65) suggests it is best to read the verbs in v. 18a–18b as gnomic.

145. For a detailed discussion of the syntax and meaning of v. 19, see Sigrid Eder, "'Broken Hearted' and 'Crushed in Spirit': Metaphors and Emotions in Psalm 34,19," *SJOT* 30 (2016): 6–10, https://doi.org/10.1080/09018328.2016.1122286.

146. For a discussion of the repetitions, see Sophie Ramond, "'Seek Peace and Pursue It' (Ps 34:15): A Call to Beleaguered Members of a Community," *JHS* 19 (2018): 1–14, https:/doi/org/10.5508/jhs.2019.v19.a. One word often noted is "all"/ כֹּל, repeated seven times (Hossfeld and Zenger, *Die Psalmen*, 211; P. J. Botha, "The Social Setting and Strategy of Psalm 34," *OTE* 10 (1997): 182).

147. God is designated exclusively by the term Yhwh (vv. 2a, 3a, 4a, 5a, 7a, 8a, 9a, 10a, 11b, 12b, 16a, 17a, 18a, 19a, 20b, 23a), though he is also present through 3ms verbs and pronouns throughout. There is a consistent pattern of appearance of Yhwh's name: Yhwh is mentioned in the first line of eight verses, then the second line of two immediately following. This pattern then appears four more times after a break with Yhwh's name in the first line of the verse, followed by one in the second line in v. 20b.

148. Kraus, *Psalms 1–59*, 384.

149. Johnson, *David in Distress*, 71. Johnson cites 1 Sam 14:24, 29; 2 Sam 3:35; Jon 3:7. Based on further examples, perhaps "sample" without the modifier is a more accurate description.

150. Luis Alonso-Schökel, "Contemplar y Gustar (Sal 34, 6.9)," *Estudios Bíblicos* 57 (1999): 17. Alonso-Schökel notes the examples of Isa 1:18; 7:15; 55:2; Jer 2:7; Prov 13:2; 15:17; 17:1; 24:13; and Song 4:10.

151. Kraus, *Psalms 1–59*, 384; DeClaissé-Walford, Jacobson, and Tanner, *Book of Psalms*, 326.

152. Leon J. Liebreich, "Psalms 34 and 145 in the Light of Their Key Words," *Hebrew Union College Annual* 27 (1956): 186.

153. Eder ("Broken Hearted," 9) notes in v. 21b an intentional repetition of the verb שׁבר (*niphal*) from v. 19a.

154. Patrick W. Skehan ("The Structure of the Song of Moses in Deuteronomy [Deut. 32:1–43]," *CBQ* 13 [1951]: 160) that both here and in Ps 25 the addition of the פ-line at the end places the ל line at the exact center of the lines, spelling out the first letter of the alphabet, and the first letter of the psalm.

155. Christine Brown Jones, "When I am Afraid: Fear in the Book of Psalms," *Review & Expositor* 115 (2018): 20.

156. Ramond, "Seek Peace," 3.

157. How (Terrien, *Psalms*, 305) concludes that the shift from plural to singular of צַדִּיק indicates that the speaker is then included in the latter category is entirely unclear.

158. Botha ("Social Setting," 186) argues on this basis that it can be assumed that the situation the righteous is in is the direct results of the actions of the wicked.

159. Brown, *Deep Calls to Deep*, 295–296.

160. See Botha, "Social Setting," 190.

161. Cheung (*Wisdom Intoned*, 54) suggests that the phrase וַעֲשֵׂה־טוֹב is explicative of trusting in Yhwh, citing *IBHS* §39.2.1b, and examples in Gen 31:13, Deut 2:24, and 2 Sam 19:8. This fits the pattern of the list of imperatives with Yhwh as the object in vv. 3a, 4a, 5a, and 7a. See also Goldingay, *Psalms*, 1:501.

162. Following the metaphorical reading in Davis, *Scripture, Culture, and Agriculture*, 116. John S. Kselman ("Two Notes on Psalm 37," *Biblica* 78 (1997): 252) suggests that this is a concrete image of food supply, though this interpretation does not relate to the image of grass in the previous verse.

163. Goldingay (*Psalms*, 1:520) notes that the metaphor of food and drink extends, pointing to Isa 55:2, 66:11.

164. The *weyiqtol* following an imperative shows a consequence (*IBHS* §33.4b; *BHRG* § 21.5.2.2; see also Cheung, *Wisdom Intoned*, 54).

165. Extending the metaphor from earlier, the light can also have the effect of drying out grasses.

166. On the phrase עוֹד מְעַט as a specific duration, see *BHRG* §40.37.(5).

167. Most translations understand כָּרִים as "pastures" (Kraus, *Psalms 1–59*, 402; Brueggemann and Bellinger, *Psalms*, 182; Hossfeld and Zenger, *Die Psalmen I*, 232 [*Auen*]). It is unclear what this metaphor would be depicting. One option, noted here, is that the use plays off of the whole burnt offerings to Yhwh, and thus, the wicked, like the sacrifices, are totally consumed. The verb כלה is used of the burnt offering (עֹלָה) in 2 Chr 29:28.

168. Psalm 102:4 also includes both words כלה and עָשָׁן with the subject "my days."

169. For the two uses of כִּי in this verse, Alonso-Schökel and Carniti (*Salmos*, 1:550) see the first as concessive and the second causal.

170. See note on v. 3a.

171. If the alphabetic acrostic pattern were retained, this line would begin with an *ayin*.

172. John A. Emerton ("Looking on One's Enemies," *VT* 51 [2001]: 195–196) argues that to "look on" an enemy with the construction of the verb ראה plus the preposition בְּ suggests triumph, and while the construction differs slightly from, a similar meaning is intended here (Emerton, "Looking on One's Enemies," 190).

173. This text is assumed to be in need of emendation or believed to be corrupt (Kraus, *Psalms 1–59*, 403; DeClaissé-Walford, Jacobson, and Tanner, *Book of Psalms*, 352), but makes sense as apposition.

174. Heb 3ms; also in v. 36b.

175. See Gerstenberger, *Psalms, Part 1*, 160 on this twofold intention.

176. The audience is addressed through a 2ms negated jussive in v. 1b, and are the subject of directive forms throughout vv. 1b–9c. The 2ms verb forms also appear in vv. 10b, 27b, 34a–34c, and 37a, with most of these references being imperative forms.

177. Goldingay, *Psalms*, 1:517. Hossfeld and Zenger (*Die Psalmen I*, 229) describe this figure as *fiktiver*. While the persona exists primarily in the poem, to describe them as fictitious distracts from the function as a representational figure.

178. The content of the "schemes" (מְזִמּוֹת) does not require violence, but the context suggests a form of illegitimate consideration or planning. This could be of ill-gotten gain or of violence.

179. They receive the designations "those who do wrong" (עֹשֵׂי עַוְלָה, v. 1c), "the one whose path is prosperous" (מַצְלִיחַ דַּרְכּוֹ, v. 7b), "a person who carries out schemes" (אִישׁ עֹשֶׂה מְזִמּוֹת, v. 7c), "those who are evil" (מְרֵעִים, v. 9a), "wicked person" (רָשָׁע; vv. 10a, 12a, 14a [pl], 16b [pl], 20a [pl], 21a, 28d [pl], 32a, 34c [pl], 35a, 38b [pl], 40b [pl]), "enemies of Yhwh" (אֹיְבֵי יְהוָה, v. 20b), "ruthless person" (עָרִיץ, v. 35b), "those who rebel" (פֹּשְׁעִים, v. 38a).

180. The offspring of the righteous person are also mentioned (זַרְעוֹ, vv. 25c, 26b).

181. W. Dennis Tucker, Jr. ("A Polysemiotic Approach to the Poor in the Psalms," *PRSt* 31 [2004]: 433) views the uses of poverty language in Ps 37:14 as a "synonym for righteousness." While they are related in a sort of synonymous relationship, the synonymy is not for "righteousness" so much as "the righteous," who are here those who suffer innocently.

182. Walter Brueggemann, "Psalm 37: Conflict of Interpretation," in *Of Prophets' Visions and the Wisdom of the Sages: Essays in Honour of R. Norman Whybray on His Seventieth Birthday*, ed. Heather A. McKay and David J. A. Clines, JSOTSup 162 (Sheffield: JSOT Press, 1993), 231.

183. Markus Witte, "Psalm 37 im Spannungsfeld von Weisheit und Eschatologie," in *Weisheit als Lebensgrundlage: Festschrift für Friedrich V. Reiterer zum 65. Geburtstag*, ed. Renate Egger-Wenzel, Karin Schöpflin, and Johannes Friedrich Diehl, Deuterocanonical and Cognate Literature Studies 15 (Berlin: De Gruyter, 2013), 419; Gerstenberger (*Psalms, Part 1*, 158).

184. Brown, "Come, O Children," 87. Brown further notes the paradox that the same posture—restraint—is required toward both deity and wicked.

185. Cheung, *Wisdom Intoned*, notes that there is an increasing intensity of destruction in the plant images from grass—which can return the next season—to the cutting down of a tree that will not regrow in vv.35–36.

186. For animals feeding on חָצִיר, see 1 Kgs 18:5; Ps 104:14; Job 40:15; for דֶּשֶׁא, see Job 6:5; Jer 14:5; for יֶרֶק, see Gen 1:30; Num 22:4.

187. Davis, *Scripture, Culture, and Agriculture*, 116.

188. Susan E. Gillingham ("'The Righteous Shall Inherit the Land, and Live in it Forever' (Ps 37:29): Towards a Theology of and Human and Divine Justice through the Reception History of Psalm 37," in *Zur Theologie des Psalters und der Psalmen*, ed. Ulrich Berges, Johannes Bremer, and Till Magnus Steiner, BBB 189 [Göttingen: V & R, 2019], 414) based on the description of the righteous as generous and on the correlations to Proverbs suggests that the author should be seen as at least moderately wealthy. This makes some difference in how the psalm is read in terms of the poverty language, though overall is a moot point considering that it is unlikely that any author of a psalm was truly in poverty.

189. Cheung, *Wisdom Intoned*, 58.

190. Patrick D. Miller, "Land in the Psalms," in *The Land of Israel in History, Bible, and Theology: Studies in Honour of Ed Noort*, ed. J. T. A. G. M. van Ruiten and Cor de Vos, VTSup 124 (Leiden: Brill, 2009), 190.

191. Mays ("Torah Psalms," 9) connects this instance of the righteous with the emphasis on Torah in Ps 1.

192. Brown, *Deep Calls to Deep*, 289–290.

193. *BHRG* §21.5.2.1.

194. Cheung, *Wisdom Intoned*, 58.

195. Alonso-Schökel and Carniti, *Salmos*, 1:552.

196. Scott C. Jones, "Psalm 37 and the Devotionalization of Instruction in the Postexilic Period," in *Prayers and the Construction of Israelite Identity*, ed. Susanne Gillmayr-Bucher and Maria Häusl, AIL 35 (Atlanta, GA: SBL, 2019), 177.

197. Kraus, *Psalms 1–59*, 408; Goldingay, *Psalms*, 1:534.

198. As in "ignore," so Marvin E. Tate, *Psalms 51–100*, WBC 20 (Dallas, TX: Word, 1990), 51.

199. For the preposition מִן in a causative function, see *IBHS* §11.2.11d (also in 4b).

200. For מִפְּנֵי functioning to as the ground for action, see *BHRG* §39.15.(2).(a).

201. Frank-Lothar Hossfeld and Erich Zenger (*Psalms 2: A Commentary on Psalms 51–100*, trans. Linda M. Maloney, Hermeneia [Minneapolis, MN: Fortress, 2005], 51) suggest without argument that the *hapax* עקה should be translated "shouts," yet also translate this phrase as "pressure."

202. Hossfeld and Zenger (*Psalms 2*, 51) note these YIQTOL forms function to clarify the past event. However, in the psalm these need not happen in the past tense.

203. Because of the YIQTOL forms describing the situation, the QATAL forms are translated here in the present tense.

204. For the meaning of "flapping" for the verb נרד, see Isa 10:14, וְלֹא הָיָה נֹדֵד כָּנָף, "and there was no flapping of a wing." The subject of a bird is also used with this verb in Isa 16:2, Jer 4:25, 9:9 with the noun עוֹף (though in the last usage, בְּהֵמָה is also a subject of the verb) and with the noun צִפּוֹר in Prov 27:8. The word can mean simply to flee in some contexts, but it appears to have a connection with the flying of birds. This usage extends the avian metaphor from above in this psalm. On the adverbial accusative function of the infinitive construct, as in this case, see *IBHS* §36.2.1d, examples 13–15.

205. Translated in present tense in line with YIQTOL in v. 11a.

206. For the adversative, see John S. Kselman and Michael L. Barré, "Psalm 55: Problems and Proposals," *CBQ* 60 (1998): 449.

207. Following *qere*. Mandolfo (*God in the Dock*, 76) suggests dividing the *kethib* to יָשִׁים מָוֶת, with the reading "He will set death." The *qere* is maintained here as it fits the parallel structure of the antagonists as the primary topic in these verses without a reference to God.

208. Heb 3ms.

209. Dahood (*Psalms*, 2:35) sees this as past referring, though in the temporal situation of the psalm it can be considered as unfolding in the text of the psalm itself. The shift to past tense in the following lines need not influence the tense of the verbs in vv. 17a–18b, as the psalm also sees the present situation of need.

210. DeClaissé-Walford, Jacobson, and Tanner (*Book of Psalms*, 476) write that the antecedent of the "many" here is time rather than people based on the preceding

mention of time in v. 18a. The shift here more likely emphasizes that while there were many "against" the speaker (v. 19a), God's salvation brought about a situation where many are not "with" them. According to Juöun §133c, the בְּ in the line does not add anything significant to the meaning.

211. The major question here is whether קֶדֶם should be understood as "East" (Hossfeld and Zenger, *Psalms 2*, 51) or "of old" (Kselman and Barré, "Psalm 55," 442, 453; DeClaissé-Walford, Jacobson, and Tanner, *Book of Psalms*, 476; Goldingay, *Psalms*, 2:163). The solution is dependent on the subject of the verb יֹשֵׁב. It is more likely here that the subject remains God, as the phrase itself has a clear meaning in relation to God.

212. The word is unclear, and so relies on parallel of the next verse. Included here a standard English idiom here in place of a phrase denoting smooth speech and using a dairy product in metaphor (following Kraus, *Psalms 1–59*, 518; cf. DeClaissé-Walford, Jacobson, and Tanner, *Book of Psalms*, 476).

213. "live half their days" NASB.

214. Human, "Tradition-Historical Analysis," 269.

215. P. J. Botha, "Psalm 55 Interpreted in View of its Textual, Metatextual and Intertextual Connections," *SJOT* 31 (2017): 123–24; Dirk J. Human, "A Tradition-Historical Analysis of Psalm 55," *SK* 18 (1997): 269–270. Hossfeld and Zenger (*Psalms 51–100*, 52) write, "Among commentators . . . the division of the psalm is on the whole undisputed." Theodor Lescow ("Die Komposition der Psalmen 6 und 55," *BN* 107/108 [2001]: 37), however, argues that there are three distinct psalms brought together, with additions in 13–15 and 21–22.

216. Kselman and Barré, "Psalm 55," 442.

217. Alastair G. Hunter, "Inside Outside Psalm 55: How Jonah Grew Out of a Psalmist's Conceit," in *Psalms and Prayers: Papers Read at the Joint Meeting of the Society for Old Testament Study and Het Oudtestamentiseh Werkgezelsehap in Nederland en België, Apeldoorn August 2006*, ed. by Bob Becking and Eric Peels, OTS 55 (Leiden: Brill, 2007), 134.

218. Human, "Tradition-Historical Analysis," 270.

219. These figures are identified also by 3mp verbs and pronouns (v. 10a).

220. Mention of the "enemy" (אוֹיֵב, v. 13a) and "one who hates me" (מְשַׂנְאִי, v. 13b) are mentioned in v. 13a–13b are also part of the description of the false friend of vv. 13a–16c.

221. Mandolfo (*God in the Dock*, 79) do not see these as requests due to her textual emendation. This is followed by Goldingay, *Psalms*, 2:173.

222. Goldingay, *Psalms*, 2:173.

223. Tate, *Psalms 51–100*, 58.

224. Hossfeld and Zenger (*Psalms II*, 55) point to similar descriptions of smooth speech in Pss 5:10, 12:3–4, and 36:4.

225. Ulrike Bail ("'O God, Hear My Prayer': Psalm 55 and Violence Against Women," in *Wisdom and Psalms*, ed. Athalya Brenner and Carole R. Fontaine, Feminist Companion to the Bible 2 [Sheffield: Sheffield Academic, 1998], 253; followed by Hossfeld and Zenger, *Psalms II*, 52) sees v. 23 as an ironic speech from the friend,

though it is difficult to see how the descriptions of the false friend as frequently past-referring allow for him to speak here, particularly without introduction.

226. Mandolfo, *God in the Dock*, 81.

227. Human ("Tradition Historical Analysis," 275, endnote on 279) also lists 2 Sam 16:15; 17:14; Jer 9:5; 20:9; Job 6:15; 19:19; Ps 38:12; Prov 2:17; 16:28; 17:9 as examples of a "treacherous friend" theme in the OT.

228. Human, "Tradition-Historical Analysis," 276.

229. The word "silence," אֵלֶם, is often repointed here as אֵלִים, a form of "gods," and interpreted either as the general council of deities mentioned elsewhere in psalms (so DeClaissé-Walford, Jacobson, and Tanner, *Book of Psalms*, 492; Kraus, *Psalms 1–59*, 534; Tate, *Psalms 51–100*, 83; Brian Doyle, "Hearts, Hands, Teeth, and Feet: From Metonymy to Metaphor and Back in Psalm 58," *The Classical Bulletin* 86 (2010): 82; Goldingay, *Psalms*, 2:201) or as human leaders J. Kenneth Kuntz ("Growling Dogs and Thirsty Deer: Uses of Animal Imagery in Psalmic Rhetoric," in *My Words are Lovely: Studies in the Rhetoric of the Psalms*, ed. Robert L. Foster and David M. Howard, LHBOTS 467 [New York: T&T Clark, 2008], 56). Christopher Begg ("Ps 58:2a: A Forschungsbericht and a Proposal," *Ephemerides Theologicae Lovanienses* 64 [1988]:.401–402) argues for the reading אֱלֹהִים and the referent of God, rather than gods, based partly on the repetition of several roots or words in 58:2–3 and 11–12. Hossfeld and Zenger (*Psalms 2*, 77–78) maintain the MT, though only tentatively. The silence of whoever is addressed is problematic as it leaves the wicked person left unchallenged until God acts against them, that is, acting as judge himself.

230. Goldingay reads דִּבְרֵי כָזָב as a title for the wicked. This is certainly possible, though even translated verbally as above, the actions are those of the רָשָׁע.

231. Reading *qere* here.

232. Heb 3ms.

233. Cf. Ps 64:4. See John A. Emerton, "The Translation of Psalm LXIV.4," *JTS* 27 (1976): 391–392.

234. Woodenly, "Withered."

235. Several scholars emend the text to שְׁכָלוּל, with the meaning "like an unborn child" (Hossfeld and Zenger, *Psalms 2*, 77–78; Adam E. Miglio, "Imagery and Analogy in Psalm 58:4–9," *VT* 65 [2015]: 123–125; Marianne Grohmann, "Metaphors of Miscarriage in the Psalms," *VT* 69 [2019]: 227).

236. For אֵשֶׁת as an absolute form, see C. Steyl, "The Construct Noun *ešet* in Ps 58:9," *Journal of Northwest Semitic Languages* 11 (1983): 133.

237. This line is notoriously difficult. Kraus (*Psalms 1–59*, 536) states that only a tentative reconstruction is possible; DeClaissé-Walford, Jacobson, and Tanner (*Book of Psalms*, 494) suggest leaving the verse untranslated. I have attempted to maintain the text as is without adjustment, though my translation emphasizes the speed in which the judgment will come. In any case, the general concept in v. 10a is the destruction of the wicked person by Yhwh.

238. For example, Kraus, *Psalms 1–59*, 533, 535.

239. Hossfeld and Zenger, *Psalms 2*, 81; Doyle, "Hearts," 94.

240. D. P. Wright ("Blown Away Like a Bramble: The Dynamics of Analogy in Psalm 58," *RB* 103 [1996]: 215) sees the first section to encompass vv. 4–6, though there is a clear shift in both content and address at v. 4a.

241. Katharine J. Dell, "The Use of Animal Imagery in the Psalms and Wisdom Literature of Ancient Israel," *Scottish Journal of Theology* 53 (2000): 278–279.

242. Miglio, "Imagery," 117.

243. Here perhaps speaking of their obstinance (so Klaus Seybold, "Psalm LVIII: Ein Losungsversuch," *VT* 30 [1980]: 57).

244. See Jer 21:14; 32:19; Amos 6:12; Ps 104:13; Prov 1:31; 12:14; 18:20.

245. Seybold, "Psalm LVIII," 61.

246. Creach, *Destiny*, 42–43.

247. Though, of course they would not be innocent if they did otherwise.

248. The text of Ps 68 is notoriously difficult. Hans-Joachim Kraus (*Psalms 60–150*, trans. by Hilton C. Oswald, CC [Minneapolis, MN: Augsburg Fortress, 1989], 47) writes, "There is hardly another song in the Psalter which in its corrupt text and its lack of coherence precipitates such serious problems for the interpreter as Psalm 68." There are numerous textual problems and an abundance of language unique to the psalm (for a list of unique words and phrases, see Israel Knohl, "Psalm 68: Structure, Composition and Geography," *JHS* 12 (2012): 3, https://doi.org/10 .5508/jhs.2012.v12.a15). Where possible, translations have been reconstructed from the MT, otherwise, traditional readings from the LXX have been utilized.

249. LXX, Jerome and some translations (NASB, NRSV, NIV2011) offer a jussive sense here. However, the description of the event of judgment at the beginning of the psalm appears to follow the pattern of a description of theophany, cf. 97:1–7, and that this theophany structurally forms the basis of the call to praise in v. 5a. Cf. Todd A. Scacewater, *The Divine Builder in Psalm 68: Jewish and Pauline Tradition*, LNTS 631 (London: T&T Clark, 2020), 37.

250. DeClaissé-Walford, Jacobson, and Tanner (*Book of Psalms*, 543) read with the BHS apparatus and NRSV a 3mp form. This smooths out the parallel structure with the verb in v. 3c. The smoothing is unnecessary. In the immediate context no other 2ms forms appear, though they appear later in the psalm (v. 8a, etc.).

251. The translation intentionally emphasizes the spatial concept of wax melting near fire. The verb is supplied for readable English. The drawback of this translation is that it does not reflect the repetition of the various uses of פָּנִים.

252. Many scholars take the phrase רֹכֵב בָּעֲרָבוֹת to be a reference to the Ugaritic phrase "Rider of the clouds" (so DeClaissé-Walford, Jacobson, and Tanner, *Book of Psalms*, 543; cf. Isa 19:1).

253. Bill T. Arnold and Brent A. Strawn ("*beyāb šemô* in Psalm 68,5: A Hebrew Gloss to an Ugaritic Epithet?" *ZAW* 115 [2003]: 428–432) argue that this is an added gloss to clarify that the "rider of the clouds," usually in reference to Baal, is in this instance Yhwh.

254. The full phrase of v. 9b also appears in Judg 5:5. Though Knohl ("Psalm 68," 17) argues that the standard function of זֶה and in its place as parallel to other names for God imply that Sinai could here be an appellative for God. This seems to force an interpretation that is far too rigid for both the term and the significance of parallelism. The

word הָז could simply function as a pronoun in construct, as Juöun (§143h) argue (also Goldingay, *Psalms*, 2:319). Robert D. Holmstedt ("Analyzing הָז Grammar and Reading הָז Texts of Ps 68:9 and Judg 5:5," *JHS* 14 [2014]: 9–16, https://doi.org/10.5508/jhs .2014.v14.a8) argues that the function of הָז never has a genitive sense, and is followed as functioning to point to the identity of the mountain or location of this section.

255. The MT includes a word of unknown meaning. A number of translations (e.g., NASB95, NIV, NRSV) follow the reading וּבְנֻת. Goldingay (*Psalms*, 2:307), Tate (*Psalms 51–100*, 165), and Hossfeld and Zenger (*Psalms 2*, 159) follow Jerome and LXX and translate this as "beauty," thought to be a construct form from נָאֶה. Kraus (*Psalms 60–150*, 44, 46) and DeClaissé-Walford, Jacobson, and Tanner (*Book of Psalms*, 544–545) take this to be derivative of נָוֶה, "meadow." None of these options are entirely satisfactory, though I have followed here the option that fits most clearly with the text and can at least make some grammatical sense.

256. "Sheepfolds" is drawn from a parallel in Judg 5:16, though the word here is not clear (see DeClaissé-Walford, Jacobson, and Tanner, *Book of Psalms*, 544).

257. This word is uncertain. Also in 17a.

258. DeClaissé-Walford, Jacobson, and Tanner, *Book of Psalms*, 545.

259. A word of uncertain meaning.

260. For a partitive reading of בְּ, see *BHRG* §39.6.(b).(iv).

261. While typically translated as "dwell," the function here in light of the preceding lines is to demonstrate that the removal of captives and taking of booty allows Yh to continue to dwell.

262. Dahood (*Psalms*, 2:131) regards Ugaritic parallels to בשׁן and believes this to be another name for Leviathan. James H. Charlesworth ("Bashan, Symbology, Haplography, and Theology in Psalm 68," in *David and Zion: Biblical Studies in Honor of J. J. M. Roberts*, ed. Bernard F. Batto and Kathryn L. Roberts [Winona Lake, IN: Eisenbrauns, 2004], 357–360) also acknowledges Ugaritic parallels, but believes due to imprecise counting of syllables that a word is missing from this line; he suggests, in parallel with Isa 11:8, that חֻר meaning "den" be added, thus creating a meaning, "from the den of the dragon-snake," which completes a sort of image between heights and the seas, both in reference to a creature. This further renders connections to themes of the dead and shifts the initial point of the quotation to immediately after "the Lord" (אֲדֹנָי, v. 22a), as noted in Charlesworth, "Bashan," 360–361. This creative and detailed reconstruction, however, interprets this as (mostly) independent from v. 16a–16b. Charlesworth ("Bashan," 367–368) addresses this question, but does not state clearly why the immediate context of the psalm should not be more significant in the interpretation than Ugaritic parallels. As such, the context here remains the best and most immediate evidence for understanding this reference to indicate the mountain of Bashan, as in v. 16a–16b.

263. Traditional reading, word is unclear.

264. The meaning of this term is uncertain, though DeClaissé-Walford, Jacobson, and Tanner (*Book of Psalms*, 546) notes that in context it relates to gathered people.

265. Or "because." The function here is unclear.

266. Uncertain.

267. Repointing the MT בְּזֻר as an imperative.

268. Following LXX; Hebrew is uncertain.

269. A rare form of מֶן, cf. Isa 30:11.

270. Heb 3ms, though the verb is 3fs.

271. Cf. Deut 33:26.

272. קֶדֶם could also be understood as "ancient time," though the spatial meaning is more appropriate here due to the imagery of place throughout the psalm.

273. The phrase "voice of strength" is retained to highlight the repetition of עֹז here and in v. 35a.

274. Robert D. Miller II, *The Dragon, the Mountain, and the Nations: An Old Testament Myth, Its Origins, and Its Afterlives*, Explorations in Ancient Near Eastern Civilizations (University Park, PA: Pennsylvania State University Press, 2018), 169.

275. Hossfeld and Zenger, *Psalms 2*, 161; the same divisions are used by Knohl ("Psalm 68," 5), though not including the sections he considers additions in vv. 1–4 and 35–36.

276. DeClaissé-Walford, Jacobson, and Tanner, *Book of Psalms*, 542, emphasis removed.

277. Scacewater, *Divine Builder*, 36.

278. Scacewater, *Divine Builder*, 39.

279. Goldingay (*Psalms*, 2:318) notes in particular the mention of rains is suggestive of ongoing activity rather than Yhwh's guiding of the people of Israel through the wilderness.

280. Scacewater, *Divine Builder*, 41.

281. Goldingay, *Psalms*, 2:310, 318.

282. Hossfeld and Zenger (*Psalms 2*, 161, 165) describe only vv. 8a–11b as a theophany, though it is unclear why v. 2a is not considered theophanic language as well.

283. Hossfeld and Zenger, *Psalms 2*, 162; Scacewater, *Divine Builder*, 37.

284. Goldingay (*Psalms*, 2:312–314) describes the unusual placement of this section.

285. The disadvantaged here are "orphans" (יְתוֹמִים, v. 6a), "widows" (אַלְמָנוֹת, v. 6a), "isolated" (יְחִידִים, v. 7a), and "imprisoned" (אֲסִירִים, v. 7b).

286. Goldingay, *Psalms*, 2:320. DeClaissé-Walford, Jacobson, and Tanner (*Book of Psalms*, 548) suggest that the rain is both destructive and nourishing, though it is only explicitly the latter. The rain in v. 9a is only described as something in response to Yhwh's presence.

287. Goldingay, *Psalms*, 2:321; Hossfeld and Zenger, *Psalms 2*, 165. Goldingay here points to the women declaring victory in battle in Exod 15:20–21 and 1 Sam 18:6–7.

288. So Hossfeld and Zenger, *Psalms 2*, 159; RSV.

289. Miller, *Dragon*, 170. John A. Emerton ("The 'Mountain of God' in Psalm 68:16," in *History and Traditions of Early Israel: Studies Presented to Edward Nielsen*, ed. André Lemaire and Bendedikt Otzen, VTSup 50 [Leiden: Brill, 1993], 304–306) argues that these lines should be rendered as a question about the mountain of Bashan's status, though the vocative meaning also resolves all of the challenges

Emerton suggests with other translations, and Emerton's solution does not clearly address the direct address of the mountain in v. 17a.

290. DeClaissé-Walford, Jacobson, and Tanner, *Book of Psalms*, 549; Goldingay, *Psalms*, 2:310.

291. Hossfeld and Zenger, *Psalms 2*, 165.

292. This description implies that the enemies Yhwh defeats are physical rather than spiritual entities, such as other gods.

293. Hossfeld and Zenger, *Psalms 2*, 167.

294. Dell, "Animal Imagery," 288.

295. Scacewater, *Divine Builder*, 37.

296. J. P. Fokkelman, "Structure of Psalm LXVIII," in *In Quest of the Past: Studies on Israelite Religion, Literature, and Prophetism: Papers Read at the Joint British-Dutch Old Testament Conference, Held at Elspeet, 1988*, ed. A. S. van der Woude, OTS 26 (Leiden: Brill, 1990), 75.

297. Levin, "Gebetbuch," 364; Hossfeld and Zenger, *Psalms 2*, 163.

298. Hossfeld and Zenger, *Psalms 2*, 164.

299. Scacewater, *Divine Builder*, 37.

300. The כִּי introduces a temporal clause, though the difference between conditional and temporal clauses of unrealized situations is not precise. See *BHRG* §40.29.1.(2).

301. For this verb meaning "to shake," see DeClaissé-Walford, Jacobson, and Tanner, *Book of Psalms*, 603. Cf. Neh 2:7.

302. Elided from the previous line.

303. The Hebrew word הָרִים can be both the plural of הַר, "mountain," or the *hiphil* infinitive construct of the verb רוּם. Both fit within the conceptual framework of the poem, with the immediate context of other geographical formations (i.e., "the wilderness") and the repetition of the verb רוּם throughout the poem. Joseph E. Jensen ("Psalm 75: Its Poetic Context and Structure," *CBQ* 63 [2001]: 418) suggests this is "an example of the rare, truly polysemantic pun in Hebrew poetry." It would be difficult to determine whether or not a wordplay is intended, but the argument is sound. However, in the logic of the poem, a verbal notion (though not necessarily a verb) would be required. An understanding of the word as "mountain" does not supply this.

304. זֶה is used here as a relative pronoun (see *BHRG* §36.3.3.(1)).

305. Meindert Dijkstra ("He Pours the Sweet Wine off, only the Dregs Are for the Wicked: An Epigraphic Note on mizzæh in Psalm 75,9," *ZAW* 107 (1995): 296–300) argues that the word מִזֶּה should rather be rendered מִזְגָּה and understood as a type of sweet wine based on epigraphic evidence on jars as well as certain comparative Semitic languages.

306. John W. Hilber, *Cultic Prophecy in the Psalms*, BZAW 352 (Berlin: De Gruyter, 2005), 174; Jensen, "Psalm 75," 419; DeClaissé-Walford, Jacobson, and Tanner, *Book of Psalms*, 605.

307. Gillingham, "New Wine," 376; Jacobson, *Many are Saying,* 109–110; Goldingay, *Psalms*, 2:439. Frank-Lothar Hossfeld ("Das Prophetische in den Psalmen: Zur Gottesrede der Asafpsalmen im Vergleich mit des der ersten und zweiten Davidpsalters," in *Ich bewirke das Heil und erschaffe das Unheil (Jesaja 45.7), Stufen zur*

Botschaft der Propheten: Festschrift für Lothar Ruppert zum 65. Geburtstag, ed. Friedrich Diedrich and Bernd Willmes, FB 65 [Würzburg: Echter, 1998], 240) offers a similar pattern, though states that the speech from God continues to verse 7. It is unclear why verse 7 would be included in the speech from God here, nor does Hossfeld explain this choice.

308. DeClaissé-Walford, Jacobson, and Tanner, *Book of Psalms*, 605.

309. Gillingham, "New Wine," 376; Jacobson, *Many are Saying*, 109–110. Hossfeld, "Das Prophetische in den Psalmen," 240; Jensen, "Psalm 75," 419; DeClaissé-Walford, Jacobson, and Tanner, *Book of Psalms*, 605.

310. Hilber, *Cultic Prophecy*, 174; Goldingay, *Psalms*, 2:439

311. For example, Pss 12:6; 60:6–8; 68:23–24; 132:18–19.

312. Elsewhere in the psalms, the creation and establishment of the earth are connected with Yhwh's taking the seat of judgment over the nations (Pss 93:1; 104:5). However, in this setting, this is done through a wordplay. The verb has the implication of a just or right standard (1 Sam 2:3; Ezek 18:25, 18:29, 33:17, 33:20; Prov 16:2, 21:2, 24:12) as well as a connection to building (2 Kgs 12:12) including creation (Job 28:25) in other locations. A similar play on words though with a different effect includes this verb in light of an act of creation and the weighing of God's motives (Isa 40:12–13). He can accurately measure the earth as well as humans.

313. Hossfeld and Zenger, *Psalms 2*, 258.

314. Kraus, *Psalms 60–150*, 105; cf. Hossfeld and Zenger, *Psalms 2*, 257.

315. Othmar Keel, *The Symbolism of the Biblical World: Ancient Near Eastern Iconography and the Book of Psalms*, trans. Timothy J. Hallett (New York: Seabury, 1978), 86. He continues "The Mesopotamian gods wear horned caps as a head covering" (Keel, *Symbolism*, 86).

316. Margit Linnéa Süring, "Horn Motifs in the Hebrew Bible and Related Ancient Near Eastern Literature and Iconography," PhD Dissertation (Berrien Springs, MI: Andrews University, 1980), 343–349.

317. Gregory R. Lanier, *Old Testament Conceptual Metaphors and the Christology of Luke's Gospel*, Library of New Testament Studies 591 (London: T&T Clark, 2018), 35–79.

318. Lanier, *Old Testament Conceptual Metaphors*, 53–54. Unfortunately, Lanier is focused on the interpretation of a New Testament text that quotes a different psalm entirely, though his work traces the conceptual metaphors beyond the instances quoted in Luke.

319. Lanier, *Old Testament Conceptual Metaphors*, 48–50.

320. Carey Ellen Walsh, *The Fruit of the Vine: Viticulture in Ancient Israel*, Harvard Semitic Monographs 60 (Winona Lake, IN: Eisenbrauns, 2000), 203–205.

321. Alonso-Schökel (*Manual*, 109) connects the language of being "full" here with the common usage of the term in other contexts of judgment and anger. The connection between a cup and blessing/judgment occurs elsewhere in the psalms (Pss 11:6, 16:5).

322. For the latter interpretation, see Tate, *Psalms 51–100*, 259, and Goldingay, *Psalms*, 2:446.

323. On the "cutting off" of horns, see also Jer 48:25.

324. Cf. 1 Sam 2:1; Pss 89:18, 25; 112:9; 148:13; Lam 2:17; 1 Chr 25:5 for the "lifting" of horns.

325. Terrien, *Psalms*, 546 simply poses the question of there being a "hidden meaning" without attempting to determine what it could be.

326. Jacobson, *Many Are Saying*, 110–111.

327. Hossfeld and Zenger (*Psalms 2*, 435) suggest the function of the מַה here extends also to v. 6b. While poetic ellipsis could account for this, Goldingay (*Psalms 3*:51) rightly notes that v. 6b functions as a straightforward indicative verbless clause.

328. Hossfeld and Zenger (*Psalms 2*, 435) argue for a past-tense reading of the WAYYIQTOL, though this does not adequately account for the clear semantic relationship with the infinitive in v. 8a.

329. The infinitive construct is used here to explain what will happen following their blossoming in v. 8b. This fits closely with the "immanent" sense (*IBHS* §36.2.3g).

330. On the modal function of the infinitive construct, see *IBHS* §36.2.3f.

331. The word בַּלֹּתִי has caused many problems for interpreters, as the meaning "I mixed" does not make sense in the context following the actions of Yhwh lifting the horn of the speaker. Nava Cohen, "Psalm 92: Structure and Meaning," *ZAW* 125 (2013): 602) argues that the word should be repointed בְלֹתִי, and infinitive construct with 1cs suffix from the verb בלה with the meaning "my old age," which is attested among some versions, but still does not make good sense of the text—in context, there is no indication of the age of the speaker (though v. 15a refers to the old age of the righteous). The theme of the ephemeral nature of the wicked is present. Th. Booij ("The Hebrew Text of Psalm XCII 11," *VT* 38 [1988]: 212), while admitting that no good solution exists, suggests a form of the *hiphil* of בלג, though this is further based on a tenuous Arabic parallel, meaning "to shine." Hossfeld and Zenger (*Psalms 2*, 435) translate the verb as transitive and amend the verbal subject to 2ms. Much of the issue is that the verb בלל does not appear in a passive form in *qal*, other than in a passive participle form (Tate, *Psalms 51–100*, 462). A scribal mistake of connecting the verb בלל with the phrase בְּשֶׁמֶן is likely, due to the numerous occasions in the Pentateuch where the verb is followed by בְּשֶׁמֶן (Exod 29:1, 40; Lev 2:4, 5; 7:10, 12; 9:4; etc.). In every case the verb בלל refers to preparation of food, and thus, there is a relative lack of breadth of evidence of the verb—37 of 44 occurrences of a verb בלל appear in this construction in texts describing ritual cooking. There is a possibility of a passive form meaning "to anoint," and has been followed in this translation.

332. Reading *qere*.

333. Nahum M. Sarna ("The Psalm for the Sabbath Day (Ps 92)," *JBL* 81 [1962]: 167) argues that the word "your works" (פָּעֳלֶךָ) draws attention to God's creative work, yet in this context the word appears more closely aligned with work God does on behalf of the speaker.

334. Goldingay, *Psalms*, 3:56.

335. Catherine Petrany ("Instruction, Performance, and Prayer: The Didactic Function of Psalmic Wisdom," in *The Shape and Shaping of the Book of Psalms: The Current State of Scholarship*, ed. Nancy L. DeClaissé-Walford, AIL 20 [Atlanta, GA:

SBL, 2014], 94) notes that while vv. 7–8 do not contain explicit address to God, they are nonetheless subsumed within the speech to God.

336. W. Dennis Tucker, Jr., "The Ordered World of Psalm 92," *OTE* 32 (2019): 368, citing *IBHS* §36.2.3f and Juöun §124.1, emphasis original.

337. See Ps 74:23 for a parallel, which functions rhetorically to connect the goals of the speaker with Yhwh's reputation. See Kevin Foth, "Psalm 74 and Social Identity," *JSOT* 47 (2022): 90–91; Goldingay, *Psalms*, 2:435–436; and a parallel in the *Hodayot* in Carol Newsom, *The Self as Symbolic Space: Constructing Identity and Community at Qumran*, Studies on the Texts of the Desert of Judah 52 (Leiden: Brill, 2004), 241.

338. Sarna, "Psalm for the Sabbath Day," 167.

339. See comments on horn metaphors under Ps 75. Peter Riede ("'Doch du erhöhtest wie einem Wildstier mein Horn': Zur Metaphorik in Ps 92,11," in *Metaphors in the Psalms*, ed. Pierre van Hecke and Antje Labahn, BETL 231 [Leuven: Peeters, 2010], 211–212) makes the connection between Ps 92:11a and Ps 75:5 in that both regard the righteous and the wicked.

340. Tucker, "Ordered World," 371.

341. Tucker, "Ordered World," 372.

342. Hossfeld and Zenger, *Psalms 2*, 436.

343. Cohen, "Psalm 92," 599.

344. Gerstenberger (*Psalms, Part 2*, 171) suggests that the "hymn" to the righteous was added to balance the negative descriptions of the wicked. Whether original or added later, the botanical metaphors express the contrast beyond the terminology.

345. Cohen, "Psalm 92."

346. Cohen, "Psalm 92," 599–603.

347. Cynthia L. Miller ("Ellipsis Involving Negation in Biblical Poetry," in *Seeking Out the Wisdom of the Ancients: Essays Offered to Honor Michael V. Fox on the Occasion of His Sixty-Fifth Birthday*, ed. Ronald L. Troxel, Kelvin G. Friebel, and Dennis R. Magary [Winona Lake, IN: Eisenbrauns, 2005], 44) notes that this is a rare case of "reverse ellipsis."

348. Howard (*Structure*, 46) argues to read the force of the עַד־מָתַי into v. 4a–4b. This is unlikely for two reasons. First, with the repetition of the phrase in both verses, one would expect the repetition to continue. Second, the content fits as the initial description of the activities of the רְשָׁעִים which continues through v. 7b.

349. See Howard (*Structure*, 44) for reading the WAYYIQTOL as a present. Cf. Kraus, *Psalms 59–150*, 237; Goldingay, *Psalms*, 3:73.

350. Hossfeld and Zenger (*Psalms 2*, 452; followed by DeClaissé-Walford, Jacobson, and Tanner, *Book of Psalms*, 711) suggests that a word is missing from this line, though only points to a comparison of the structure. With Tate (*Psalms 51–100*, 484), I read the lack of verb to point to an ellipsis for the verb יֹכִיחַ.

351. See comments on Ps 1:1.

352. Heb 3ms.

353. Some manuscripts include צַדִּיק here (followed by Tate, *Psalms 51–100*, 484–485; Howard, *Structure*, 48), though it is not necessary to amend. With the

interpretive decision in the following footnote, the noun צֶדֶק/"righteousness" makes sense within the parallel structure of the line.

354. The antecedent of the pronominal suffix on וְאַחֲרָיו is understood as "righteousness" (צֶדֶק) in the previous line. *BHRG* §39.2.(1).d–e show the function of preposition אַחַר having the sense of devotion to a person in several cases, as I interpret it here. Cf. also Hossfeld and Zenger, *Psalms 2*, 452.

355. Gerstenberger, *Psalms, Part 2*, 180 writes that לוּלֵי expresses an unreal situation and even suggests that God could fail.

356. Hossfeld and Zenger, *Psalms 51–100*, 453.

357. In this case, these should be considered coreferential with those who speak in v. 7a–7b. Petrany ("Instruction," 97) rightly notes that these figures "parallel" the wicked figures. Hossfeld and Zenger (*Psalms 2*, 454) suggest "they must be identical with the wicked/evildoers" here. Cf. Gerstenberger, *Psalms, Part 2*, 178.

358. Petrany, "Instruction," 97.

359. Brown, *Seeing the Psalms*, 170.

360. The "upright in heart" (יִשְׁרֵי־לֵב, v. 15b) function on the side of justice, though they do not have the same function as those who are attacked by the enemies.

361. See *IBHS* §36.2.3d.

362. Broyles, *Psalms*, 372.

363. On the self-destruction of the wicked see Pss 9:17, 141:10, or for the opponent of the speaker, see e.g., Ps 35:7–8. On the destruction of the wicked by Yhwh, see e.g., Pss 3:8; 9:6; 11:6; 129:4; 145:20; and 147:6.

364. Neumann, *Schriftgelehrte Hymnen*, 98.

365. Hossfeld and Zenger, *Psalms 2*, 453.

366. Neumann, *Schriftgelehrte Hymnen*, 98.

367. Tate (*Psalms 51–100*, 516) translates as "islands," noting either option is possible and both express the metaphorical landscape of distant places connected to water.

368. Howard (*Structure*, 68) notes that the pronoun "him" is implied by the context, though this is unnecessary to supply in the translation.

369. The term can be understood as indicative (Goldingay, *Psalms*, 3:110; Tate, *Psalms 51–100*, 517; Hossfeld and Zenger, *Psalms 2*, 469) or imperative (LXX, DeClaissé-Walford, Jacobson, and Tanner, *Book of Psalms*, 723). I take the indicative due to the context of the psalm as a declaration of God's power rather than as a prayer.

370. Some scholars (Kraus, *Psalms 59–150*, 156; Howard, *Structure*, 72–73) repoint as a form of "dawns" (זרח) following the reading in LXX and parallel to Ps 112:4. However, most recent interpreters rightly accept the MT as the *lectio difficilior* and have no issue viewing this as metaphor (Hossfeld and Zenger, *Psalms 2*, 469; Goldingay, *Psalms*, 3:117; DeClaissé-Walford, Jacobson, and Tanner, *Book of Psalms*, 724).

371. Hossfeld and Zenger, *Psalms 2*, 479.

372. Reinhard Müller, "The Origins of Yhwh in Light of the Earliest Psalms," in *The Origins of Yahwism*, ed. Jürgen van Oorschot and Markus Witte, BZAW 484 (Berlin: De Gruyter, 2017), 213.

373. E. N. Ortlund, "An Intertextual Reading of Theophany of Psalm 97," *SJOT* 20 (2006): 273.

374. See Mowinckel, *Psalms*, 1:107–109. I do not take this position here, though it has been influential in scholarship.

375. Joerstad argues that "inanimate" is not an appropriate term for the created world in the ancient Hebrew mentality (Mari Joerstad, *The Hebrew Bible and Environmental Ethics: Humans, Nonhumans, and the Living Landscape* [Cambridge: Cambridge University Press, 2019], 158–171 for a treatment of the psalms). However, I use inanimate here to demonstrate that these features do not typically move nor give verbal declarations. Other objects that are described in action in the psalm participate through activities that are not necessarily personifications, though they still are part of the general description of the results of Yhwh's reign (vv. 2a, 3a–3b, 4a, 5a).

376. Beth LaNeel Tanner, *The Book of Psalms Through the Lens of Intertextuality*, Studies in Biblical Literature 26 (New York: Peter Lang, 2001), 120.

377. Ortlund, "Intertextual Reading," 278.

378. Differentiated from the deity Yhwh through the modifier לכֹּ.

379. For the metaphor of light as salvation in psalms, see Bernd Janowski, "Das Licht des Lebens: Zur Lichtmetaphorik in den Psalmen," in *Metaphors in the Psalms*, ed. Pierre van Hecke and Antje Labahn, BETL 231 (Leuven: Peeters, 2010), 98–100. Janowski points out that light in this context makes Yhwh visible to those who are saved ("Licht," 100). Here, in this psalm, it leads directly into the peoples' praise.

380. While the canonical placement of the psalms is not a concern for this work, it is important to note that Ps 111 is closely related to Ps 112 in structure. One is either written in light of the other or they were written in conjunction. The direction of borrowing cannot be determined. See Raymond C. Van Leeuwen, "Form Criticism, Wisdom, and Psalms 111–112," in *The Changing Face of Form Criticism for the Twenty-First Century*, ed. Marvin A. Sweeney and Ehud Ben Zvi (Grand Rapids, MI: Eerdmans, 2003).

381. Hebrew 3ms here and throughout the psalm

382. Allen (*Psalms 101–150*, 94) and Kraus (*Psalms 60–150*, 361) translate the יכִּ as emphatic. This may be the case here, but rather than a purely emphatic function, the clause following יכִּ provides the reasons for the statements in 1b–5b.Cf. *BHRG* §40.29.2.(2).(b), and Ps 1:6a.

383. See *BHRG* §39.19.(3) for the use of the preposition דעַ to indicate a circumstance extending "to an extreme dimension." In this case, it would make little sense that the commendable person would be afraid only to the point of their enemy appearing.

384. P. J. Botha, "'Wealth and Riches are in His House' (Ps 112:3): Acrostic Wisdom Psalms and the Development of Antimaterialism," in *The Shape and Shaping of the Book of Psalms: The Current State of Scholarship*, ed. Nancy L. DeClaissé-Walford, AIL 20 (Atlanta, GA: SBL, 2014), 114.

385. Rainer Kessler ("Khirbet el-Kôm und Psalm 112—ein Fall von Intertextualität," *VT* 61 [2011]: 678–679) notes that the reception of blessing, that of salvation

from enemies, and wealth from Yhwh forms a conceptual constellation that is present here as well as in the Khirbet el-Kōm inscription.

386. In this case, the righteous and the poor are clearly delineated.

387. Schaefer, *Psalms*, 278.

388. See the comments on horn metaphors in the section on Ps 75.

389. Schaefer, *Psalms*, 279.

390. Kraus, *Psalms 60–150*, 365. In Ps 37:12, the רָשָׁע similarly gnashes their teeth against the צַדִּיק. See also Pss 35:16; Job 16:9; Lam 2:16)

391. Tanner, *The Book of Psalms Through the Lens of Intertextuality*, 144.

392. Some MT manuscripts, LXX, and 11QPsᵃ include the definite article. Frank-Lothar Hossfeld and Erich Zenger (*Psalms 3: A Commentary on Psalms 101–150*, trans. Linda M. Maloney, Hermeneia [Minneapolis, MN: Fortress, 2011], 549) suggest that this is more likely to occur as a gloss from a phrase common to the Psalter.

393. Interestingly, Egbert Ballhorn (*Zum Telos des Psalters: der Textzusammenhang des Vierten und Fünften Psalmenbuches (Ps 90–150)*, BBB 138 [Berlin: Philo, 2004], 277) notes that *selah* appears with regular frequency in the first three books of the Psalter but only in four total times in two psalms of books 4–5, with three of four total references in Ps 140.

394. Woodenly, "Push my foot."

395. Hossfeld and Zenger (*Psalms 3*, 549) see this verb introducing a repetition of something said earlier, thus "I said." In favor of a present-time translation, this quote appears in medias res, and as such, introduces a statement of commitment prior to Yhwh's rescue in the midst of the trial.

396. Heb 3ms.

397. Heb ms.

398. Heb 3ms.

399. Following *qere*.

400. This word is *hapax legomenon,* and while there is no clear answer as to its meaning, some have suggested a continuation of the hunting imagery. Moshe Greenberg ("Two New Hunting Terms in Psalm 140, 12," *Hebrew Annual Review* 1 [1977]: 151) suggests that "corral" is the meaning here, drawing on ancient hunting practices. This is followed by Wilton Gerardo Sánchez-Castelblanco, "'Que les caigan brasas de fuego' (Sal 140,11): Comentario exegético del salmo 140," *Franciscanum* 54 (2012): 304.

401. Following *qere*.

402. And, as Kraus (*Psalms 60–150*, 521) notes: "not a word is said about the reason for these hostilities."

403. 1cs verbal subjects and pronouns appear in vv. 2a–2b, 5a–8b, 10a, 13a.

404. Gerstenberger, *Psalms, Part 2 and Lamentations*, 409.

405. The structure of the psalm is coherent and linear, against Allen (*Psalms 101–150*, 267) and DeClaissé-Walford, Jacobson, and Tanner (*Book of Psalms*, 967) who see a chiastic structure centered on vv. 7a–8b. Apart from the chiasm, the structural divisions here agree.

406. Hauge, *Between Sheol and Temple*, 10.

407. Tova Forti, "Of Snakes and Sinners: An Intertextual Reading of *Ba'al ha-lashon* in Ecclesiastes 10:11 in Light of *'ish lashon* in Psalm 140:12 (11)," in *Reading Ecclesiastes Intertextually*, ed. Katharine Dell and Will Kynes, LHBOTS 574 (New York: T&T Clark, 2013), 89–90. For example, Prov 18:6; 10:18, 29:13.

408. So DeClaissé-Walford, Jacobson, and Tanner, *Book of Psalm*, 970.

409. Hossfeld and Zenger, *Psalms 3*, 553.

410. Kraus, *Psalms 60–150*, 523.

411. For the argument of worshiping activities as part of the ethical vision of psalms, see Joshua T. James, *The Storied Ethics of the Thanksgiving Psalms*, LHBOTS 658 (London: Bloomsbury T&T Clark, 2017), 19–38.

412. See Exod 30:8.

413. Nearly all commentators translate מַשְׂאַת with a version of the verbal concept of "lifting/lifting up" of hands (See e.g., DeClaissé-Walford, Jacobson, and Tanner, *Book of Psalms*, 973; Hossfeld and Zenger, *Psalms 3*, 555; Kraus, *Psalms 60–150*, 525). The phrase appears to be understood as a synonym for prayer, which, as noted by Hossfeld and Zenger (*Psalms 3*, 558), has been used by more traditional scholars as a way of devaluing the sacrificial system. DCH (5:499) understands the instance of the word in Ps 141:2 to refer to a gift or offering, as the term does in many contexts (2 Sam 11:8; Jer 40:5; Ezek 20:40; Esth 2:18). In fact, understanding this term as a synonym for prayer would be unique. It is more likely that the line expands on the concept of sacrifice, forming an extended simile comparing the act of prayer to regular sacrificial acts. However, this second line emphasizes a second situation related to the temple cult, which could be referring to the daily evening sacrifice. The only time that the explicit phrase מִנְחַת־עָרֶב appears elsewhere is Dan 9:21. Though this may be later than Ps 141, it reflects terminology used in the early second temple period, a likely historical situation for Ps 141. In a few cases, the word denotes the rising of smoke (Judg 20:38, 20:40, Jer 6:1), which could connect to the act of incense rising, which would further parallel the previous line.

414. Th. Booij ("Psalm 141: A Prayer for Discipline and Protection," *Bib* 86 [2005]: 97–106, 98) argues that here the root should be עוֹלֵל, "child," and thus point to a meaning of to "think up (frivolously), devise." Booij has made too much of a parallel relationship, seeing here the need for a sort of synonymous parallelism with "mind"/לֵב.

415. This is not typically a transitive verb.

416. Reading רָאשִׁי as the object and omitting the repetition for רֹאשׁ to smooth the translation.

417. Raymond Jacques Tournay ("Psaume CXLI: Nouvelle Interprétation," *RB* 90 [1983]: 322) follows the LXX in reading רָשָׁע in the first instance of רֹאשׁ here (ἁμαρτωλοῦ), establishing an antithetical parallelism, giving the meaning "Let not the oil of the wicked adorn my head" ("Que l'huile de l'impie n'orne pas ma tête"). Text critically, reading רֹאשׁ or רֹשׁ have advantages or disadvantages, particularly that both are repeated elsewhere in the immediate context. רֹאשׁ is maintained as the *lectio difficilior*.

418. On כִּי as a modal adverb, see *BHRG* §40.9.2.(4).

419. Michael D. Goulder (*The Psalms of the Return [Book V, Psalms 107–150]*, vol. 2, *Studies in the Psalter*, JSOTSup 258 (Sheffield: Sheffield Academic, 1998), 259) compares Prov 24:27 for a comparable use of the ו to signal a later temporal situation. Tournay ("Psaume CXLI," 324) suggests repointing עוֹד to עֵד in light of Deut 31:26, though this is unnecessary in the context drawing on the context of judgment, though this is unnecessary to amend.

420. Understanding the idiom to refer to the portion of a trap that closes against a capture animal.

421. Hebrew pronoun suffix is 3ms, which Hossfeld and Zenger (*Psalms 3*, 557) and Allen (*Psalms 101–150*, 272) suggest a distributive sense.

422. Hossfeld and Zenger (*Psalms 4*, 555), Goldingay (*Psalms*, 3:653), Allen (*Psalms 101–150*, 272) understand the word יַחַד to modify the entrapment of the wicked, though the MT places it on a separate line. This would create a quite imbalanced line, both in terms of length and content. *DCH* 4:197 suggests that the use here may emphasize exclusivity of escape for the speaker.

423. See e.g., Dahood, *Psalms*, 3:309.

424. Booij ("Psalm 141," 97) argues that it must not mean incense here because of the parallelism with מִנְחַת־עָרֶב, which he interprets to mean either a grain offering (2 Kgs 16:15) or the evening sacrifice (Exod 29:38–42, Num 28:3–9). However, the continual offerings and incense that are burned at the altar are themselves connected semantically. The parallelism thus serves rather to further connect the idea of incense and both images are used to describe the continual nature of the prayer.

425. For example, Judg 5:26; Prov 23:35 for the use of the term relating to violence. The term is also used specifically of an end deserving of fools in Prov 18:6, 19:29. Though it is not something the wicked ever do in the psalm, conceptually it is related to the activities of those who oppose the speaker rather than those who help him.

426. Holt, "Psalm 141," 190.

427. So DeClaissé-Walford, Jacobson, and Tanner, *Book of Psalms*, 974.

428. Following Allen, *Psalms 101–150*, 18 and 299, emphasizing the focus on the metonymic use of נֶפֶשׁ for the person.

429. Woodenly, "Son of a Man." Hossfeld and Zenger (*Psalms 3*, 609) note an important wordplay between אָדָם in v. 3b and אַדְמָתוֹ in v. 4.

430. Following Hossfeld and Zenger, *Psalms 3*, 609, who write that רוּחַ here connotes a "life force," the absence of which clearly leads to death in the context of the poem.

431. The 3ms pronoun suffix appears to make this term reflexive, "his ground," though this sounds awkward in English translation.

432. The presence of a clear subject suggests the predicative sense of the participles, yet I have maintained the earlier sentence structure to reveal the repetition of participles in vv. 6–9 and due to the focus of this section on describing Yhwh's character through his activities.

433. With the frequency of references, the density of the divine name in Ps 146 is one of the highest in the Psalter (Patrick D. Miller, "The End of the Psalter: A Response to Erich Zenger," *JSOT* 80 [1998]: 108–109).

434. Neumann, *Schriftgelherte Hymnen*, 110.

435. John S. Kselman, "Psalm 146 in Its Context," *CBQ* 50 (1988): 592. Willgren (*Formation*, 280) argues that the uses of *Hallelujah* in vv. 1a and 10c are original, rather than a liturgical note or editorial addition.

436. Jacqueline E. Lapsley, "Reading Psalm 146 in the Wild: A Feminist Biblical Theology of Praise," in *After Exegesis: Feminist Biblical Theology: Essays in Honor of Carol A. Newsom*, ed. Patricia K. Tull and Jacqueline E. Lapsley (Waco, TX: Baylor University Press, 2015), 86.

437. Hossfeld and Zenger, *Psalms 3*, 609.

438. Lapsley, "Reading Psalm 146," 93. Dahood (*Psalms*, 3:341) views these two as a merism, indicating those with or without power, though the second line is more likely to refer either to the leaders or to humanity in general.

439. Brodersen, *End of the Psalter*, 241.

440. Goldingay (*Psalms*, 3:709) notes that the leaders "may not belong to the faithless [רָשָׁע] or come short in moral values," yet that their death is inevitable provides grounds enough for their unreliability. Goldingay sees the wicked (which he calls "faithless") to be a more specific designation rather than generally bad.

441. Broyles (*Psalms*, 510) notes that the expression of אַשְׁרֵי reveals both a reality and a teaching to follow regarding how one would accomplish that state.

442. Gerstenberger (*Psalms, Part 2, and Lamentations*, 439) notes that this is a rare occurrence where the beatitude does not emphasize an individual's actions, here instead highlighting the association with Yhwh and his people.

443. W. Dennis Tucker, Jr., *Constructing and Deconstructing Power in Psalms 107–150*, AIL 19 (Atlanta, GA: SBL, 2014), 194.

444. Ballhorn, *Zum Telos des Psalters*, 308: "Als Personengruppe, der man sich bewußt zuordnen kann, kommen nur die Gerechten in Frage; zu den anderen Bedürftigen gehört man nicht per voluntativem Akt."

445. Hossfeld and Zenger (*Psalms 3*, 615) suggests that this is a concrete metaphor wherein those who are enslaved in chains are able to walk upright.

446. Reindl ("Gotteslob," 124) notes that it is only here that Yhwh is said to "love"/אהב the righteous in the Old Testament.

447. Neumann, *Schriftgelherte Hymnen*, 142.

448. Kraus, *Psalms 60–150*, 552.

449. Kselman, "Psalm 146," 595.

450. Brodersen, *End of the Psalter*, 233.

451. Gerstenberger, *Psalms, Part 2*, 439.

452. Neumann, *Schriftgelehrte Hymnen*, 127.

Conclusion

This work has shown that greater care can be taken to understand conventional language in Hebrew psalms. Poetics and semantics are closely related, and much more language in the psalms can be understood from within the conventions of psalmody, rather than imposed from other works in the Hebrew Bible or assumed by the canonical placement of certain psalms. Drawing the boundary around convention rather than theological influence or canonical placement has allowed for a more nuanced articulation of the theme of the righteous and the wicked in psalms. The research presented here has yielded results regarding the function of these figures, and ultimately, their identity more broadly.

Rooted in the semantics of the terms צַדִּיק and רָשָׁע, I have shown that individual uses of these terms signal a range of meanings, though within the individual psalm these figures rely on the set literary pattern of the judgment of the wicked and the salvation or blessing of the righteous. These meanings and functions are unique to the individual context of a single psalm rather than, as scholarship has often assumed, in a singular or programmatic way. They relate to other poetic features as part of the psalmic rhetoric to contribute to the overall meaning of the psalm.

I have shown that the semantic functions of צַדִּיק and רָשָׁע must be determined in the context of the individual psalm. These terms do not equate to the meanings and functions of the terms as they appear elsewhere in the Hebrew Bible, especially in Proverbs. Even across psalms, however, the uses of these terms are not consistent. Further, I have shown that the deed-consequence or character-consequence paradigms are not proper labels for all of the psalms that contrast צַדִּיק and רָשָׁע. In several instances, both figures are judged, either positively or negatively, respectively. However, the designation צַדִּיק is often given because they are innocently threatened by others. In connection with this, the רָשָׁע often functions as an opponent rather than simply as one who does wrong. As such, it is not so much their character that is central to the paradigm of their salvation, but the fairness or justice of God to eventually elevate their position and to destroy the wicked.

It is thus more accurate to say that there is no distinct "paradigm" of the צַדִּיק and רָשָׁע apart from its usage as a binary contrast. This conclusion allows for a much more fluid interpretation of these figures within individual psalms. Because there are no distinct markers within psalms about who represents the righteous or the wicked, the context remains essential for understanding the meaning of the terms.

This semantic distinction allows for the contrast of these two terms to serve various ends within the poetry of a psalm. The language of the psalms is rich in imagery and formal features. Some of these features are unique to or more frequent in psalms than in other Hebrew poetic texts. These features highlight not only meaning, but beauty, and ultimately, the cognitive experience of the readers who encounter these texts, both ancient and modern. Poetics, as applied to psalms, often includes limited recognition of less formal features, such as that of character. The use of figural representation as a poetic tool itself leads to claims for readers of the text. In binary opposition and through consistent character patterning of the righteous and the wicked, the description of the righteous is exemplified, though not necessarily in the same way as is often assumed from Psalm 1 or from Proverbs. For the readers, the righteous are those to be emulated by the readers, but frequently not in the ethical attributes ascribed to the righteous, but in their reliance on Yhwh for his protection in times of need.

As shown in the analyses of the psalms, in a majority of cases the righteous and the wicked contrast is used to affirm a reality about the world wherein the innocent are offered hope that their persecutors will one day be destroyed. In some cases, notably Pss 37 and 112, activities of what it means to be righteous are more clearly articulated without reference to their plight. Namely, they are noted for their generosity (Pss 37:21, 26; 112:5, 9) and speaking wisdom (Ps 37:30). Further, in Ps 92:13–15, the righteous person is described by their flourishing. However, with the contrast between the figures, the destruction of the רָשָׁע in every case affirms a principle of justice. The claim that is most generally true of the righteous and the wicked in psalms is: The righteous suffer at the hands of the wicked. Secondarily, the theology expressed is: The righteous are protected by Yhwh, the wicked are condemned, either by Yhwh or their own devices.

The most common feature of the contrast between the צַדִּיק and רָשָׁע relates to their respective ends. The ends of the figures are contrasted in Pss 1:4–6; 7:10 (in a request); 32:10–11; 34:20–22; 37:16–18, 28–29, 38–40; 55:23–24;[1] 58:11–12; 68:3–4; 75:9–11; 92:8, 13–15; 97:10–12; 112:6, 10;

140:9–12 (in a request), 14; and 146:6–9. The end of the wicked alone appears in Pss 11:6; 31:18 (in a request); 37:10, 34–36; 94:13; 141:9–10. While not every mention of רָשָׁע is directly associated with their destruction, the theme unfolds in every psalm which contains both figures. This pattern is significant. Not only does it show that there is a common portrayal, but the use of these contrasting ends lies at the core of the poetic functions of their contrast.

The רָשָׁע in the psalms in this study is not directly associated with the "prototypically bad person" in every case, but rather, most often identified as an opponent of the righteous, the psalmist, or another innocent victim. They are described by their illegitimate activities. A majority of these activities involve committing some form of violence (Pss 11:2, 37:12, 13, 32; 55:4; 94:3–7; 97:10; 140:5–6; 141:9–10). In some instances, the רָשָׁע are characterized by their speech, which also occurs in the context of a threat to the righteous or the speaker (Pss 55:4; 58:4; 75:5). Their greed is mentioned as well, in contrast with the צַדִּיק (Ps 37:21). In a couple of instances, their temporary flourishing is highlighted (Pss 37:25, 92:8). Even in these last instances, and as noted above, their deserved destruction is described. In nearly every psalm studied, the wicked somehow receive a bitter end. This is sometimes in general judgment of getting what they deserve (Pss 55:4, 24; 75:9, 11; 94:3; 141:10, 146:9), though sometimes in a vaguer sense (e.g., Pss 32:10; 37:28, 34, 38; 112:10). Their death is imagined in most of the psalms studied (Pss 1:6; 11:6; 34:22; 37:10, 20; 58:11; 68:3; 92:8). This end is sometimes spoken of in a request for Yhwh to judge them (Pss 7:10; 31:18; 140:5). The exception to this rule is Ps 97:10, which speaks of Yhwh's salvation of the faithful from the רְשָׁעִים. Even in this final instance, they are those who deserve judgment for their wrongdoing.

One of the major contributions of this study is the distinction between the uses of צַדִּיק in individual psalms. The צַדִּיק (or צַדִּיקִים) can be understood through context as one who is (or those who are) in need in ten of the psalms studied here (Pss 7:10; 11:3, 5; 31:19; 34:16, 20, 22; 37:12, 32, 39; 55:23; 58:11–12; 94:21; 97:11; 146:8).[2] Significantly, in all the cases listed that unambiguously use the term צַדִּיק to designate innocence, the term is singular. This pattern extends to psalms not studied here (Pss 5:14; 14:5). In two cases listed above (Ps 34:16 and Ps 146:8), the usage of "righteous" as innocent is tied to the context of the psalm or to other uses present in the psalm.

In six psalms, the צַדִּיק can be understood as those who are prototypically good (1:6; 32:11; 37:21; 25, 29–30; 92:13; 112:6; 141:5). In four psalms, the meaning could be determined as either those in need or those who are prototypically good, as the immediate context does not supply enough information (Pss 37:16–17; 68:3; 75:10; 140:14). However, in three of these psalms, there is the broader context of enmity (Pss 37, 75, 140). This indicates that the contrast of the righteous and the wicked is often understood to be opposing, rather than simply contrasting, figures within psalms.

Because of these clear differences, the meaning of the term צַדִּיק, either in plural or singular forms, must not be assumed as a description of character but must be drawn from the immediate context. In some cases, more than one meaning is possible. In every case, careful attention to both meaning and poetic function clarifies the creativity and conventionality of each use of the term צַדִּיק.

There is also a significant relationship between the צַדִּיק and Yhwh, often in relation to their identity. In a majority of psalms, the צַדִּיק is one whom Yhwh saves (Pss 7:10; 11:3–7; 31:19 [in a request]; 34:16; 37:17, 39–40; 55:23–24; 58:11–12; 75:11; 94:21–23; 97:11; 146:8). In other examples, the righteous are those who praise Yhwh in response to or following a description of Yhwh's action in the context of the psalm (Pss 32:11; 68:4; 97:11–12; 140:14). Even in the examples of Pss 1:5–6 and 92:13–16, their flourishing comes from their connection with Yhwh. In the broad context of Ps 112, they are also associated with blessings from Yhwh. To varying degrees in the kind of activity, though with great consistency in terms of the broad theme, Yhwh's activity toward the righteous is significant. Only in Ps 141, where the צַדִּיק is the one who might rebuke the speaker, is there no connection to beneficent activity from Yhwh. In terms of the literary pattern, the righteous are both those whom Yhwh blesses and those whom Yhwh saves.

As shown through the preceding argument, conventional language in the psalms can be employed in uniquely psalmic ways. Character and characterization play a significant role as part of the poetics of individual psalms, even apart from features of characterization derived from the "shape" of the Psalter. The righteous and the wicked are present throughout the Psalter because they are part of the conventional language of psalms, and as such, are presented in both stereotypical and creative ways throughout. These figures, alongside other figures and features present in the psalms, contribute to the psalmic imagination that draws the reader into experiencing the textual world of the psalm to compare or contrast the reality of the text with the reality the reader inhabits.

NOTES

1. Psalm 55 does not explicitly state that רָשָׁע will be destroyed, but in context, the רָשָׁע in v. 4 should be associated with the figure in v. 24. This is also the case in the mention of Ps 55:24 in the paragraph below.
2. It must be noted that different instances of צַדִּיק in Ps 37 fit into each of these categories.

Appendix

CATEGORIZATION OF צַדִּיק AND רָשָׁע IN PSALMS

This appendix categorizes the appearances of צַדִּיק and רָשָׁע in broad categorizations explored throughout this book. Instances in italics represent psalms in which both figures are present, and thus, are included in chapter 4 of this book. Passages marked with an asterisk indicate the possibility of multiple intended meanings. All references follow Hebrew versification.

צַדִּיק as Innocent

Ps 5:13
Ps 7:10 [2x]
Ps 11:3
Ps 11:5*
Ps 14:5
Ps 31:19
Ps 34:20
Ps 34:22
Ps 37:12
Ps 37:32
Ps 37:39* [pl]
Ps 55:23
Ps 58:11
Ps 58:12
Ps 64:11
Ps 94:21
Ps 97:11*
Ps 146:8* [pl]

צַדִּיק as General Description

Ps 1:5 [pl]
Ps 1:6 [pl]
Ps 32:11 [pl]
Ps 33:1 [pl]
Ps 34:16 [pl]*
*Ps 37:16**
Ps 37:17 [pl]*
Ps 37:21
Ps 37:25
Ps 37:29 [pl]
Ps 37:30
Ps 52:8 [pl]
Ps 68:4 [pl]
Ps 69:29 [pl]
Ps 75:11*
Ps 92:13
Ps 97:12 [pl]
Ps 112:4
Ps 112:6
Ps 118:15 [pl]
Ps 118:20 [pl]
Ps 125:3 [2x, pl]
Ps 140:14 [pl]
Ps 141:5
Ps 142:8 [pl]

רָשָׁע as Antagonist/Violent Perpetrator

Ps 3:8 [pl]
Ps 7:10
Ps 9:6
Ps 9:17
Ps 9:18 [pl]
Ps 10:2
Ps 10:3
Ps 10:4
Ps 10:13
Ps 10:15
Ps 11:2 [pl]
Ps 11:5

Ps 11:6 [pl]
Ps 14:9 [pl]
Ps 14:13
Ps 17:9 [pl]
Ps 17:13 [pl]
Ps 31:18 [pl]
Ps 34:22
Ps 36:12 [pl]
Ps 37:10
Ps 37:12
Ps 37:14 [pl]
Ps 37:20 [pl]
Ps 37:32
Ps 37:38
Ps 37:40 [pl]
Ps 55:4
Ps 58:4 [pl]
Ps 58:11
Ps 71:4
Ps 94:3 [2x, pl]
Ps 94:13
Ps 97:10 [pl]
Ps 109:2
Ps 109:6
Ps 109:7
Ps 119:95 [pl]
Ps 119:110 [pl]
Ps 139:19
Ps 140:5
Ps 140:9
Ps 141:10 [pl]

רָשָׁע as General Description

Ps 1:1 [pl]
Ps 1:4 [pl]
Ps 1:5 [pl]
Ps 1:6 [pl]
Ps 12:9 [pl]
Ps 26:5 [pl]
Ps 28:3 [pl]
Ps 32:10

Ps 36:2
Ps 37:16 [pl]
Ps 37:17 [pl]
Ps 37:21
Ps 37:28 [pl]
Ps 37:34 [pl]
Ps 37:35
Ps 39:2
Ps 50:16
Ps 68:3 [pl]
Ps 73:3 [pl]
Ps 73:12 [pl]
Ps 75:5 [pl]
Ps 75:9 [pl]
Ps 75:11 [pl]
Ps 82:2 [pl]
Ps 82:4* [pl]
Ps 91:8 [pl]
Ps 92:8 [pl]
Ps 101:8 [pl]
Ps 104:35 [pl]
Ps 106:18 [pl]
Ps 112:10 [2x; 1x sgl, 1x pl]
Ps 119:53 [pl]
Ps 119:61 [pl]
Ps 119:119 [pl]
Ps 119:155
Ps 129:4 [pl]
Ps 145:20 [pl]
Ps 146:9 [pl]
Ps 147:6 [pl]

Bibliography

Abernethy, Andrew T. "'Right Paths' and/or 'Paths of Righteousness'? Examining Psalm 23.3b within the Psalter." *JSOT* 39 (2015): 299–318.

Abrams, M. H., and Geoffrey Galt Harpham. *A Glossary of Literary Terms*. 10th ed. Boston, MA: Wadsworth Cengage Learning, 2012.

Achtemeier, E. R. "Righteousness in the OT." In *The Interpreter's Dictionary of the Bible*, edited by George Arthur Buttrick, 4:80–85. Nashville, TN: Abingdon, 1962.

Allen, Leslie C. *Psalms 101-150*. 2nd ed. WBC 21. Waco, TX: Word, 1983.

Alonso-Schökel, Luis. "Contemplar y Gustar (Sal 34, 6.9)." *Estudios Bíblicos* 57 (1999): 11–21.

———. "En la mano de Dios (Salmo 31)." *Estudios Bíblicos* 56 (1998): 405–415.

———. *A Manual of Hebrew Poetics*. Translated by Adrian Graffy. Subsidia Biblica 11. Rome: Editrice Pontificio Istituto Biblico, 1988.

———. *Treinta Salmos: Poesía y Oración*. 2nd ed. Madrid: Christiandad, 1986.

Alonso-Schökel, Luis, and Cecilia Carniti. *Salmos: Traducción, introducciones y comentario*. 2 vols. Estella: Verbo Divino, 1993.

Alter, Robert. *The Art of Biblical Poetry*. Rev. ed. New York: Basic Books, 2011.

———. *The Book of Psalms: A Translation with Commentary*. New York: W. W. Norton, 2007.

Andersen, Francis I. *Habakkuk: A New Translation with Introduction and Commentary*. AB 25. New York: Doubleday, 2001.

Ansberry, Christopher B. *Be Wise, My Son, and Make My Heart Glad: An Exploration of the Courtly Nature of the Book of Proverbs*. BZAW 422. Berlin: De Gruyter, 2010.

Apple, Raymond. "Psalm 34—Does the Heading Fit?" *JBQ* 46 (2018): 97–103.

Aristotle. *Poetics*. Edited by John Baxter and Patrick Atherton. Translated by George Whalley. Montreal: McGill-Queen's University Press, 1997.

Arnold, Bill T. *Genesis*. NCBC. Cambridge: Cambridge University Press, 2009.

Arnold, Bill T., and Brent A. Strawn. "*bᵉyāb šᵉmô* in Psalm 68,5: A Hebrew Gloss to an Ugaritic Epithet?" *ZAW* 115 (2003): 428–432.

Aurelius, Erik. "Davids Unschuld: Die Hofgeschichte und Psalm 7." In *Gott und Mensch im Dialog: Fetschrift für Otto Kaiser zum 80. Geburtstag*, edited by Markus Witte, 391–412. BZAW 345. Berlin: De Gruyter, 2004.

Bail, Ulrike. "'O God, Hear My Prayer': Psalm 55 and Violence Against Women." In *Wisdom and Psalms*, edited by Athalya Brenner and Carole R. Fontaine, 242–263. Feminist Companion to the Bible 2. Sheffield: Sheffield Academic, 1998.

Bal, Mieke. *Narratology: Introduction to the Theory of Narrative*. 4th ed. Translated by Christine van Boheemen. Toronto: University of Toronto Press, 2017.

Balentine, Samuel. *Job*. Smyth & Helwys Bible Commentary. Macon, GA: Smyth & Helwys, 2006.

———. "Proverbs." In *The Oxford Handbook of Wisdom and the Bible*, edited by Will Kynes, 495–514. Oxford: Oxford University Press, 2021.

Ballhorn, Egbert. *Zum Telos des Psalters: der Textzusammenhang des Vierten und Fünften Psalmenbuches (Ps 90–150)*. BBB 138. Berlin: Philo, 2004.

Baldick, Chris. *The Oxford Dictionary of Literary Terms*. 4th ed. Oxford: Oxford University Press, 2015.

Barr, James. *The Semantics of Biblical Language*. Oxford: Oxford University Press, 1961.

Bartholomew, Craig G. *Ecclesiastes*. BCOTWP. Grand Rapids, MI: Baker Academic, 2009.

Bartholomew, Craig G., and Ryan O'Dowd. *Old Testament Wisdom Literature: A Theological Introduction*. Downers Grove, IL: IVP Academic, 2011.

Basson, Alec. "The Path Image Schema as Underlying Structure for the Metaphor *Moral Life is a Journey* in Psalm 25." *OTE* 24 (2011): 19–29.

———. "'You are My Rock and Fortress': Refuge Metaphors in Psalm 31; A Perspective From Cognitive Metaphor Theory." *Acta Theologica* 2 (2005): 1–17.

Begg, Christopher. "Ps 58:2a: A *Forschungsbericht* and a Proposal." *Ephemerides Theologicae Lovanienses* 64 (1988): 397–404.

Bellinger, William H. *Psalmody and Prophecy*. JSOTSup 27. Sheffield: JSOT, 1984.

———. "Psalms and the Question of Genre." In *The Oxford Handbook of the Psalms*, edited by William P. Brown, 313–325. Oxford: Oxford University Press, 2014.

Berlin, Adele. *Dynamics of Biblical Parallelism*. 2nd ed. Grand Rapids, MI: Eerdmans, 2008.

———. "On Reading Biblical Poetry: The Role of Metaphor." In *Congress Volume: Cambridge, 1995*, edited by J. A. Emerton, 25–35. Leiden: Brill, 1997.

———. *Poetics and Interpretation of Biblical Narrative*. Bible and Literature Series 9. Sheffield: Almond Press, 1983.

Blenkinsopp, Joseph. *The Beauty of Holiness: Re-reading Isaiah in Light of the Psalms*. London: T&T Clark, 2019.

———. *Isaiah 1–39: A New Translation with Introduction and Commentary*. AB 19. New York: Doubleday, 2000.

———. *Isaiah 40–55: A New Translation with Introduction and Commentary*. AB 19A. New York: Doubleday, 2002.

———. *Wisdom and Law in the Old Testament: The Ordering of Life in Israel and Early Judaism*. Oxford Bible Series. Oxford: Oxford University Press, 1995.

Block, Daniel. *The Book of Ezekiel: Chapters 1–24*. NICOT. Grand Rapids, MI: Eerdmans, 1997.

Boda, Mark J. ———. *The Book of Zechariah*. NICOT. Grand Rapids, MI: Eerdmans, 2016.

———. *A Severe Mercy: Sin and Its Remedy in the Old Testament*. Siphrut 1. Winona Lake, IN: Eisenbrauns, 2009.

———. "'Varied and Resplendid Riches': Exploring the Breadth and Depth of Worship in the Psalter." In *Rediscovering Worship: Past, Present, and Future*, edited by Wendy J. Porter. McMaster New Testament Studies. Eugene, OR: Pickwick, 2015.

———. *Praying the Tradition: The Origin and Use of Tradition in Nehemiah 9*. BZAW 277. Berlin: De Gruyter, 1999.

Booij, Th. "The Hebrew Text of Psalm XCII 11." *VT* 38 (1988): 210–214.

———. "Psalm 141: A Prayer for Discipline and Protection." *Bib* 86 (2005): 97–106.

Boström, Lennart. "Retribution and Wisdom Literature." In *Interpreting Old Testament Wisdom Literature*, edited by David G. Firth and Lindsay Wilson, 134–154. Downers Grove, IL: IVP Academic, 2017.

Botha, P. J. "Annotated History—The Implications of Reading Psalm 34 in Conjunction with 1 Samuel 21–26 and Vice Versa." *OTE* 21 (2008): 593–617.

———. "The Function of the Polarity Between the Pious and the Enemies in Psalm 119." *OTE* 5 (1992): 252–263.

———. "Intertextuality and the Interpretation of Psalm 1." *OTE* 18 (2005): 503–520.

———. "The Junction of the Two Ways: The Structure and Theology of Psalm 1." *OTE* 4 (1991): 381–396.

———. "Psalm 55 Interpreted in View of its Textual, Metatextual and Intertextual Connections." *SJOT* 31 (2017): 118–141.

———. "The Social Setting and Strategy of Psalm 34." *OTE* 10 (1997): 178–197.

———. "'Wealth and Riches are in His House' (Ps 112:3): Acrostic Wisdom Psalms and the Development of Antimaterialism." In *The Shape and Shaping of the Book of Psalms: The Current State of Scholarship*, edited by Nancy L. DeClaissé-Walford, 105–128. AIL 20. Atlanta, GA: SBL, 2014.

Brodersen, Alma. *The End of the Psalter: Psalms 146–150 in the Masoretic Text, the Dead Sea Scrolls, and the Septuagint*. 2017. Reprint, Waco, TX: Baylor University Press, 2018.

Brown, William P. *Character in Crisis: A Fresh Approach to the Wisdom Literature of the Old Testament*. Grand Rapids, MI: Eerdmans, 1996.

———. "Come, O Children . . . I Will Teach You the Fear of the Lord" (Psalm 34:12): Comparing Psalms and Proverbs." In *Seeking Out the Wisdom of the Ancients: Essays Offered to Honor Michael V. Fox on the Occasion of His Sixty-Fifth Birthday*, edited by Ronald L. Troxel, Kelvin G. Friebel, and Dennis R. Magary, 85–102. Winona Lake, IN: Eisenbrauns, 2005.

———. *Deep Calls to Deep: The Psalms in Dialogue amid Disruption*. Nashville, TN: Abingdon, 2021.

———. *Psalms*. Interpreting Biblical Texts. Nashville, TN: Abingdon, 2010.

———. "The Psalms and 'I': The Dialogical Self and the Disappearing Psalmist." In *Diachronic and Synchronic: Reading the Psalms in Real time: Proceedings of the Baylor Symposium on the Book of Psalms*, edited by Joel S. Burnett, W. H. Bellinger, Jr., and W. Dennis Tucker, 26–44. LHBOTS 488. New York: T&T Clark, 2007.

———. "Reading the Psalms Sapientially in the Writings." In *The Oxford Handbook of the Writings of the Hebrew Bible*, edited by Donn F. Morgan, 151–168. Oxford: Oxford University Press, 2018.

———. *Seeing the Psalms: A Theology of Metaphor*. Louisville, KY: Westminster John Knox, 2002.

Broyles, Craig C. *Psalms*. NIBC. Peabody, MA: Hendrickson, 1999.

Brueggemann, Walter. "Psalm 37: Conflict of Interpretation." In *Of Prophets' Visions and the Wisdom of the Sages: Essays in Honour of R. Norman Whybray on His Seventieth Birthday*, edited by Heather A. McKay and David J. A. Clines, 229–256. JSOTSup 162. Sheffield: JSOT Press, 1993.

———. "Psalms and Life of Faith: A Suggested Typology of Function." *JSOT* 17 (1980): 3–32.

———. "Some Aspects of Theodicy in Old Testament Faith." *PRSt* 26 (1999): 253–268.

Brueggemann, Walter, and William H. Bellinger, Jr. *Psalms*. NCBC. New York: Cambridge University Press, 2014.

Burger, J. A. "Psalm 1 and Wisdom." *OTE* 8 (1995): 327–339.

Burton, Marilyn. *The Semantics of Glory: A Cognitive, Corpus-Based Approach to Hebrew Word Meaning*. SSN 68. Leiden: Brill, 2017.

Byun, Paul. "A Paradoxical Situation and God's Righteousness in Ezra 9:15." *ZAW* 131 (2019): 467–473.

Charlesworth, James H. "Bashan, Symbology, Haplography, and Theology in Psalm 68." In *David and Zion: Biblical Studies in Honor of J. J. M. Roberts*, edited by Bernard F. Batto and Kathryn L. Roberts. Winona Lake, IN: Eisenbrauns, 2004.

Charney, Davida. "Maintaining Innocence Before a Divine Hearer: Deliberative Rhetoric in Psalm 22, Psalm 17, and Psalm 7." *BibInt* 21 (2013): 33–63.

Chatman, Seymour. *Story and Discourse: Narrative Structure in Fiction and Film*. Ithaca, NY: Cornell University Press, 1978.

Cheung, Simon Chi-Chung. *Wisdom Intoned: A Reappraisal of the Genre 'Wisdom Psalms.'* LHBOTS 613. London: Bloomsbury, 2015.

Childs, Brevard. *Introduction to the Old Testament as Scripture*. Philadelphia, PA: Fortress, 1979.

———. *Isaiah: A Commentary*. OTL. Louisville, KY: Westminster John Knox, 2001.

Clines, David J. A. "The Arguments of Job's Three Friends." In *Art and Meaning: Rhetoric in Biblical Literature*, edited by David J. A. Clines, David M. Gunn, and Alan J. Hauser, 199–214. JSOTSup 19. Sheffield: JSOT, 1982.

———. *Job 1–20*. WBC 17. Dallas, TX: Word, 1989.

———. *Job 21–37*. WBC 18a. Nashville, TN: Thomas Nelson, 2006.

Cohen, Nava. "Psalm 92: Structure and Meaning." *ZAW* 125 (2013): 593–606.

Cole, Robert L. "An Integrated Reading of Psalms 1 and 2." *JSOT* 98 (2002): 75–88.

Collins, C. John. "Psalm 1: Structure and Rhetoric." *Presbyterion* 31 (2005): 37–48.

Creach, Jerome F. D. *The Destiny of the Righteous in the Psalms*. St. Louis, MO: Chalice, 2008.

———. "The Destiny of the Righteous and the Theology of the Psalms." In *Soundings in the Theology of the Psalms: Perspectives and Methods in Contemporary Scholarship*, edited by Rolf A. Jacobson, 49–61. Minneapolis, MN: Fortress, 2011.

———. "Like a Tree Planted by the Temple Stream: The Portrait of the Righteous in Psalm 1:3." *CBQ* 61 (1999): 34–46.

———. "The Righteous and the Wicked." In *The Oxford Handbook of the Psalms*, edited by William P. Brown, 529–541. Oxford: Oxford University Press, 2014.

———. *Yahweh as Refuge and the Editing of the Hebrew Psalter*. JSOTSup 217. Sheffield: Sheffield Academic, 1996.

Crenshaw, James L. "Gold Dust or Nuggets? A Brief Response to J. Kenneth Kuntz." *Currents in Biblical Research* 1/2 (2003): 155–158.

———. *The Psalms: An Introduction*. Grand Rapids, MI: Eerdmans, 2001.

———. "Wisdom Psalms?" *Currents in Research: Biblical Studies* 8 (2010): 9–17.

Culler, Jonathan. *Literary Theory: A Very Short Introduction*. 2nd ed. Oxford: Oxford University Press, 2011.

Culpepper, Jonathan. *Language and Characterisation: People in Plays and Other Texts*. 2001. Textual Explorations. Reprint, London: Routledge, 2014.

Daffern, Megan I. J. "Imagining Prayer: Deepening Awareness of Audiences in the Psalms." In *Psalms and the Use of the Critical Imagination: Essays in Honour of Professor Susan Gillingham*, edited by Katherine E. Southwood and Holly Morse, 81–96. LHBOTS 710. London: T&T Clark, 2022.

———. "The Semantic Field of 'Remembering' in the Psalms." *JSOT* 41 (2016): 79–97.

Dahood, Mitchell. *Psalms*. 3 vols. AB. Garden City, NY: Doubleday, 1966–1970.

Darr, Katheryn Pfisterer. "Proverb Performance and Transgenerational Retribution in Ezekiel 18." In *Ezekiel's Hierarchical World: Wrestling with a Tiered Reality*, edited by Stephen L. Cook and Corrine L. Patton, 199–223. SBL Symposium Series 31. Atlanta, GA: SBL, 2004.

Davis, Ellen F. *Scripture, Culture, and Agriculture: An Agrarian Reading of the Bible*. Cambridge: Cambridge University Press, 2009.

DeClaissé-Walford, Nancy L., Rolf Jacobson, and Beth LaNeel Tanner. *The Book of Psalms*. NICOT. Grand Rapids, MI: Eerdmans, 2014.

Dell, Katharine J. *The Book of Job as Sceptical Literature*. BZAW 197. Berlin: De Gruyter, 1991.

———. "The Use of Animal Imagery in the Psalms and Wisdom Literature of Ancient Israel." *Scottish Journal of Theology* 53 (2000): 275–291.

Dijkstra, Meindert. "He Pours the Sweet Wine off, only the Dregs Are for the Wicked: An Epigraphic Note on *mizzæh* in Psalm 75,9." *ZAW* 107 (1995): 296–300.

Dobbs-Allsopp, F. W. *On Biblical Poetry*. Oxford: Oxford University Press, 2015.

Doyle, Brian. "Hearts, Hands, Teeth, and Feet: From Metonymy to Metaphor and Back in Psalm 58." *The Classical Bulletin* 86 (2010): 81–100.

Duggan, Michael W. "Ezra 9:6–15: A Penitential Prayer within Its Literary Setting." In *The Origins of Penitential Prayer in Second Temple Judaism*, vol. 1 of *Seeking the Favor of God*, edited by Mark J. Boda, Daniel K. Falk, and Rodney A. Werline, 165–180. EJL 21. Atlanta: SBL, 2006.

Eaton, John. *The Psalms: A Historical and Spiritual Commentary with an Introduction and New Translation*. London: Continuum, 2005.

Eder, Jens, Fotis Jannidis, and Ralf Schneider. "Characters in Fictional Worlds: An Introduction." In *Characters in Fictional Worlds: Understanding Imaginary Beings in Literature, Film, and Other Media*, edited by Jens Eder, Fotis Jannidis, and Ralf Schneider, 3–64. Berlin: De Gruyter, 2010.

Eder, Sigrid. "'Broken Hearted' and 'Crushed in Spirit': Metaphors and Emotions in Psalm 34,19." *SJOT* 30 (2016): 1–15, https://doi.org/10.1080/09018328.2016.1122286.

———. *Identifikationspotenziale in den Psalmen: Emotionen, Metaphern und Textdynamik in den Psalmen 30, 64, 90 und 147*. BBB 183. Göttigen: V & R, 2018.

———. "Storytelling in the Psalter? Chances and Limits of a Narrative Psalm Analysis—Shown Exemplarily in Psalm 64." *OTE* 32 (2019): 343–357.

Egger-Wenzel, Renate. *Von der Freiheit Gottes, anders zu sein: Die zentrale Rolle der Kaptiel 9 und 10 für das Ijobbuch*. FB 83. Würzburg: Echter, 1998.

Emerton, John A. "Looking on One's Enemies." *VT* 51 (2001): 186–196.

———. "The 'Mountain of God' in Psalm 68:16." In *History and Traditions of Early Israel: Studies Presented to Edward Nielsen*, edited by André Lemaire and Bendedikt Otzen, 24–37. VTSup 50. Leiden: Brill, 1993.

———. "The Translation of Psalm LXIV.4." *JTS* 27 (1976): 391–392.

Fohrer, Georg. "Form und Funktion in der Hiobdichtung." *Zeitschrift der Deutschen Morgenländischen Gesellschaft* 109 (1959): 31–49.

Fokkelman, J. P. *Reading Biblical Poetry: An Introductory Guide*. Louisville, KY: Westminster John Knox, 2001.

———. "Structure of Psalm LXVIII." In *In Quest of the Past: Studies on Israelite Religion, Literature, and Prophetism: Papers Read at the Joint British-Dutch Old Testament Conference, Held at Elspeet, 1988*, edited by A. S. van der Woude, 72–83. OTS 26. Leiden: Brill, 1990.

Forti, Tova. "*Gattung* and *Sitz im Leben*: Methodological Vagueness in Defining Wisdom Psalms." In *Was There a Wisdom Tradition? New Prospects in Israelite Wisdom Studies*, edited by Mark R. Sneed, 205–220. AIL 23. Atlanta: SBL, 2015.

———. *"Like a Lone Bird on a Roof": Animal Imagery and the Structure of Psalms*. Critical Studies in the Hebrew Bible 10. University Park, PA: Eisenbrauns, 2018.

———. "Of Snakes and Sinners: An Intertextual Reading of *Ba'al ha-lashon* in Ecclesiastes 10:11 in Light of *'ish lashon* in Psalm 140:12 (11)." In *Reading Ecclesiastes Intertextually*, edited by Katharine Dell and Will Kynes, 84–93. LHBOTS 574. New York: T&T Clark, 2013.

Foth, Kevin. "Psalm 74 and Social Identity." *JSOT* 47 (2022): 82–97.

———. "A Solution to the Subject(s) of Psalm 7:13–14." *VT* 74 (2024): 594–602, https:/doi/org/10.1163/15685330-bja10140.

Fox, Michael V. *Ecclesiastes*. JPS Bible Commentary. Philadelphia, PA: Jewish Publication Society, 2004.

———. *Proverbs 10–31*. Anchor Yale Bible 18b. New Haven, CT: Yale University Press, 2009.

———. "What is the Book of Proverbs About?" In *Congress Volume: Cambridge, 1995*, edited by J. A. Emerton, 153–167. Leiden: Brill, 1997.

Fried, Lisbeth S. *Ezra: A Commentary*. Critical Commentaries. Sheffield: Sheffield Phoenix, 2015.

Gelander, Shamai. "The Language of the Wicked in the Psalms." *Proceedings of the World Congress of Jewish Studies* 10 (1989): 37–42. [Hebrew]

Genette, Gérard. *Narrative Discourse: An Essay in Method*. Translated by Jane E. Lewin. 1972. Reprint, Ithaca, NY: Cornell University Press, 1980.

Giffone, Benjamin. "A 'Perfect' Poem: The Use of the QATAL Verbal Form in the Biblical Acrostics." *HS* 51 (2010): 49–72.

Gillingham, Susan E. "New Wine and Old Wineskins: Three Approaches to Prophecy and Psalmody." In *Prophecy and Prophets and Ancient Israel: Proceedings of the Oxford Old Testament Seminar*, edited by John Day, 370–390. LHBOTS 531. London: T&T Clark, 2010.

———. *The Poems and Psalms of the Hebrew Bible*. Oxford Bible Series. Oxford: Oxford University Press, 1994.

———. "'The Righteous Shall Inherit the Land, and Live in it Forever': (Ps 37:29). Towards a Theology of and Human and Divine Justice through the Reception History of Psalm 37." In *Zur Theologie des Psalters und der Psalmen*, edited by Ulrich Berges, Johannes Bremer, and Till Magnus Steiner, 411–427. BBB 189. Göttingen: V & R, 2019.

———. "The Wisdom Tradition and the Psalms." In *Perspectives on Israelite Wisdom: Proceedings of the Oxford Old Testament Seminar*, edited by John Jarick, 277–309. LHBOTS 618. New York: T&T Clark, 2016.

Gitay, Yehoshua. "Psalm 1 and the Rhetoric of Religious Argumentation." In *Literary Structures and Rhetorical Strategies in the Hebrew Bible*, edited by L. J. de Regt, J. de Waard, and Jan P. Fokkelman, 232–240. Assen: Van Gorcum, 1996.

Goldingay, John. "The Arrangement of Sayings in Proverbs 10–15." *JSOT* 61 (1994): 75–83.

———. *Psalms*. 3 vols. BCOTWP. Grand Rapids, MI: Baker, 2006–2008.

Goldingay, John, and David Payne. *Isaiah 40–55*. 2 vols. ICC. New York: T&T Clark, 2006.

Gossai, Hemchand. "Ṣaddîq in Theological and Economic Perspectives." *SEÅ* 53 (1988): 7–13.

Goswell, Gregory. "A Theocratic Reading of Zechariah 9:9." *BBR* 26 (2016): 7–19.

Goulder, Michael D. *The Psalms of the Return (Book V, Psalms 107–150)*. Vol. 4 of *Studies in the Psalter*. JSOTSup 258. Sheffield: Sheffield Academic, 1998.

Grant, Jamie A. *The King as Exemplar: The Function of Deuteronomy's Kingship Law in the Shaping of the Book of Psalms*. AcBib 17. Atlanta, GA: SBL, 2004.

Gray, Alison Ruth. *Psalm 18 in Words and Pictures*. BibInt 127. Leiden: Brill, 2014.

Greenberg, Moshe. "Two New Hunting Terms in Psalm 140, 12." *Hebrew Annual Review* 1 (1977): 149–153.

Greimas, Algirdas Julien. *On Meaning: Selected Writings in Semiotic Theory*. Translated by Paul J. Perron and Frank H. Collins. Theory and History of Literature 38. Minneapolis, MN: University of Minnesota Press, 1987.

Grohmann, Marianne. "Ambivalent Images of Birth in Psalm vii 15." *VT* 55 (2005): 439–449.

———. "Metaphors of Miscarriage in the Psalms." *VT* 69 (2019): 219–231.

Gunkel, Hermann. "Psalm 1: An Interpretation." *The Biblical World* 21 (1903): 120–123.

Gunkel, Hermann, and Joachim Begrich. *Introduction to Psalms: The Genre of the Religious Lyric of Israel*. Translated by James D. Nogalski. Macon, GA: Mercery University Press, 1998.

Habel, Norman C. "The Symbolism of Wisdom in Proverbs 1–9." *Interpretation* 26 (1972): 131–157.

Hauge, Martin Ravndal. *Between Sheol and Temple: Motif Structure and Function in the I-Psalms*. JSOTSup 178. Sheffield: Sheffield Academic, 1995.

Hawley, Lance. *Metaphor Competition in the Book of Job*. Journal of Ancient Judaism Supplements 26. Göttingen: Vandenhoeck & Ruprecht, 2018.

———. "The Rhetoric of Condemnation in the Book of Job." *JBL* 139 (2020): 459–478, https://doi.org/10/15699/jbl.1393.2020.2.

Heim, Knut Martin. *Like Grapes of Gold Set in Silver: An Interpretation of Proverbial Clusters in Proverbs 10:1–22:16*. BZAW 273. Berlin: De Gruyter, 2001.

Hernández, Dominick S. "'Evil' or 'Agitated': The Meaning of רֹגֶז in Job 3:17." In *Ve-'Ed Ya'aleh (Gen 2:6): Essays in Biblical and Ancient Near Eastern Studies Presented to Edward L. Greenstein*, volume 2, edited by Peter Machinist, Robert A. Harris, Joshua A. Berman, Nili Samet, and Noga Ayali-Darshan, 789–808. Atlanta, GA: SBL, 2021.

Hilber, John W. *Cultic Prophecy in the Psalms*. BZAW 352. Berlin: De Gruyter, 2005.

Hildebrandt, Samuel. "Whose Voice is Heard? Speaker Ambiguity in the Psalms." *CBQ* 82 (2020): 197–213.

Hillebrandt, Claudia. "Figur und Person im Gedicht: Zum Stand der lyrikologischen Figurenforschung und zur Funktion von Figuren in lyrischen Gebilden." In *Lyrisches Ich, Textsubjekt, Sprecher?* vol. 1 of *Grundfragen der Lyrikologie*, edited by Claudia Hillebrandt, Sonja Klimek, Ralph Müller, and Rüdiger Zymner, 148–163. Berlin: De Gruyter, 2019.

Hoffman, Yair. *A Blemished Perfection: The Book of Job in Context*. JSOTSup 213. Sheffield: Sheffield Academic, 1996.

Holmstedt, Robert D. "Analyzing זֶה Grammar and Reading זֶה Texts of Ps 68:9 and Judg 5:5." *JHS* 14 (2014): 1–26, https://doi.org/10.5508/jhs.2014.v14.a8.

———. "Hebrew Poetry and the Appositive Style: Parallelism, *Requiescat in Pace*." *VT* 69 (2019): 617–648.

Holt, Else K. "'Let the Righteous Strike Me; Let the Faithful Correct Me': Psalm 141 and the Enclave of the *Ṣaddiqîm*." *SJOT* 33 (2019): 185–202, https://doi.org/10.1080/09018328.2019.1686282.

Hossfeld, Frank-Lothar. "Das Prophetische in den Psalmen: Zur Gottesrede der Asafpsalmen im Vergleich mit des der ersten und zweiten Davidpsalters." In *Ich bewirke das Heil und erschaffe das Unheil (Jesaja 45.7), Stufen zur Botschaft der Propheten: Festschrift für Lothar Ruppert zum 65. Geburtstag*, edited by Friedrich Diedrich and Bernd Willmes, 223–243. FB 65. Würzburg: Echter, 1998.

Hossfeld, Frank-Lothar, and Erich Zenger. *Die Psalmen I: Psalm 1–50*. Die Neue Echter Bibel 29. Würzburg: Echter, 1993.

———. *Psalms 2: A Commentary on Psalms 51–100*. Translated by Linda M. Maloney. Hermeneia. Minneapolis, MN: Fortress, 2005.

———. *Psalms 3: A Commentary on Psalms 101–150*. Translated by Linda M. Maloney. Hermeneia. Minneapolis, MN: Fortress, 2011.

Howard, David M. Jr. "The Proto-MT Psalter, the King, and Psalms 1 and 2: A Response to Klaus Seybold." In *Jewish and Christian Approaches to the Psalms: Conflict and Convergence*, edited by Susan Gillingham, 182–189. Oxford: Oxford University Press, 2013.

———. *The Structure of Psalms 93–100*. Biblical and Judaic Studies from the University of California San Diego 5. Winona Lake, IN: Eisenbrauns, 1997.

Hubbard, Robert L. "Dynamistic and Legal Processes in Psalm 7." *ZAW* 94 (1982): 267–279.

Human, Dirk J. "A Tradition-Historical Analysis of Psalm 55." *SK* 18 (1997): 267–279.

Hunter, Alastair G. "Inside Outside Psalm 55: How Jonah Grew Out of a Psalmist's Conceit." In *Psalms and Prayers: Papers Read at the Joint Meeting of the Society for Old Testament Study and Het Oudtestamentiseh Werkgezelsehap in Nederland en België, Apeldoorn August 2006*, edited by Bob Becking and Eric Peels, 129–139. OTS 55. Leiden: Brill, 2007.

Hurvitz, Avi. "Wisdom Vocabulary in the Hebrew Psalter: A Contribution to the Study of 'Wisdom Psalms.'" *VT* 38 (1988): 41–51.

Irons, Charles Lee. "Is 'Righteousness' a Relational Concept in the Hebrew Bible?" In *Reflections on Lexicography: Explorations in Ancient Syriac, Hebrew, and Greek Sources*, edited by Richard A. Taylor and Craig E. Morrison, 135–146. Perspectives on Linguistics and Ancient Languages 4. Piscataway, NJ: Gorgias, 2014.

Jacobs, Mignon R. *The Books of Haggai and Malachi*. NICOT. Grand Rapids, MI: Eerdmans, 2017.

———. "Sin, Silence, Suffering, and Confession in the Conceptual Landscape of Psalm 32." In *Text and Community: Essays in Memory of Bruce M. Metzger*, vol. 2, edited by J. Harold Ellens, 14–34. Sheffield: Sheffield Phoenix, 2007.

Jacobson, Rolf A. *"Many Are Saying": The Function of Direct Discourse in the Hebrew Psalter*. JSOTSup 397. London: T&T Clark, 2004.

Jannidis, Fotis. *Figur und Person: Beitrag zu einer historischen Narratologie*. Narratologia 3. Berlin: De Gruyter, 2004.

———. "Character." In *Handbook of Narratology*, edited by Peter Hühn, John Pier, Wolf Schmid, and Jörg Schönert et al., 14–29. Narratologia 19. Berlin: De Gruyter, 2009.

Janowski, Bernd. "JHWH der Richter—ein rettender Gott." *JBTh* 9 (1994): 53–85.

————. "Das Licht des Lebens: Zur Lichtmetaphorik in den Psalmen." In *Metaphors in the Psalms*, edited by Pierre van Hecke and Antje Labahn, 87–113. BETL 231. Leuven: Peeters, 2010.

Janzen, Waldemar. "'*ašrê* in the Old Testament." *Harvard Theological Review* 58 (1965): 215–226.

James, Joshua T. *The Storied Ethics of the Thanksgiving Psalms*. LHBOTS 658. London: Bloomsbury T&T Clark, 2017.

Jensen, Joseph E. "Psalm 75: Its Poetic Context and Structure." *CBQ* 63 (2001): 416–429.

Joerstad, Mari. *The Hebrew Bible and Environmental Ethics: Humans, Nonhumans, and the Living Landscape*. Cambridge: Cambridge University Press, 2019.

Johnson, B. "צָדִיק." In *Theological Dictionary of the Old Testament*, volume 4, edited by G. Johannes Botterweck and Helmer Ringgren, 239–64. Translated by David E. Green. Grand Rapids, MI: Eerdmans, 1980.

Johnson, Mark. *Moral Imagination: Implications of Cognitive Science for Ethics*. Chicago, IL: University of Chicago Press, 1994.

Johnson, Vivian L. *David in Distress: His Portrait Through the Historical Psalms*. LHBOTS 505. New York: T&T Clark, 2009.

Jones, Christine Brown. "When I am Afraid: Fear in the Book of Psalms." *Review & Expositor* 115 (2018): 15–25.

Jones, Scott C. "Psalm 37 and the Devotionalization of Instruction in the Postexilic Period." In *Prayers and the Construction of Israelite Identity*, edited by Susanne Gillmayr-Bucher and Maria Häusl, 167–187. AIL 35. Atlanta, GA: SBL, 2019.

Kaminski, Carol M. *Was Noah Good? Finding Favour in the Flood Narrative*. LHBOTS 563. New York: T&T Cark, 2014.

Kaminsky, Joel S. "Would You Impugn My Justice? A Nuanced Approach to the Hebrew Bible's Theology of Divine Recompense." *Interpretation* 69 (2015): 299–310.

Kartje, John. *Wisdom Epistemology in the Psalms: A Study of Psalms 1, 73, 90, and 107*. BZAW 472. Berlin: De Gruyter, 2014.

Keel, Othmar. *The Symbolism of the Biblical World: Ancient Near Eastern Iconography and the Book of Psalms*. Translated by Timothy J. Hallett. New York: Seabury, 1978.

Kessler, Rainer. "Khirbet el-Köm und Psalm 112—ein Fall von Intertextualität." *VT* 61 (2011): 677–684.

Kim, Ee Kon. "Holy War Ideology and the Rapid Shift of Mood in Psalm 3." In *On the Way to Nineveh: Studies in Honor of George M. Landes*, edited by Stephen L. Cook and S. C. Winter, 77–93. ASOR Books 4. Atlanta, GA: Scholars, 1999.

Klein, Ralph W. *2 Chronicles: A Commentary*. Edited by Paul D. Hanson. Hermeneia. Minneapolis, MN: Fortress, 2012.

Knohl, Israel. "Psalm 68: Structure, Composition and Geography." *JHS* 12 (2012): 1–21, https://doi.org/10.5508/jhs.2012.v12.a15.

Koch, Klaus. *Um das Prinzip der Vergeltung in Religion und Recht des Alten Testaments*. Wege der Forschung 125. Darmstadt: Wissenschaftliche Buchgesellschaft, 1972.

Krašovec, Jože. *God's Righteousness and Justice in the Old Testament*. Grand Rapids, MI: Eerdmans, 2022.

———. *Reward, Punishment, and Forgiveness: The Thinking and Beliefs of Ancient Israel in the Light of Greek and Modern Views*. VTSup 78. Leiden: Brill, 1999.

Kratz, Reinhard Gregor. "Gerechte und Frevler: die Auslegung von Psalm 37 in Qumran und bei Martin Luther." *Zeitschrift für Theologie und Kirche* 114 (2017): 367–397.

Kraus, Hans-Joachim. *Psalms 1–59*. CC. Translated by Hilton C. Oswald. Minneapolis, MN: Augsburg, 1988.

———. *Psalms 60–150*. Translated by Hilton C. Oswald. CC. Minneapolis, MN: Augsburg Fortress, 1989.

———. *Theology of the Psalms*. Translated by Keith R. Crim. Minneapolis, MN: Augsburg, 1986.

Kselman, John S. "Psalm 146 in Its Context." *CBQ* 50 (1988): 587–599.

———. "Two Notes on Psalm 37." *Biblica* 78 (1997): 252–254.

Kselman, John S., and Michael L. Barré. "Psalm 55: Problems and Proposals." *CBQ* 60 (1998): 440–462.

Kugel, James L. *The Idea of Hebrew Poetry: Parallelism and Its History*. New Haven, CT: Yale University Press, 1981.

Kuntz, J. Kenneth. "The Canonical Wisdom Psalms of Ancient Israel: Their Rhetorical, Thematic, and Formal Dimensions." In *Rhetorical Criticism, Essays in Honor of James Muilenburg*, edited by Jared J. Jackson and Martin Kessler, 186–222. Pittsburgh Theological Monograph Series 1. Pittsburgh, PA: Pickwick, 1974.

———. "Growling Dogs and Thirsty Deer: Uses of Animal Imagery in Psalmic Rhetoric." In *My Words are Lovely: Studies in the Rhetoric of the Psalms*, edited by Robert L. Foster and David M. Howard, 46–62. LHBOTS 467. New York: T&T Clark, 2008.

———. "The Retribution Motif in Psalmic Wisdom." *ZAW* 89 (1977): 223–233.

Kwakkel, Gert. *According to My Righteousness: Upright Behaviour as Grounds for Deliverance in Psalms 7, 17, 18, 26 and 44*. OTS 46. Leiden: Brill, 2002.

Kynes, Will. *My Psalm Has Turned into Weeping: Job's Dialogue with the Psalms*. BZAW 437. Berlin: De Gruyter, 2012.

———. *An Obituary for "Wisdom Literature": The Birth, Death, and Intertextual Reintegration of a Biblical Corpus*. Oxford: Oxford University Press, 2019.

Laberge, Léo. "A Literary Analysis of Psalm 31." *Église et théologie* 16 (1985): 147–168.

Lanier, Gregory R. *Old Testament Conceptual Metaphors and the Christology of Luke's Gospel*. LNTS 591. London: T&T Clark, 2018.

Lapsley, Jacqueline E. *Can These Bones Live? The Problem of the Moral Self in the Book of Ezekiel*. BZAW 301. Berlin: de Gruyter, 2000.

———. "Reading Psalm 146 in the Wild: A Feminist Biblical Theology of Praise." In *After Exegesis: Feminist Biblical Theology: Essays in Honor of Carol A. Newsom*, edited by Patricia K. Tull and Jacqueline E. Lapsley, 77–90. Waco, TX: Baylor University Press, 2015.

LeFebvre, Michael. "'On His Law He Meditates': What is Psalm 1 Introducing?" *JSOT* 40 (2016): 439–450.

Lescow, Theodor. "Die Komposition der Psalmen 6 und 55." *BN* 107/108 (2001): 32–40.

Leveen, Jacob. "The Textual Problems of Psalm VII." *VT* 16 (1996): 439–445.

Levin, Cristoph. "Das Gebetbuch der Gerechten: Literargeschichtliche Beobachtungen am Psalter." *Zeitschrift für Theologie und Kirche* 90 (1993): 356–381.

Liebreich, Leon J. "Psalms 34 and 145 in the Light of Their Key Words." *Hebrew Union College Annual* 27 (1956): 181–192.

Lohfink, Norbert. "Ps 7,2–6—vom Löwen gejagt." In *Die Freude an Gott, unsere Kraft: Festschrift für Otto Bernhard Knoch zum 65. Geburtstag*, edited by Johannes Joachim Degenhardt and Otto Bernhard Knoch, 60–67. Stuttgart: Katholisches Bibelwerk, 1991.

Longman, Tremper III. *Job*. BCOTWP. Grand Rapids, MI: Baker Academic, 2012.

———. "The Psalms and Ancient Near Eastern Prayer Genres." In *Interpreting the Psalms: Issues and Approaches*, edited by Philip S. Johnston and David G. Firth, 41–59. Downers Grove, IL: InterVarsity, 2005.

———. *Psalms: An Introduction and Commentary*. TOTC. Downers Grove, IL: InterVarsity, 2014.

Loretz, Oswald. *Psalmstudien: Kolometrie, Strophik, und Theologie ausgewählter Psalmen*. BZAW 309. Berlin: De Gruyter, 2002.

Lugt, P. van der. *Psalms 90–150 and Psalm 1*. Vol. 3 of *Cantos and Strophes in Biblical Hebrew Poetry*. OTS 63. Leiden: Brill, 2014.

Lyu, Sun Myung. *Righteousness in the Book of Proverbs*. FAT 2.55. Tübingen: Mohr Siebeck, 2012.

Mandolfo, Carleen. *God in the Dock: Dialogic Tension in the Psalms of Lament*. JSOTSup 357. London: Sheffield Academic, 2002.

Margolin, Uri. "Character." In *The Cambridge Companion to Narrative*, edited by David Herman, 66–79. Cambridge Companions to Narrative. Cambridge: Cambridge University Press, 2007.

———. "Characters in Literary Narrative: Representation and Signification." *Semiotica* 106 (1995): 373–392.

———. "The Doer and the Deed: Action as a Basis for Characterization in Narrative." *Poetics Today* 7 (1986): 205–225.

Marlowe, W. Creighton. "Righteous People in Proverbs." In *Das heilige Herz der Tora: Festschrift fur Hendrik Koorevaar zu seinem 65. Geburtstag*, edited by Siegbert Riecker and Julius Steinberg, 267–283. Aachen: Shaker, 2011.

———. "The Wicked Wealthy in Isaiah 53:9." *Asbury Journal* 64 (2009): 68–81.

Martilla, Marko. *Collective Reinterpretation in the Psalms: A Study of the Redaction History of the Psalter*. FAT 2.13. Tübigen: Mohr Siebeck, 2006.

Mays, James Luther. "The Place of the Torah-Psalms in the Psalter." *JBL* 106 (1987): 3–12.

———. *Psalms*. Interpretation. Louisville, KY: John Knox, 1994.

McCann, J. Clinton. *A Theological Introduction to the Psalter: The Psalms as Torah*. Nashville, TN: Abingdon, 1993.

Mein, Andrew. *Ezekiel and the Ethics of Exile*. Oxford Theological Monographs. Oxford: Oxford University Press, 2001.

Miglio, Adam E. "Imagery and Analogy in Psalm 58:4–9." *VT* 65 (2015): 114–135.

Millar, Suzanna R. *Genre and Openness in Proverbs 10:1–22:16*. AIL 39. Atlanta, GA: SBL, 2020.

Miller, Cynthia L. "Ellipsis Involving Negation in Biblical Poetry." In *Seeking Out the Wisdom of the Ancients: Essays Offered to Honor Michael V. Fox on the Occasion of His Sixty-Fifth Birthday*, edited by Ronald L. Troxel, Kelvin G. Friebel, and Dennis R. Magary, 37–52. Winona Lake, IN: Eisenbrauns, 2005.

Miller, Patrick D. "The Beginning of the Psalter." In *The Shape and Shaping of the Psalter*, edited by J. Clinton McCann, 83–92. JSOTSup 159. Sheffield: JSOT, 1993.

———. "The End of the Psalter: A Response to Erich Zenger." *JSOT* 80 (1998): 103–110.

———. "Land in the Psalms." In *The Land of Israel in History, Bible, and Theology: Studies in Honour of Ed Noort*, edited by J. T. A. G. M. van Ruiten and Cor de Vos, 183–196. VTSup 124. Leiden: Brill, 2009.

———. "Who Are the Bad Guys in the Psalms?" In *Let Us Go up to Zion: Essays in Honour of H. G. M. Williamson on the Occasion of His Sixty-Fifth Birthday*, edited by Iain W. Provan and Mark J. Boda, 424–430. VTSup 153. Leiden: Brill, 2012.

Miller, Robert D. II. *The Dragon, the Mountain, and the Nations: An Old Testament Myth, Its Origins, and Its Afterlives*. Explorations in Ancient Near Eastern Civilizations. University Park, PA: Pennsylvania State University Press, 2018.

Mol, Jurrien. *Collective and Individual Responsibility: A Description of Corporate Personality in Ezekiel 18 and 20*. SSN 53. Leiden: Brill, 2009.

Mowinckel, Sigmund. *The Psalms in Israel's Worship*. Translated by D. R. Ap-Thomas. 2 vols. Oxford: Blackwell, 1962.

Müller, Reinhard. "The Origins of Yhwh in Light of the Earliest Psalms." In *The Origins of Yahwism*, edited by Jürgen van Oorschot and Markus Witte, 207–238. BZAW 484. Berlin: De Gruyter, 2017.

Muraoka, T. *Emphatic Words and Structures in Biblical Hebrew*. Jerusalem: Magnes Press, 1985.

Murphy, Roland E. "A Consideration of the Classification, 'Wisdom Psalm.'" In *Congress Volume Bonn 1962*, edited by G. W. Anderson, P. A. H. de Boer, G. R. Castellino, Henry Cazelles, E. Hammershaimb, H. G. May, and W. Zimmerli, 156–167. VTSup 9. Leiden: Brill, 1963.

Musy, Meghan D. "Hearing Voices: Exploring Psalmic Multivocality as Lyric Poetry." PhD Dissertation, McMaster Divinity College, Hamilton, 2018.

Nasuti, Harry P. *Defining the Sacred Songs: Genre, Tradition and the Post-Critical Interpretation of the Psalms*. JSOTSup 218. Sheffield: Sheffield Academic, 1999.

Nel, Philip J. "Righteousness from the Perspective of the Wisdom Literature of the Old Testament." *OTE* 13 (2000): 309–328.

Neumann, Friederike. *Schriftegelehrte Hymnen: Gestalt, Theologie und Intention der Psalmen 145 und 146–150*. BZAW 491. Berlin: De Gruyter, 2016.

Newsom, Carol. *The Book of Job: A Contest of Moral Imaginations*. Oxford: Oxford University Press, 2009.

———. *The Self as Symbolic Space: Constructing Identity and Community at Qumran*. Studies on the Texts of the Desert of Judah 52. Leiden: Brill, 2004.

Niehaus, Jeffrey J. "Righteousness and the Created Order: Appreciation and Critique of a Novel Idea." *JETS* 63 (2020): 233–254.

Noll, Sonja. *The Semantics of Silence in Biblical Hebrew*. Studies in Semitic Languages and Linguistics 100. Leiden: Brill, 2020.

Nõmmik, Urmas. "Die Gerechtigkeitsbearbeitungen in den Psalmen: Eine Hypothese von Christoph Levin formgeschichtlich und kolometrish überprüft." *Ugarit Forschungen* 31 (1999): 443–533.

Nõmmik, Urmas, and Anu Põldsam. "Psalm 86, Its Place in the Psalter, and group Identity in the Second Temple Period." *ZAW* 130 (2018): 398–417.

Olley, John W. "'Righteous' and Wealthy? The Description of the *ṣaddîq* in Wisdom Literature." *Colloquium* 22 (1990): 38–45.

———. "'Righteousness'—Some Issues in Old Testament Translation into English." *Bible Translator* 38 (1987): 307–315.

Ortlund, E. N. "An Intertextual Reading of Theophany of Psalm 97." *SJOT* 20 (2006): 273–285.

Overland, Paul. *Proverbs*. Apollos Old Testament Commentary 15. London: Apollos, 2022.

Owens, Daniel C. *Portraits of the Righteous in the Psalms: An Exploration of the Ethics of Book I*. Eugene, OR: Pickwick, 2013.

Pelham, Abigail. *Contested Creations in the Book of Job: The-World-as-It-Ought t-and-Ought-Not-to-Be*. BibInt 113. Leiden: Brill, 2012.

Perdue, Leo G. "Cosmology and the Social Order of the Wisdom Tradition." In *The Sage in Israel and the Ancient Near East*, edited by John G. Gammie and Leo G. Perdue, 457–478. Winona Lake, IN: Eisenbrauns, 1990.

———. *Proverbs*. Interpretation. Louisville, KY: Westminster John Knox, 2012.

———. *The Sword and the Stylus: An Introduction to Wisdom in the Age of Empires*. Grand Rapids, MI: Eerdmans, 2008.

Peters, Kurtis. *Hebrew Lexical Semantics and Daily Life in Ancient Israel: What's Cooking in Ancient Israel?* BibInt 146. Leiden: Brill, 2016.

Petrany, Catherine. "Instruction, Performance, and Prayer: The Didactic Function of Psalmic Wisdom." In *The Shape and Shaping of the Book of Psalms: the Current State of Scholarship*, edited by Nancy L. DeClaissé-Walford, 87–103. AIL 20. Atlanta, GA: SBL, 2014.

———. *Pedagogy, Prayer, and Praise: The Wisdom of the Psalms and Psalter*. FAT 2.83. Tübingen: Mohr Siebeck, 2015.

Phelan, James. "Character, Progression, and the Mimetic-Didactic Distinction." *Modern Philology* 84 (1987): 282–299.

———. *Reading People, Reading Plots: Character, Progression, and the Interpretation of Narrative*. Chicago, IL: University of Chicago Press, 1989.

Pinker, Aron. "The Wicked in Ambush (Job 27:18–19)." *BBR* 25 (2015): 295–310.

Poe Hays, Rebecca W. *The Function of Story in the Hebrew Psalter*. Lanham, MD: Lexington Books, 2021.

Prinsloo, Gert T. M. "Psalm 5: A Theology of Tension and Reconciliation." *SK* 19 (1998): 628–643.

Propp, Vladimir. *Morphology of the Folktale*. Edited by Louis A. Wagner. Translated by Laurence Scott. 2nd ed. American Folklore Society Bibliographical and Special Series 9. Austin, TX: University of Texas Press, 1968.

Quine, Cat. "The Bird and the Mountains: A Note on Psalm 11." *VT* 67 (2017): 470–479.

Raabe, Paul R. "Deliberate Ambiguity in the Psalter." *JBL* 110 (1991): 213–227.

Rad, Gerhard von. *The Theology of Israel's Historical Traditions*. Vol. 1 of *Old Testament Theology*. Translated by D. M. G. Stalker. Louisville, KY: Westminster John Knox, 1962.

———. *Wisdom in Israel*. Translated by James D. Martin. London: SCM, 1972.

Ramond, Sophie. "'Seek Peace and Pursue It' (Ps 34:15): A Call to Beleaguered Members of a Community." *JHS* 19 (2018): 1–14, https:/doi/org/10.5508/jhs.2019.v19.a.

Rendtorff, Rolf. "The Psalms of David: David in the Psalms." In *The Book of Psalms: Composition and Reception*, edited by Peter W. Flint and Patrick D. Miller, 53–64. VTSup 99. Leiden: Brill, 2005.

Reventlow, Henning Graf. "Righteousness as Order of the World: Some Remarks Towards a Program." In *Justice and Righteousness: Biblical Themes and Their Influence*, edited by Henning Graf Reventlow and Yair Hoffman, 163–172. JSOTSup 137. Sheffield: JSOT, 1992.

Richards, Kent Harold. "Psalm 34." *Interpretation* 40 (1986): 175–180.

Ricouer, Paul. *Narrative and Time*. Vol. 1. Translated by Kathleen McLaughlin and David Pellauer. Chicago, IL: University of Chicago Press, 1984.

Riede, Peter. "'Doch du erhöhtest wie einem Wildstier mein Horn': Zur Metaphorik in Ps 92,11." In *Metaphors in the Psalms*, edited by Pierre van Hecke and Antje Labahn, 209–216. BETL 231. Leuven: Peeters, 2010.

Roberts, J. J. M. "The Young Lions of Psalm 34,11." *Bib* 54 (1973): 265–267.

Rubin, Aaron D. "The Form and Meaning of Hebrew *'ašrê*." *VT* 60 (2010): 366–372.

Sánchez-Castelblanco, Wilton Gerardo. "'Que les caigan brasas de fuego' (Sal 140,11): Comentario exegético del salmo 140." *Franciscanum* 54 (2012): 299–331.

Sarna, Nahum M. "The Psalm for the Sabbath Day (Ps 92)." *JBL* 81 (1962): 155–168.

Scacewater, Todd A. *The Divine Builder in Psalm 68: Jewish and Pauline Tradition*. LNTS 631. London: T&T Clark, 2020.

Schaefer, Konrad. *Psalms*. Berit Olam. Collegeville, MN: Liturgical Press, 2001.

Schipper, Bernd U. *The Hermeneutics of Torah: Proverbs 2, Deuteronomy, and the Composition of Proverbs 1–9*. AIL 43. Atlanta, GA: SBL, 2021.

———. *Proverbs 1–15*. Edited by Thomas Krüger. Translated by Stephen Germany. Hermeneia. Minneapolis, MN: Fortress, 2019.

Schmid, H. H. "Creation, Righteousness, and Salvation: 'Creation Theology' as the Broad Horizon of Biblical Theology." In *Creation in the Old Testament*, edited by

Bernhard W. Anderson, 102–117. Issues in Religion and Theology 6. Philadelphia, PA: Fortress, 1984.

———. *Gerechtigkeit als Weltordnung: Hintergrund und Geschichte der alttesta- mentlichen Gerechtigkeitsbegriffes.* Beiträge zur historischen Theologie 40. Tübingen: Mohr Siebeck, 1968.

Schneider, Ralf. "Toward a Cognitive Theory of Literary Character: The Dynamics of Mental-Model Construction." *Style* 35 (2001): 607–639.

Schwarz, Daniel. "Character and Characterization: An Inquiry." *Journal of Narrative Technique* 19 (1989): 85–105.

Schwienhorst-Schönberger, Ludiger. "Order: Wisdom, Retribution, and Skepticism." In *The Oxford Handbook of Wisdom in the Bible*, edited by Will Kynes, 83–99. Oxford: Oxford University Press, 2021.

Scoralick, Ruth. *Einzelspruch und Sammlung: Komposition im Buch der Sprichwörter Kapitel 10–15.* BZAW 232. Berlin: De Gruyter, 1995.

Scott, R. B. Y. *The Way of Wisdom in the Old Testament.* New York: Macmillan, 1971.

———. "Wise and Foolish, Righteous and Wicked." In *Studies in the Religion of Ancient Israel*, edited by G. W. Anderson et al., 146–165. VTSup 23. Leiden: Brill, 1972.

Scullion, J. J. "Righteousness (OT)." In *Anchor Bible Dictionary*, edited by David Noel Freedman, 5:724–736. New York: Doubleday, 1992.

Seed, David. *Science Fiction: A Very Short Introduction.* New York: Oxford University Press, 2011.

Seifrid, Mark A. "Righteousness Language in the Hebrew Scriptures and Early Judaism." In *The Complexities of Second Temple Judaism*, vol. 1 of *Justification and Variegated Nomism*, edited by D. A. Carson, Peter T. O'Brien, and Mark A. Seifrid, 415–442. Wissenschaftliche Untersuchungen zum Neuen Testament 2.140. Tübingen: Mohr Siebeck, 2001.

Seitz, Christopher R. "Psalm 34: Redaction, Inner-Biblical Exegesis and the Longer Psalm Superscriptions—'Mistake' Making and Theological Significance." In *The Bible As Christian Scripture: The Work of Brevard S. Childs*, edited by Christopher R. Seitz and Kent Harold Richards, 279–298. Biblical Scholarship in North America 25. Atlanta, ga: SBL, 2013.

Seo, J. Mira. *Exemplary Traits: Reading Characterization in Roman Poetry.* Oxford: Oxford University Press, 2013.

Seow, Choon-Leong. *Ecclesiastes: A New Translation with Introduction and Commentary.* AB 18c. New York: Doubleday, 1997.

Seybold, Klaus. *Introducing the Psalms.* Translated by R. Graeme Dunphy. London: T&T Clark, 1990.

———. "Psalm LVIII: Ein Losungsversuch." *VT* 30 (1980): 53–66.

Shead, Stephen L. *Radical Frame Semantics and Biblical Hebrew: Exploring Lexical Semantics.* BibInt 108. Leiden: Brill, 2011.

Skehan, Patrick W. "A Note on Psalm 34:1." *CBQ* 14 (1952): 226.

———. "The Structure of the Song of Moses in Deuteronomy (Deut. 32:1–43)." *CBQ* 13 (1951): 153–163.

Smith, Ralph L. *Micah–Malachi.* WBC 32. Nashville, TN: Thomas Nelson, 1984.

Sneed, Mark R. "'Grasping After the Wind'": The Elusive Attempt to Define and Delimit Wisdom." In *Was There a Wisdom Tradition? New Prospects in Israelite Wisdom Studies*, edited by Mark R. Sneed, 39–67. AIL 23. Atlanta, GA: SBL, 2015.

———. "Is the 'Wisdom Tradition' a Tradition?" *CBQ* 73 (2011): 50–71.

Snyman, Stephanus D. "Psalm 32: Structure, Genre, Intent and Liturgical Use." In *Psalms and Liturgy*, edited by Dirk J. Human and Cas J. A. Vos, 155–167. JSOT-Sup 410. London: T&T Clark, 2004.

Spero, Shubert. "Variations on a Theme in Biblical Psalmody." *JBQ* 45 (2017): 115–118.

Stewart, Anne W. *Poetic Ethics in Proverbs: Wisdom Literature and the Shaping of the Moral Self*. Cambridge: Cambridge University Press, 2016.

Steyl, C. "The Construct Noun *ešet* in Ps 58:9." *Journal of Northwest Semitic Languages* 11 (1983): 133–134.

Sticher, Claudia. *Die Rettung der Guten durch Gott und die Selbstzerstörung der Bösen: ein theologisches Denkmuster im Psalter*. BBB 137. Berlin: Philo, 2002.

Stocks, Simon P. "'Children, Listen to Me': The Voicing of Wisdom in the Psalms." In *Interpreting Old Testament Wisdom Literature*, edited by David G. Firth and Lindsay Wilson, 194–204. Downers Grove, IL: IVP Academic, 2017.

Strawn, Brent A. "Lyric Poetry." In *Dictionary of the Old Testament: Wisdom, Poetry & Writings*, edited by Tremper Longman and Peter Enns, 437–446. Downers Grove, IL: IVP Academic, 2008.

Sumner, Stephen T. "A Reanalysis of Psalm 11." *ZAW* 131 (2019): 77–90.

Süring, Margit Linnéa. "Horn Motifs in the Hebrew Bible and Related Ancient Near Eastern Literature and Iconography." PhD Dissertation, Andrews University, Berrien Springs, MI, 1980.

Talmon, Shemaryahu. *Literary Motifs and Patterns in the Hebrew Bible: Collected Studies*. Winona Lake, IN: Eisenbrauns, 2013.

Tanner, Beth LaNeel. *The Book of Psalms Through the Lens of Intertextuality*. Studies in Biblical Literature 26. New York: Peter Lang, 2001.

Tate, Marvin E. *Psalms 51–100*. WBC 20. Dallas, TX: Word, 1990.

Terrien, Samuel. *The Psalms: Strophic Structure and Theological Commentary*. Eerdmans Critical Commentary. Grand Rapids, MI: Eerdmans, 2003.

Tournay, Raymond Jacques. "Psaume CXLI: Nouvelle Interprétation." *RB* 90 (1983): 321–333.

Tsumura, David Toshio. "Vertical Grammar of Parallelism in Hebrew Poetry." *JBL* 128 (2009): 167–181.

Tucker, W. Dennis Jr. *Constructing and Deconstructing Power in Psalms 107–150*. AIL 19. Atlanta, GA: SBL, 2014.

———. "The Ordered World of Psalm 92." *OTE* 32 (2019): 358–377.

———. "A Polysemiotic Approach to the Poor in the Psalms." *PRSt* 31 (2004): 424–439.

Van Grol, Harm. "David and His Chasidim: Place and Function of Psalms 138–145." In *The Composition of the Book of Psalms*, edited by Erich Zenger, 309–337. BETL 238. Leuven: Peeters, 2010.

Van Leeuwen, Raymond C. "Form Criticism, Wisdom, and Psalms 111–112." In *The Changing Face of Form Criticism for the Twenty-First Century*, edited by Marvin A. Sweeney and Ehud Ben Zvi, 51–72. Grand Rapids, MI: Eerdmans, 2003.

———. "Liminality and Worldview in Proverbs 1–9." *Semeia* 50 (1990): 111–144.

———. "Theology: Creation, Wisdom, and Covenant." In *The Oxford Handbook of Wisdom in the Bible*, edited by Will Kynes, 65–82. Oxford: Oxford University Press, 2021.

———. "Wealth and Poverty: System and Contradiction in Proverbs." *HS* 33 (1992): 25–36.

Vayntrub, Jacqueline. *Beyond Orality: Biblical Poetry on Its Own Terms*. The Ancient Word. London: Routledge, 2019.

———. "Hearing the Voice of Biblical Poetry." *SEÅ* 86 (2021): 20–38.

Villanueva, Federico G. *The 'Uncertainty of a Hearing': A Study of the Sudden Change of Mood in the Psalms of Lament*. VTSup 121. Leiden: Brill, 2008.

Vint, Sherryl. *Science Fiction*. MIT Essential Knowledge Series. Cambridge, MA: MIT Press, 2021.

Walsh, Carey Ellen. *The Fruit of the Vine: Viticulture in Ancient Israel*. Harvard Semitic Monographs 60. Winona Lake, IN: Eisenbrauns, 2000.

Waltke, Bruce K. *The Book of Proverbs: 1–15*. NICOT. Grand Rapids, MI: Eerdmans, 2004.

Watson, Wilfred G. E. *Classical Hebrew Poetry: A Guide to Its Techniques*. 2nd ed. JSOTSup 26. Sheffield: Sheffield Academic, 1986.

Watts, James W. *Psalm and Story: Inset Hymns in Hebrew Narrative*. JSOTSup 139. Sheffield: JSOT: 1992.

Weber, Beat. "'Dann wird er sein wie ein Baum . . . ' (Psalm 1,3): Zu den Sprachbildern von Psalm 1." *OTE* 23 (2010): 406–426.

Weeks, Stuart. "Wisdom Psalms." In *Temple and Worship in Biblical Israel*, edited by John Day, 292–307. LHBOTS 422. London: T&T Clark, 2005.

Wenham, Gordon J. "The Ethics of the Psalms." In *Interpreting the Psalms: Issues and Approaches*, edited by David Firth and Philip S. Johnston, 175–194. Downers Grove, IL: InterVarsity, 2005.

———. *Genesis 1–15*. WBC 1. Waco, TX: Word, 1987.

Westermann, Claus. *Praise and Lament in the Psalms*. Translated by Keith R. Crim and Richard N. Soulen. Atlanta, GA: John Knox, 1981.

———. *Roots of Wisdom: The Oldest Proverbs of Israel and Other Peoples*. Translated by J. Daryl Charles. Louisville, KY: Westminster John Knox, 1995.

Whybray, Norman. *Reading the Psalms as a Book*. JSOTSup 222. Sheffield: Sheffield Academic, 1996.

Wildberger, Hans. *Isaiah 13–27*. Translated by Thomas H. Trapp. CC. Minneapolis, MN: Fortress, 1997.

Willgren, David. *The Formation of the "Book" of Psalms: Reconsidering the Transmission and Canonization of Psalmody in Light of Material Culture and the Poetics of Anthologies*. FAT 2.88. Tübingen: Mohr Siebeck, 2016.

Williamson, H. G. M. "Semantics and Lexicography: A Methodological Conundrum." In *Biblical Lexicology: Hebrew and Greek*, edited by Eberhard Bons, Jan Joosten, and Regine Hunziker-Rodewald, 327–339. BZAW 443. Berlin: De Gruyter, 2015.

Wilson, Gerald H. *The Editing of the Hebrew Psalter*. SBLDS 76. Chico, CA: Scholars, 1985.

———. "Shaping the Psalter: A Consideration of Editorial Linkage in the Book of Psalms." In *The Shape and Shaping of the Psalter*, edited by J. Clinton McCann, 72–82. JSOTSup 159. Sheffield: JSOT, 1993.

Wilson, Lindsay. *Proverbs: An Introduction and Commentary*. TOTC 17. Downers Grove, IL: IVP Academic, 2018.

Winko, Simone. "On the Constitution of Characters in Poetry." In *Characters in Fictional Worlds: Understanding Imaginary Beings in Literature, Film, and Other Media*, edited by Jens Eder, Fotis Jannidis, and Ralf Schneider, 208–231. Revisionen 3. Berlin: De Gruyter, 2010.

Witte, Markus. "Psalm 37 im Spannungsfeld von Weisheit und Eschatologie." In *Weisheit als Lebensgrundlage: Festschrift für Friedrich V. Reiterer zum 65. Geburtstag*, edited by Renate Egger-Wenzel, Karin Schöpflin, and Johannes Friedrich Diehl, 411–436. Deuterocanonical and Cognate Literature Studies 15. Berlin: De Gruyter, 2013.

Wong, Ka Leung. *The Idea of Retribution in the Book of Ezekiel*. VTSup 87. Leiden: Brill, 2001.

Wright, D. P. "Blown Away Like a Bramble: The Dynamics of Analogy in Psalm 58." *RB* 103 (1996): 213–236.

Wright, N. T. "Righteousness." In *New Dictionary of Theology*, edited by Sinclair B. Ferguson, David F. Wright, and J. I. Packer, 590–592. Downers Grove, IL: InterVarsity, 1988.

Wu, Daniel Y. *Honor, Shame, and Guilt: Social Scientific Approaches to the Book of Ezekiel*. BBRSup 14. Winona Lake, IN: Eisenbrauns, 2016.

Zehnder, Markus Philipp. *Wegmetaphorik im Alten Testament: Eine semantische Untersuchung der alttestamentlichen und altorientalischen Weg-Lexeme mit besonderer Berücksichtigung ihrer metaphorischen Verwendung*. BZAW 268. Berlin: De Gruyter, 1999.

Zernecke, Anna Elise. "Der Feind und die Hexe: Die Widersacher in mesopotamischen und biblischen Gebeten." *Die Welt des Orients* 49 (2019): 109–123.

Zewi, Tamar. *Parenthesis in Biblical Hebrew*. Studies in Semitic Languages and Linguistics 50. Leiden: Brill, 2007.

Index

Scripture Index

About the Author

Kevin Foth (PhD, McMaster Divinity College) is Adjunct Professor of Old Testament at Denver Seminary and Upper Grades Teacher at Ambleside School of Colorado. His current projects include a book on the concept of "wisdom" in the Bible and a commentary on Isaiah.

www.ingramcontent.com/pod-product-compliance
Ingram Content Group UK Ltd.
Pitfield, Milton Keynes, MK11 3LW, UK
UKHW031313250425
457881UK00002B/26